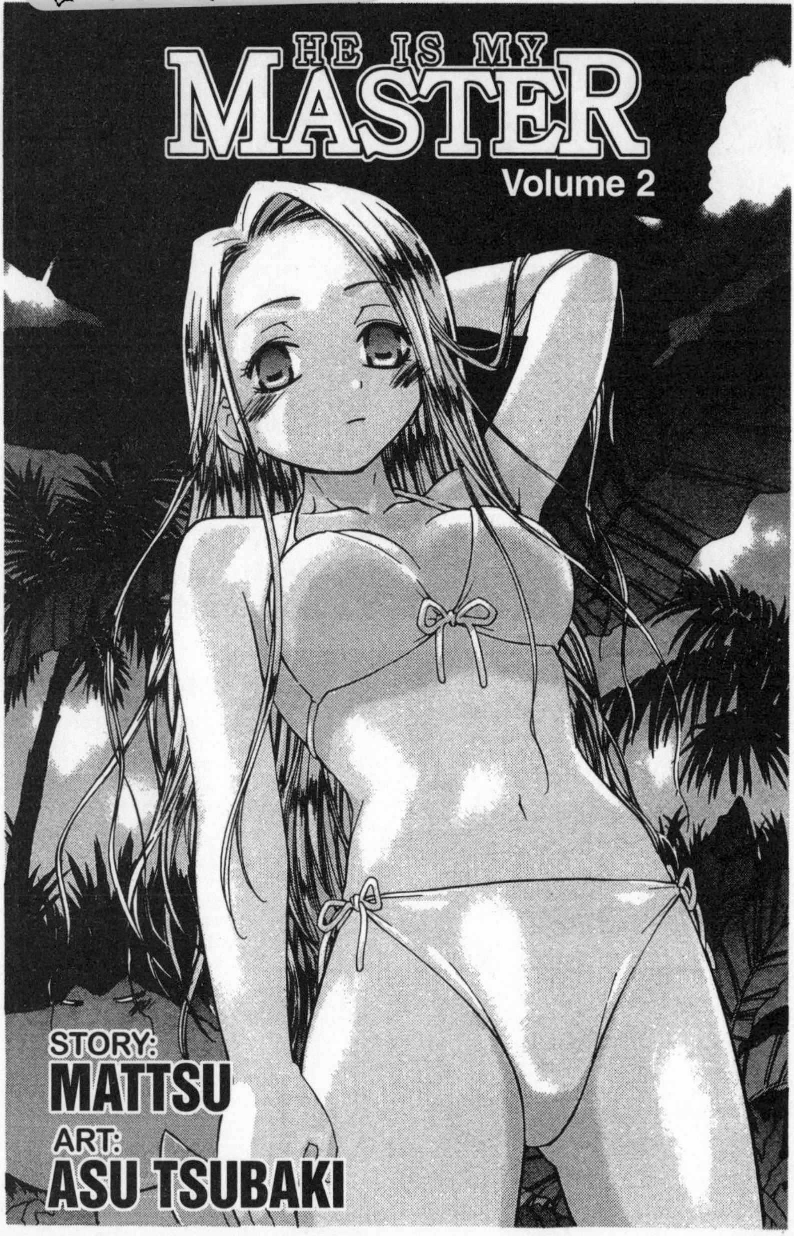
HE IS MY
MASTER
Volume 2
STORY:
MATTSU
ART:
ASU TSUBAKI

HE IS MY MASTER
Volume 2

story by Mattsu   art by Asu Tsubaki

STAFF CREDITS

translation	**Beni Axia Conrad**
adaptation	**Janet Houck,**
	Bambi Eloriaga
retouch & lettering	**Roland Amago**
cover design	**Nicky Lim**
design	**Roland Amago**
layout	**Bambi Eloriaga**
editor	**Adam Arnold**

publisher   **Seven Seas Entertainment**

HE IS MY MASTER VOL. 2
© 2004 Mattsu & Asu Tsubaki / SQUARE ENIX. All rights reserved.
First published in Japan in 2004 by SQUARE ENIX CO., LTD.
English translation rights arranged with SQUARE ENIX CO., LTD. and
Seven Seas Entertainment, LLC. through Tuttle-Mori Agency, Inc.

Visit us online at www.gomanga.com

ISBN: 978-1-933164-62-5

Printed in Canada

Second Printing: August 2008

10 9 8 7 6 5 4 3 2

CONTENTS

CHARACTER INTRODUCTIONS

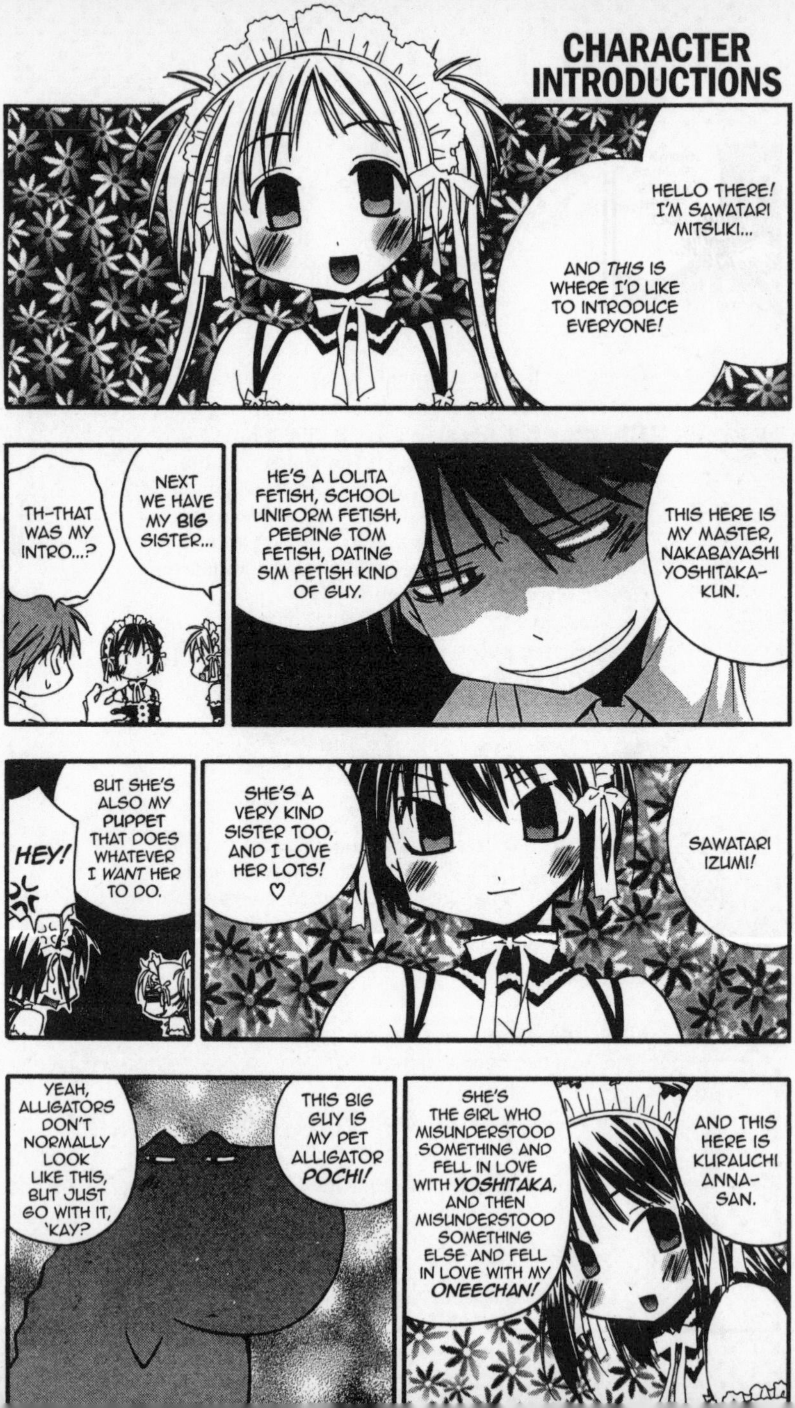

HELLO THERE! I'M SAWATARI MITSUKI...
AND *THIS* IS WHERE I'D LIKE TO INTRODUCE EVERYONE!
THIS HERE IS MY MASTER, NAKABAYASHI YOSHITAKA-KUN.
HE'S A LOLITA FETISH, SCHOOL UNIFORM FETISH, PEEPING TOM FETISH, DATING SIM FETISH KIND OF GUY.
NEXT WE HAVE MY **BIG** SISTER...
TH-THAT WAS MY INTRO...?
SAWATARI IZUMI!
SHE'S A VERY KIND SISTER TOO, AND I LOVE HER LOTS! ♡
BUT SHE'S ALSO MY **PUPPET** THAT DOES WHATEVER I *WANT* HER TO DO.
HEY!
AND THIS HERE IS KURAUCHI ANNA-SAN.
SHE'S THE GIRL WHO MISUNDERSTOOD SOMETHING AND FELL IN LOVE WITH ***YOSHITAKA***, AND THEN MISUNDERSTOOD SOMETHING ELSE AND FELL IN LOVE WITH MY ***ONEECHAN!***
THIS BIG GUY IS MY PET ALLIGATOR ***POCHI!***
YEAH, ALLIGATORS DON'T NORMALLY LOOK LIKE THIS, BUT JUST GO WITH IT, 'KAY?

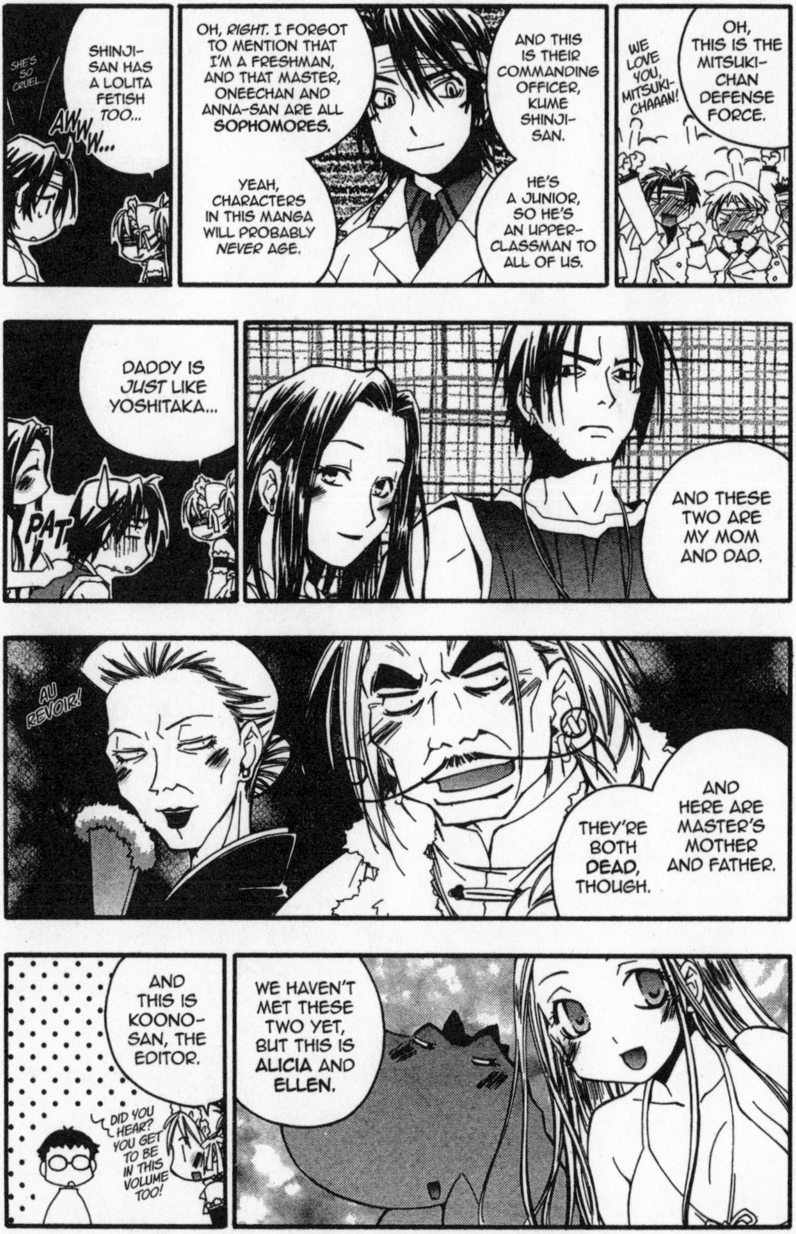
OH, THIS IS THE MITSUKI-CHAN DEFENSE FORCE.
WE LOVE YOU, MITSUKI-CHAAAN!
AND THIS IS THEIR COMMANDING OFFICER, KUME SHINJI-SAN.
HE'S A JUNIOR, SO HE'S AN UPPER-CLASSMAN TO ALL OF US.
OH, *RIGHT.* I FORGOT TO MENTION THAT I'M A FRESHMAN, AND THAT MASTER, ONEECHAN AND ANNA-SAN ARE ALL **SOPHOMORES.**
YEAH, CHARACTERS IN THIS MANGA WILL PROBABLY *NEVER* AGE.
SHINJI-SAN HAS A LOLITA FETISH TOO...
SHE'S SO CRUEL...
AWWW...
AND THESE TWO ARE MY MOM AND DAD.
DADDY IS *JUST* LIKE YOSHITAKA...
PAT
AND HERE ARE MASTER'S MOTHER AND FATHER.
THEY'RE BOTH **DEAD,** THOUGH.
AU REVOIR!
WE HAVEN'T MET THESE TWO YET, BUT THIS IS **ALICIA** AND **ELLEN.**
AND THIS IS KOONO-SAN, THE EDITOR.
DID YOU HEAR? YOU GET TO BE IN THIS VOLUME TOO!

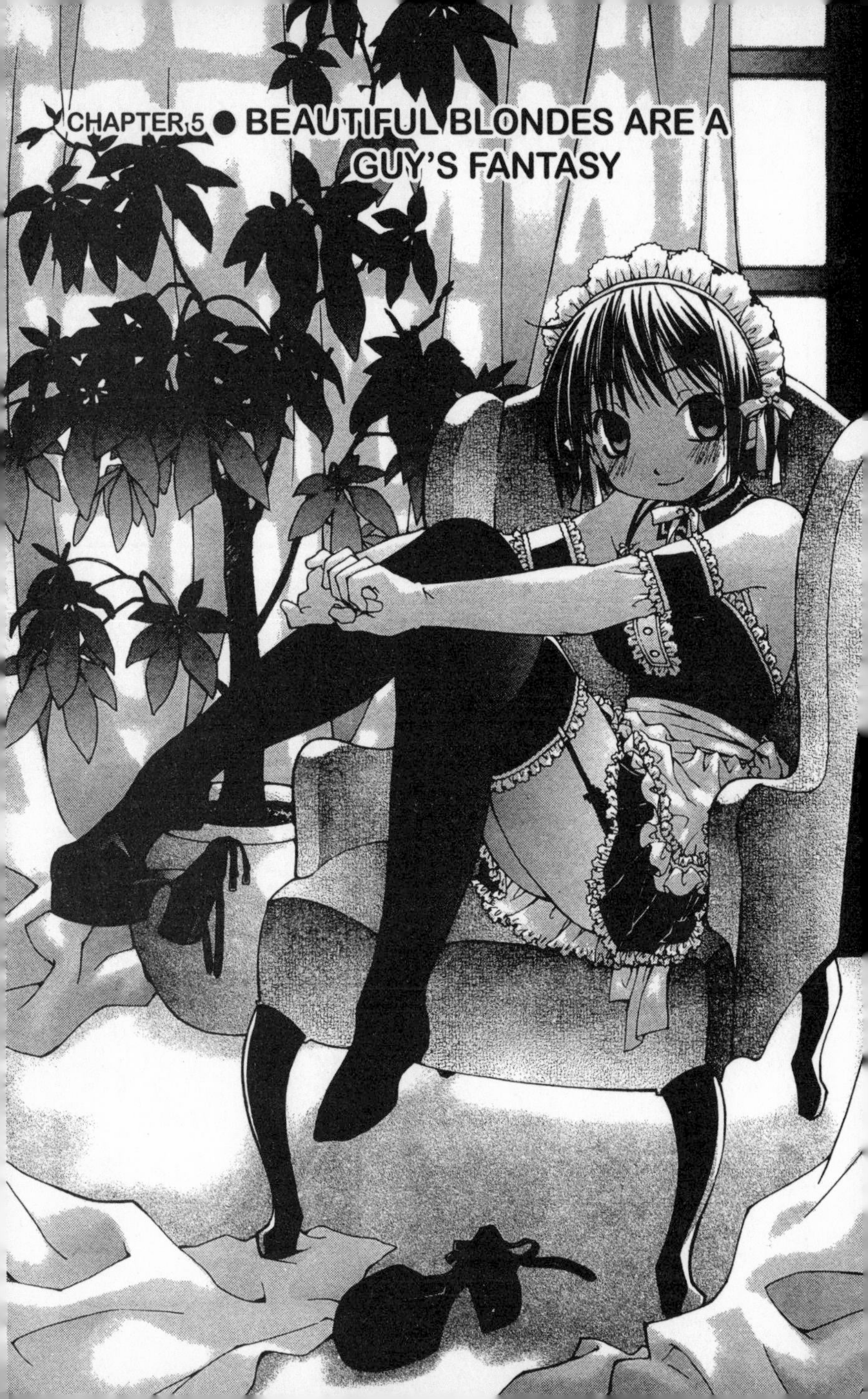
CHAPTER 5 ● BEAUTIFUL BLONDES ARE A GUY'S FANTASY

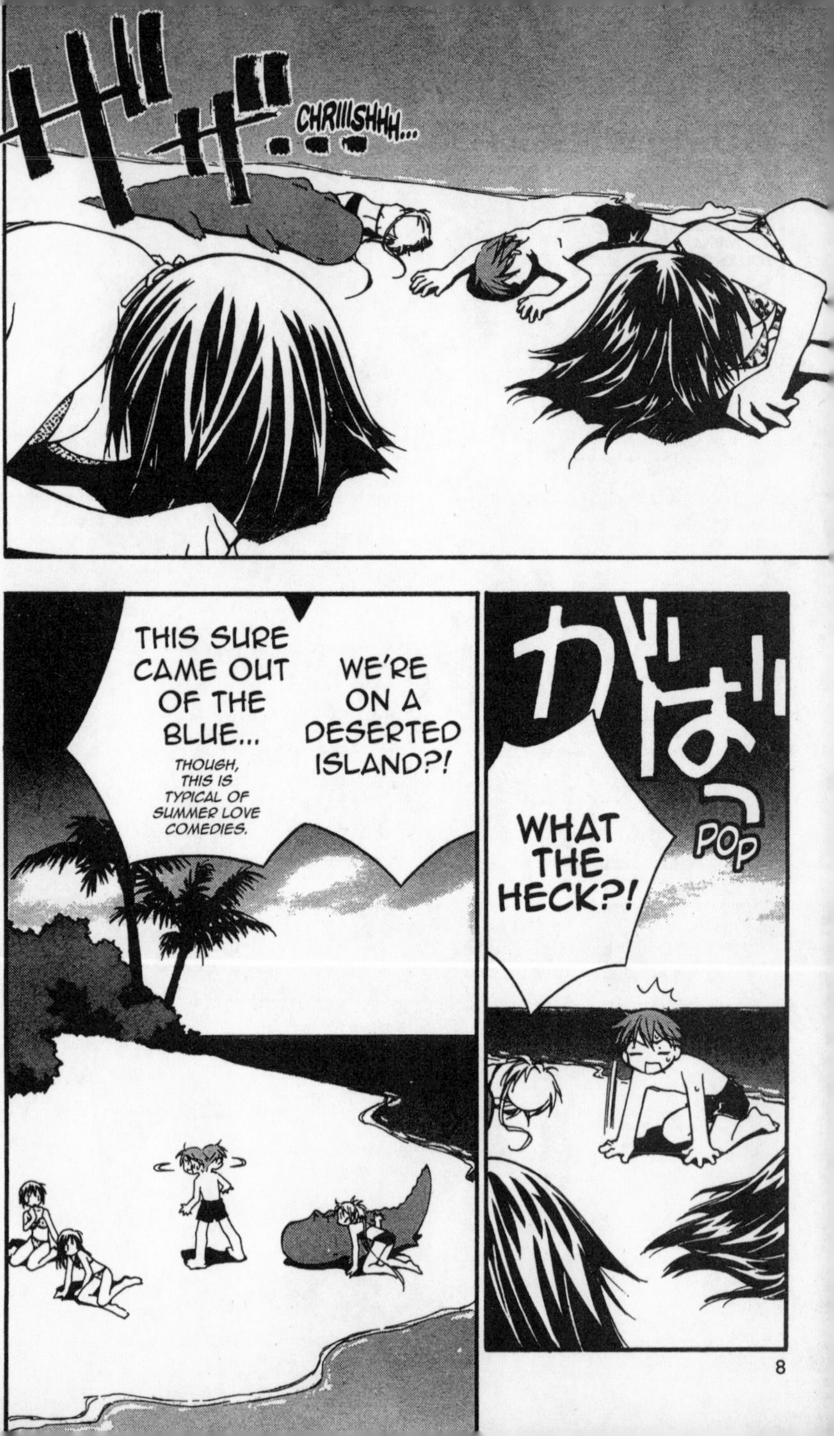
ザザ…
CHRIIISHHH...
がばっ
POP
WHAT THE HECK?!
WE'RE ON A DESERTED ISLAND?!
THIS SURE CAME OUT OF THE BLUE...
THOUGH, THIS IS TYPICAL OF SUMMER LOVE COMEDIES.

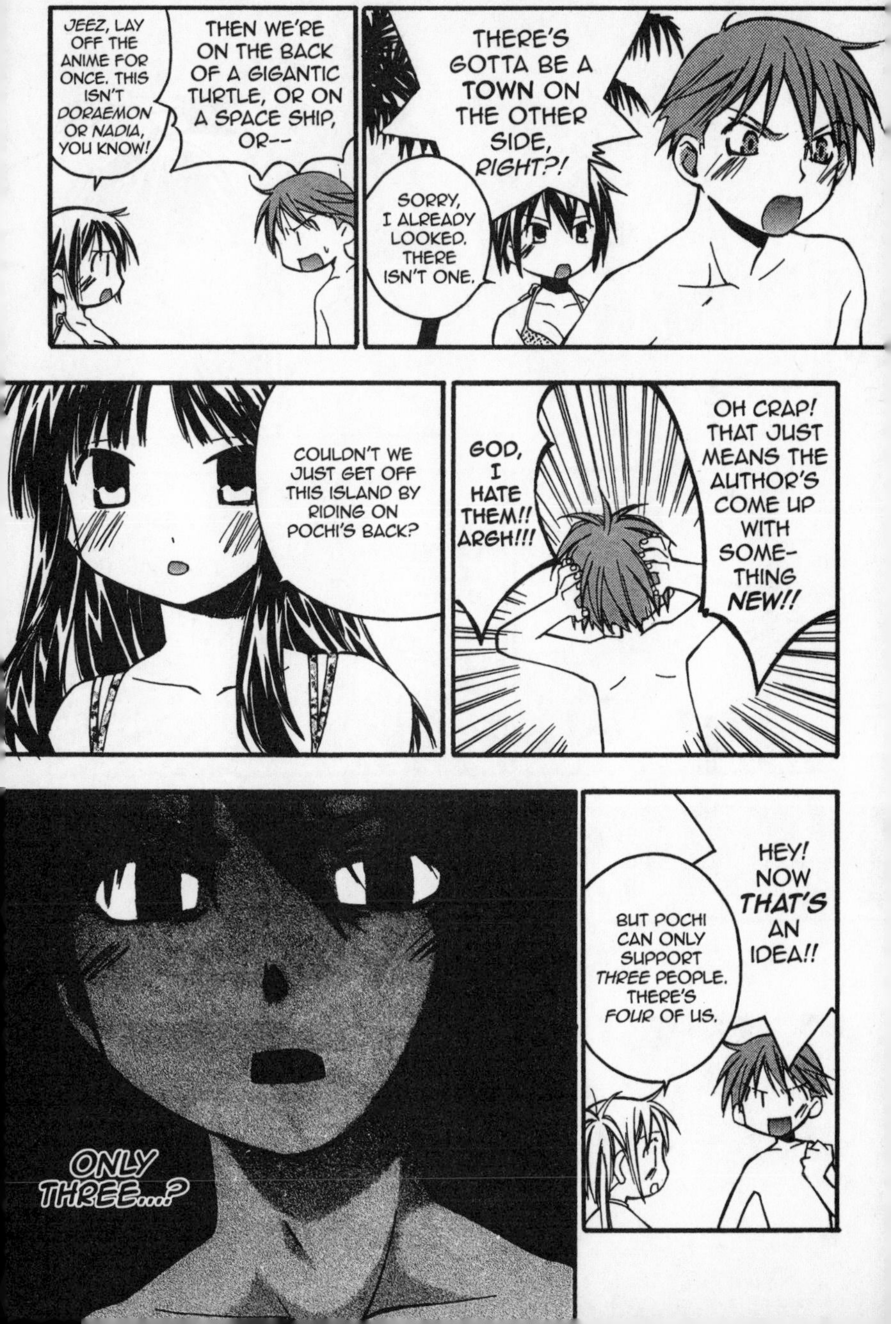
THERE'S GOTTA BE A TOWN ON THE OTHER SIDE, RIGHT?!
SORRY, I ALREADY LOOKED. THERE ISN'T ONE.
THEN WE'RE ON THE BACK OF A GIGANTIC TURTLE, OR ON A SPACE SHIP, OR--
JEEZ, LAY OFF THE ANIME FOR ONCE. THIS ISN'T DORAEMON OR NADIA, YOU KNOW!
OH CRAP! THAT JUST MEANS THE AUTHOR'S COME UP WITH SOME-THING NEW!!
GOD, I HATE THEM!! ARGH!!!
COULDN'T WE JUST GET OFF THIS ISLAND BY RIDING ON POCHI'S BACK?
HEY! NOW THAT'S AN IDEA!!
BUT POCHI CAN ONLY SUPPORT THREE PEOPLE. THERE'S FOUR OF US.
ONLY THREE...?

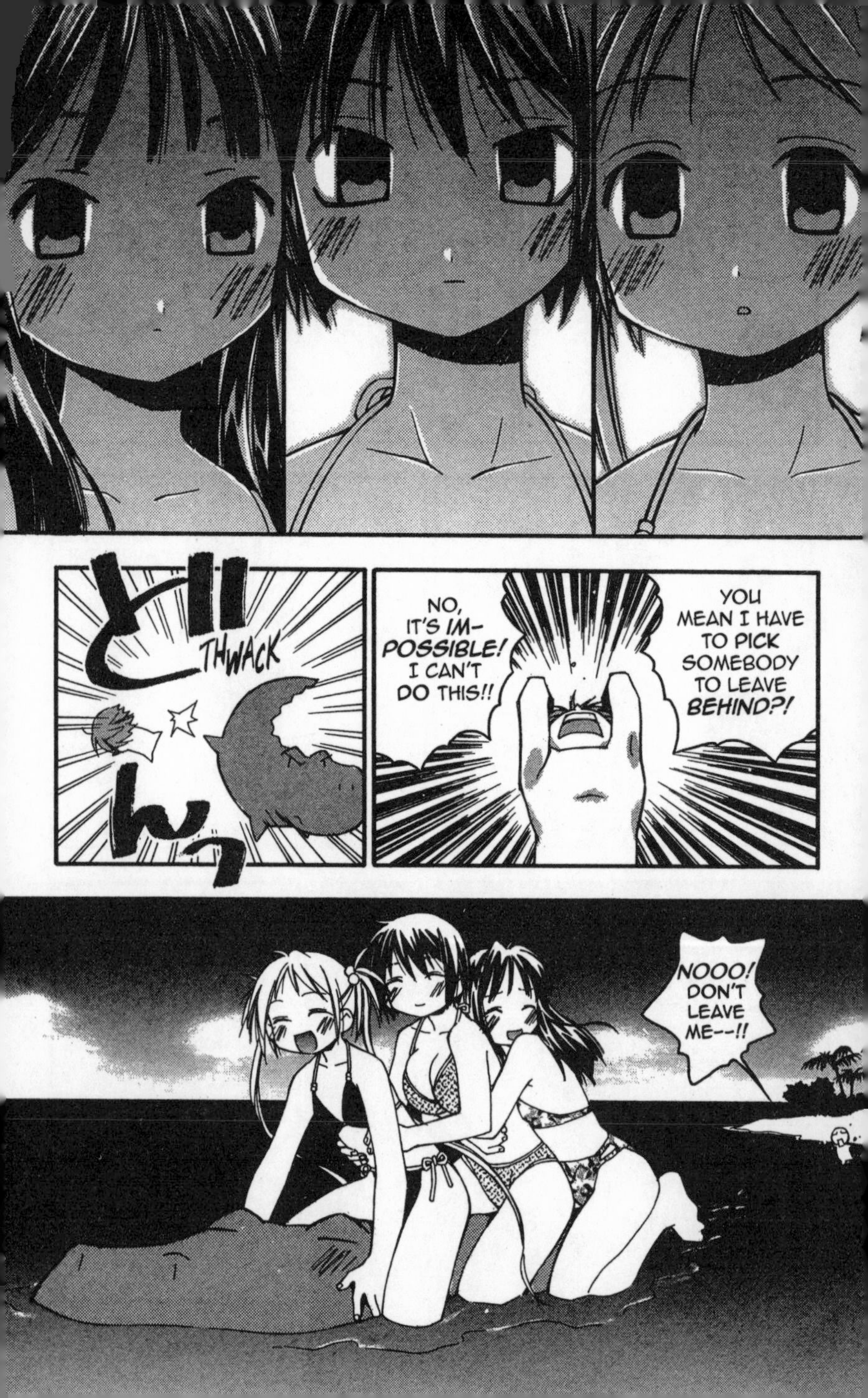
YOU MEAN I HAVE TO PICK SOMEBODY TO LEAVE BEHIND?!
NO, IT'S IM-POSSIBLE! I CAN'T DO THIS!!
どんっ
THWACK
NOOO! DON'T LEAVE ME--!!

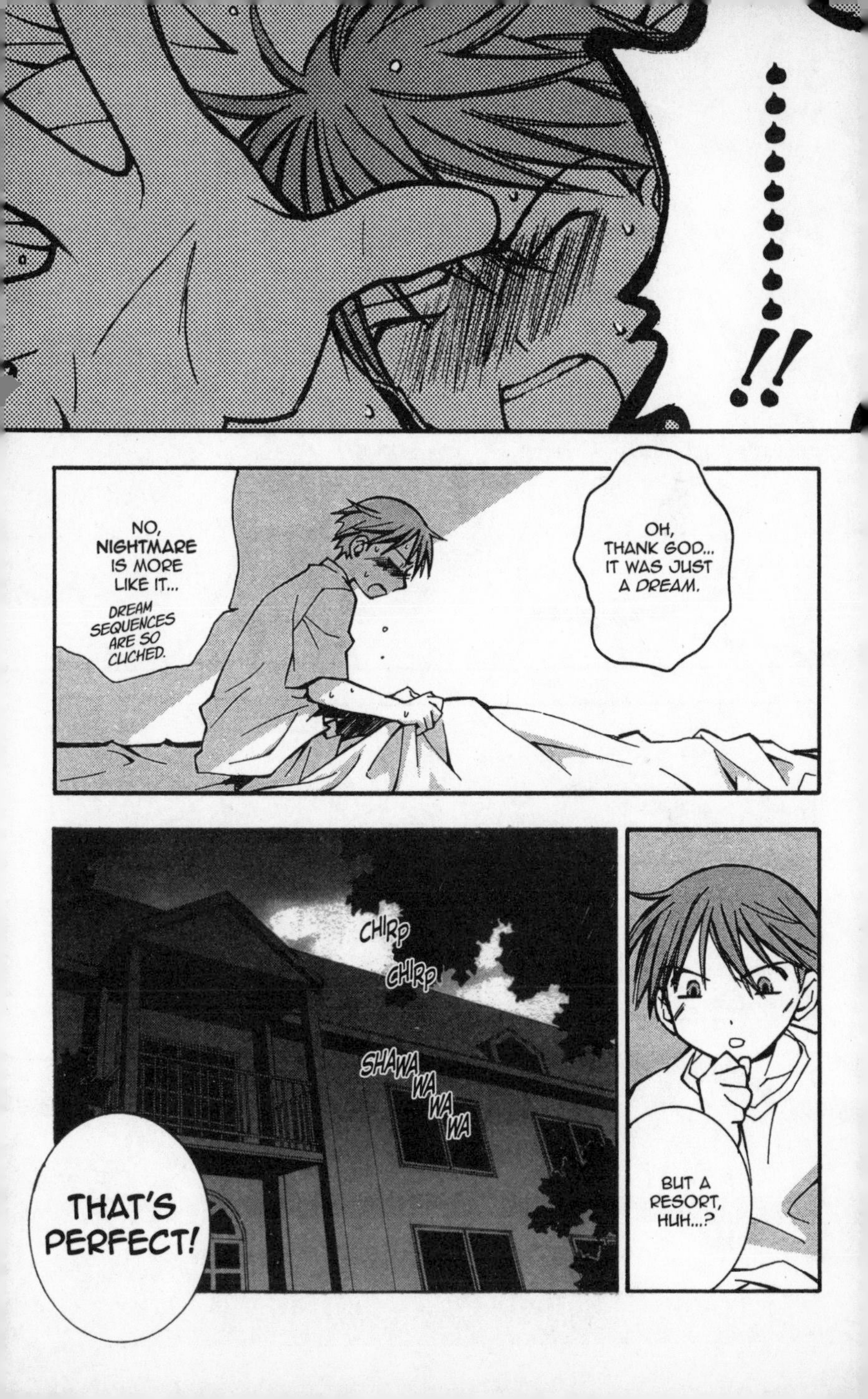
..........!!
OH, THANK GOD... IT WAS JUST A *DREAM*.
NO, NIGHTMARE IS MORE LIKE IT...
DREAM SEQUENCES ARE SO CLICHED.
BUT A RESORT, HUH...?
CHIRP
CHIRP
SHAWAWAWAWA
THAT'S PERFECT!

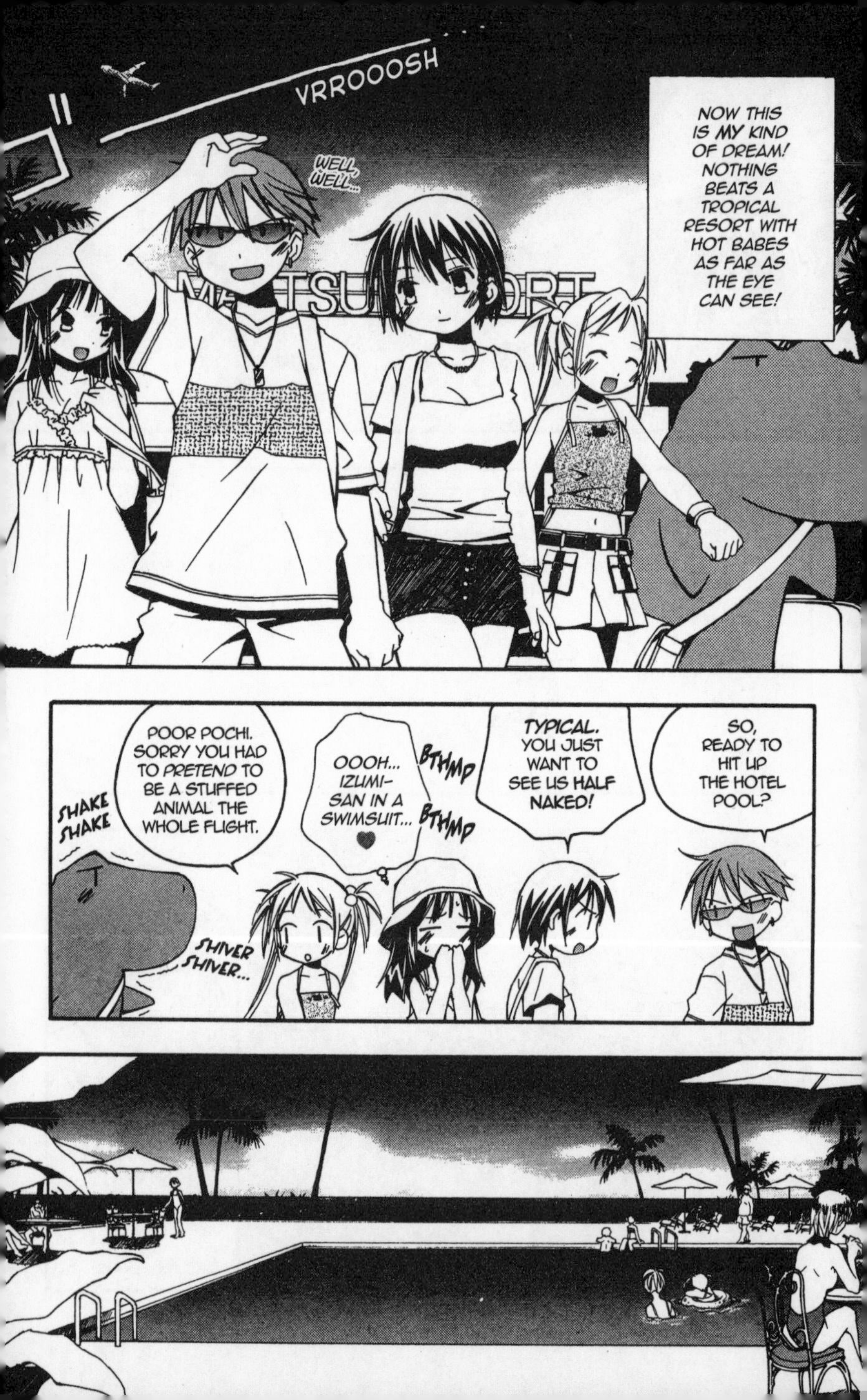
NOW THIS IS MY KIND OF DREAM! NOTHING BEATS A TROPICAL RESORT WITH HOT BABES AS FAR AS THE EYE CAN SEE!
VRROOOSH
WELL, WELL...
SO, READY TO HIT UP THE HOTEL POOL?
TYPICAL. YOU JUST WANT TO SEE US HALF NAKED!
BTHMP
BTHMP
OOOH... IZUMI-SAN IN A SWIMSUIT...
POOR POCHI. SORRY YOU HAD TO PRETEND TO BE A STUFFED ANIMAL THE WHOLE FLIGHT.
SHAKE SHAKE
SHIVER SHIVER...

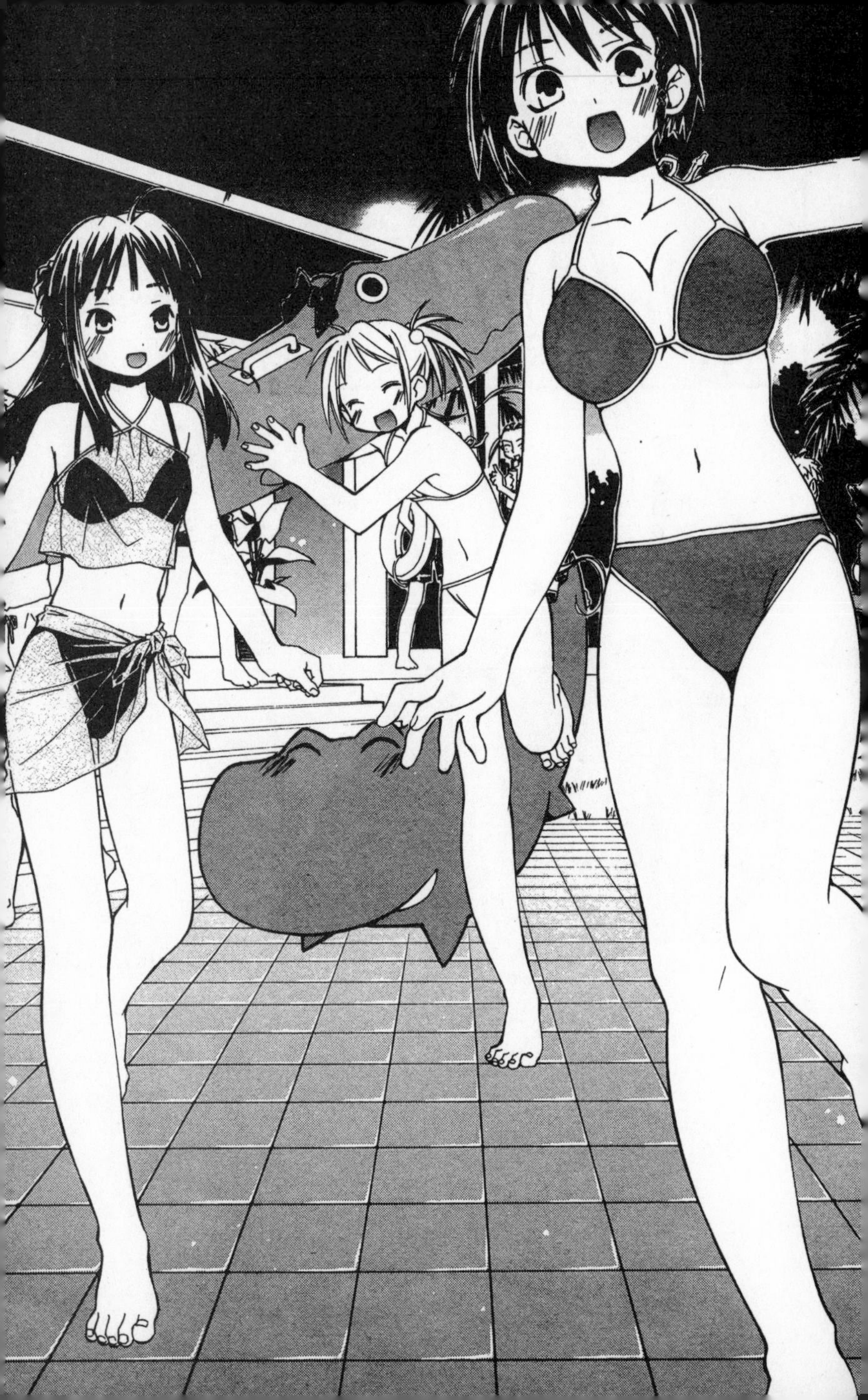

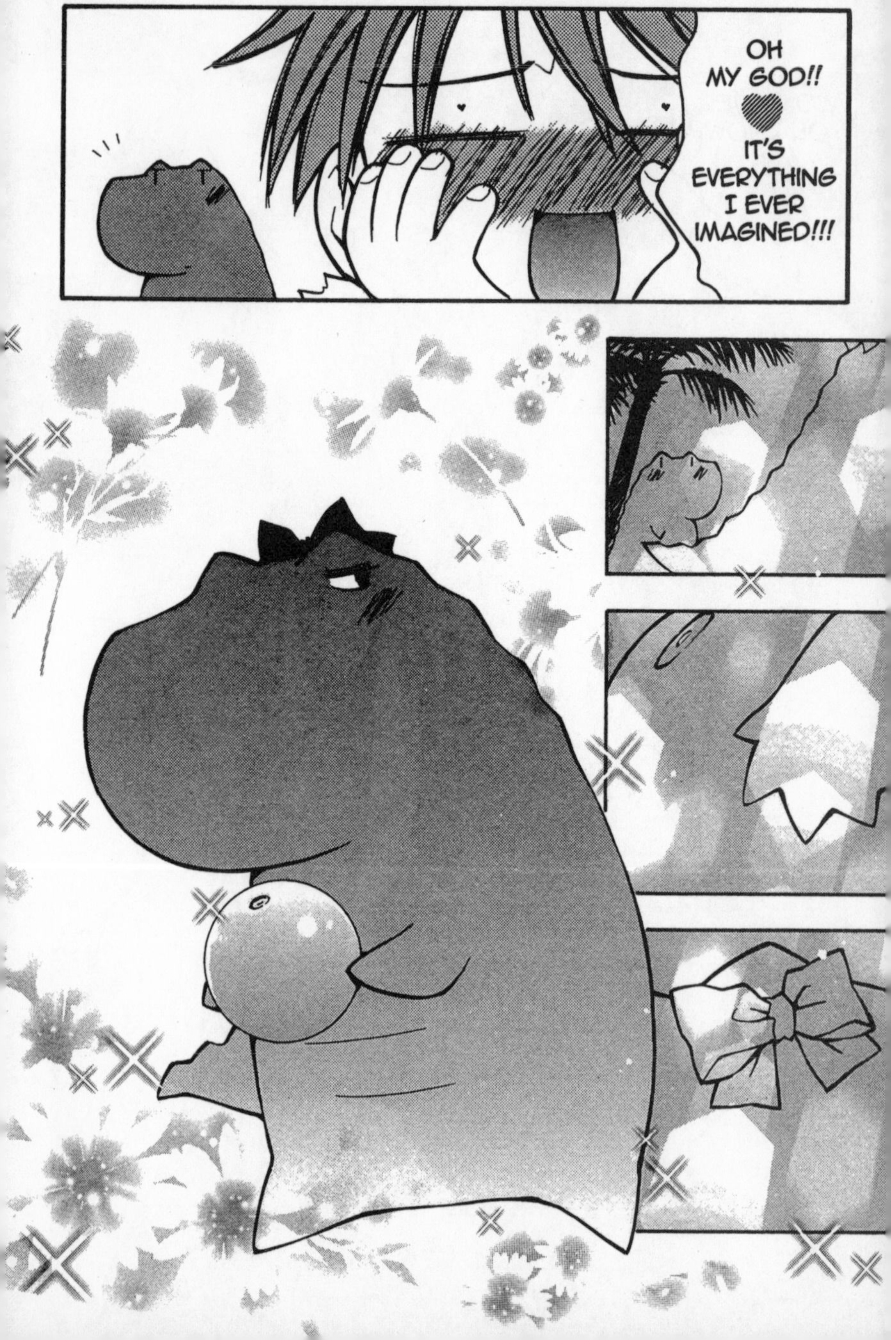
OH MY GOD!! ♥ IT'S EVERYTHING I EVER IMAGINED!!!

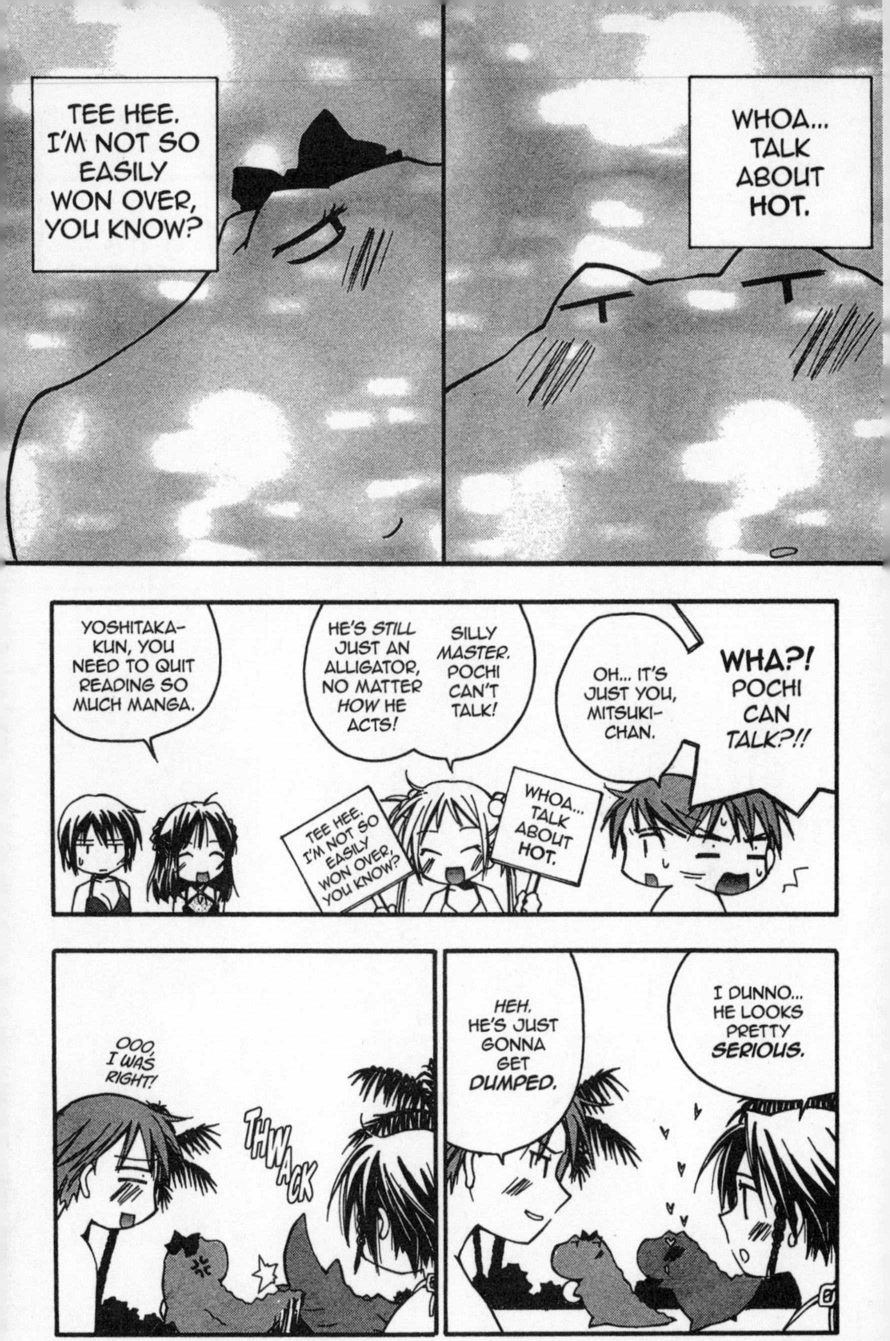
WHOA... TALK ABOUT HOT.
TEE HEE. I'M NOT SO EASILY WON OVER, YOU KNOW?
WHA?! POCHI CAN TALK?!!
OH... IT'S JUST YOU, MITSUKI-CHAN.
WHOA... TALK ABOUT HOT.
SILLY MASTER. POCHI CAN'T TALK!
HE'S STILL JUST AN ALLIGATOR, NO MATTER HOW HE ACTS!
TEE HEE. I'M NOT SO EASILY WON OVER, YOU KNOW?
YOSHITAKA-KUN, YOU NEED TO QUIT READING SO MUCH MANGA.
I DUNNO... HE LOOKS PRETTY SERIOUS.
HEH. HE'S JUST GONNA GET DUMPED.
THWACK
OOO, I WAS RIGHT!

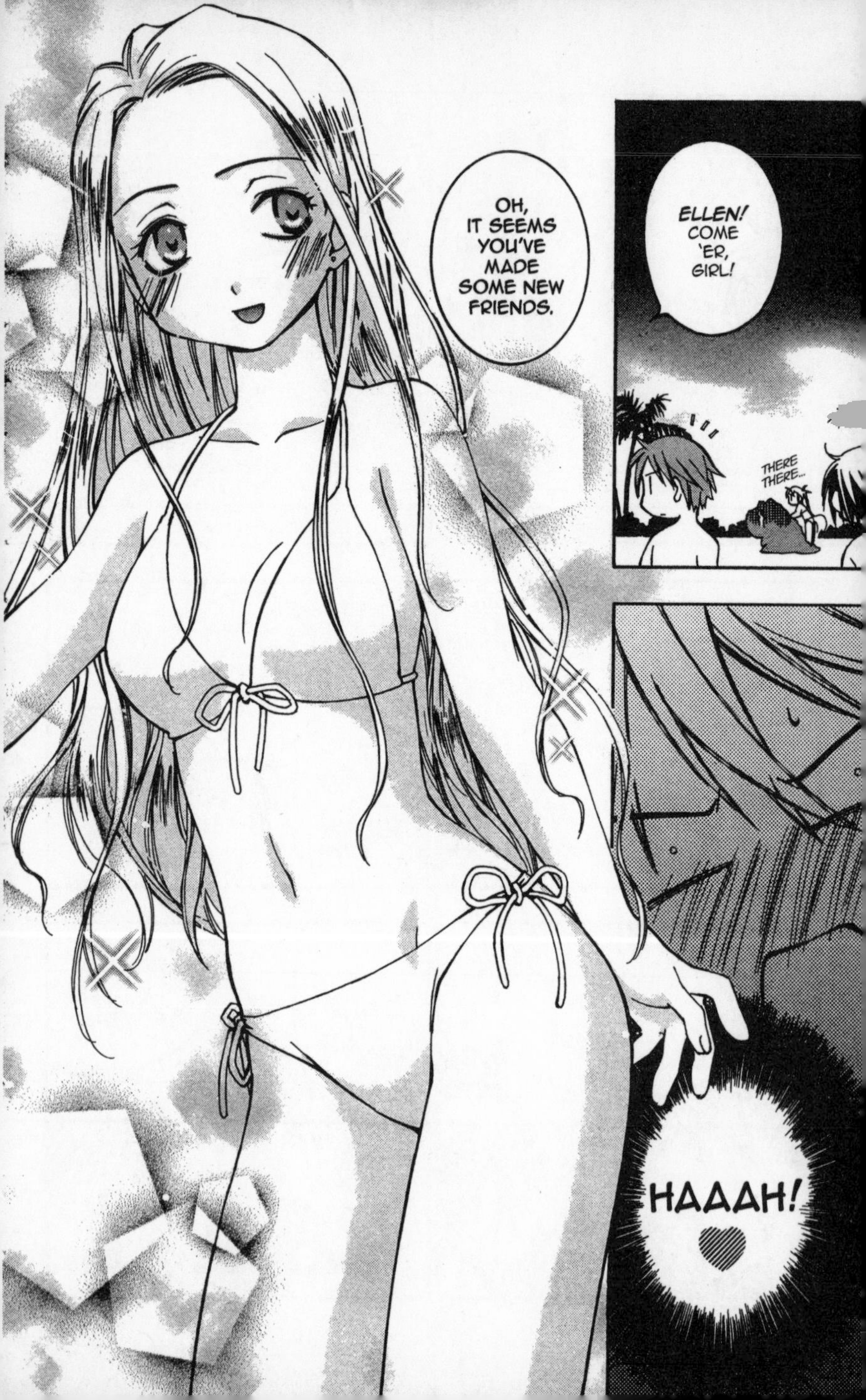
ELLEN! COME 'ER, GIRL!
THERE THERE...
HAAAH!
OH, IT SEEMS YOU'VE MADE SOME NEW FRIENDS.

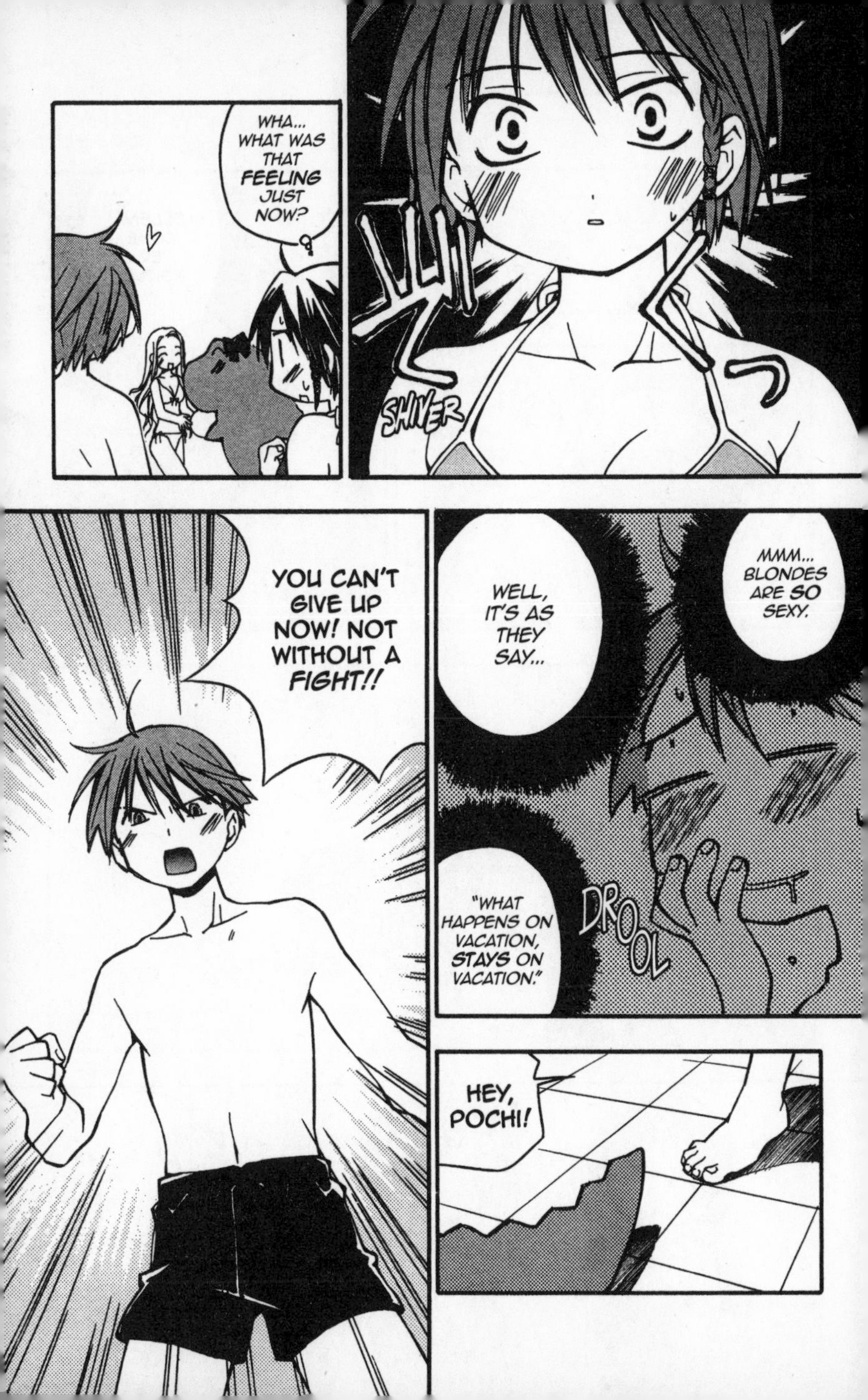
SHIVER
WHA... WHAT WAS THAT FEELING JUST NOW?
MMM... BLONDES ARE SO SEXY.
WELL, IT'S AS THEY SAY...
"WHAT HAPPENS ON VACATION, STAYS ON VACATION."
DROOL
HEY, POCHI!
YOU CAN'T GIVE UP NOW! NOT WITHOUT A FIGHT!!

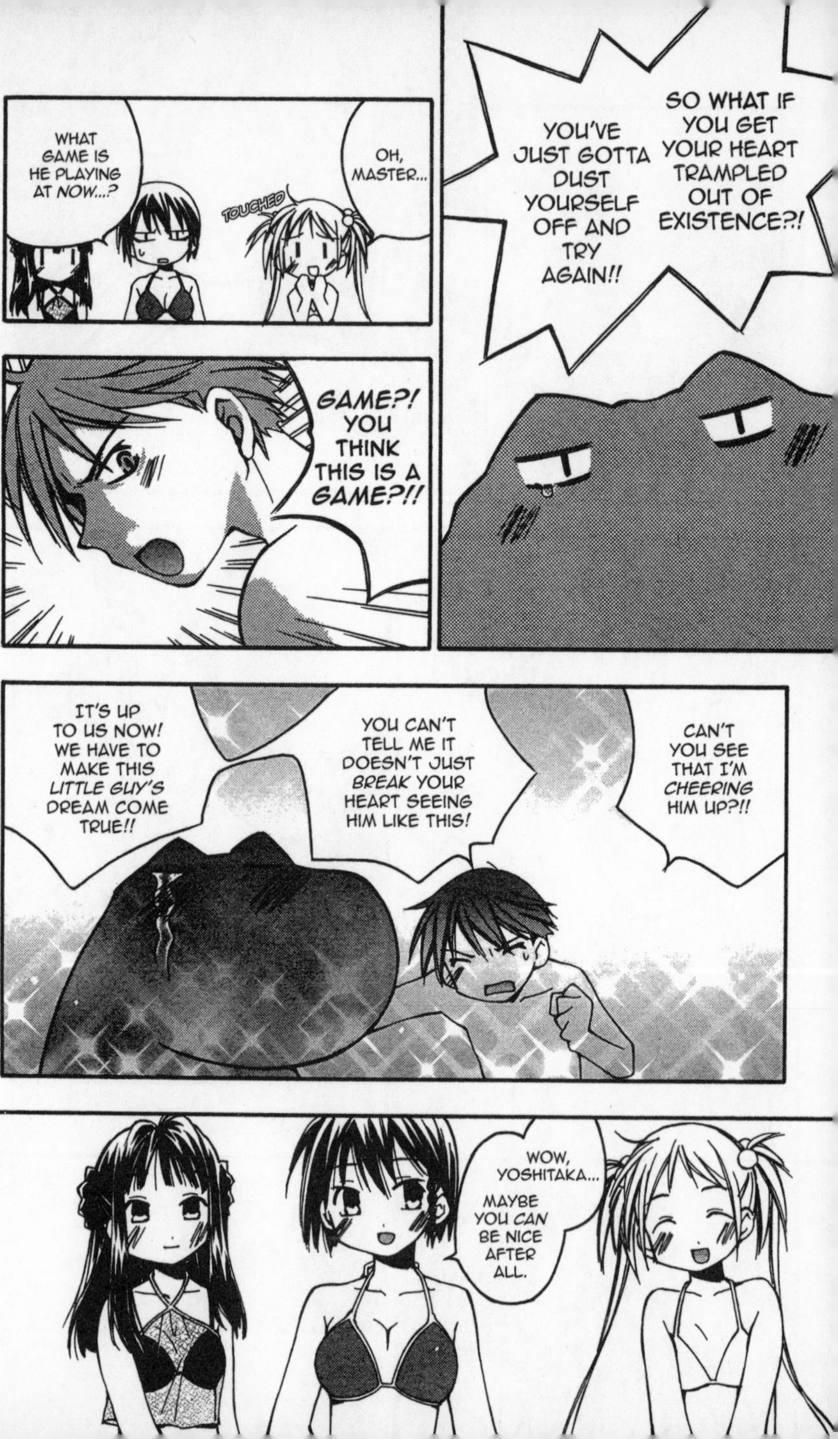
SO WHAT IF YOU GET YOUR HEART TRAMPLED OUT OF EXISTENCE?!
YOU'VE JUST GOTTA DUST YOURSELF OFF AND TRY AGAIN!!
OH, MASTER...
TOUCHED
WHAT GAME IS HE PLAYING AT NOW...?
GAME?! YOU THINK THIS IS A GAME?!!
CAN'T YOU SEE THAT I'M CHEERING HIM UP?!!
YOU CAN'T TELL ME IT DOESN'T JUST BREAK YOUR HEART SEEING HIM LIKE THIS!
IT'S UP TO US NOW! WE HAVE TO MAKE THIS LITTLE GUY'S DREAM COME TRUE!!
WOW, YOSHITAKA...
MAYBE YOU CAN BE NICE AFTER ALL.

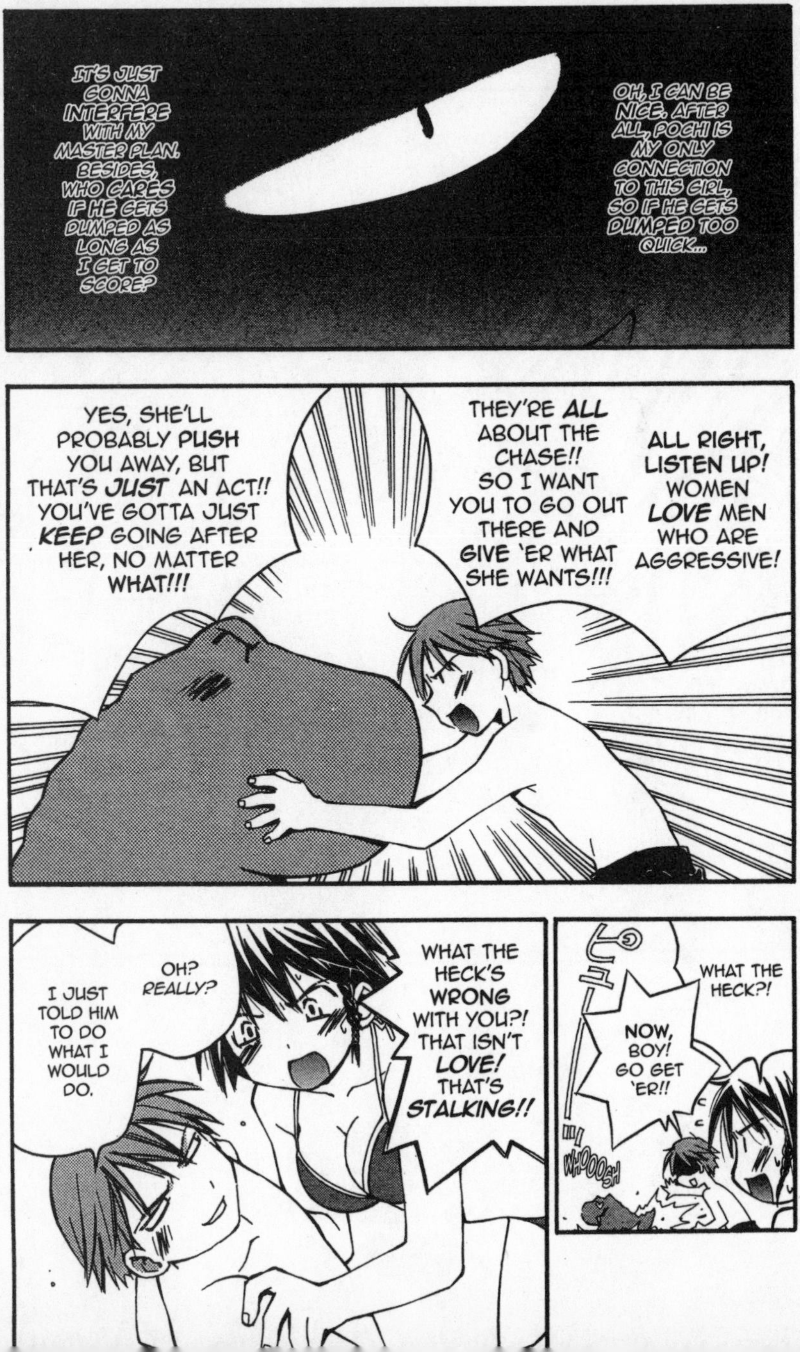
OH, I CAN BE NICE. AFTER ALL, POCHI IS MY ONLY CONNECTION TO THIS GIRL, SO IF HE GETS DUMPED TOO QUICK...
IT'S JUST GONNA INTERFERE WITH MY MASTER PLAN. BESIDES, WHO CARES IF HE GETS DUMPED AS LONG AS I GET TO SCORE?
ALL RIGHT, LISTEN UP! WOMEN LOVE MEN WHO ARE AGGRESSIVE!
THEY'RE ALL ABOUT THE CHASE!! SO I WANT YOU TO GO OUT THERE AND GIVE 'ER WHAT SHE WANTS!!!
YES, SHE'LL PROBABLY PUSH YOU AWAY, BUT THAT'S JUST AN ACT!! YOU'VE GOTTA JUST KEEP GOING AFTER HER, NO MATTER WHAT!!!
WHAT THE HECK?!
NOW, BOY! GO GET 'ER!!
WHOOOSH
WHAT THE HECK'S WRONG WITH YOU?! THAT ISN'T LOVE! THAT'S STALKING!!
OH? REALLY?
I JUST TOLD HIM TO DO WHAT I WOULD DO.

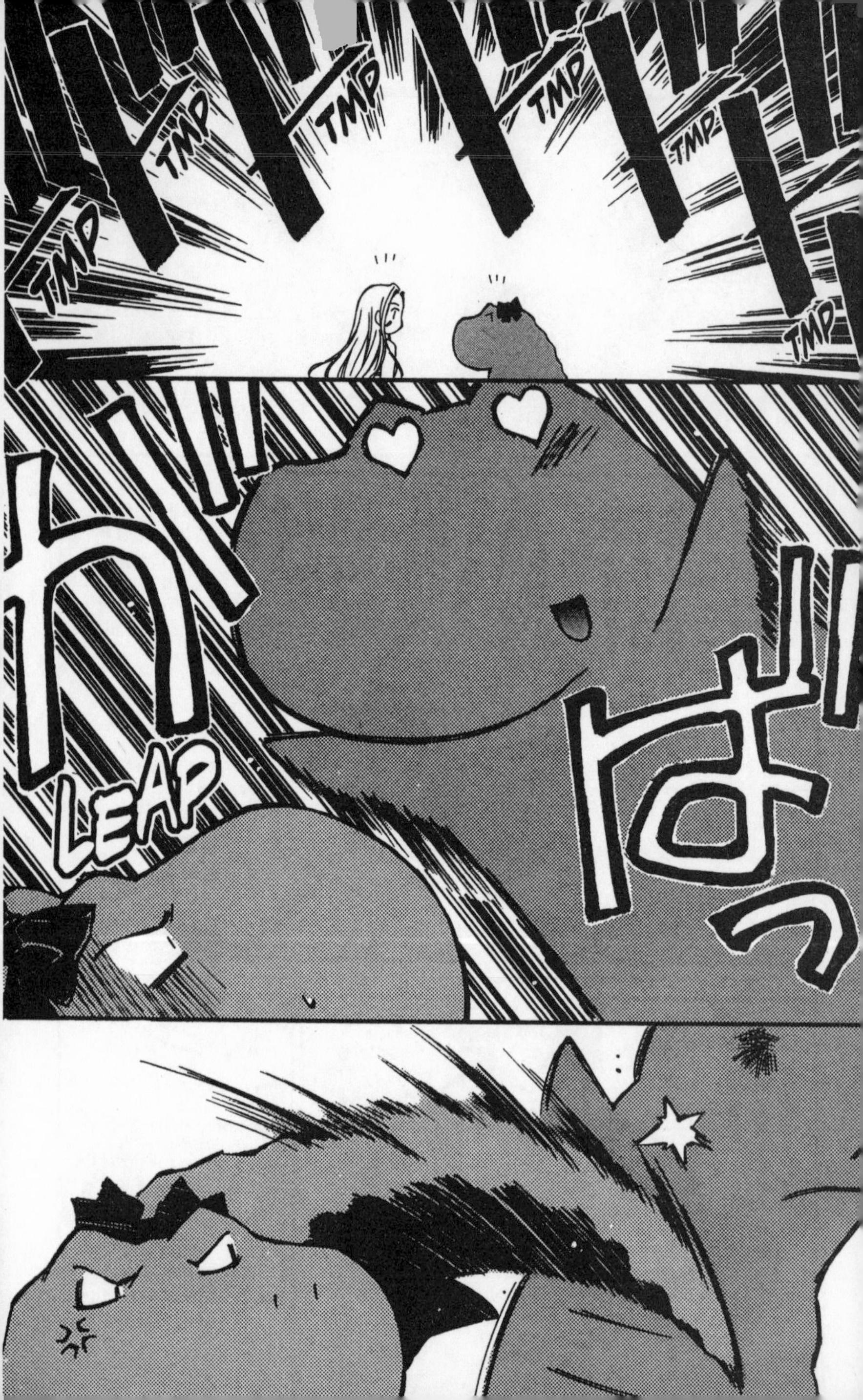
TMP
TMP
TMP
TMP
TMP
TMP
TMP
はっ
LEAP

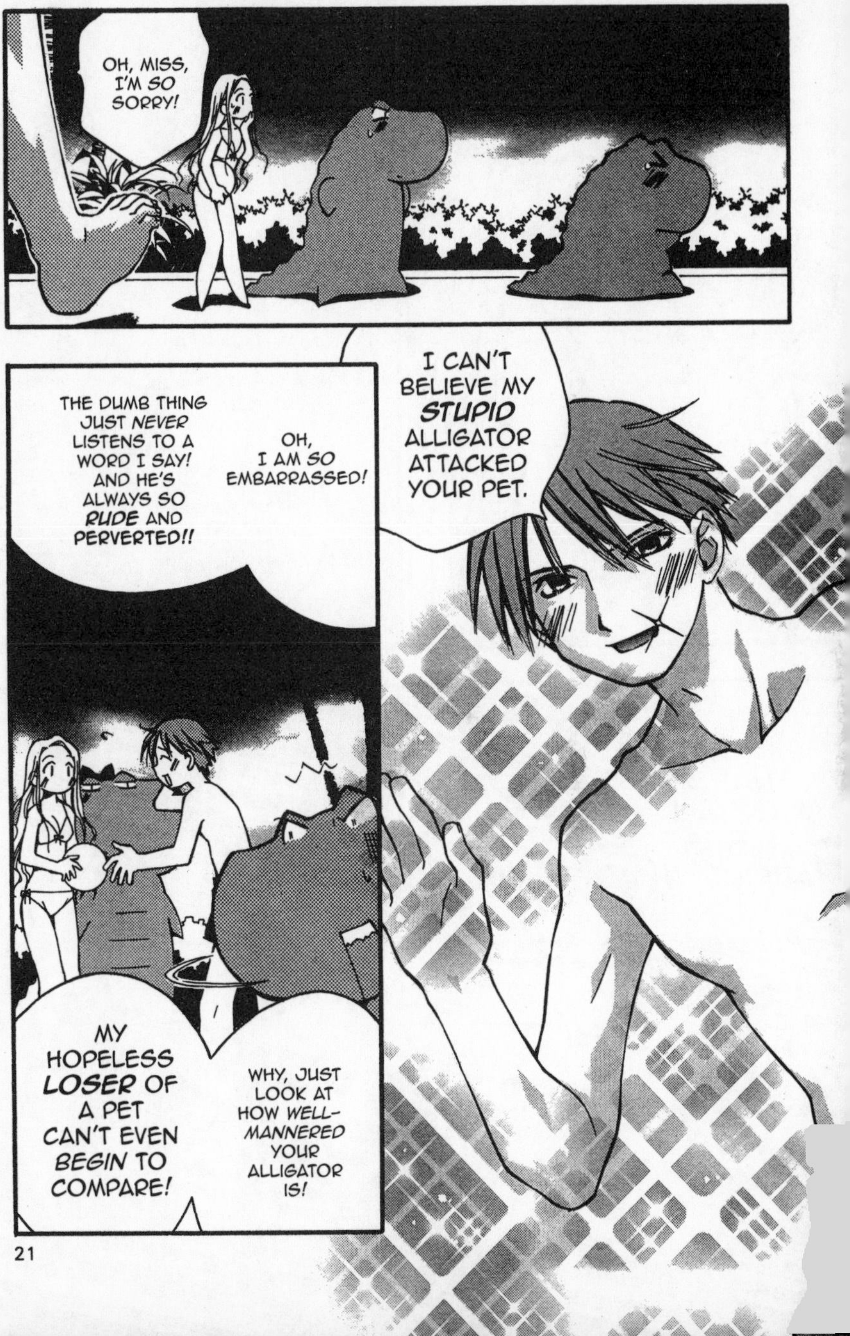
OH, MISS, I'M SO SORRY!
I CAN'T BELIEVE MY STUPID ALLIGATOR ATTACKED YOUR PET.
OH, I AM SO EMBARRASSED!
THE DUMB THING JUST NEVER LISTENS TO A WORD I SAY! AND HE'S ALWAYS SO RUDE AND PERVERTED!!
WHY, JUST LOOK AT HOW WELL-MANNERED YOUR ALLIGATOR IS!
MY HOPELESS LOSER OF A PET CAN'T EVEN BEGIN TO COMPARE!

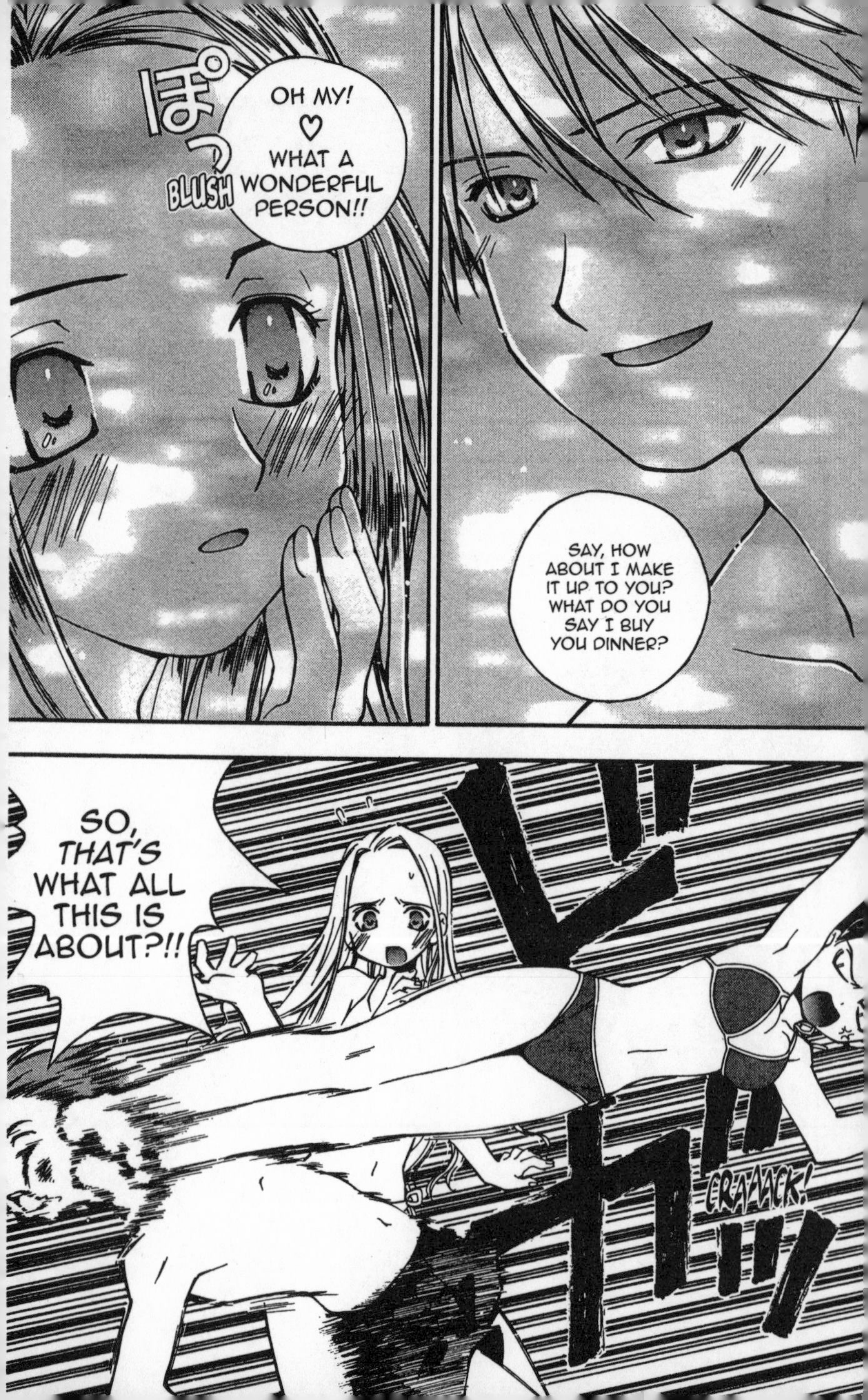
SAY, HOW ABOUT I MAKE IT UP TO YOU? WHAT DO YOU SAY I BUY YOU DINNER?
ぽっ
BLUSH
OH MY! ♡ WHAT A WONDERFUL PERSON!!
SO, THAT'S WHAT ALL THIS IS ABOUT?!!
CRAAACK!

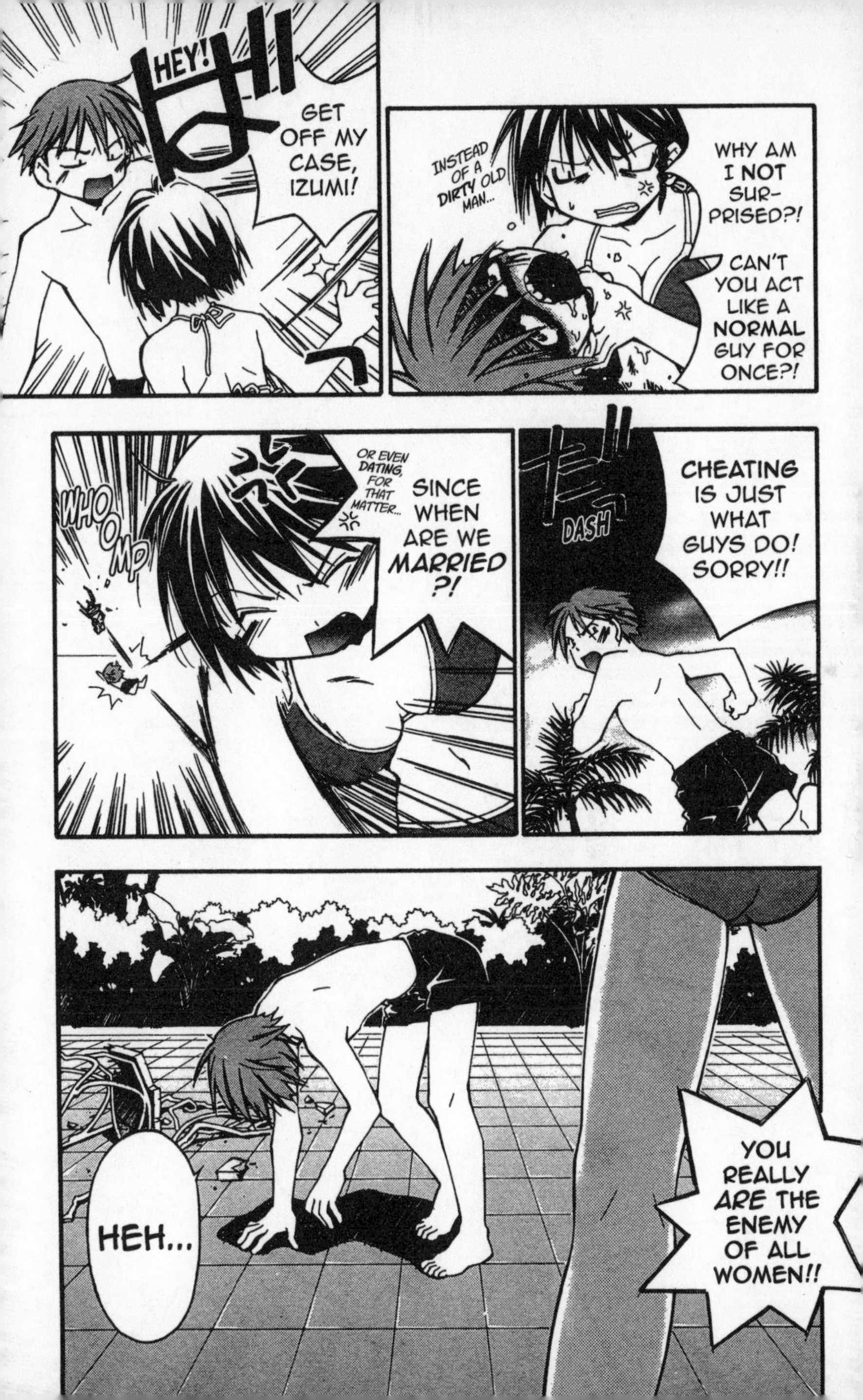
WHY AM I NOT SUR-PRISED?!
CAN'T YOU ACT LIKE A NORMAL GUY FOR ONCE?!
INSTEAD OF A DIRTY OLD MAN...
HEY!
GET OFF MY CASE, IZUMI!
CHEATING IS JUST WHAT GUYS DO! SORRY!!
DASH
SINCE WHEN ARE WE MARRIED?!
OR EVEN DATING, FOR THAT MATTER...
WHOOMP
YOU REALLY ARE THE ENEMY OF ALL WOMEN!!
HEH...

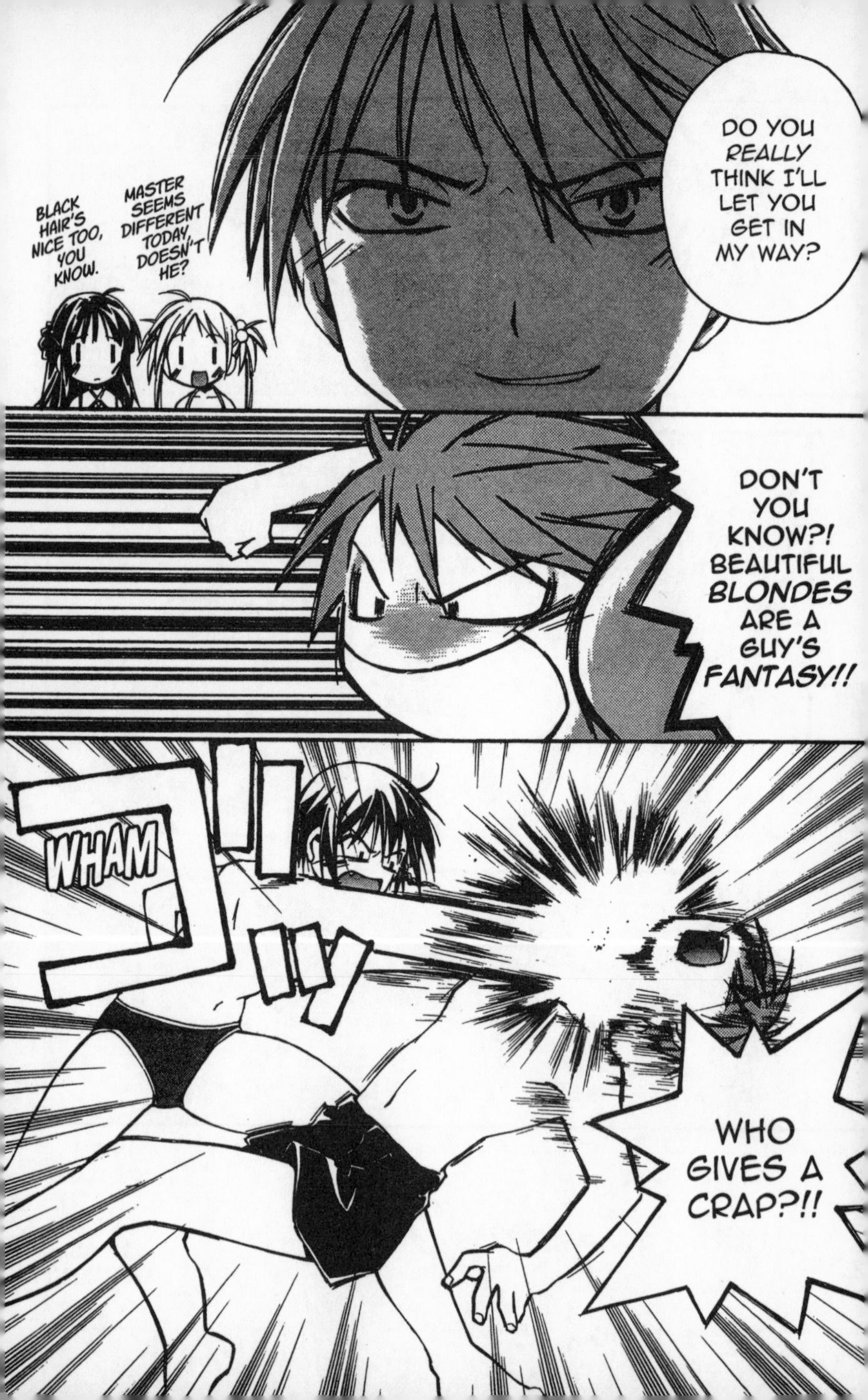
DO YOU REALLY THINK I'LL LET YOU GET IN MY WAY?
MASTER SEEMS DIFFERENT TODAY, DOESN'T HE?
BLACK HAIR'S NICE TOO, YOU KNOW.
DON'T YOU KNOW?! BEAUTIFUL BLONDES ARE A GUY'S FANTASY!!
WHO GIVES A CRAP?!!
WHAM

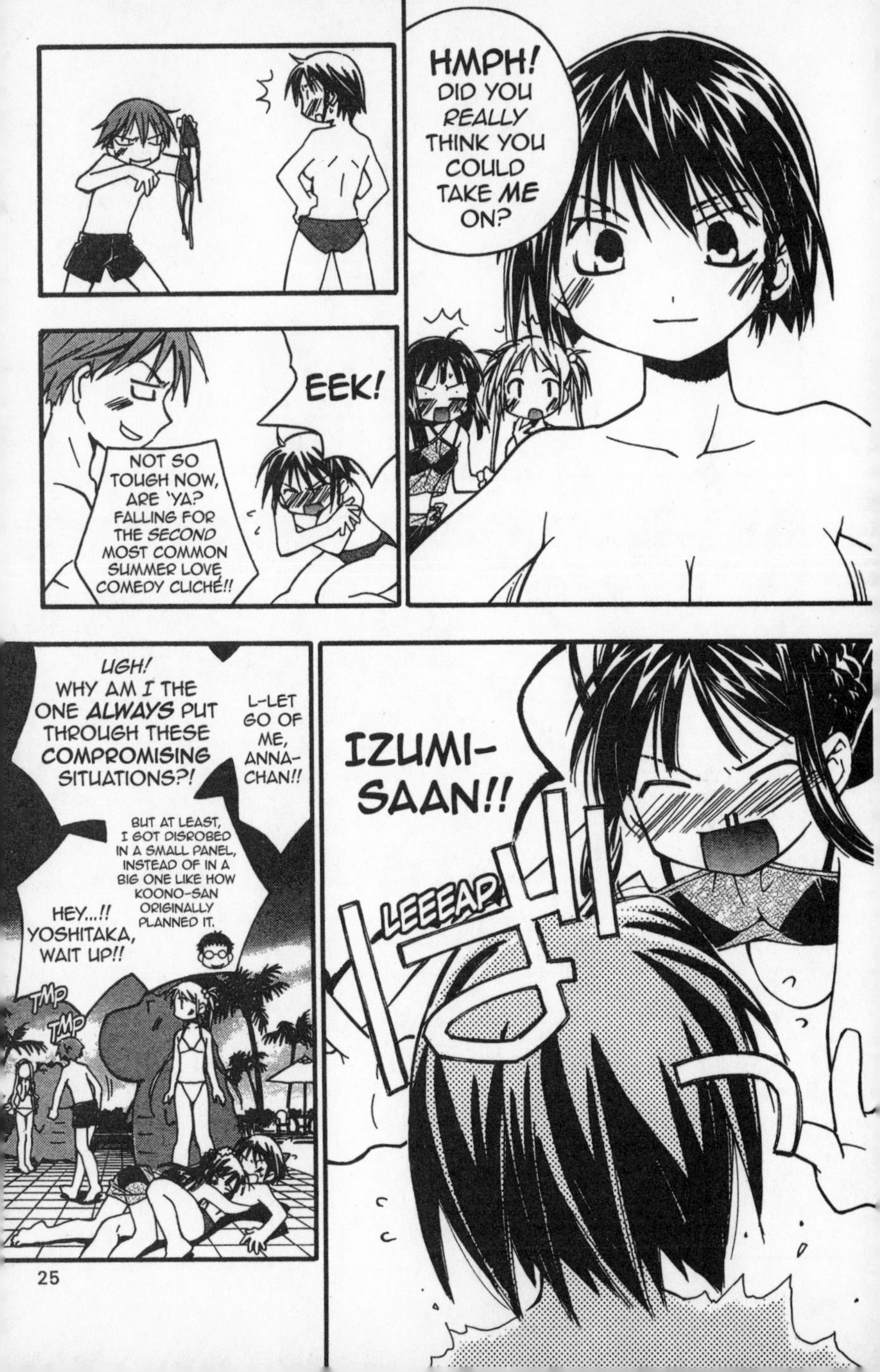
HMPH! DID YOU *REALLY* THINK YOU COULD TAKE *ME* ON?
EEK!
NOT SO TOUGH NOW, ARE 'YA? FALLING FOR THE *SECOND* MOST COMMON SUMMER LOVE COMEDY CLICHÉ!!
IZUMI-SAAN!!
LEEEAP
L-LET GO OF ME, ANNA-CHAN!!
UGH! WHY AM *I* THE ONE **ALWAYS** PUT THROUGH THESE **COMPROMISING** SITUATIONS?!
BUT AT LEAST, I GOT DISROBED IN A SMALL PANEL, INSTEAD OF IN A BIG ONE LIKE HOW KOONO-SAN ORIGINALLY PLANNED IT.
HEY...!! YOSHITAKA, WAIT UP!!
TMP
TMP

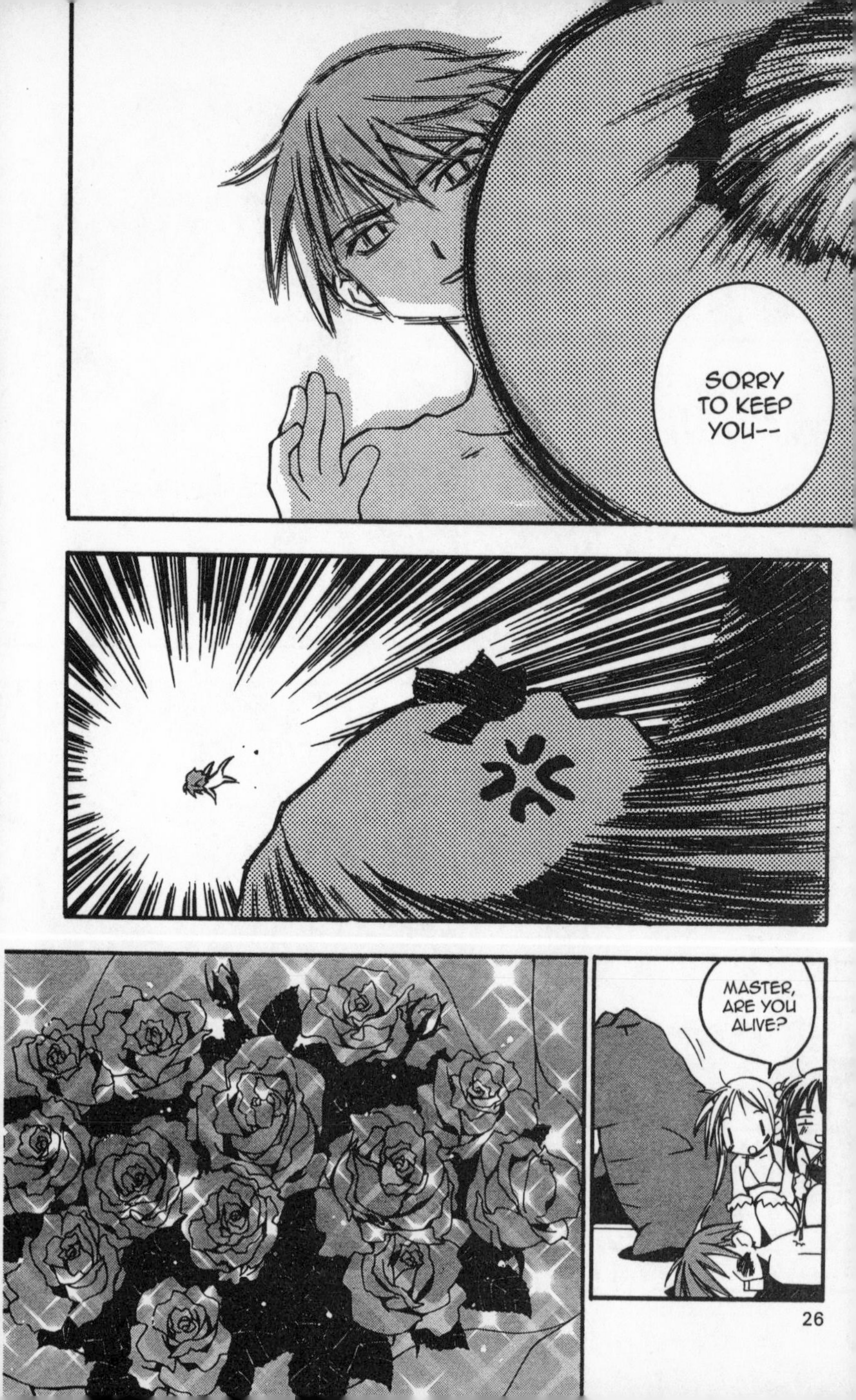
SORRY TO KEEP YOU--
MASTER, ARE YOU ALIVE?

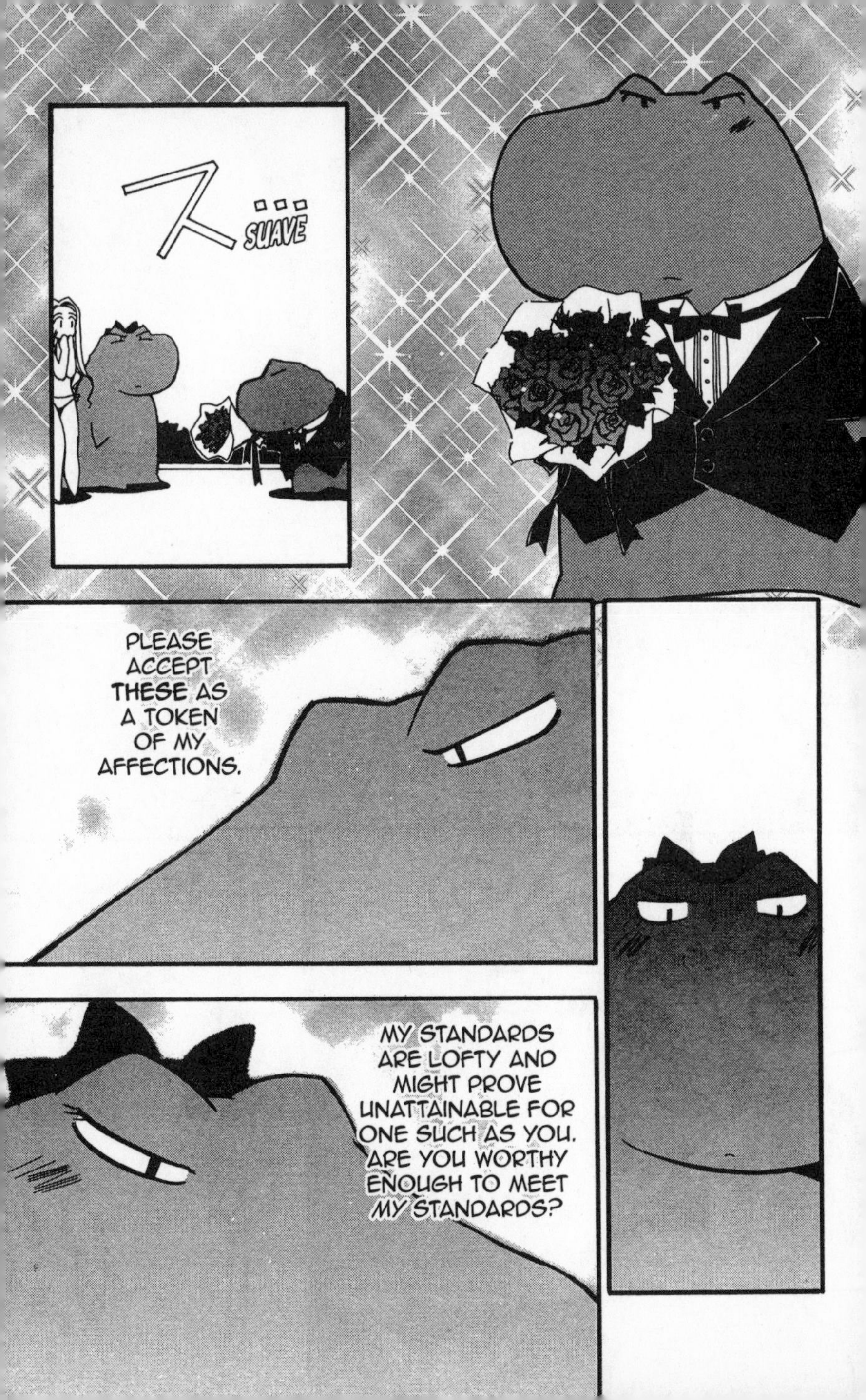
ス...
SUAVE
PLEASE ACCEPT THESE AS A TOKEN OF MY AFFECTIONS.
MY STANDARDS ARE LOFTY AND MIGHT PROVE UNATTAINABLE FOR ONE SUCH AS YOU. ARE YOU WORTHY ENOUGH TO MEET MY STANDARDS?

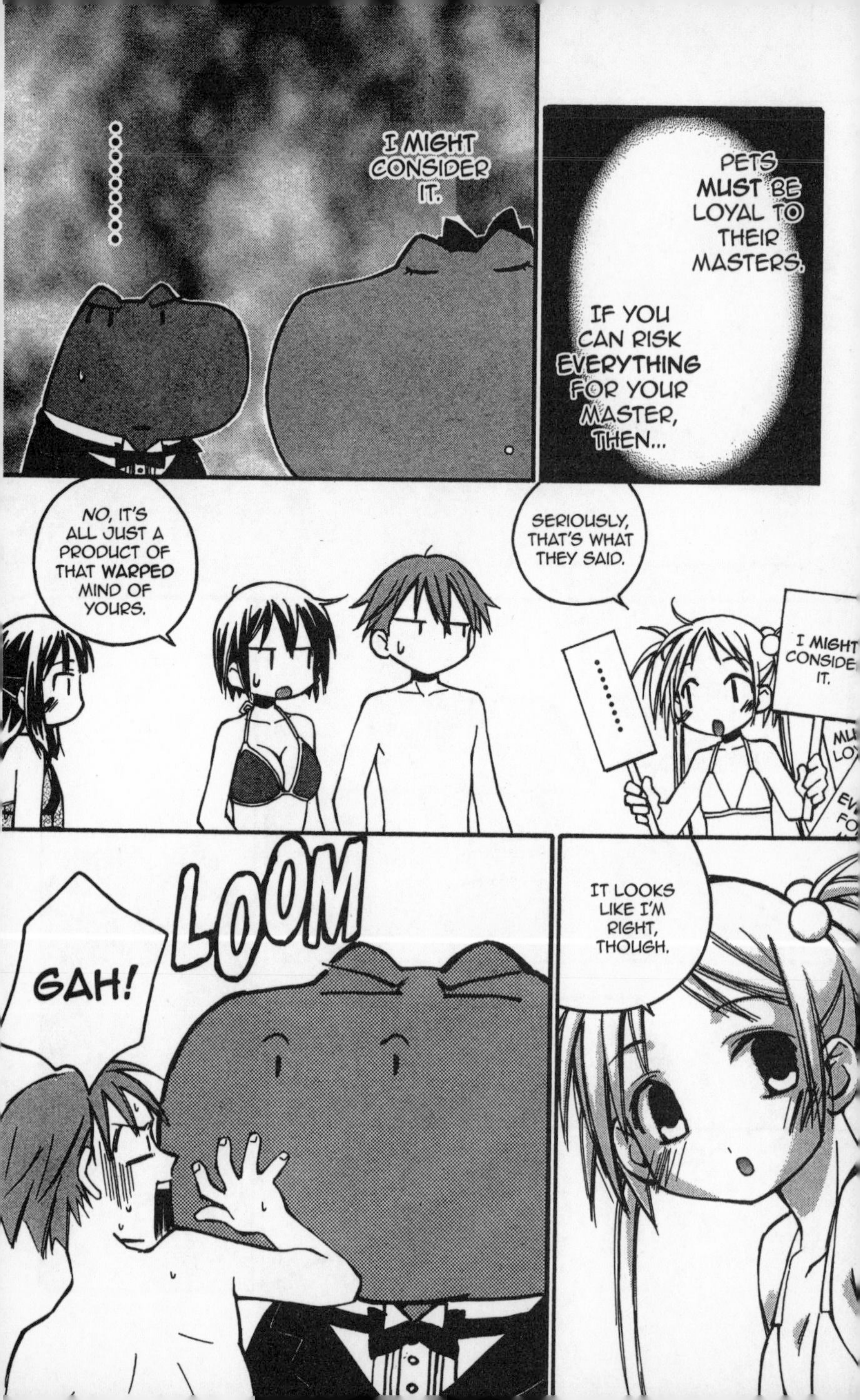
PETS MUST BE LOYAL TO THEIR MASTERS.
IF YOU CAN RISK EVERYTHING FOR YOUR MASTER, THEN...
I MIGHT CONSIDER IT.
....
SERIOUSLY, THAT'S WHAT THEY SAID.
NO, IT'S ALL JUST A PRODUCT OF THAT WARPED MIND OF YOURS.
IT LOOKS LIKE I'M RIGHT, THOUGH.
LOOM
GAH!

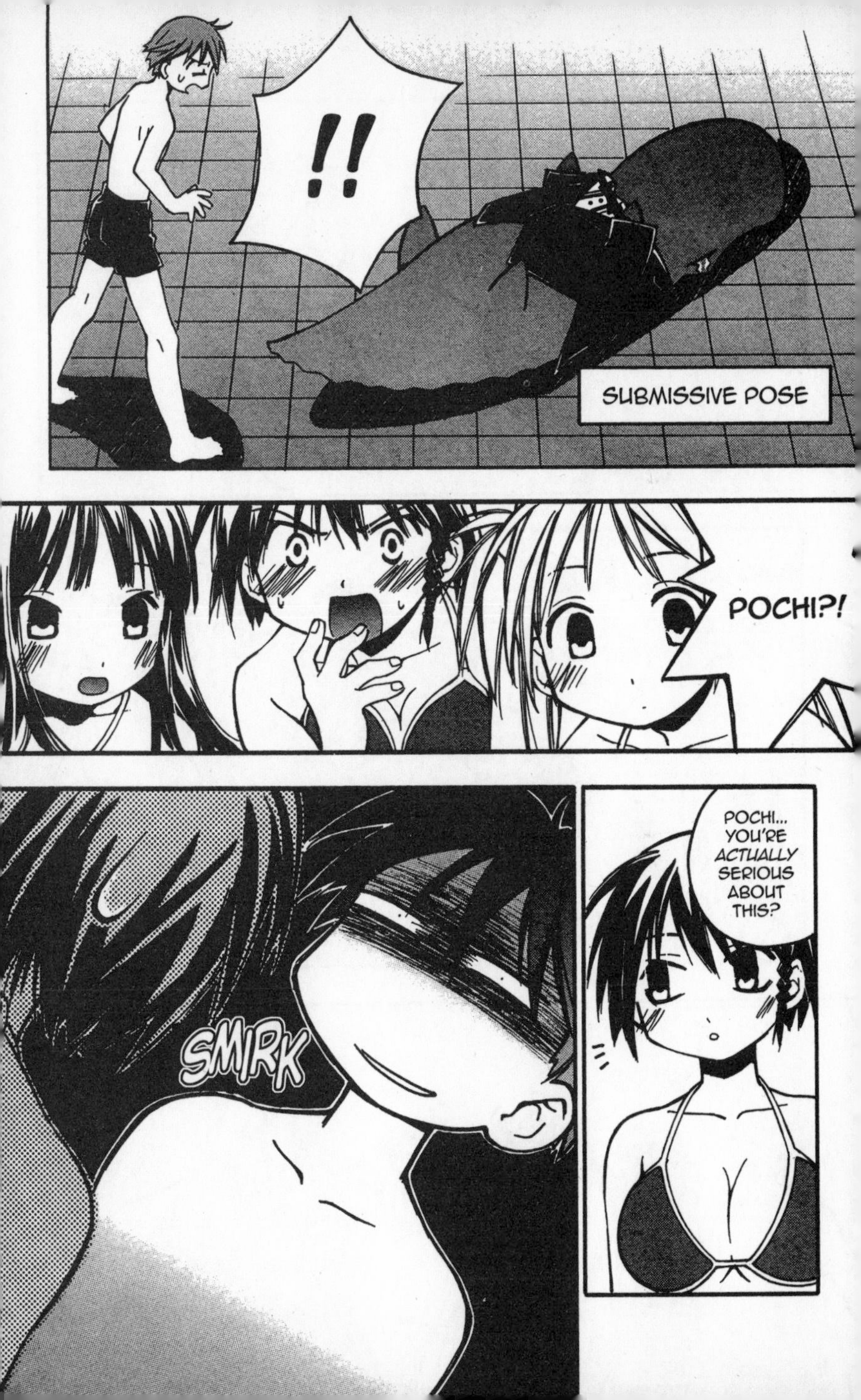
!!
SUBMISSIVE POSE
POCHI?!
POCHI... YOU'RE ACTUALLY SERIOUS ABOUT THIS?
SMIRK

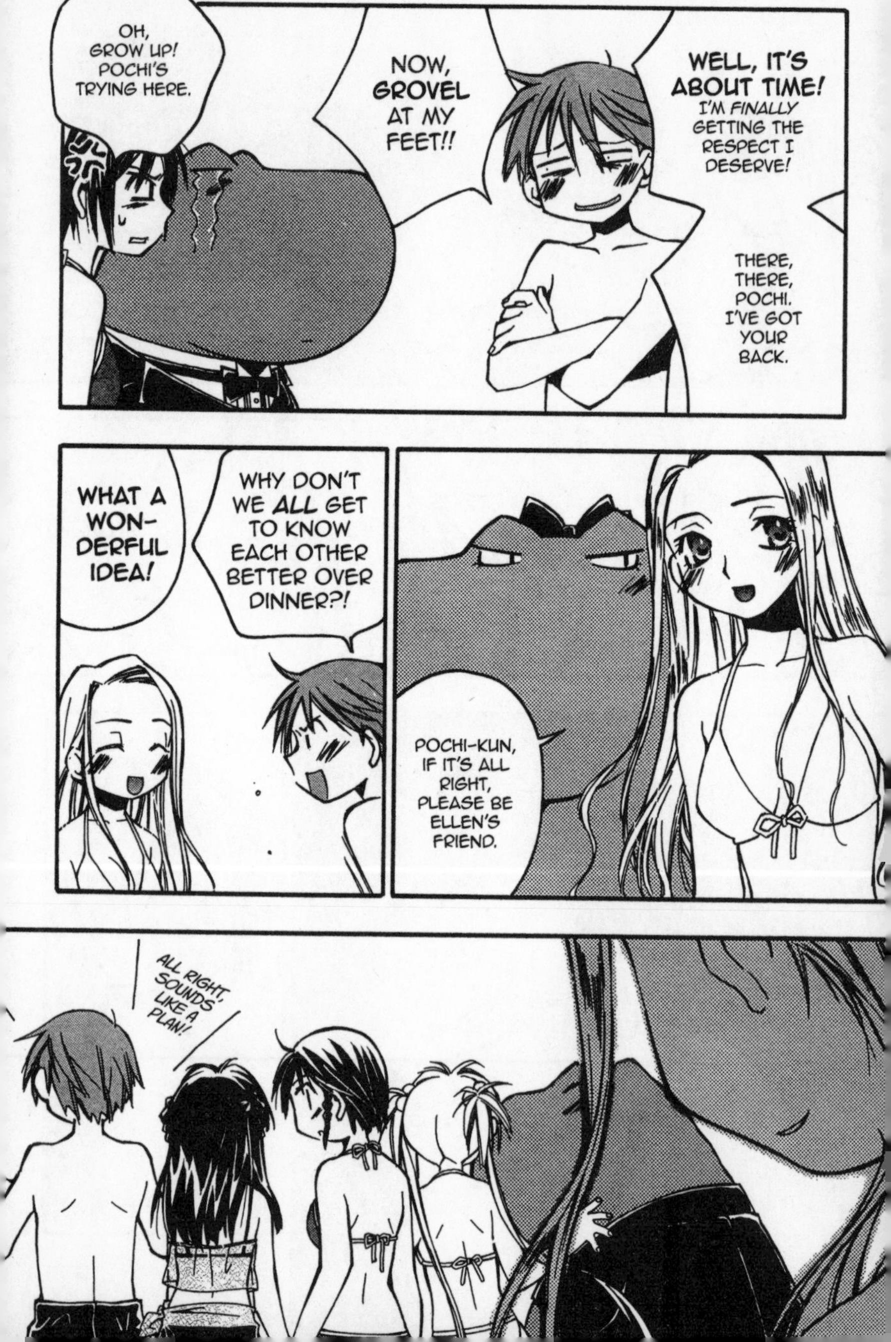
WELL, IT'S ABOUT TIME! I'M FINALLY GETTING THE RESPECT I DESERVE!
NOW, GROVEL AT MY FEET!!
THERE, THERE, POCHI. I'VE GOT YOUR BACK.
OH, GROW UP! POCHI'S TRYING HERE.
POCHI-KUN, IF IT'S ALL RIGHT, PLEASE BE ELLEN'S FRIEND.
WHY DON'T WE ALL GET TO KNOW EACH OTHER BETTER OVER DINNER?!
WHAT A WONDERFUL IDEA!
ALL RIGHT, SOUNDS LIKE A PLAN!

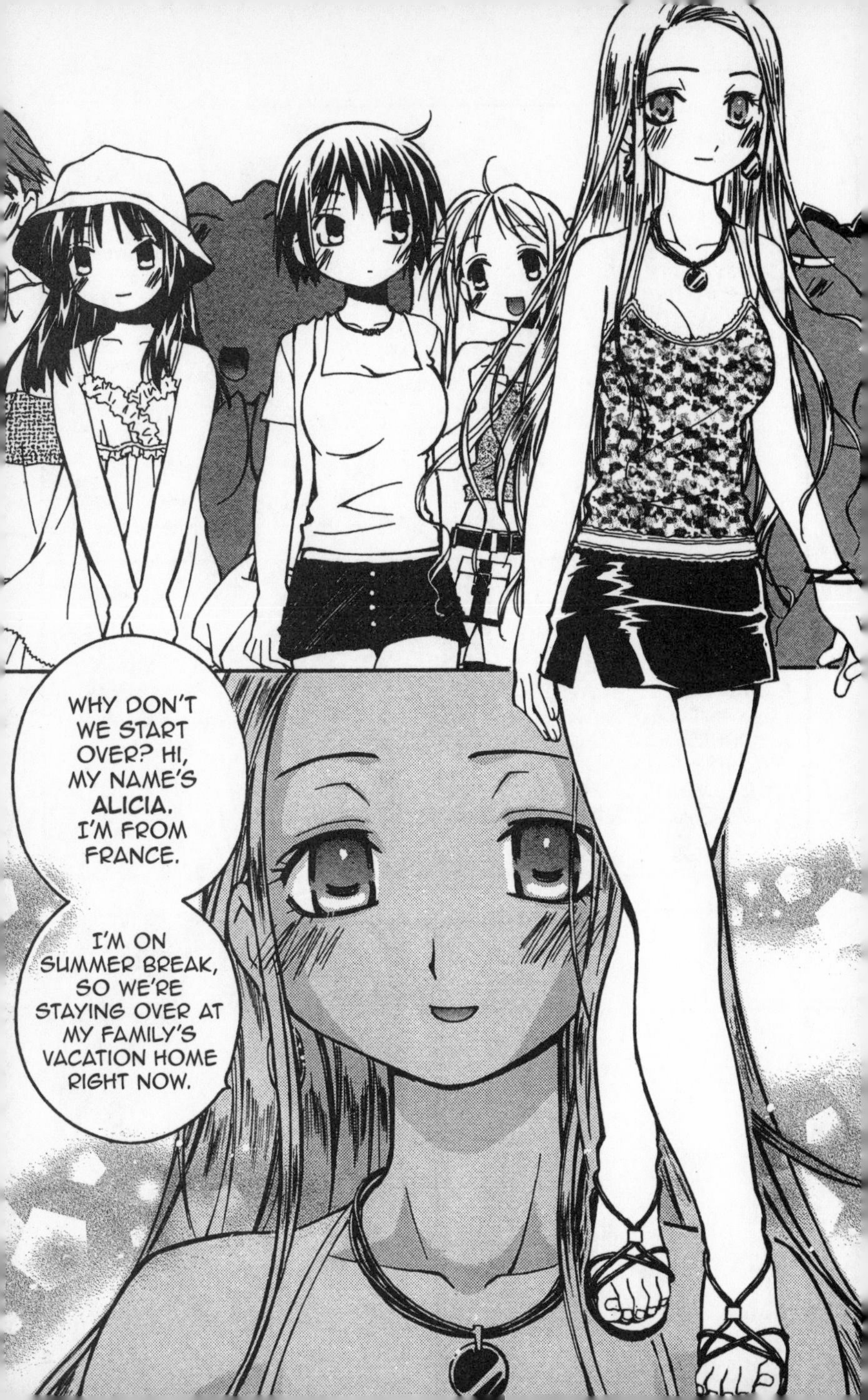
WHY DON'T WE START OVER? HI, MY NAME'S **ALICIA**. I'M FROM FRANCE.
I'M ON SUMMER BREAK, SO WE'RE STAYING OVER AT MY FAMILY'S VACATION HOME RIGHT NOW.

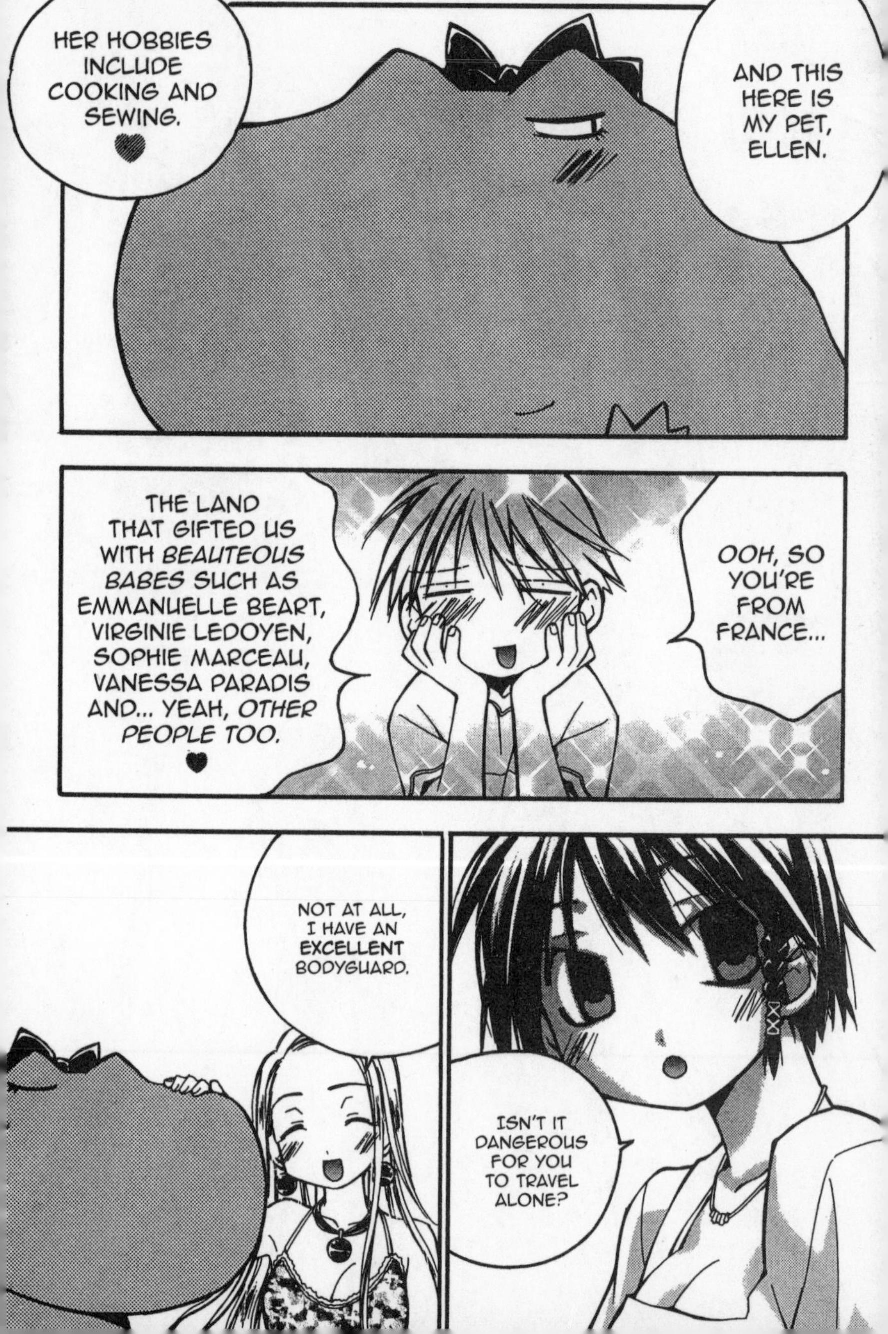
AND THIS HERE IS MY PET, ELLEN.
HER HOBBIES INCLUDE COOKING AND SEWING. ♥
OOH, SO YOU'RE FROM FRANCE...
THE LAND THAT GIFTED US WITH *BEAUTEOUS BABES* SUCH AS EMMANUELLE BEART, VIRGINIE LEDOYEN, SOPHIE MARCEAU, VANESSA PARADIS AND... YEAH, *OTHER PEOPLE TOO.* ♥
ISN'T IT DANGEROUS FOR YOU TO TRAVEL ALONE?
NOT AT ALL, I HAVE AN EXCELLENT BODYGUARD.

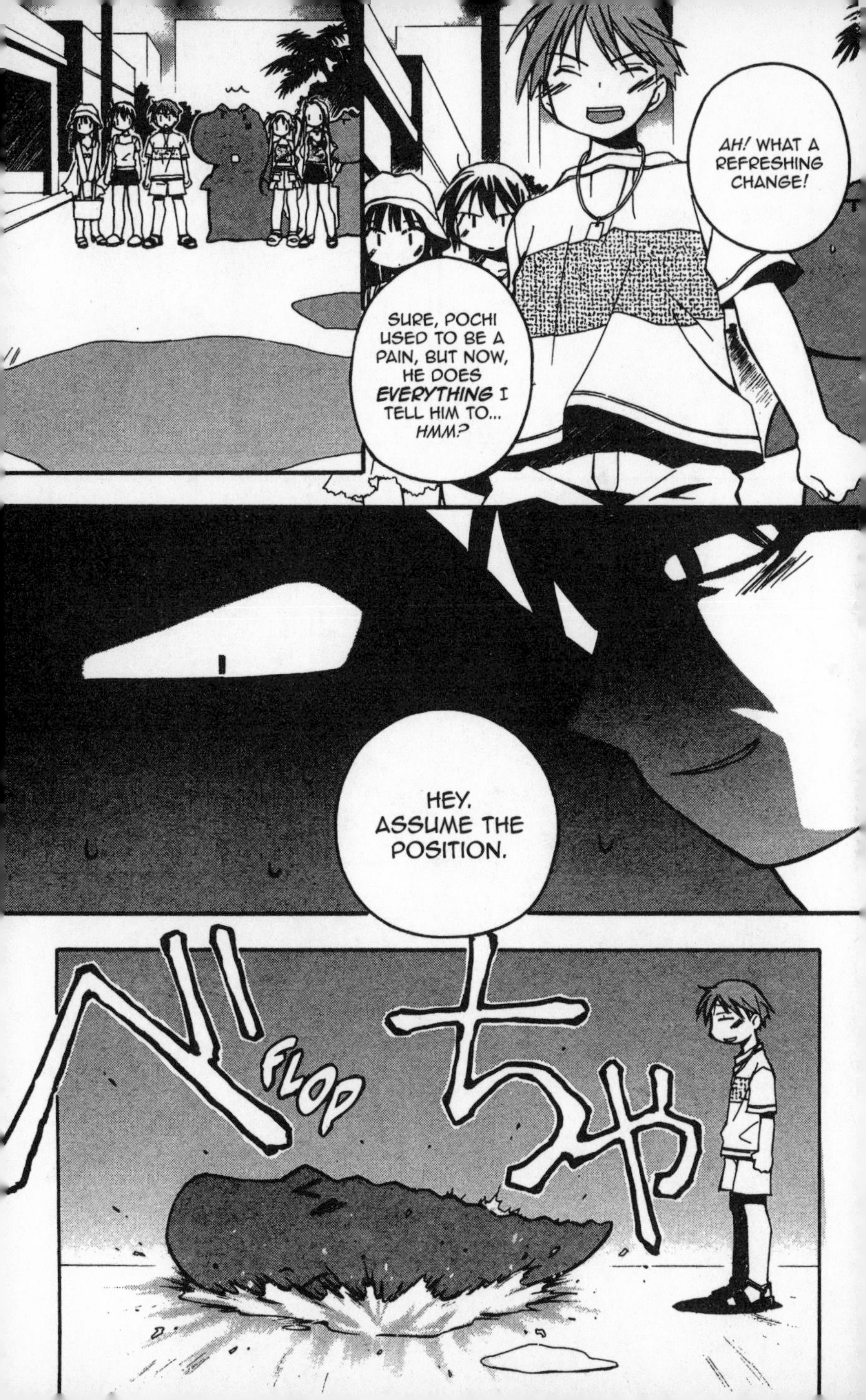

AH! WHAT A REFRESHING CHANGE!
SURE, POCHI USED TO BE A PAIN, BUT NOW, HE DOES *EVERYTHING* I TELL HIM TO... *HMM?*
HEY. ASSUME THE POSITION.
ベちゃ
FLOP

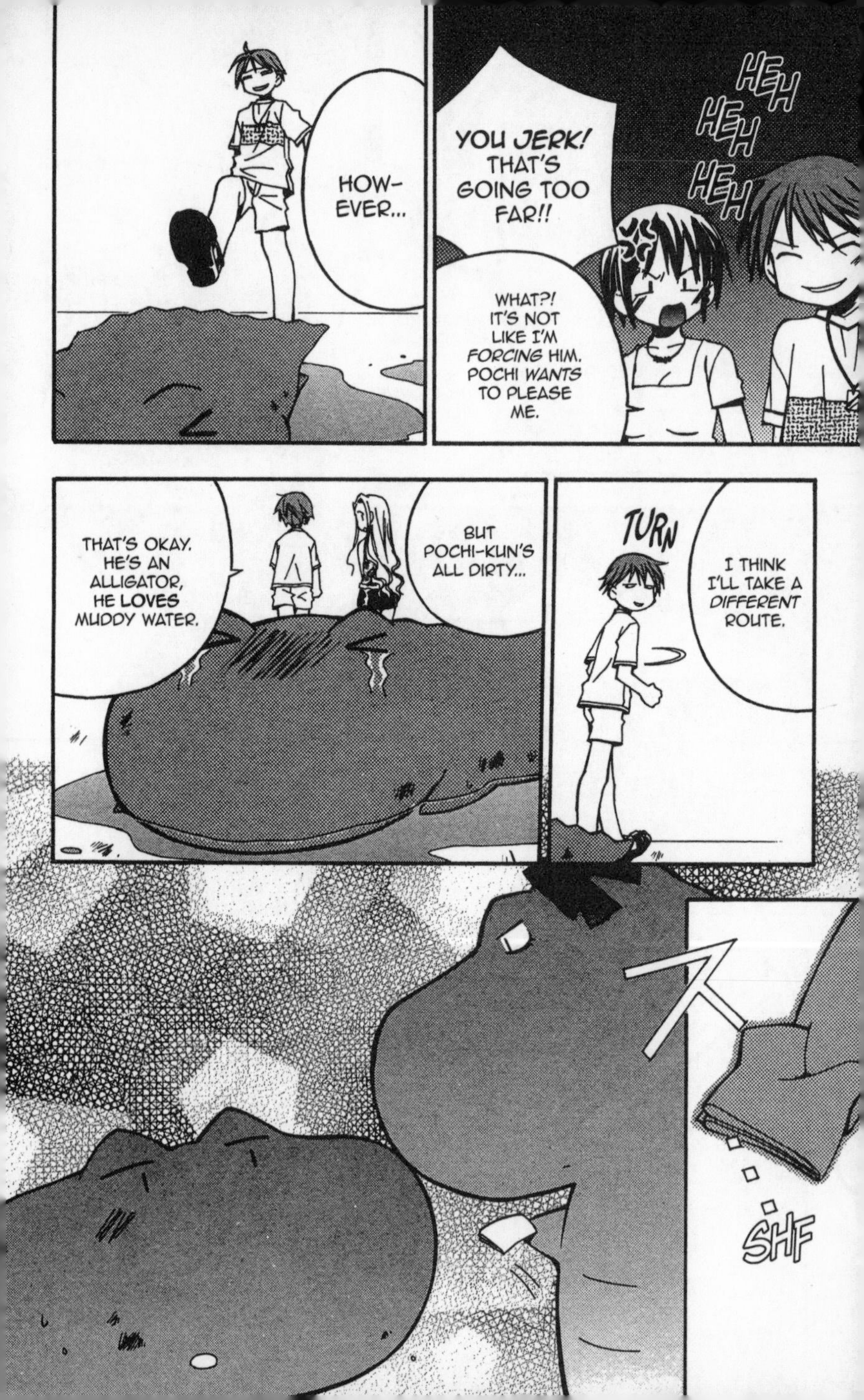

HEH HEH HEH
YOU JERK! THAT'S GOING TOO FAR!!
WHAT?! IT'S NOT LIKE I'M FORCING HIM. POCHI WANTS TO PLEASE ME.
HOW-EVER...
TURN
I THINK I'LL TAKE A DIFFERENT ROUTE.
BUT POCHI-KUN'S ALL DIRTY...
THAT'S OKAY. HE'S AN ALLIGATOR, HE LOVES MUDDY WATER.
SHF

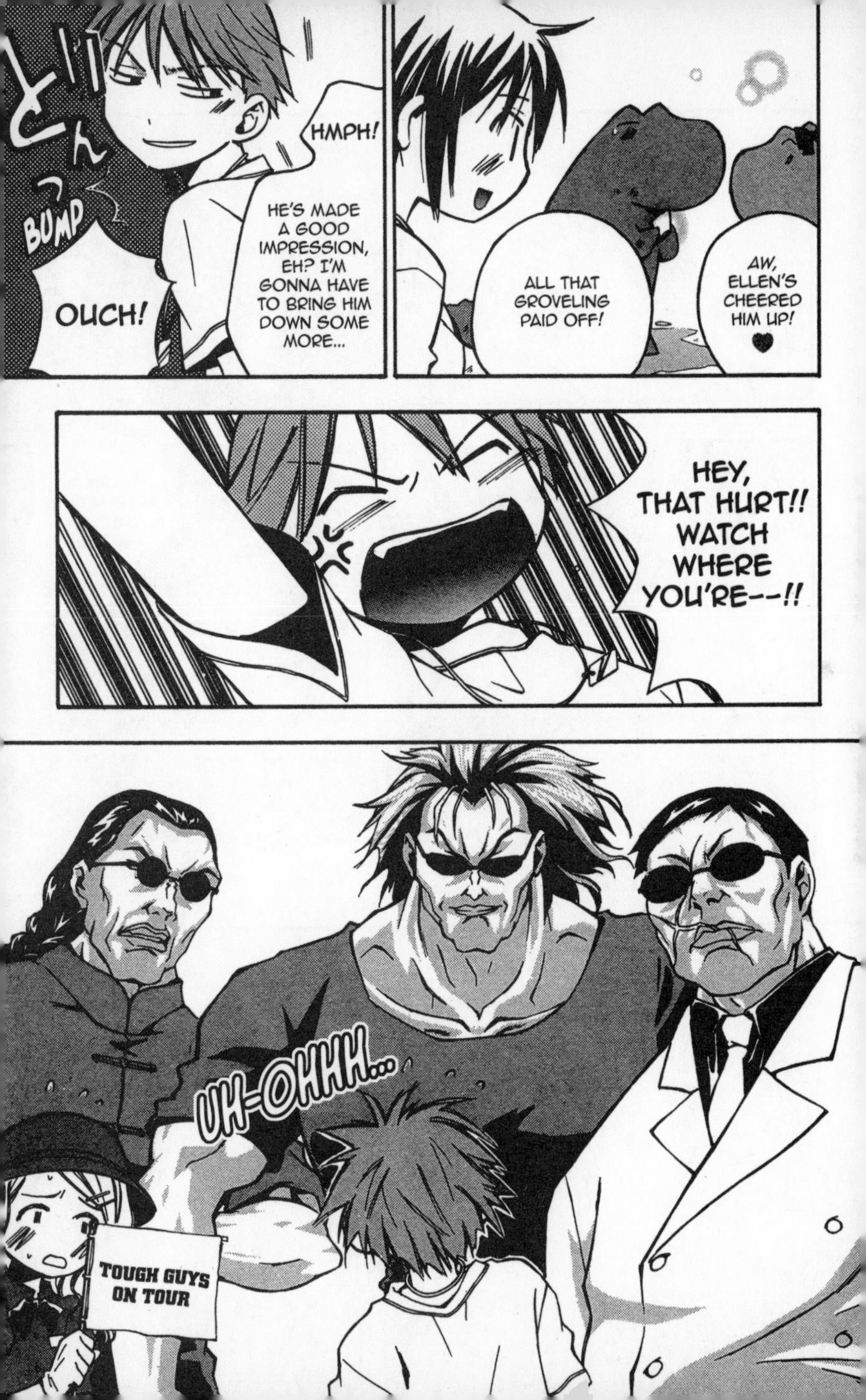
AW, ELLEN'S CHEERED HIM UP! ♥
ALL THAT GROVELING PAID OFF!
HMPH!
HE'S MADE A GOOD IMPRESSION, EH? I'M GONNA HAVE TO BRING HIM DOWN SOME MORE...
BUMP
OUCH!
HEY, THAT HURT!! WATCH WHERE YOU'RE--!!
UH-OHHH...
TOUGH GUYS ON TOUR

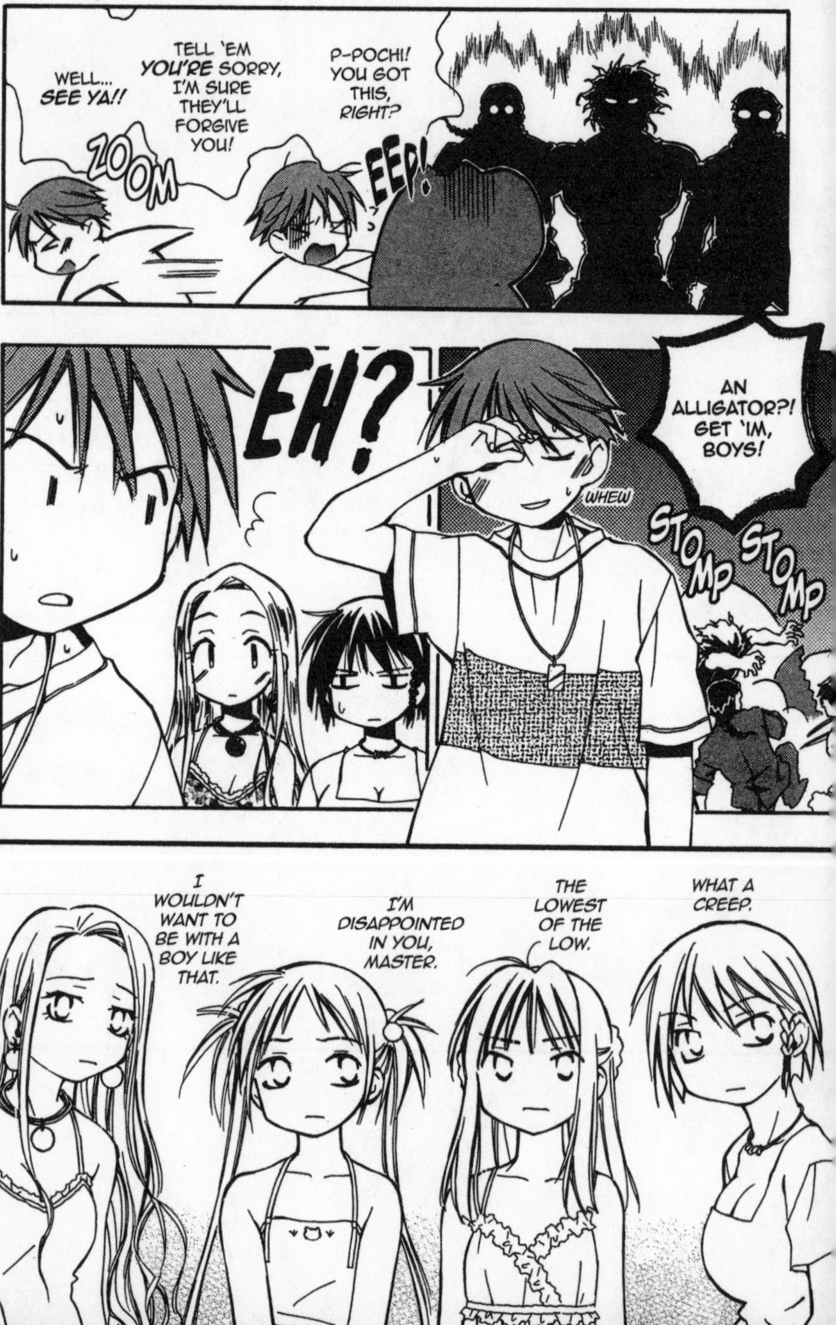
P-POCHI! YOU GOT THIS, RIGHT?
EEP!
TELL 'EM YOU'RE SORRY, I'M SURE THEY'LL FORGIVE YOU!
WELL... SEE YA!!
ZOOM
AN ALLIGATOR?! GET 'IM, BOYS!
STOMP STOMP
WHEW
EH?
WHAT A CREEP.
THE LOWEST OF THE LOW.
I'M DISAPPOINTED IN YOU, MASTER.
I WOULDN'T WANT TO BE WITH A BOY LIKE THAT.

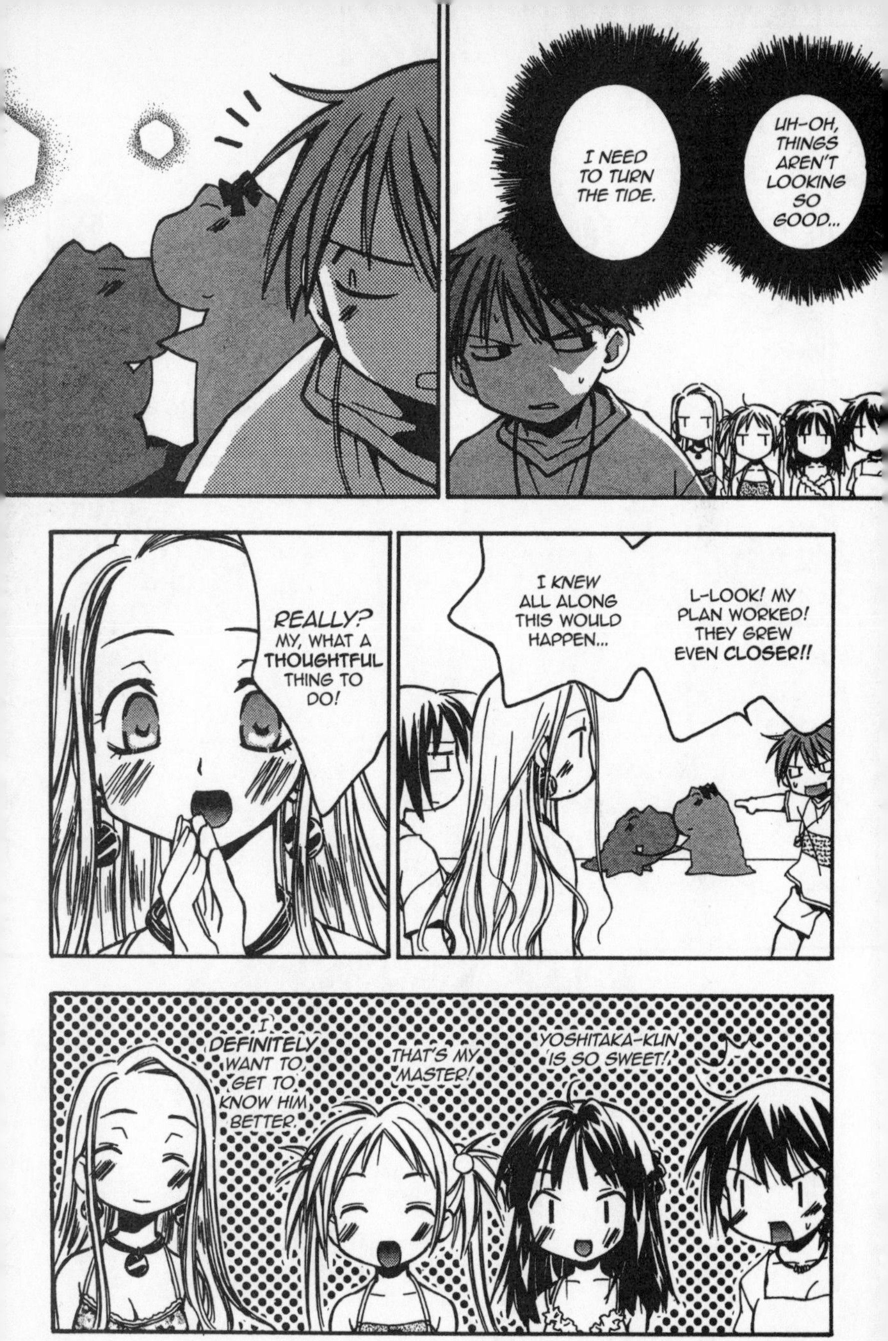
UH-OH, THINGS AREN'T LOOKING SO GOOD...
I NEED TO TURN THE TIDE.
L-LOOK! MY PLAN WORKED! THEY GREW EVEN CLOSER!!
I KNEW ALL ALONG THIS WOULD HAPPEN...
REALLY? MY, WHAT A THOUGHTFUL THING TO DO!
YOSHITAKA-KUN IS SO SWEET!
THAT'S MY MASTER!
I DEFINITELY WANT TO GET TO KNOW HIM BETTER.

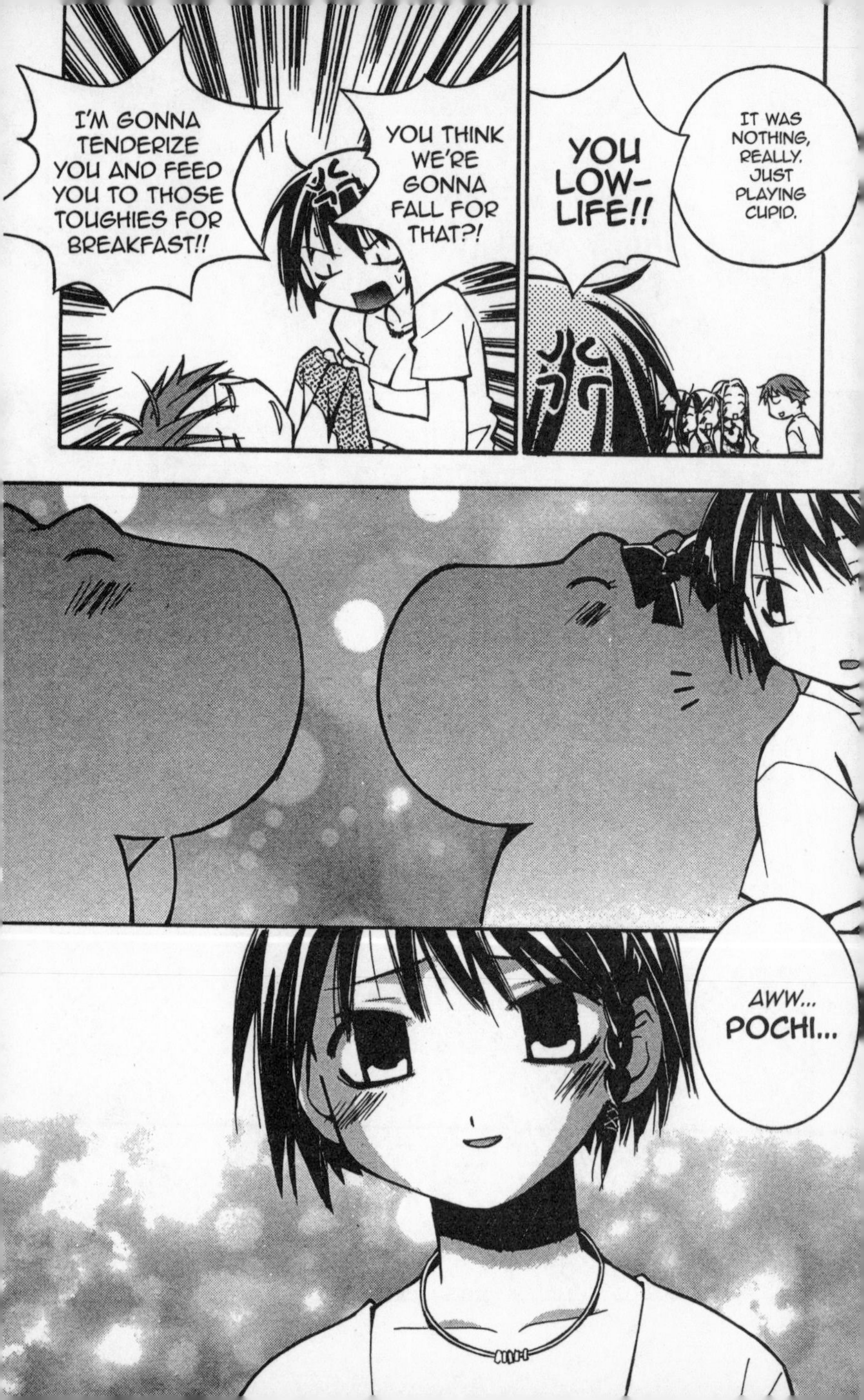
IT WAS NOTHING, REALLY. JUST PLAYING CUPID.
YOU LOW-LIFE!!
YOU THINK WE'RE GONNA FALL FOR THAT?!
I'M GONNA TENDERIZE YOU AND FEED YOU TO THOSE TOUGHIES FOR BREAKFAST!!
AWW... POCHI...

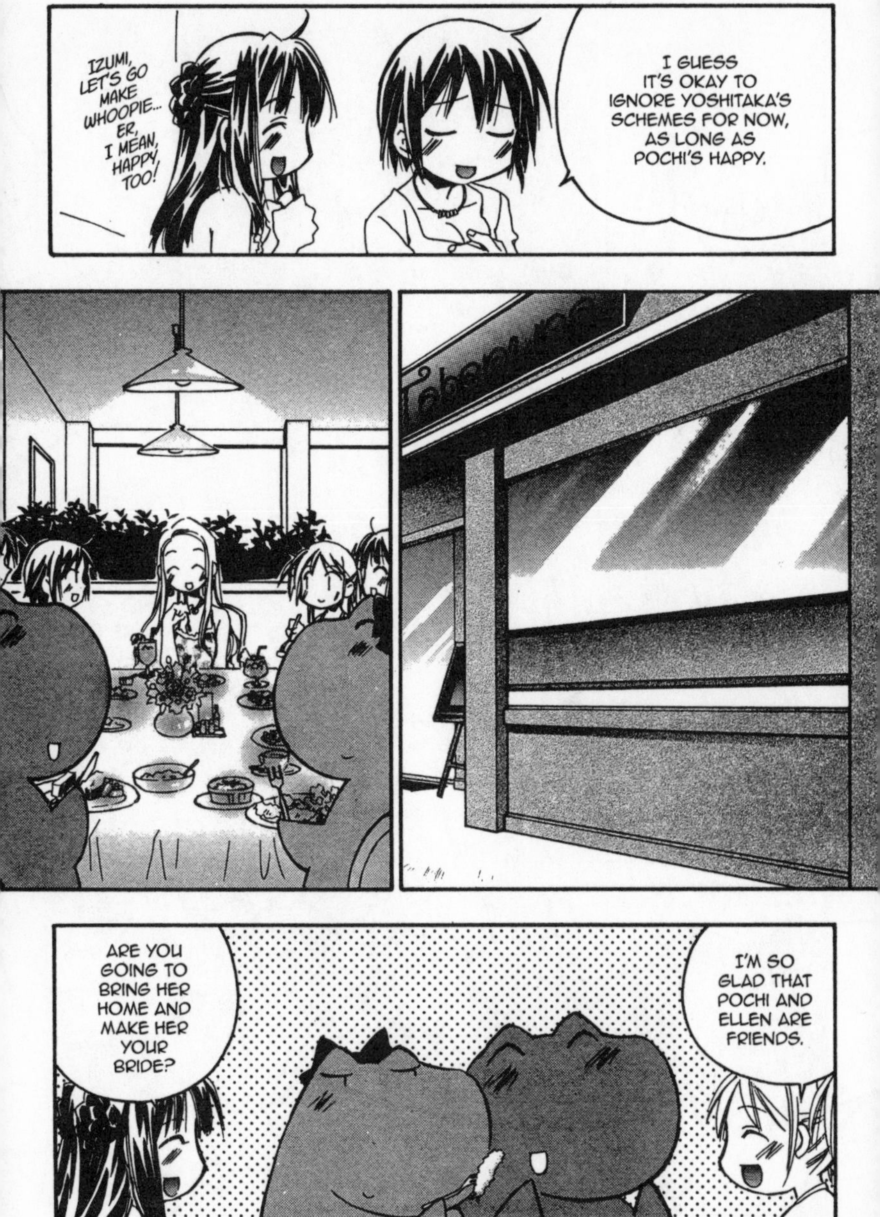
I GUESS IT'S OKAY TO IGNORE YOSHITAKA'S SCHEMES FOR NOW, AS LONG AS POCHI'S HAPPY.
IZUMI, LET'S GO MAKE WHOOPIE... ER, I MEAN, HAPPY, TOO!
I'M SO GLAD THAT POCHI AND ELLEN ARE FRIENDS.
ARE YOU GOING TO BRING HER HOME AND MAKE HER YOUR BRIDE?

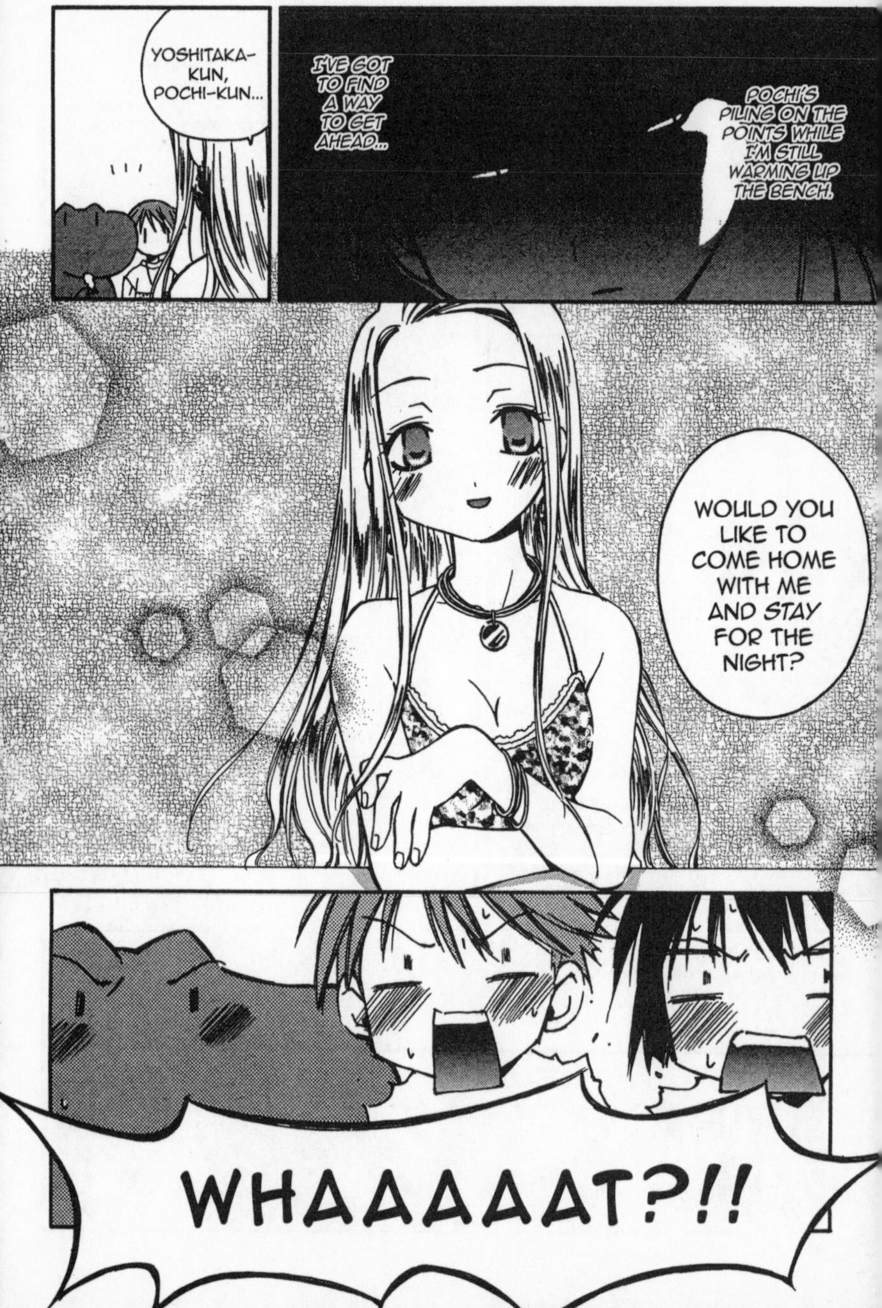
POCHI'S PILING ON THE POINTS WHILE I'M STILL WARMING UP THE BENCH.
I'VE GOT TO FIND A WAY TO GET AHEAD...
YOSHITAKA-KUN, POCHI-KUN...
WOULD YOU LIKE TO COME HOME WITH ME AND *STAY* FOR THE NIGHT?
WHAAAAAAT?!!

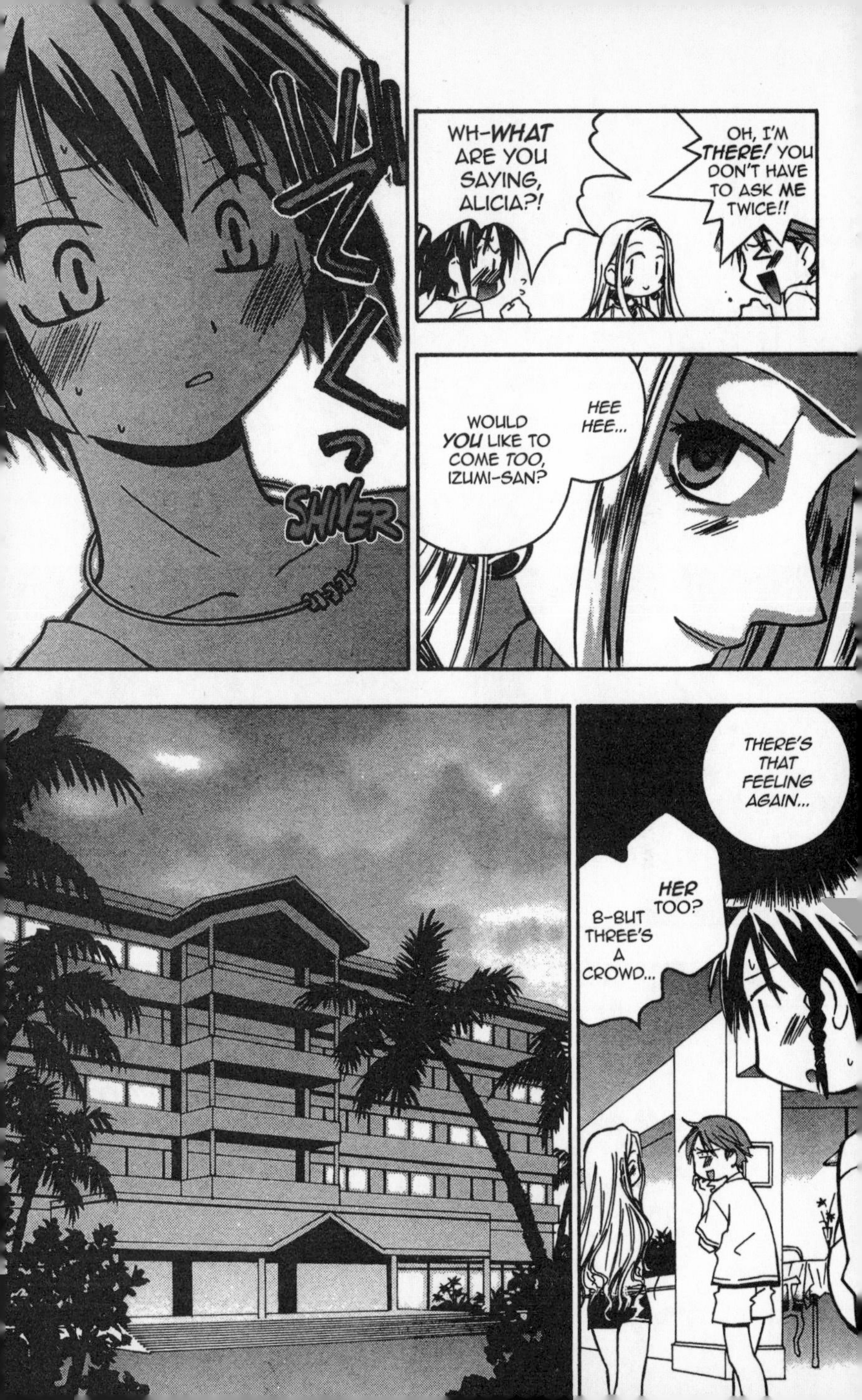
OH, I'M THERE! YOU DON'T HAVE TO ASK ME TWICE!!
WH-WHAT ARE YOU SAYING, ALICIA?!
HEE HEE...
WOULD YOU LIKE TO COME TOO, IZUMI-SAN?
SHIVER
THERE'S THAT FEELING AGAIN...
HER TOO?
B-BUT THREE'S A CROWD...

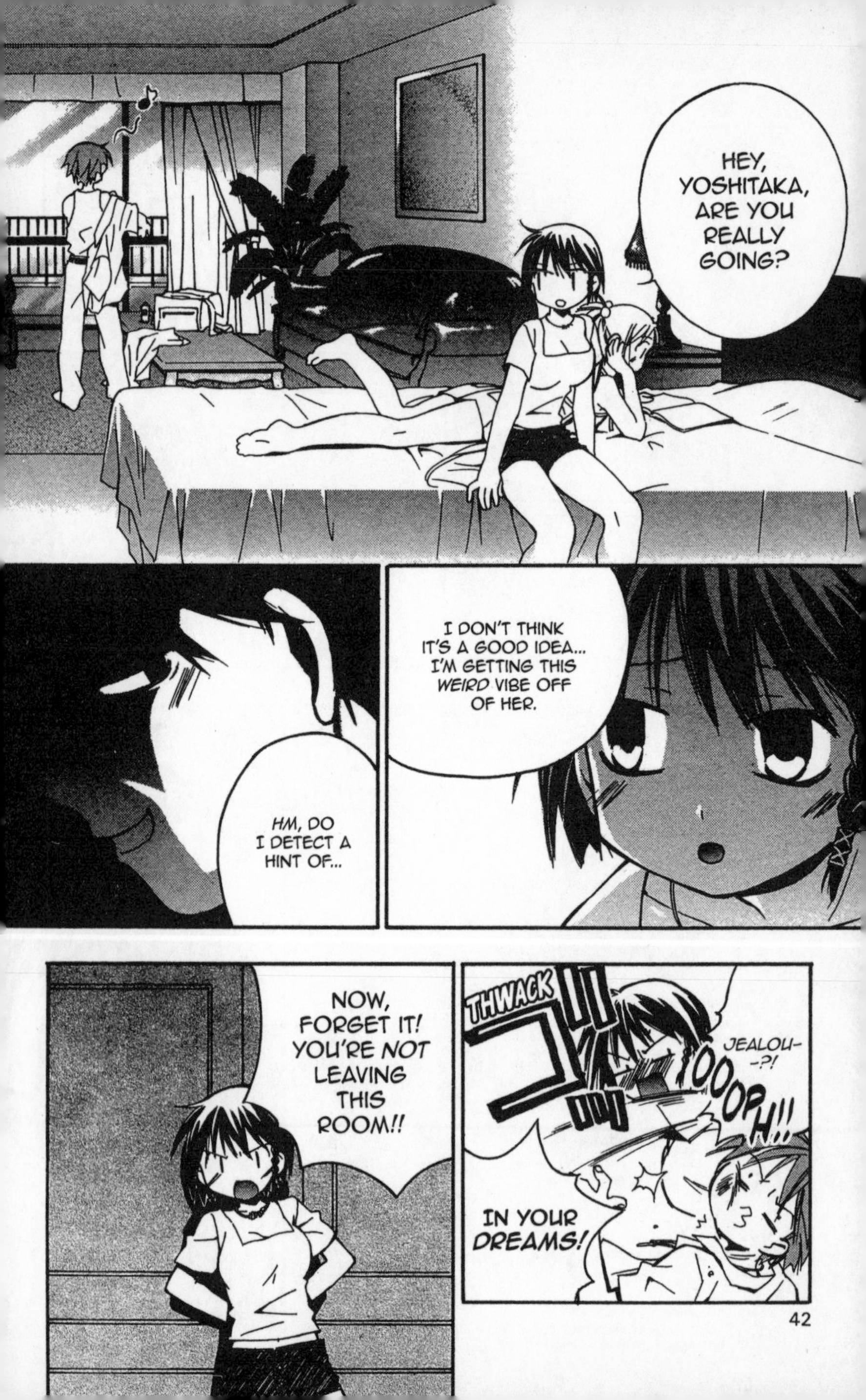
HEY, YOSHITAKA, ARE YOU REALLY GOING?
I DON'T THINK IT'S A GOOD IDEA... I'M GETTING THIS *WEIRD* VIBE OFF OF HER.
HM, DO I DETECT A HINT OF...
THWACK
JEALOU--?!
OOOPH!!
IN YOUR *DREAMS*!
NOW, FORGET IT! YOU'RE *NOT* LEAVING THIS ROOM!!

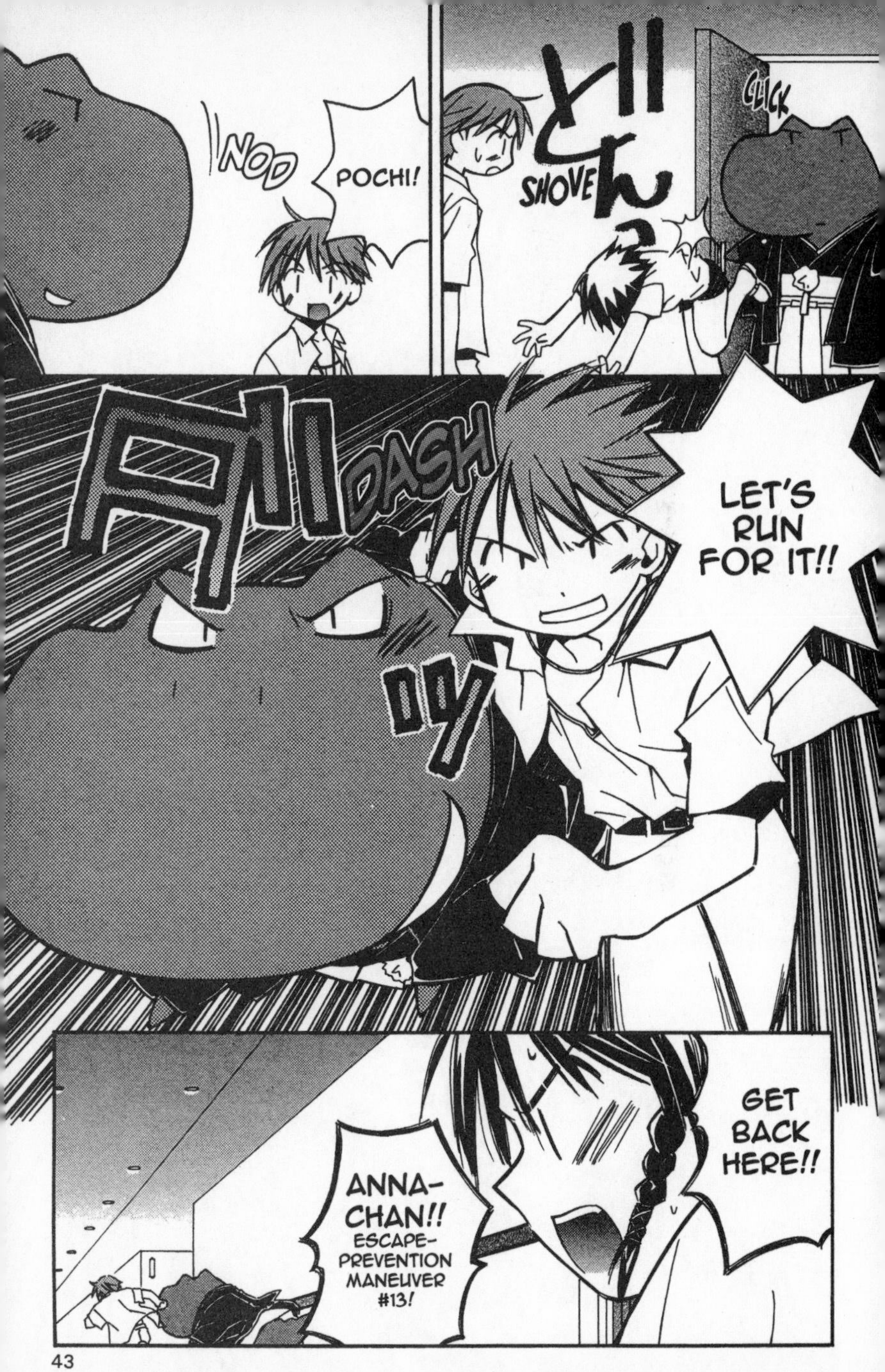
CLICK
とん
SHOVE
POCHI!
NOD
LET'S RUN FOR IT!!
DASH
GET BACK HERE!!
ANNA-CHAN!!
ESCAPE-PREVENTION MANEUVER #13!

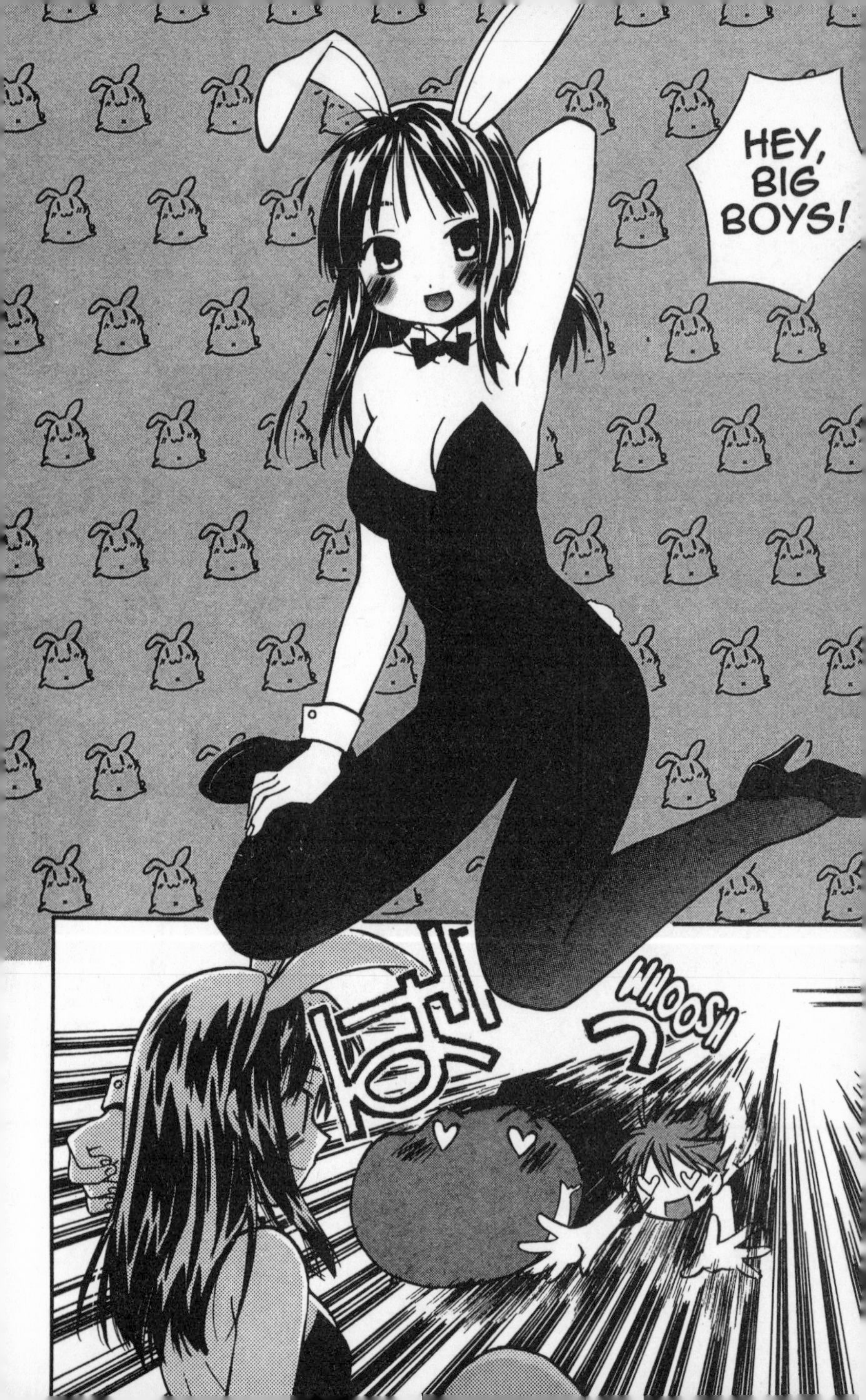
HEY, BIG BOYS!
はっ
WHOOSH

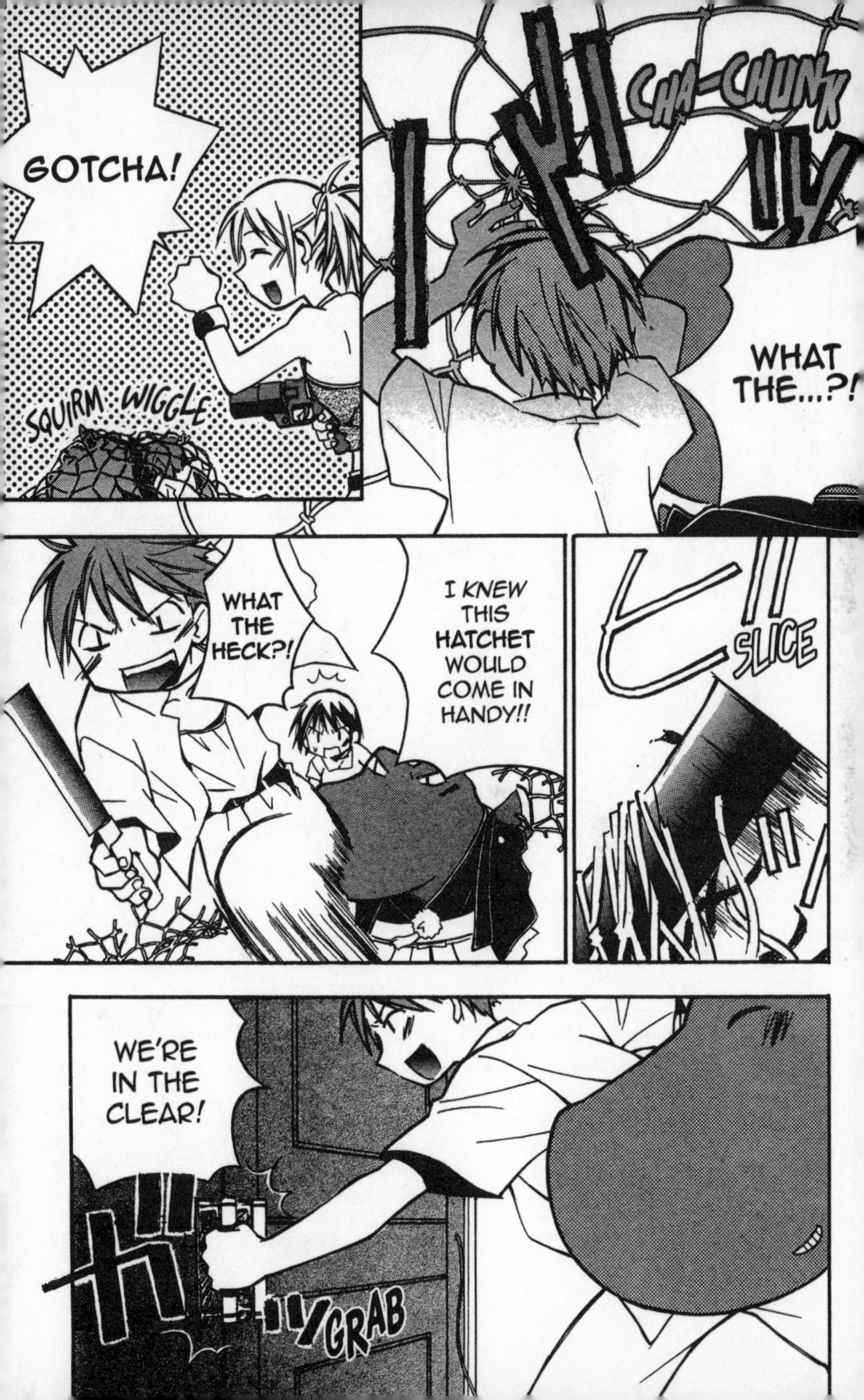
CHA-CHUNK
WHAT THE...?!
GOTCHA!
SQUIRM WIGGLE
SLICE
I KNEW THIS HATCHET WOULD COME IN HANDY!!
WHAT THE HECK?!
WE'RE IN THE CLEAR!
GRAB

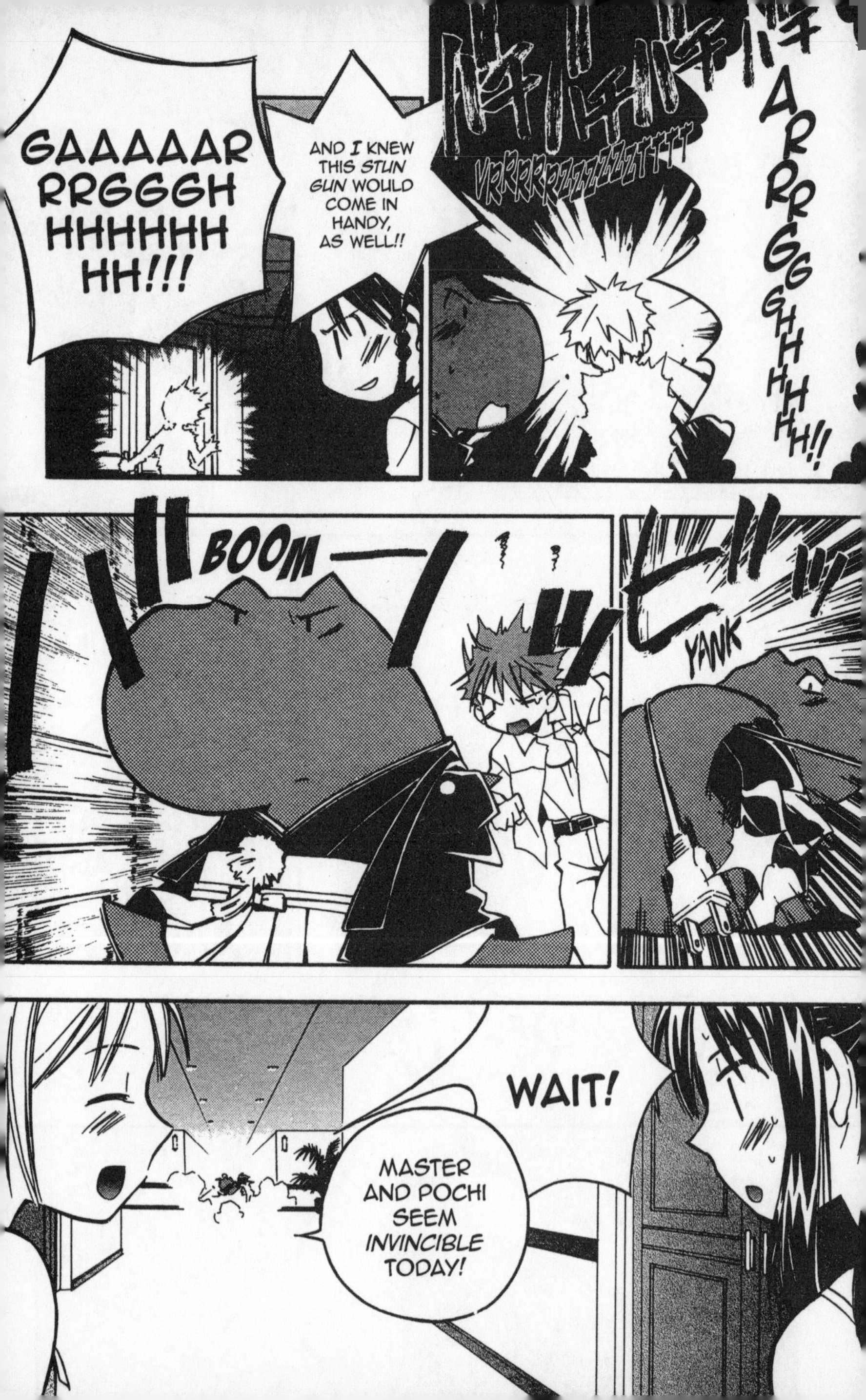
バチバチバチ
VRRRRRZZZZZZZTTTTT
ARRRGGGHHHHHH!!
AND I KNEW THIS STUN GUN WOULD COME IN HANDY, AS WELL!!
GAAAAARRRGGGHHHHHHHH!!!
YANK
BOOM
WAIT!
MASTER AND POCHI SEEM INVINCIBLE TODAY!

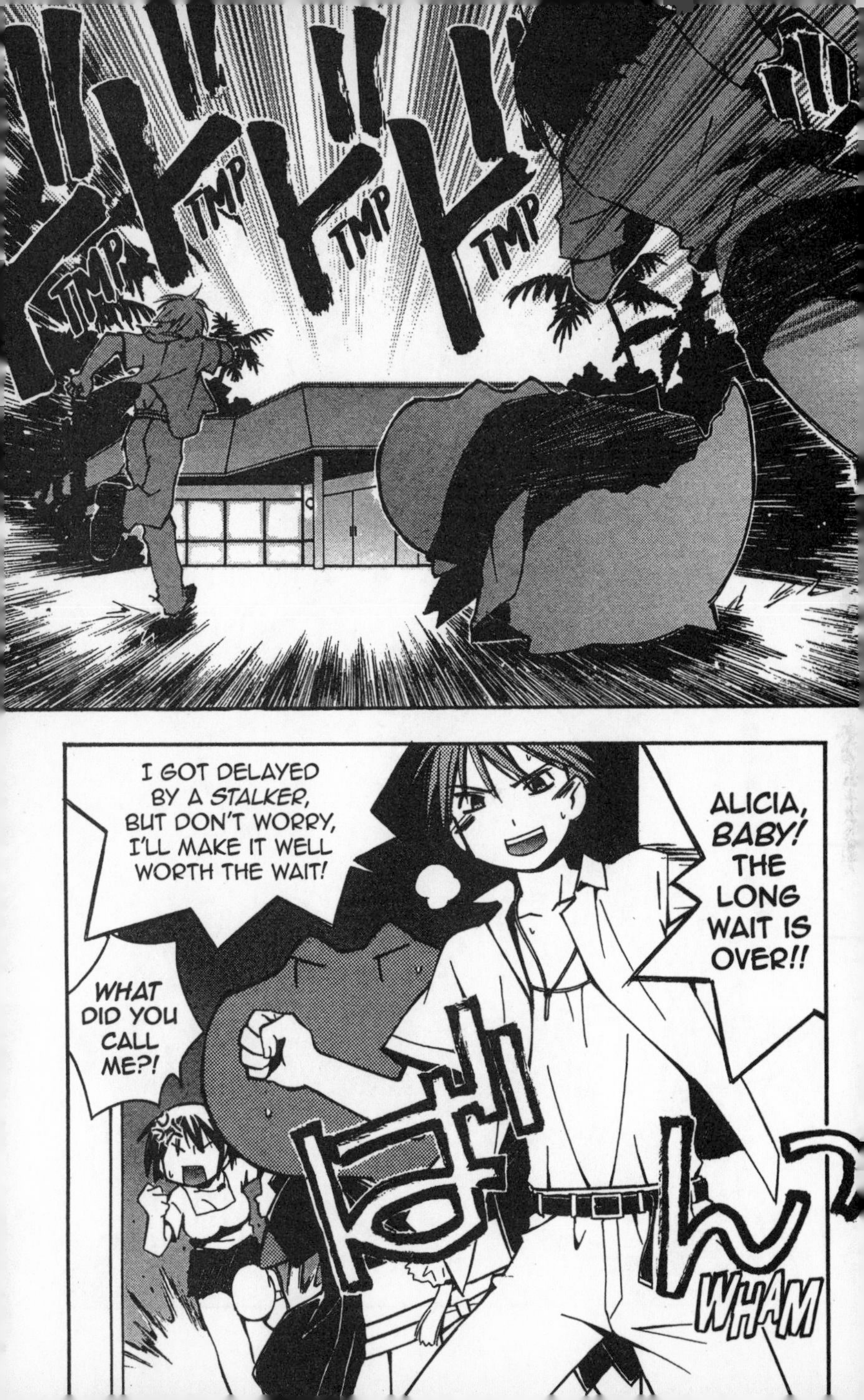
TMP
TMP
TMP
TMP
TMP
ALICIA, BABY! THE LONG WAIT IS OVER!!
I GOT DELAYED BY A STALKER, BUT DON'T WORRY, I'LL MAKE IT WELL WORTH THE WAIT!
WHAT DID YOU CALL ME?!
WHAM

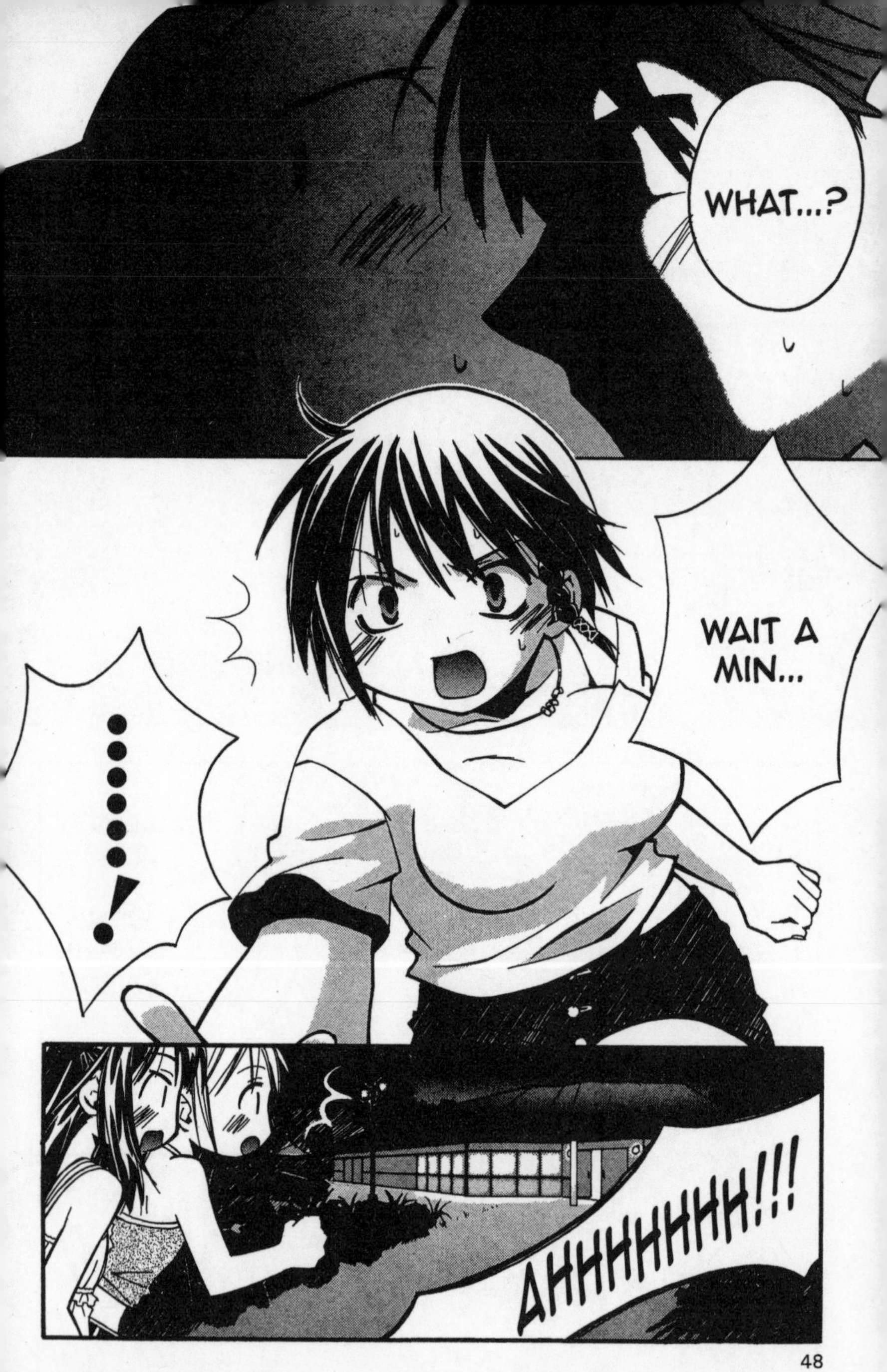
WHAT...?
WAIT A MIN...
......!
AHHHHHHH!!!

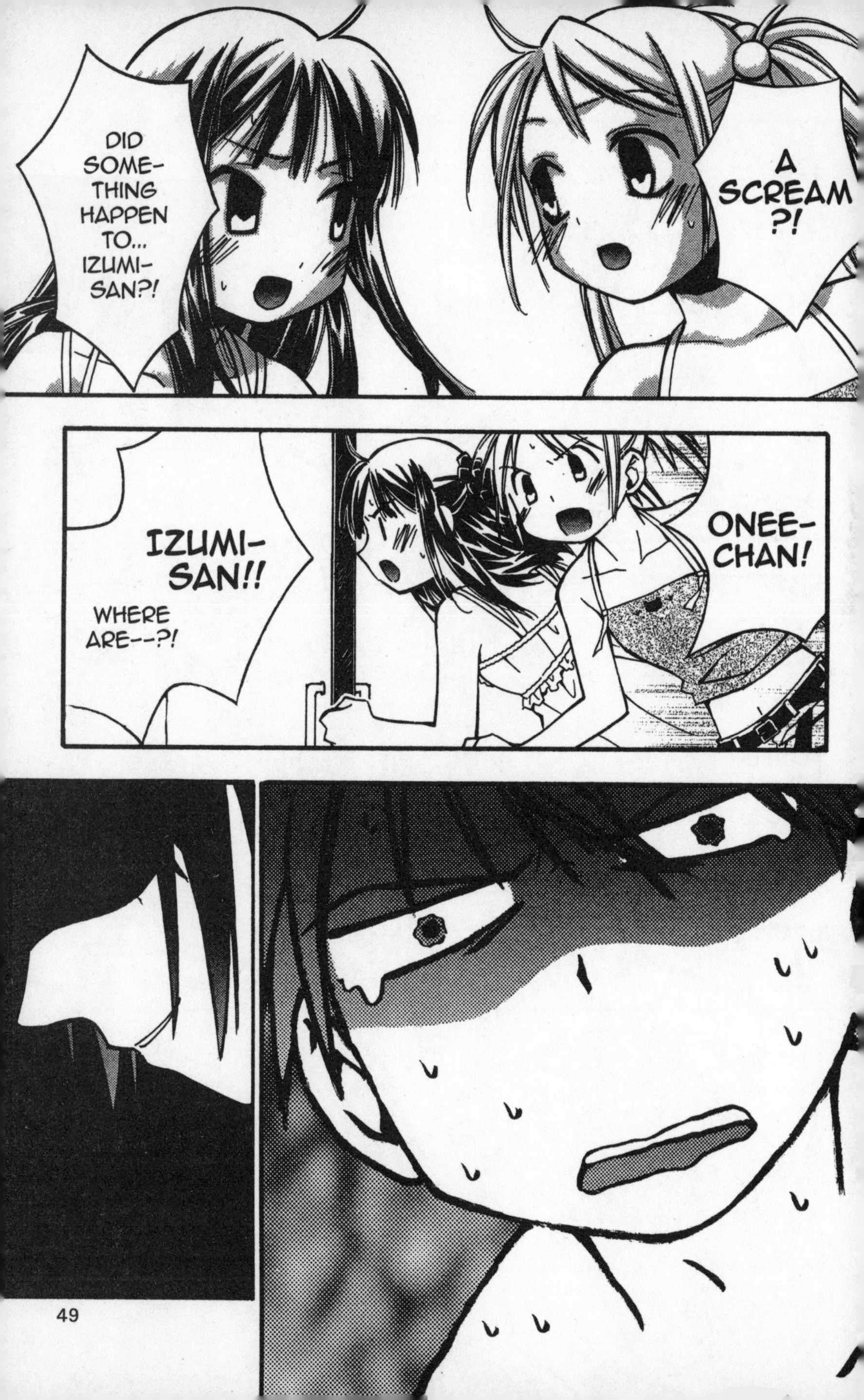
A SCREAM?!
DID SOMETHING HAPPEN TO... IZUMI-SAN?!
ONEE-CHAN!
IZUMI-SAN!!
WHERE ARE--?!

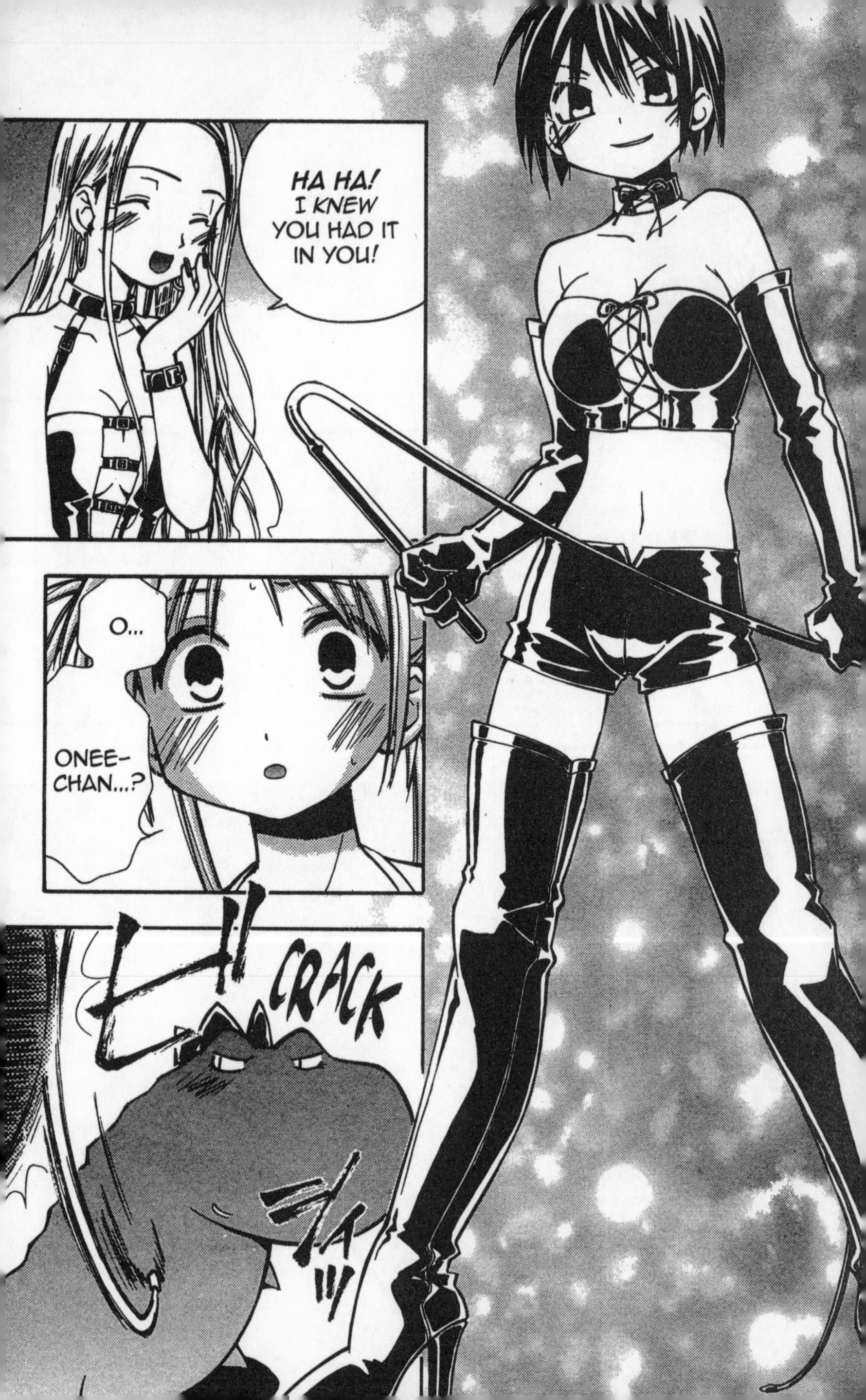
HA HA! I KNEW YOU HAD IT IN YOU!
O...
ONEE-CHAN...?
CRACK

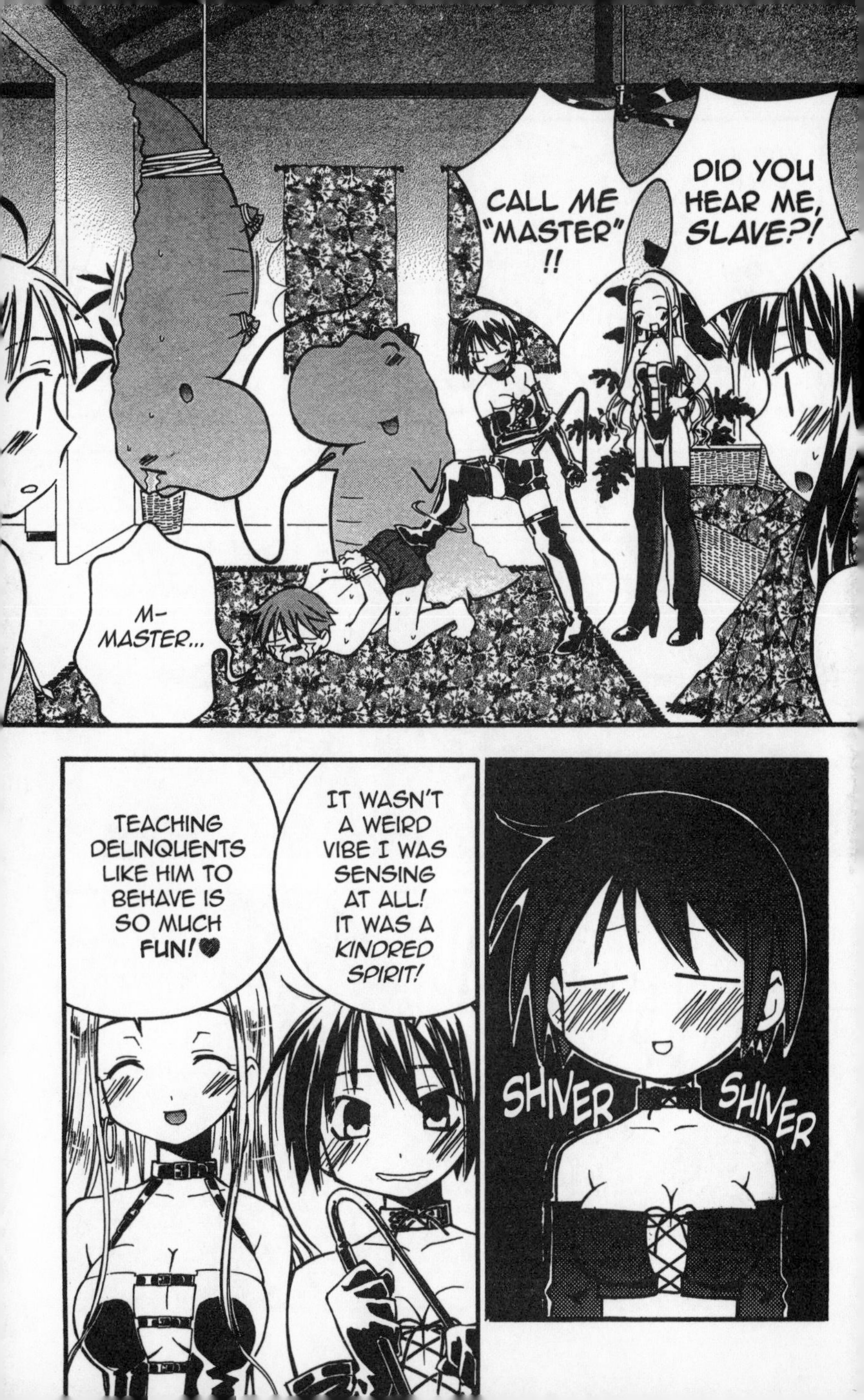
DID YOU HEAR ME, SLAVE?!
CALL ME "MASTER" !!
M-MASTER...
SHIVER
SHIVER
IT WASN'T A WEIRD VIBE I WAS SENSING AT ALL! IT WAS A KINDRED SPIRIT!
TEACHING DELINQUENTS LIKE HIM TO BEHAVE IS SO MUCH FUN!♥

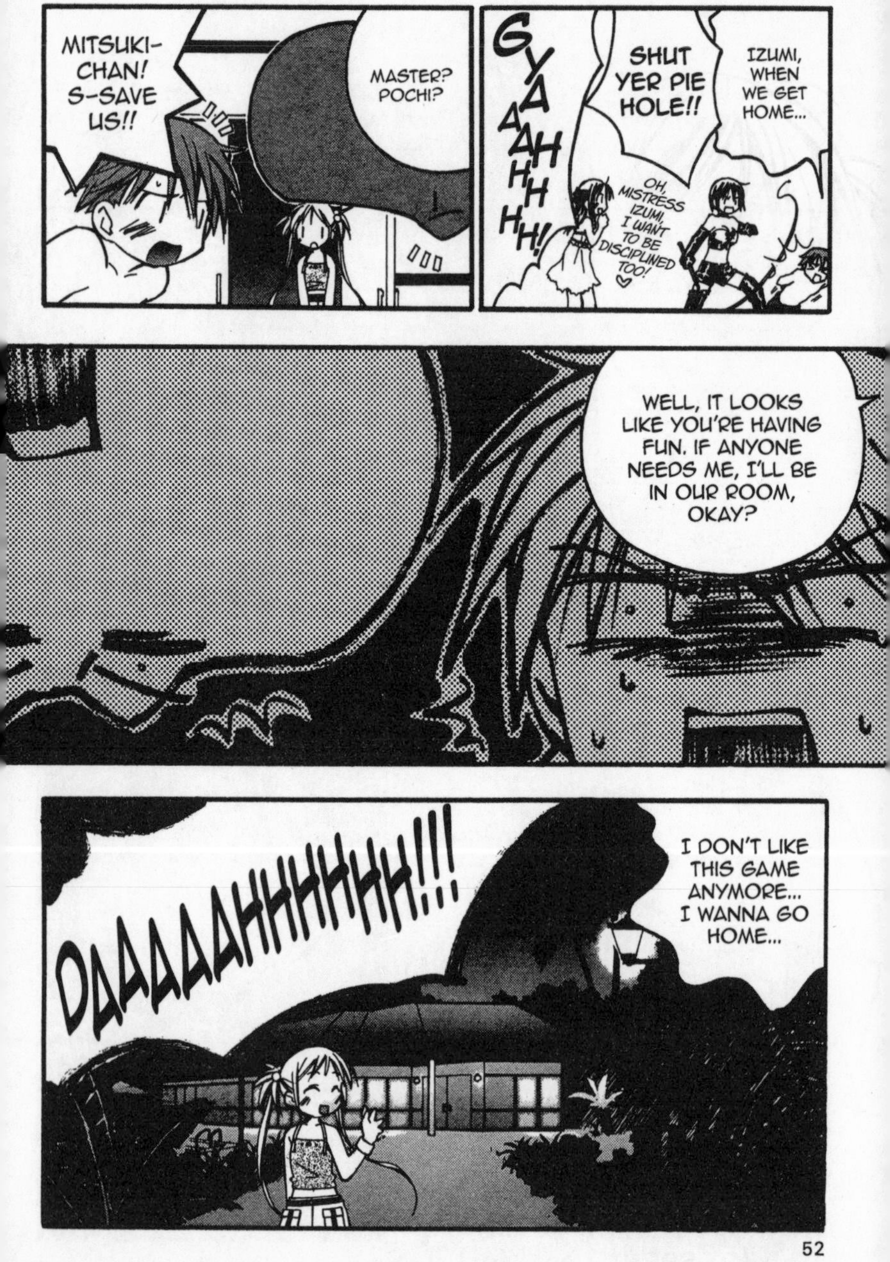
IZUMI, WHEN WE GET HOME...
SHUT YER PIE HOLE!!
GYAAAHHHHH!
OH, MISTRESS IZUMI, I WANT TO BE DISCIPLINED TOO! ♡
MASTER? POCHI?
MITSUKI-CHAN! S-SAVE US!!
WELL, IT LOOKS LIKE YOU'RE HAVING FUN. IF ANYONE NEEDS ME, I'LL BE IN OUR ROOM, OKAY?
I DON'T LIKE THIS GAME ANYMORE... I WANNA GO HOME...
OAAAAAHHHHHH!!!

THE OTHER DAY, I WENT TO THE BEER GARDEN ON THE ROOF OF HAKATA STATION. IT WAS A BUD GIRL GARDEN AND THERE WERE *LOTS* OF PRETTY LADIES (*PANT, PANT*). AND IT WAS THERE THAT THIS IMAGE CAME TO MIND: "NEXT TIME, I'VE GOT TO GO WITH BUD GIRLS FOR THE TITLE PAGE."

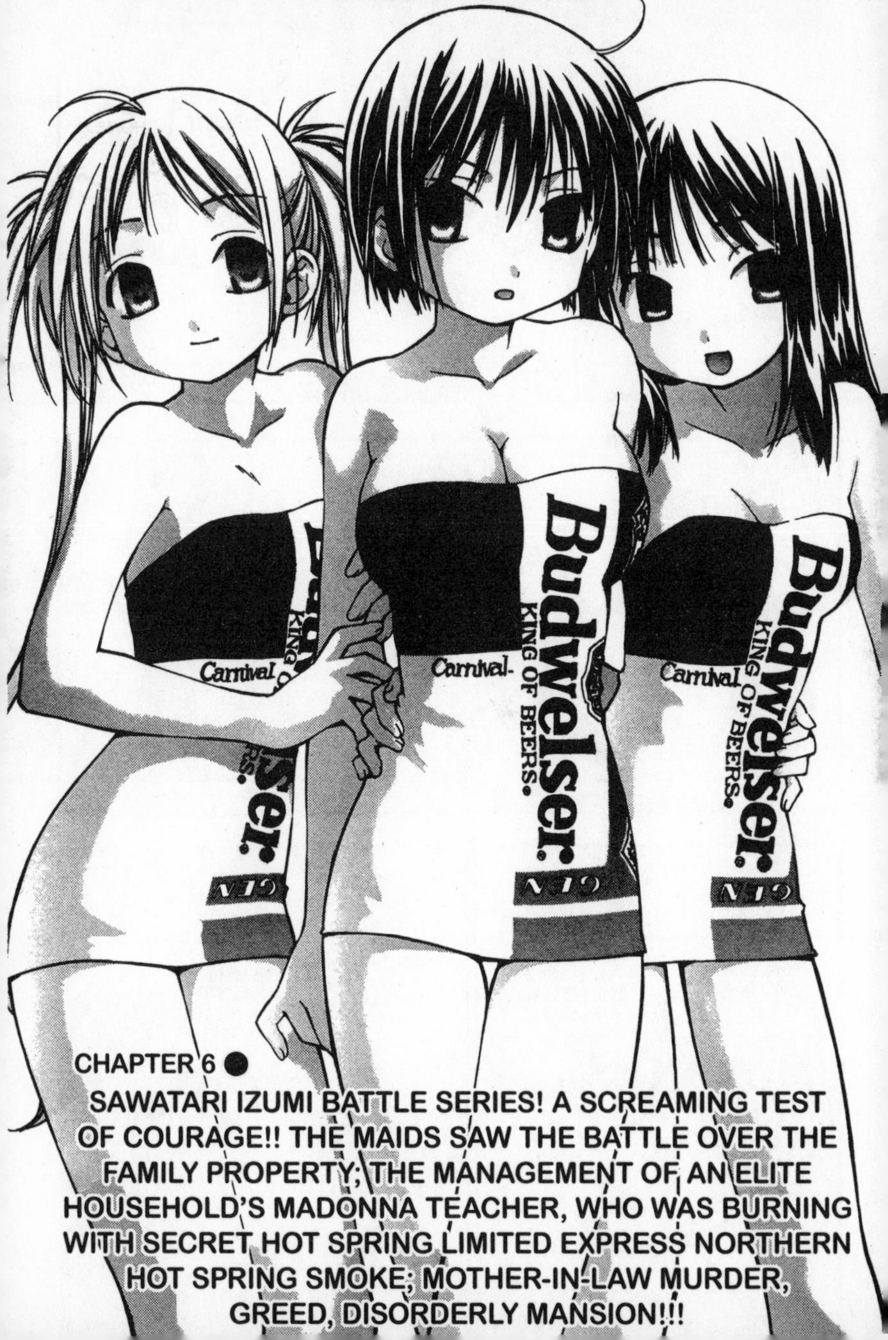
Budweiser
KING OF BEERS.
Carnival
Budweiser
KING OF BEERS.
Carnival
Carnival

CHAPTER 6 ●

SAWATARI IZUMI BATTLE SERIES! A SCREAMING TEST OF COURAGE!! THE MAIDS SAW THE BATTLE OVER THE FAMILY PROPERTY; THE MANAGEMENT OF AN ELITE HOUSEHOLD'S MADONNA TEACHER, WHO WAS BURNING WITH SECRET HOT SPRING LIMITED EXPRESS NORTHERN HOT SPRING SMOKE; MOTHER-IN-LAW MURDER, GREED, DISORDERLY MANSION!!!

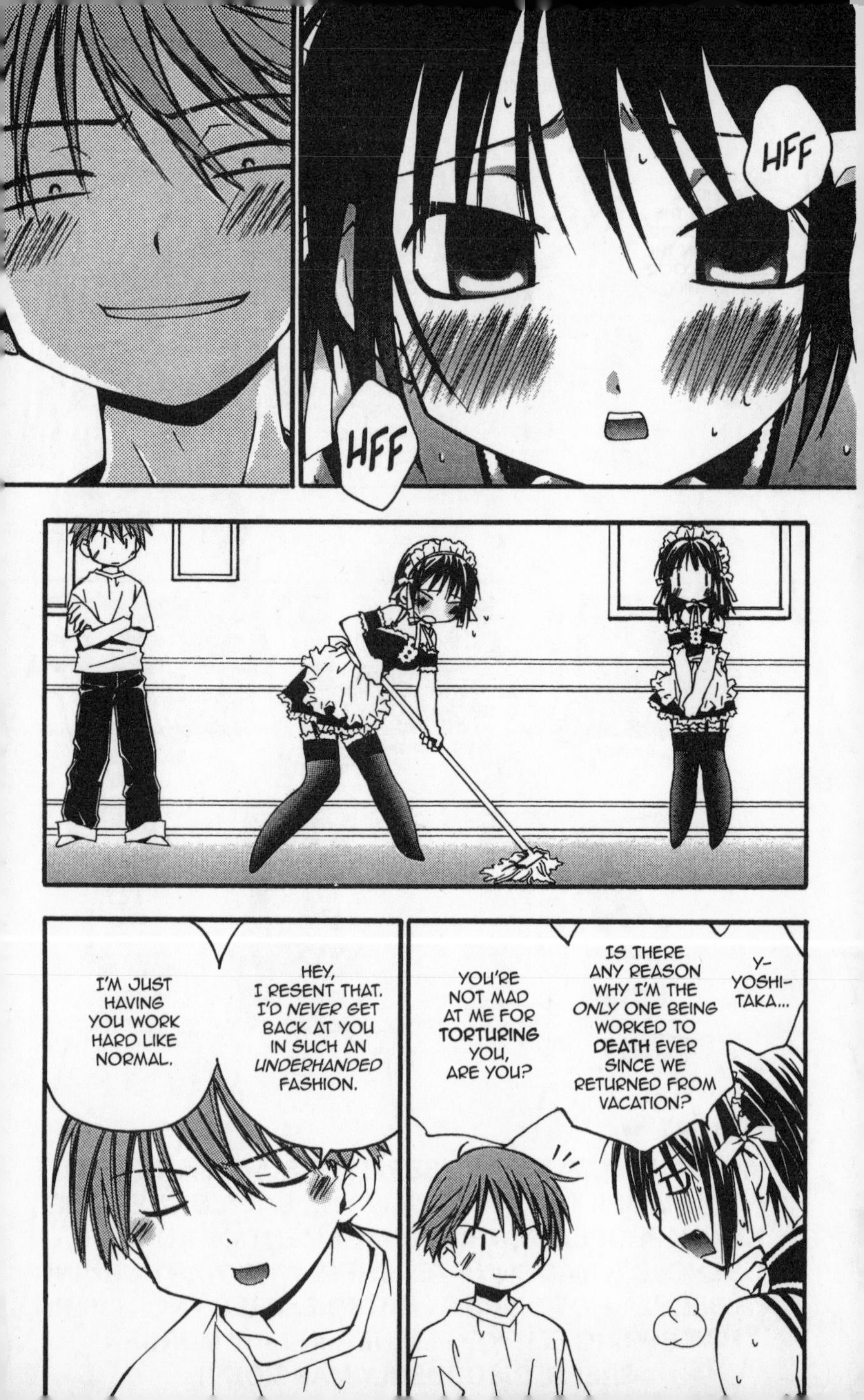
HFF
HFF
Y-YOSHI-TAKA...
IS THERE ANY REASON WHY I'M THE *ONLY* ONE BEING WORKED TO **DEATH** EVER SINCE WE RETURNED FROM VACATION?
YOU'RE NOT MAD AT ME FOR **TORTURING** YOU, ARE YOU?
HEY, I RESENT THAT. I'D *NEVER* GET BACK AT YOU IN SUCH AN *UNDERHANDED* FASHION.
I'M JUST HAVING YOU WORK HARD LIKE NORMAL.

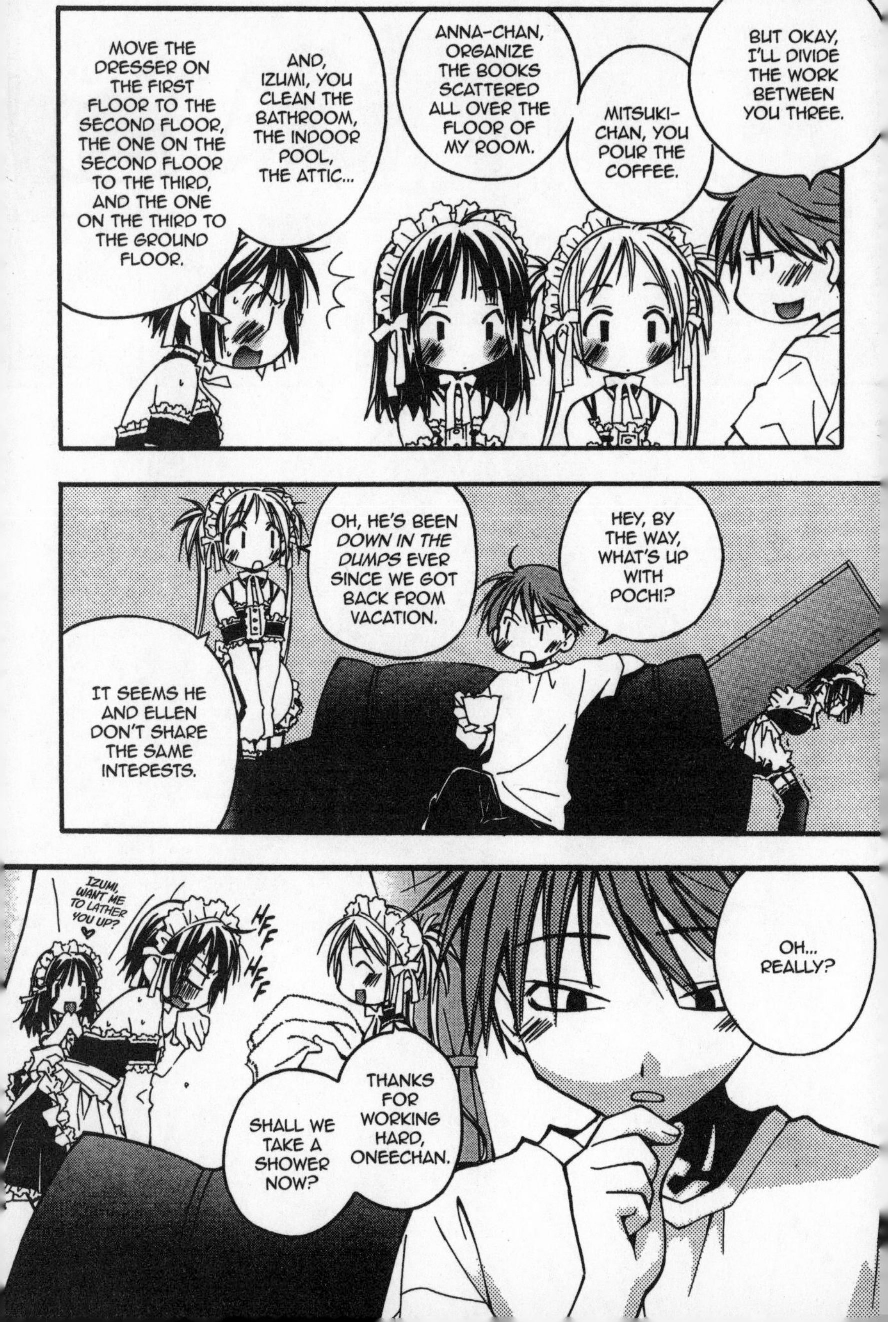
BUT OKAY, I'LL DIVIDE THE WORK BETWEEN YOU THREE.
MITSUKI-CHAN, YOU POUR THE COFFEE.
ANNA-CHAN, ORGANIZE THE BOOKS SCATTERED ALL OVER THE FLOOR OF MY ROOM.
AND, IZUMI, YOU CLEAN THE BATHROOM, THE INDOOR POOL, THE ATTIC...
MOVE THE DRESSER ON THE FIRST FLOOR TO THE SECOND FLOOR, THE ONE ON THE SECOND FLOOR TO THE THIRD, AND THE ONE ON THE THIRD TO THE GROUND FLOOR.
HEY, BY THE WAY, WHAT'S UP WITH POCHI?
OH, HE'S BEEN *DOWN IN THE DUMPS* EVER SINCE WE GOT BACK FROM VACATION.
IT SEEMS HE AND ELLEN DON'T SHARE THE SAME INTERESTS.
OH... REALLY?
HFF HFF
THANKS FOR WORKING HARD, ONEECHAN.
SHALL WE TAKE A SHOWER NOW?
IZUMI, WANT ME TO LATHER YOU UP? ♥

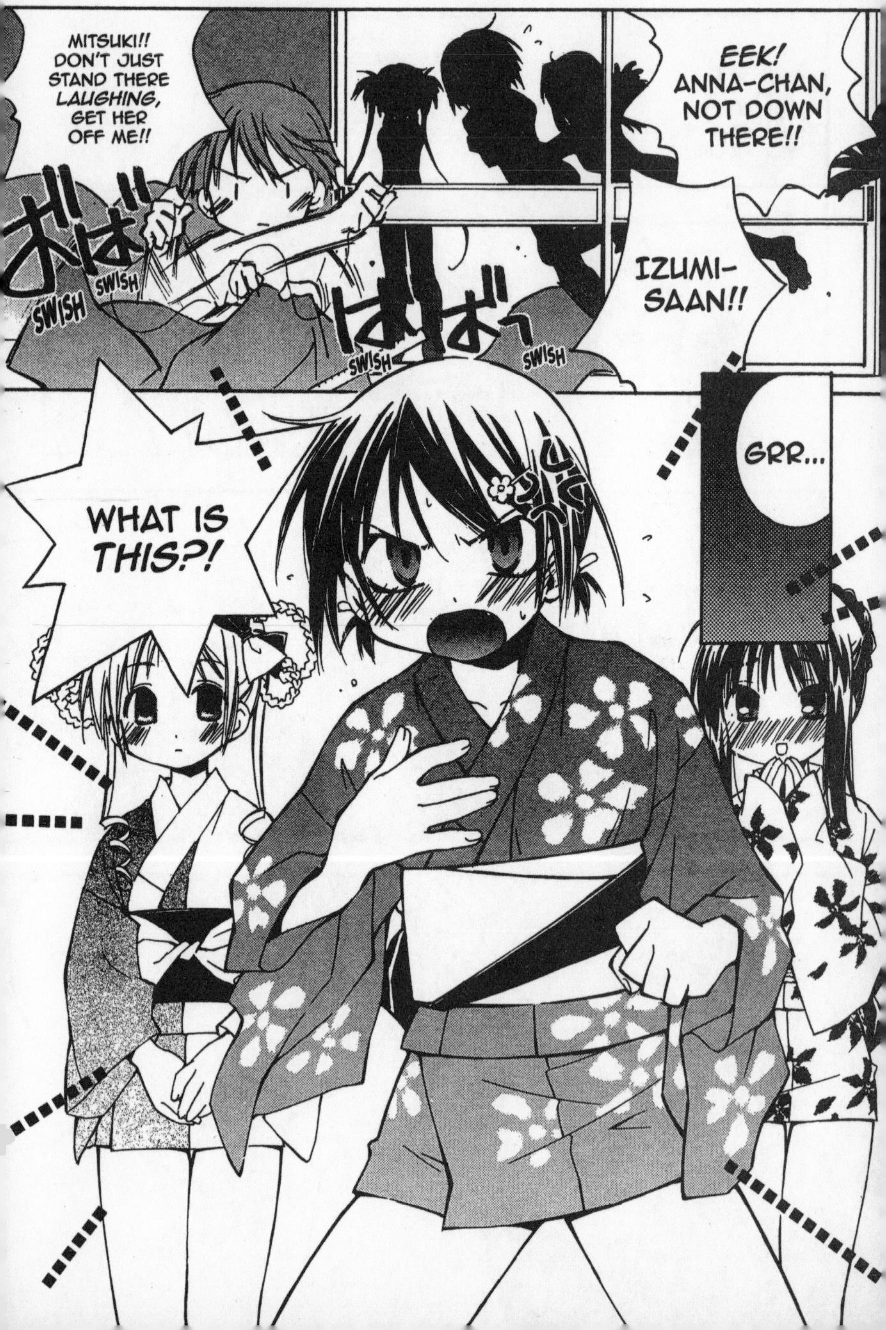
EEK! ANNA-CHAN, NOT DOWN THERE!!
IZUMI-SAAN!!
SWISH
ばばっ
SWISH
MITSUKI!! DON'T JUST STAND THERE LAUGHING, GET HER OFF ME!!
おば
SWISH
SWISH
GRR...
WHAT IS THIS?!

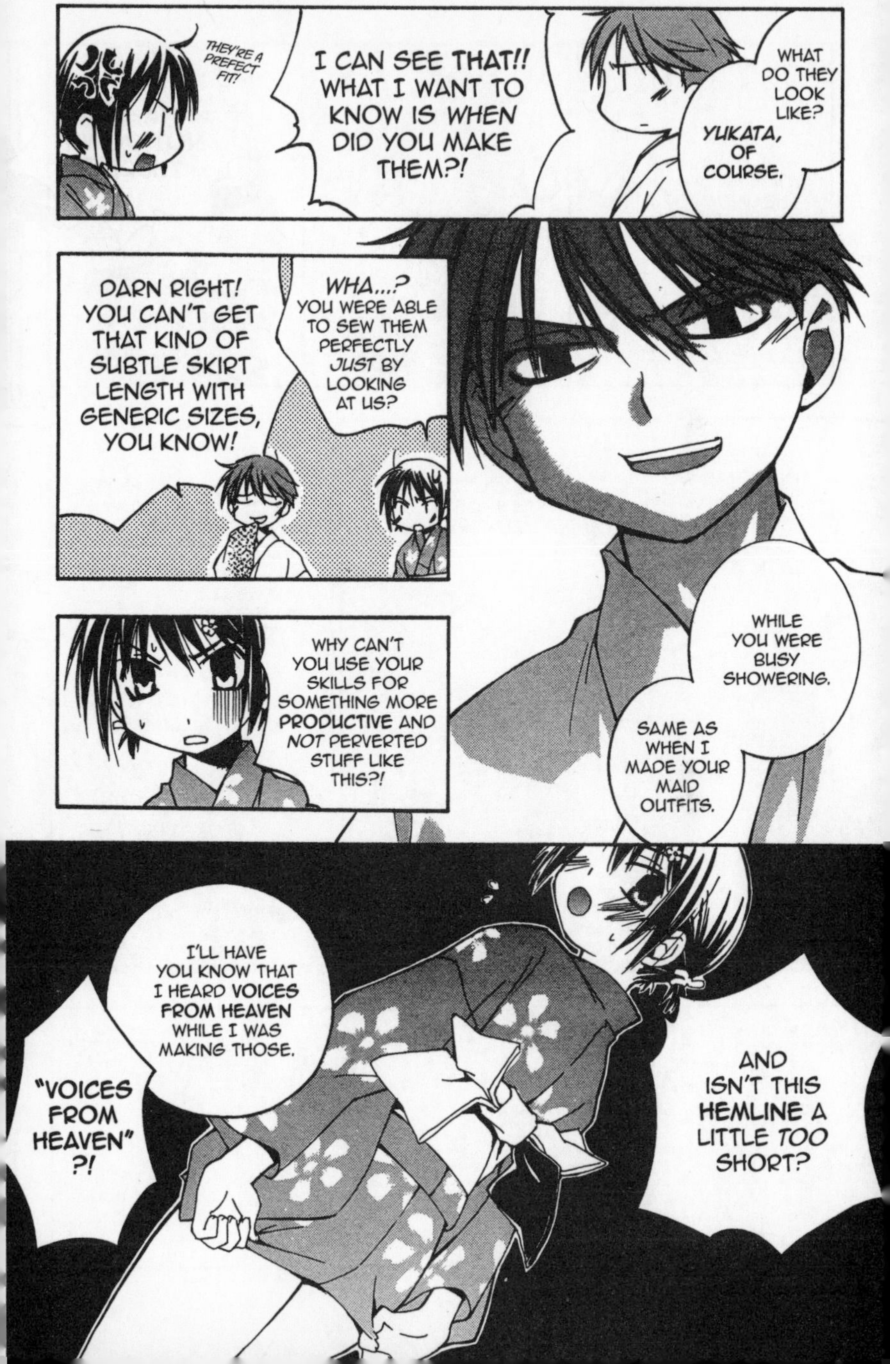
WHAT DO THEY LOOK LIKE?
YUKATA, OF COURSE.
I CAN SEE THAT!! WHAT I WANT TO KNOW IS WHEN DID YOU MAKE THEM?!
THEY'RE A PREFECT FIT!
WHILE YOU WERE BUSY SHOWERING.
SAME AS WHEN I MADE YOUR MAID OUTFITS.
WHA...? YOU WERE ABLE TO SEW THEM PERFECTLY JUST BY LOOKING AT US?
DARN RIGHT! YOU CAN'T GET THAT KIND OF SUBTLE SKIRT LENGTH WITH GENERIC SIZES, YOU KNOW!
WHY CAN'T YOU USE YOUR SKILLS FOR SOMETHING MORE PRODUCTIVE AND NOT PERVERTED STUFF LIKE THIS?!
I'LL HAVE YOU KNOW THAT I HEARD VOICES FROM HEAVEN WHILE I WAS MAKING THOSE.
"VOICES FROM HEAVEN"?!
AND ISN'T THIS HEMLINE A LITTLE TOO SHORT?

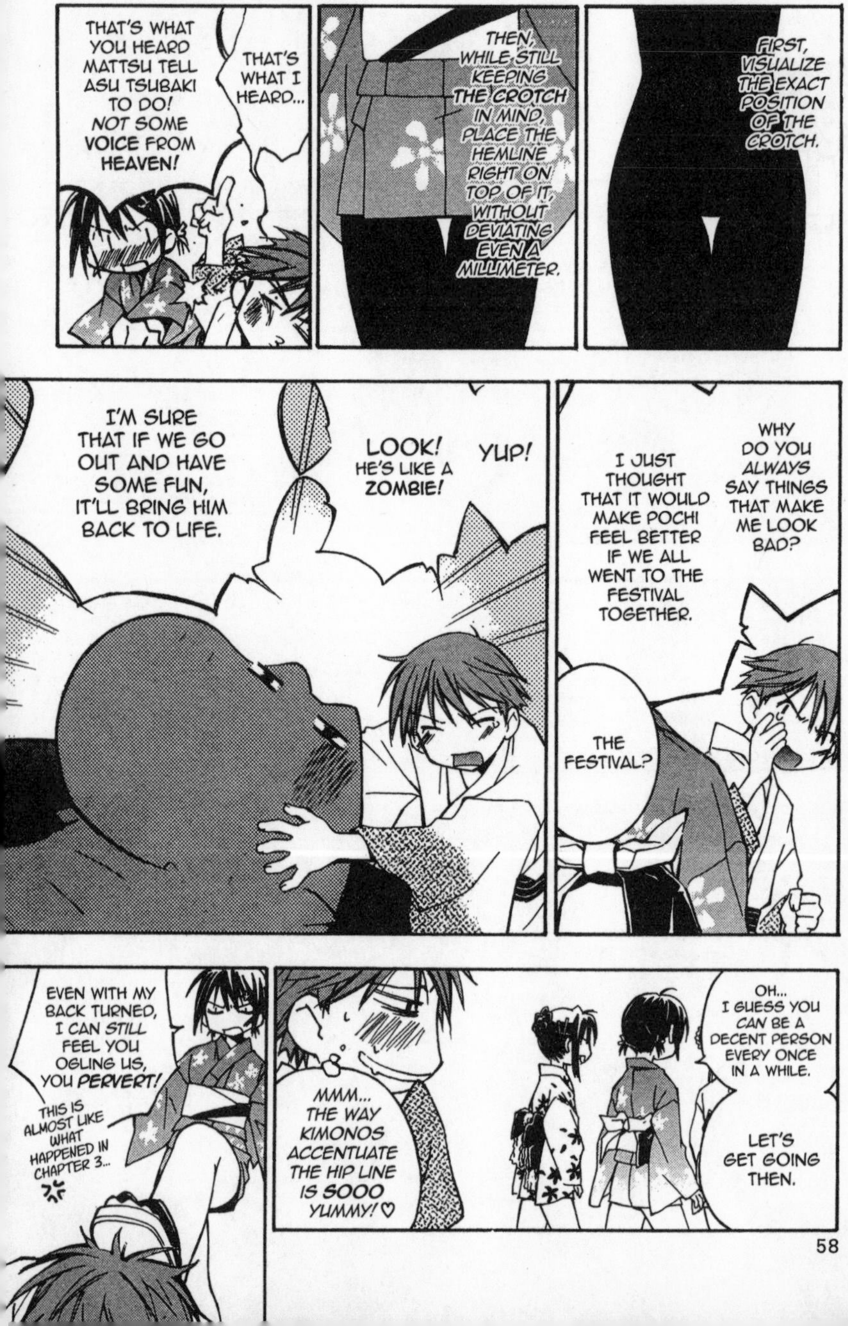
FIRST, VISUALIZE THE EXACT POSITION OF THE CROTCH.
THEN, WHILE STILL KEEPING THE CROTCH IN MIND, PLACE THE HEMLINE RIGHT ON TOP OF IT, WITHOUT DEVIATING EVEN A MILLIMETER.
THAT'S WHAT I HEARD...
THAT'S WHAT YOU HEARD MATTSU TELL ASU TSUBAKI TO DO! NOT SOME VOICE FROM HEAVEN!
WHY DO YOU ALWAYS SAY THINGS THAT MAKE ME LOOK BAD?
I JUST THOUGHT THAT IT WOULD MAKE POCHI FEEL BETTER IF WE ALL WENT TO THE FESTIVAL TOGETHER.
THE FESTIVAL?
YUP!
LOOK! HE'S LIKE A ZOMBIE!
I'M SURE THAT IF WE GO OUT AND HAVE SOME FUN, IT'LL BRING HIM BACK TO LIFE.
OH... I GUESS YOU CAN BE A DECENT PERSON EVERY ONCE IN A WHILE.
LET'S GET GOING THEN.
MMM... THE WAY KIMONOS ACCENTUATE THE HIP LINE IS SOOO YUMMY! ♡
EVEN WITH MY BACK TURNED, I CAN STILL FEEL YOU OGLING US, YOU PERVERT!
THIS IS ALMOST LIKE WHAT HAPPENED IN CHAPTER 3...

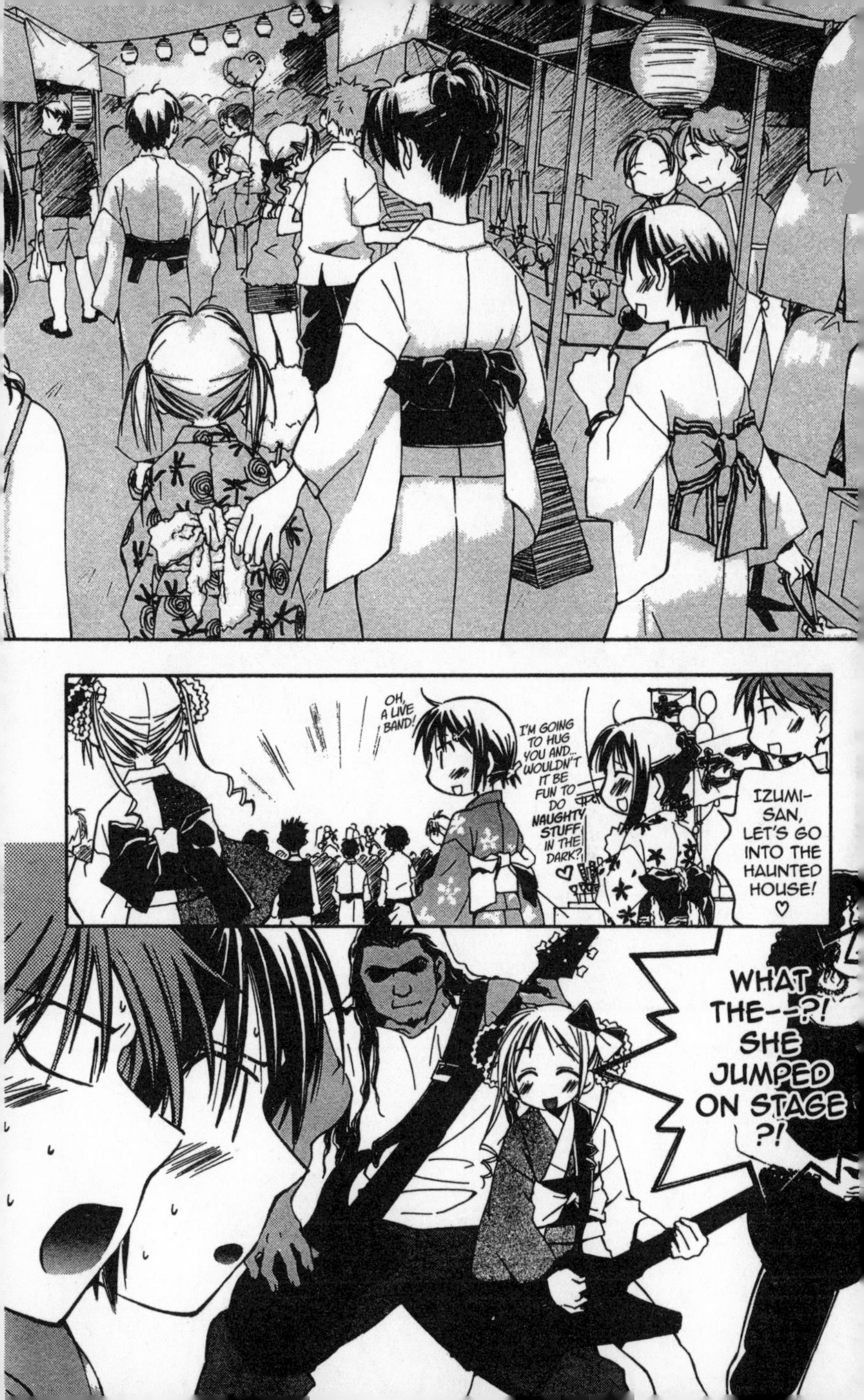
IZUMI-SAN, LET'S GO INTO THE HAUNTED HOUSE! ♡
I'M GOING TO HUG YOU AND... WOULDN'T IT BE FUN TO DO NAUGHTY STUFF IN THE DARK? ♡
OH, A LIVE BAND!
WHAT THE--?! SHE JUMPED ON STAGE?!

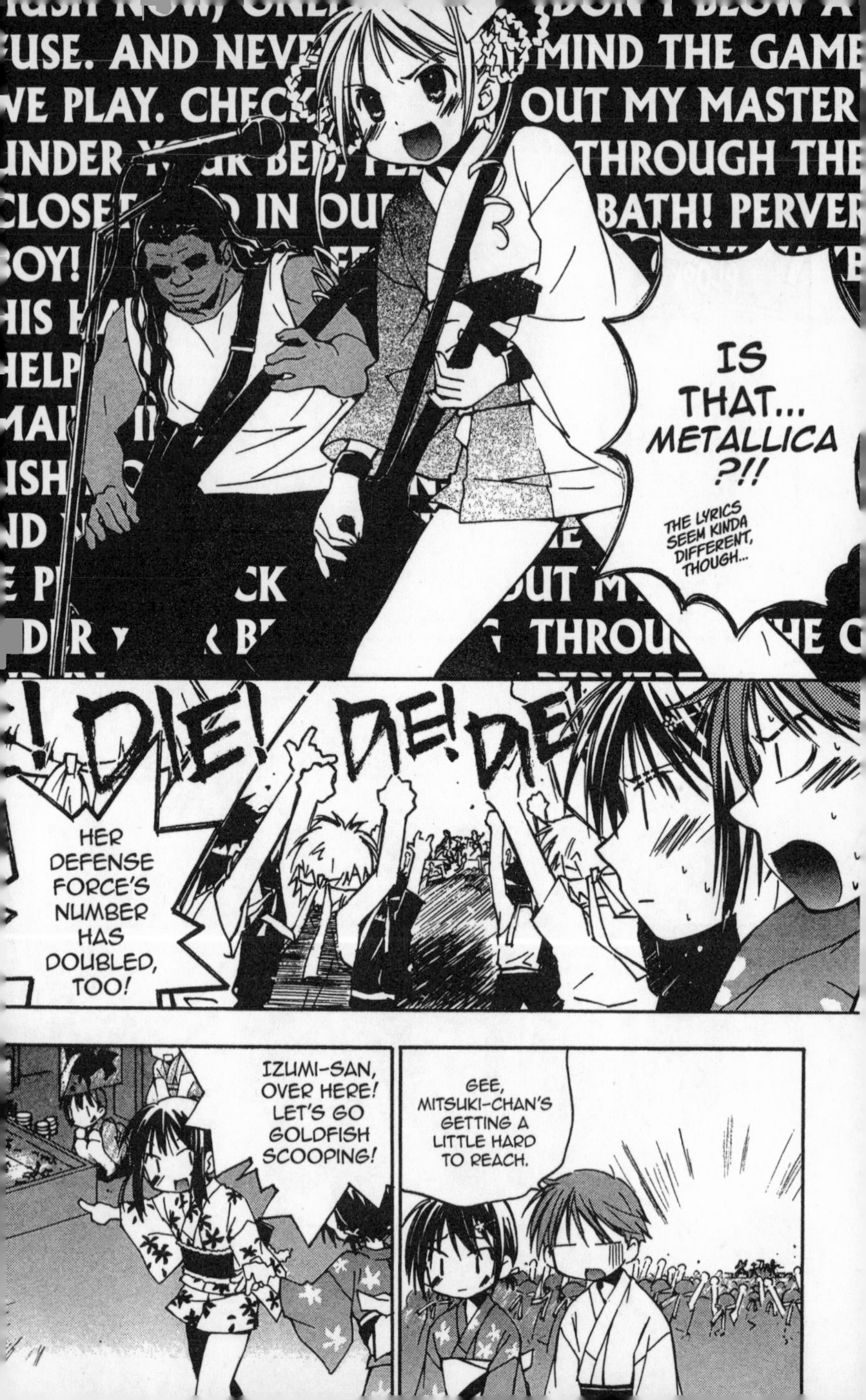
USE. AND NEVE
MIND THE GAME
WE PLAY. CHEC
OUT MY MASTER
THROUGH THE
BATH! PERVER
IS THAT... METALLICA ?!!
THE LYRICS SEEM KINDA DIFFERENT, THOUGH...
DIE! DIE! DIE!
HER DEFENSE FORCE'S NUMBER HAS DOUBLED, TOO!
GEE, MITSUKI-CHAN'S GETTING A LITTLE HARD TO REACH.
IZUMI-SAN, OVER HERE! LET'S GO GOLDFISH SCOOPING!

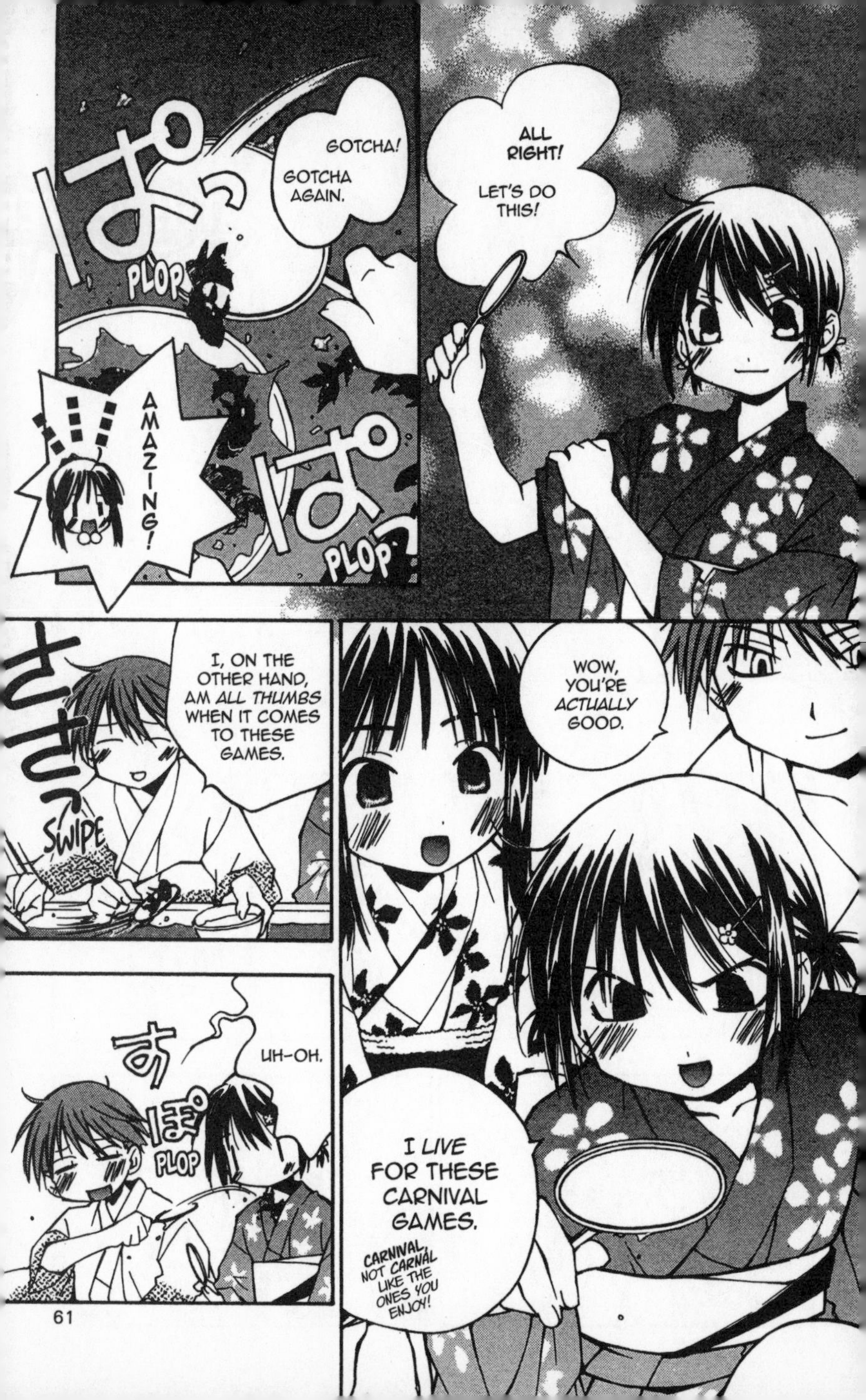
ALL RIGHT!
LET'S DO THIS!
ぱっ
PLOP
GOTCHA!
GOTCHA AGAIN.
AMAZING!
ぱっ
PLOP
WOW, YOU'RE ACTUALLY GOOD.
I LIVE FOR THESE CARNIVAL GAMES.
CARNIVAL, NOT CARNAL LIKE THE ONES YOU ENJOY!
I, ON THE OTHER HAND, AM ALL THUMBS WHEN IT COMES TO THESE GAMES.
さっ
SWIPE
すぽ
PLOP
UH-OH.

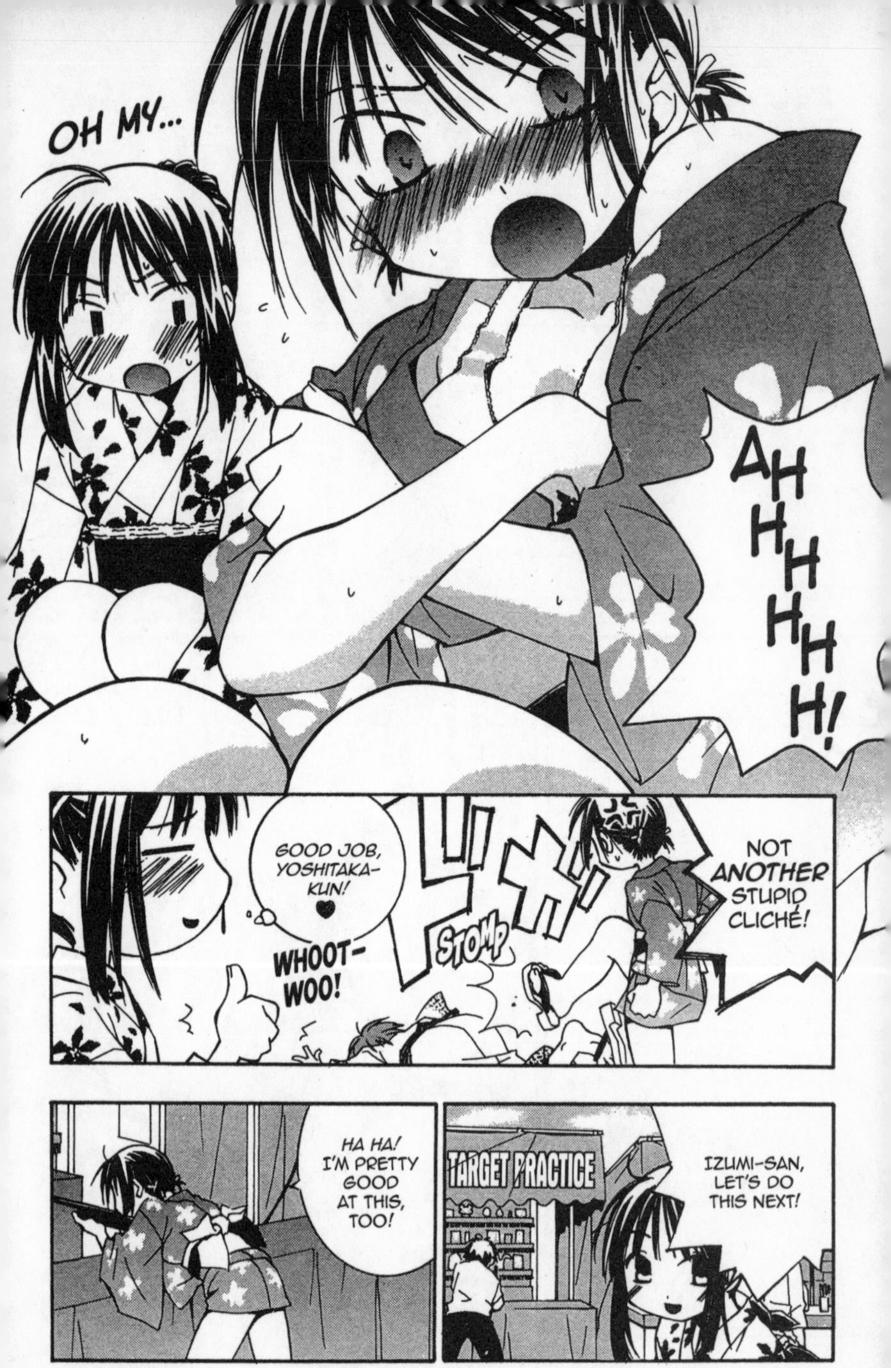

AHHHHHH!
OH MY...
NOT ANOTHER STUPID CLICHÉ!
STOMP
GOOD JOB, YOSHITAKA-KUN! ♥
WHOOT-WOO!
IZUMI-SAN, LET'S DO THIS NEXT!
TARGET PRACTICE
HA HA! I'M PRETTY GOOD AT THIS, TOO!

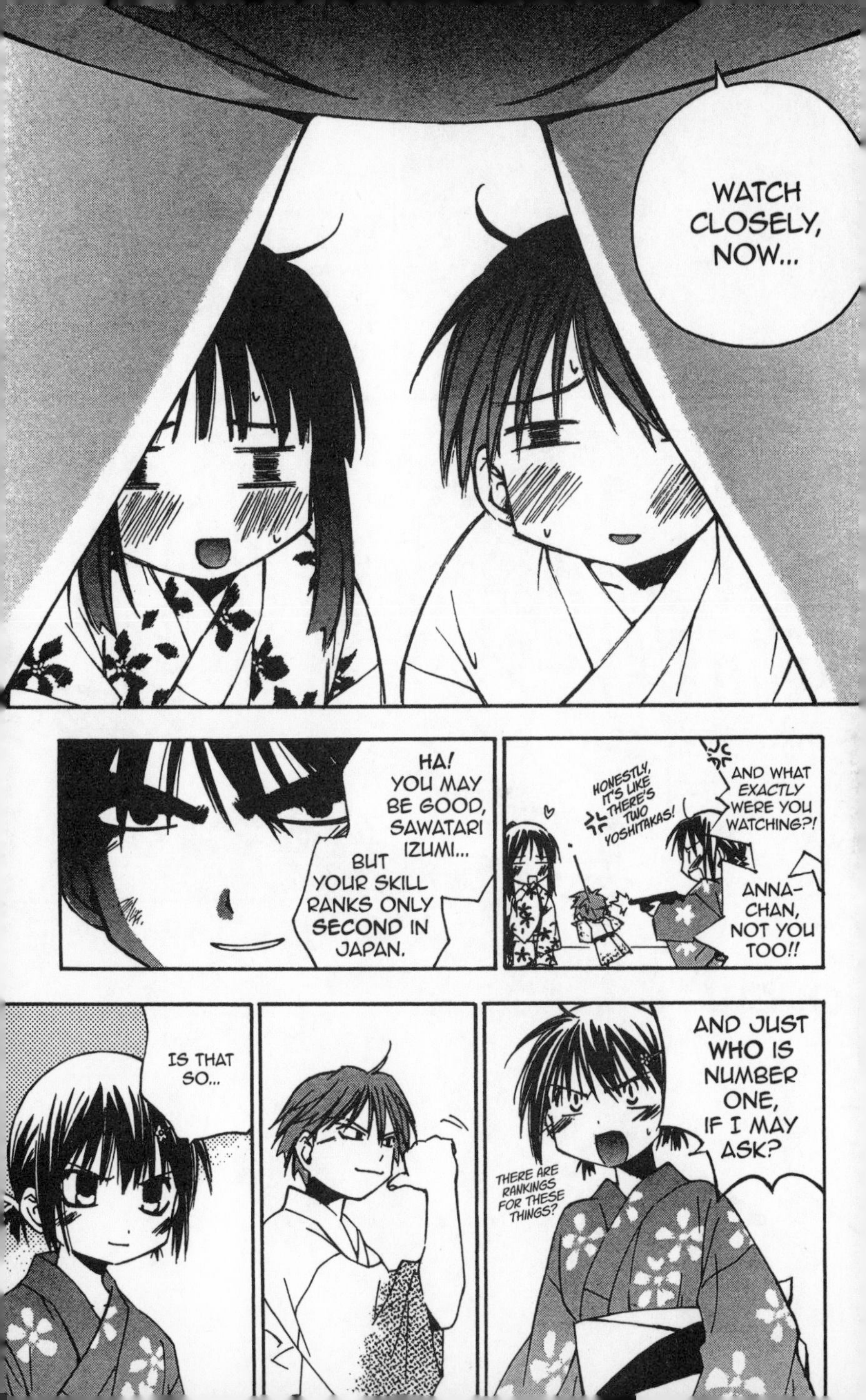
WATCH CLOSELY, NOW...
AND WHAT EXACTLY WERE YOU WATCHING?!
HONESTLY, IT'S LIKE THERE'S TWO YOSHITAKAS!
ANNA-CHAN, NOT YOU TOO!!
HA! YOU MAY BE GOOD, SAWATARI IZUMI...
BUT YOUR SKILL RANKS ONLY SECOND IN JAPAN.
AND JUST WHO IS NUMBER ONE, IF I MAY ASK?
THERE ARE RANKINGS FOR THESE THINGS?
IS THAT SO...

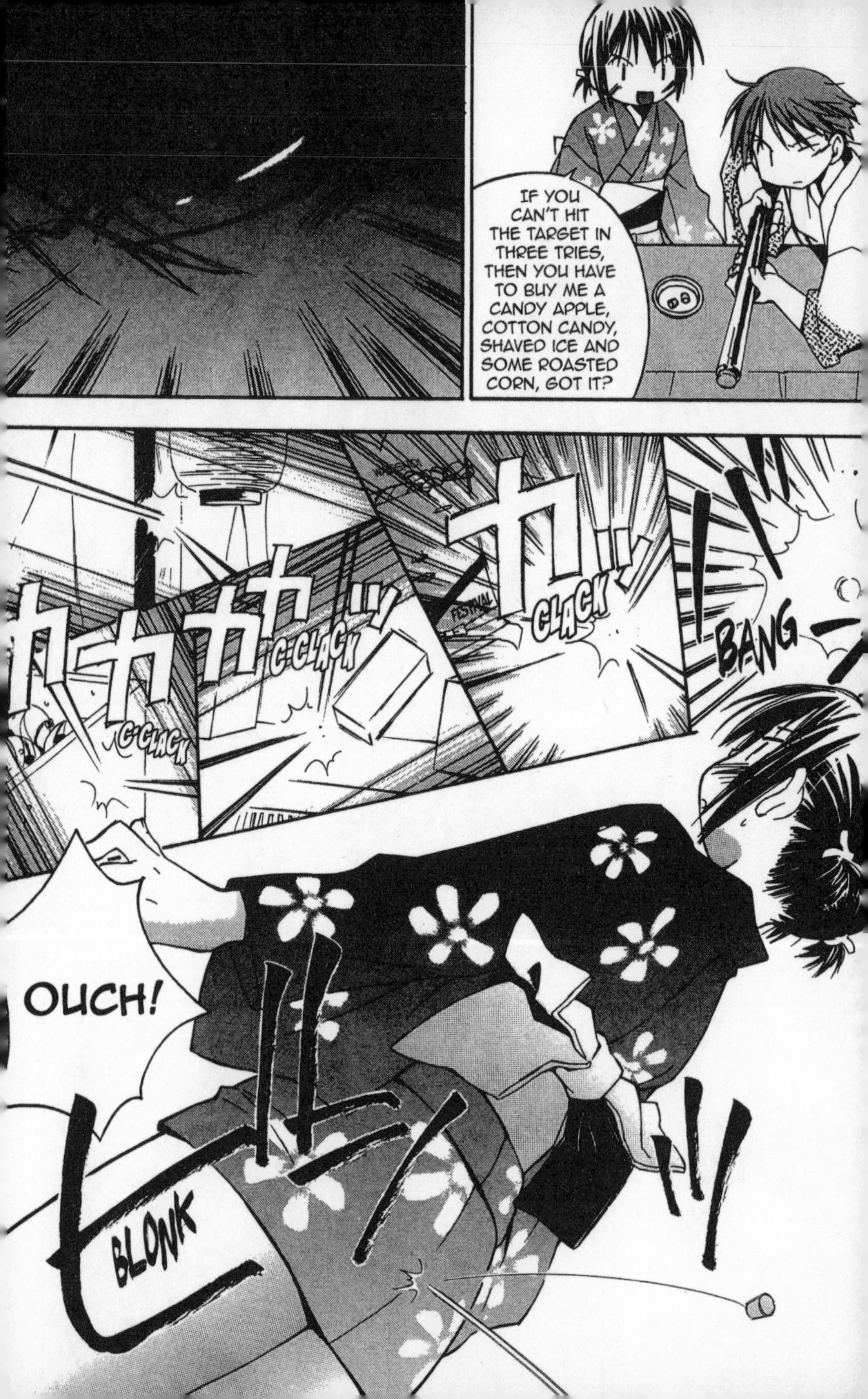

IF YOU CAN'T HIT THE TARGET IN THREE TRIES, THEN YOU HAVE TO BUY ME A CANDY APPLE, COTTON CANDY, SHAVED ICE AND SOME ROASTED CORN, GOT IT?
BANG
CLACK
C-CLACK
C-CLACK
OUCH!
BLONK

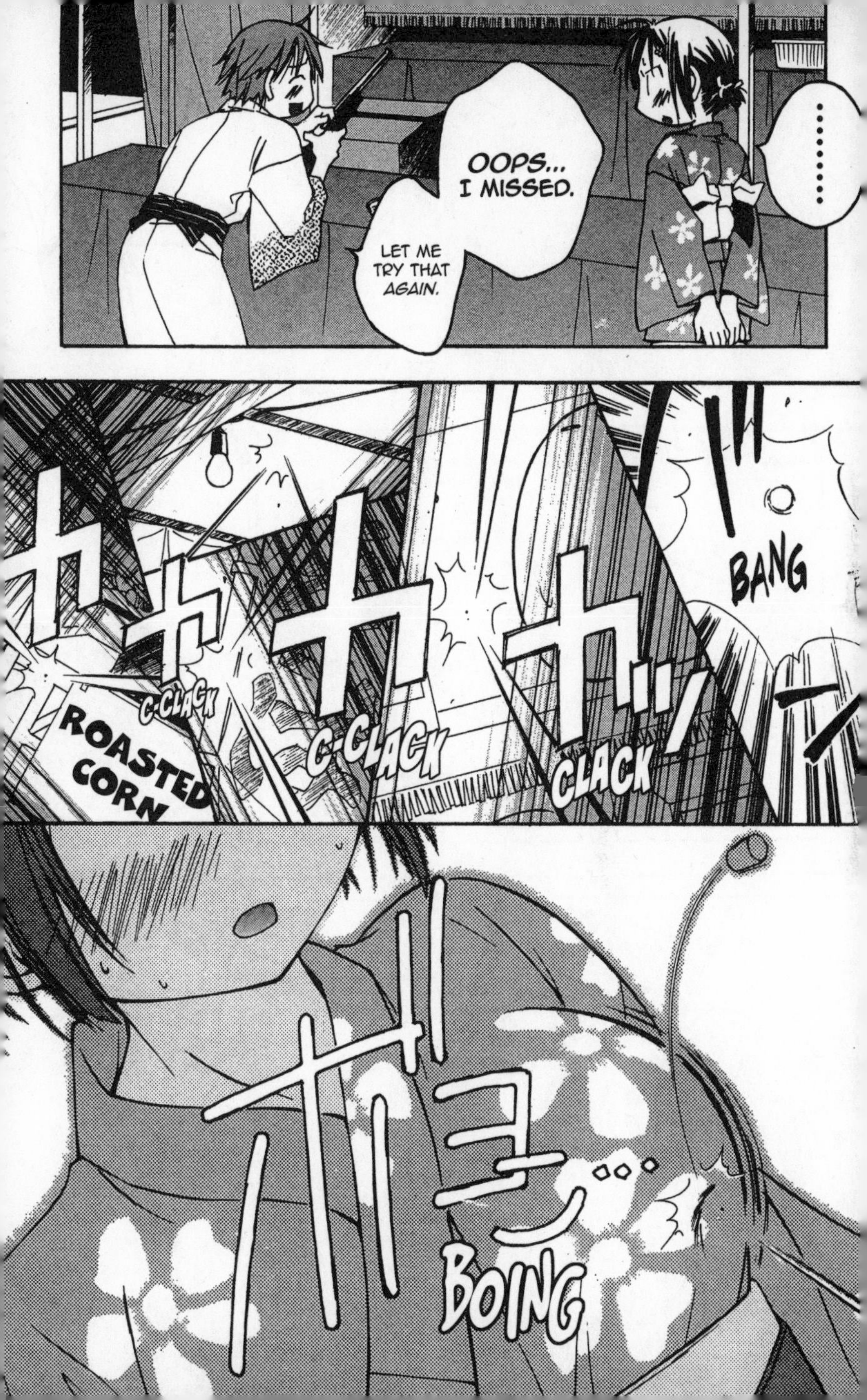
......
OOPS... I MISSED.
LET ME TRY THAT AGAIN.
BANG
CLACK
C-CLACK
C-CLACK
ROASTED CORN
BOING

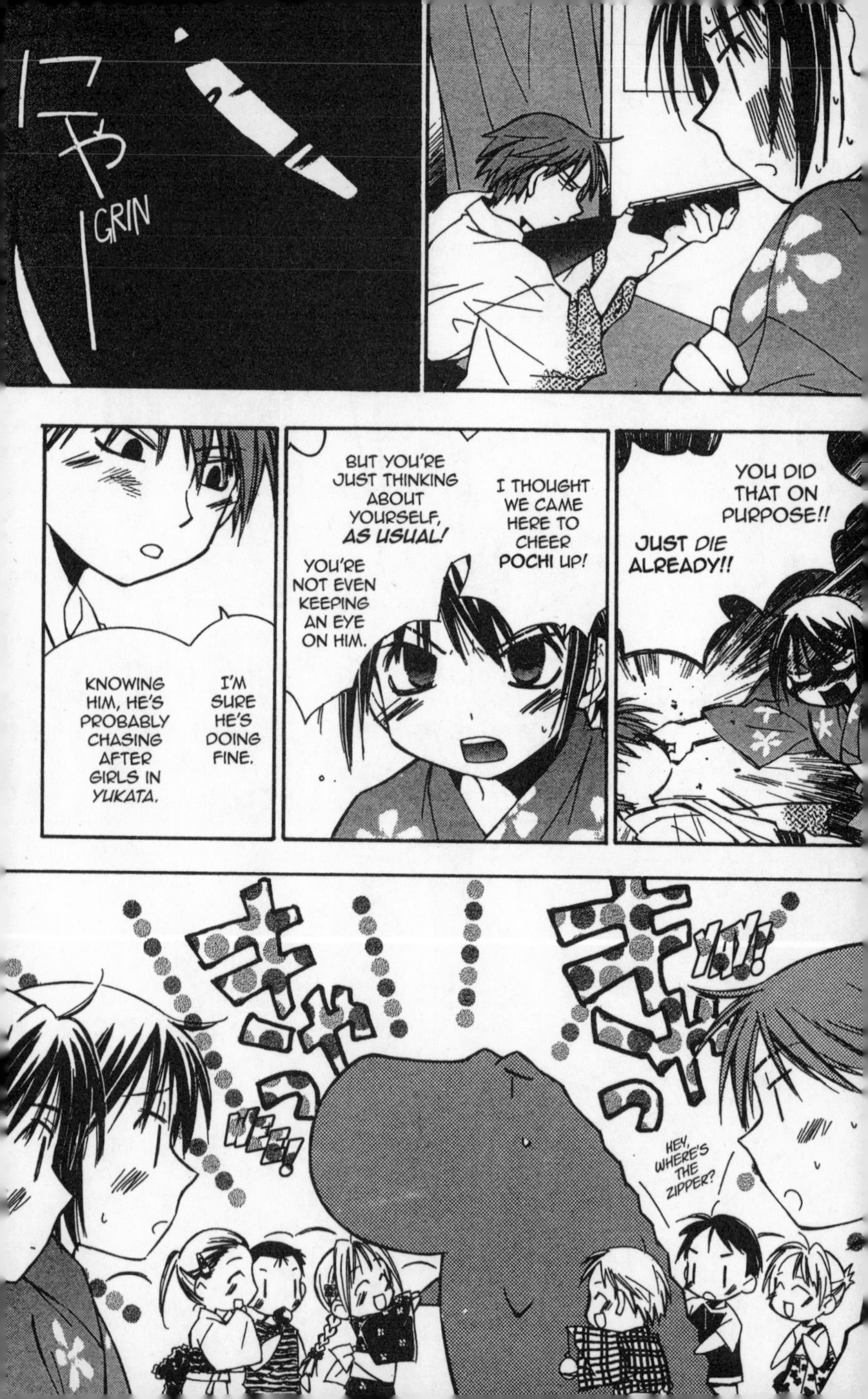
ニヤ
GRIN
YOU DID THAT ON PURPOSE!!
JUST DIE ALREADY!!
I THOUGHT WE CAME HERE TO CHEER POCHI UP!
BUT YOU'RE JUST THINKING ABOUT YOURSELF, AS USUAL!
YOU'RE NOT EVEN KEEPING AN EYE ON HIM.
I'M SURE HE'S DOING FINE.
KNOWING HIM, HE'S PROBABLY CHASING AFTER GIRLS IN YUKATA.
YAY!
HEY, WHERE'S THE ZIPPER?
WEE!

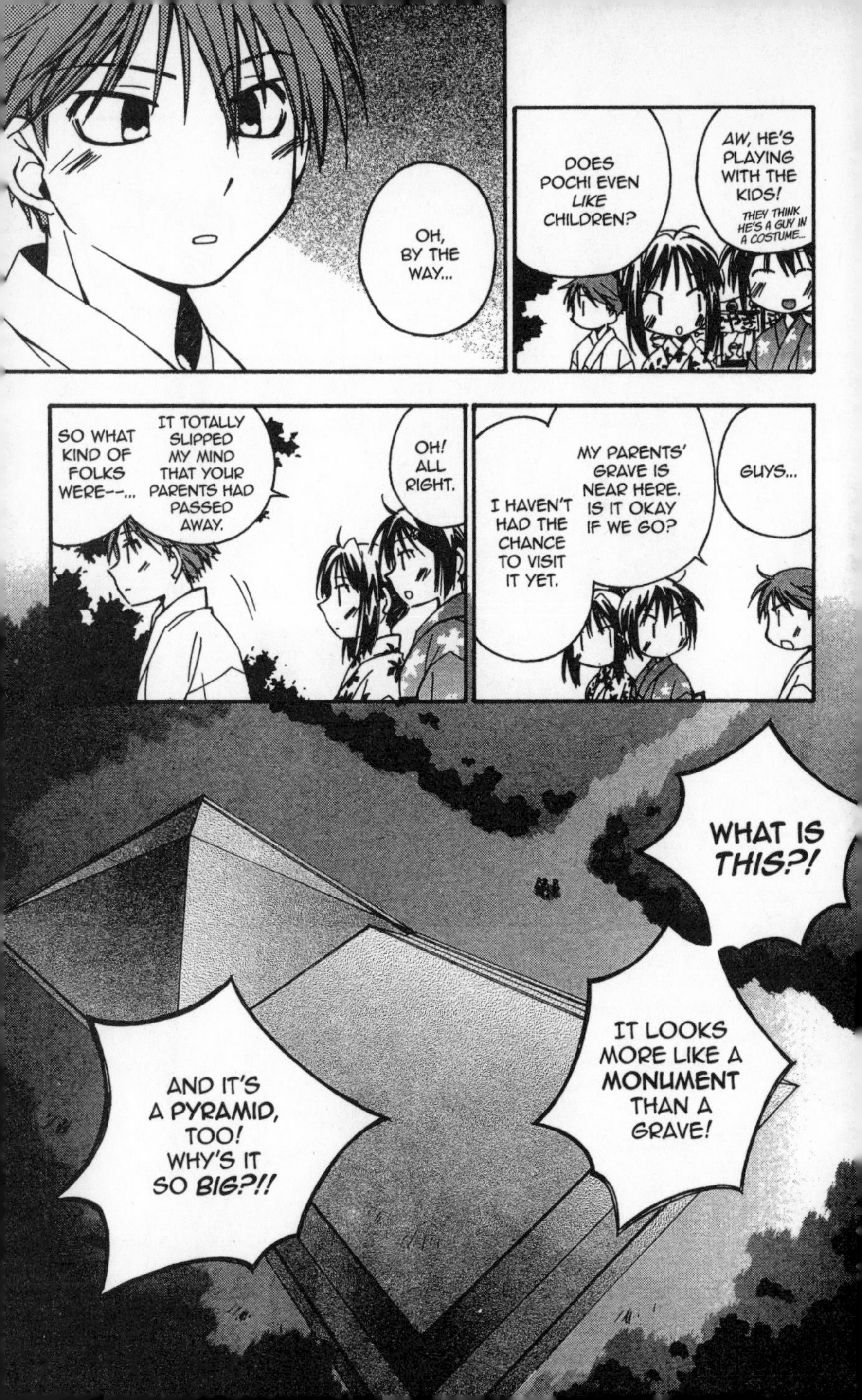
AW, HE'S PLAYING WITH THE KIDS!
THEY THINK HE'S A GUY IN A COSTUME...
DOES POCHI EVEN LIKE CHILDREN?
OH, BY THE WAY...
GUYS...
MY PARENTS' GRAVE IS NEAR HERE. IS IT OKAY IF WE GO?
I HAVEN'T HAD THE CHANCE TO VISIT IT YET.
OH! ALL RIGHT.
IT TOTALLY SLIPPED MY MIND THAT YOUR PARENTS HAD PASSED AWAY.
SO WHAT KIND OF FOLKS WERE--...
WHAT IS THIS?!
IT LOOKS MORE LIKE A MONUMENT THAN A GRAVE!
AND IT'S A PYRAMID, TOO! WHY'S IT SO BIG?!!

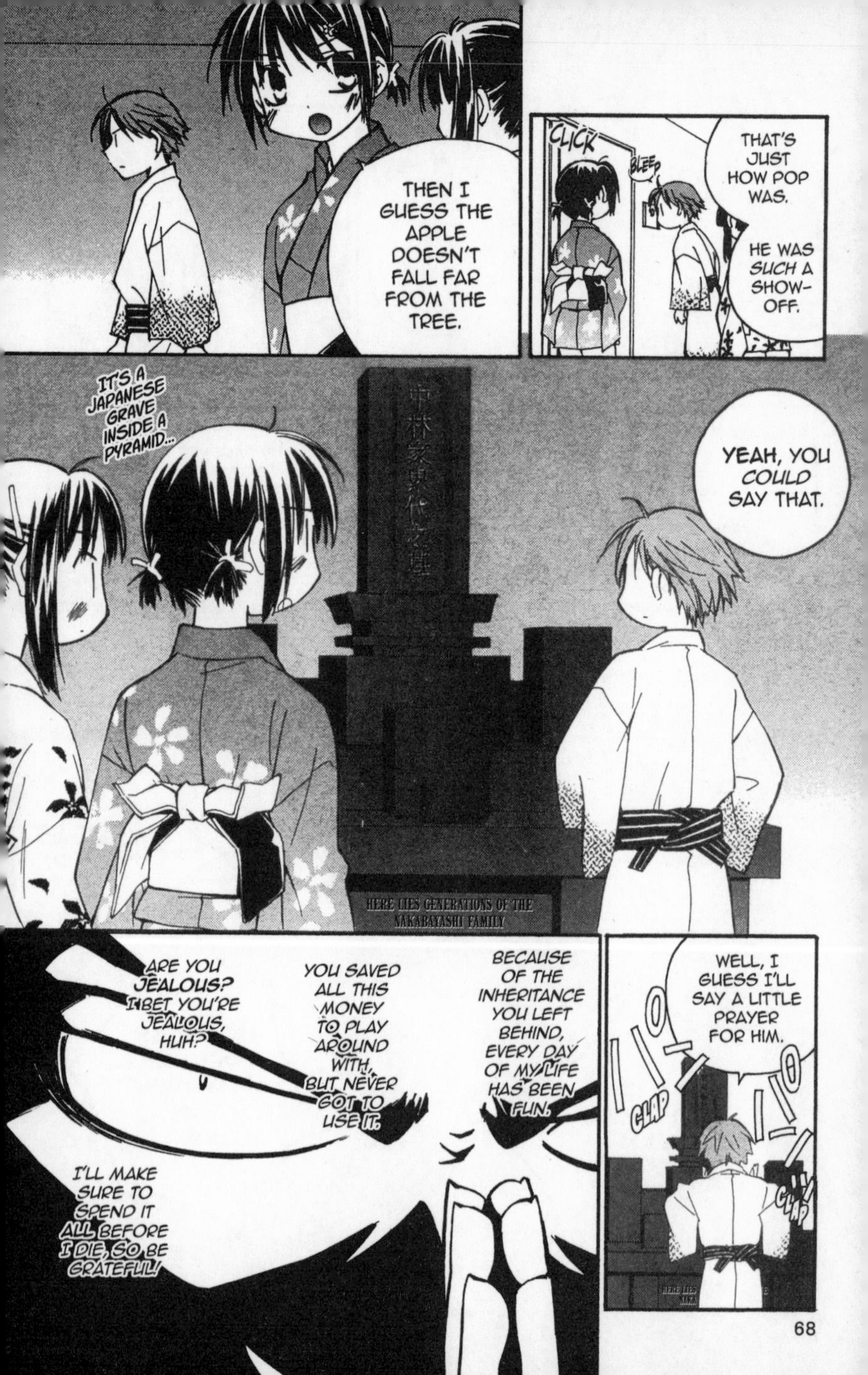
CLICK
BLEEP
THAT'S JUST HOW POP WAS.
HE WAS SUCH A SHOW-OFF.
THEN I GUESS THE APPLE DOESN'T FALL FAR FROM THE TREE.
YEAH, YOU COULD SAY THAT.
IT'S A JAPANESE GRAVE INSIDE A PYRAMID...
HERE LIES GENERATIONS OF THE NAKABAYASHI FAMILY
WELL, I GUESS I'LL SAY A LITTLE PRAYER FOR HIM.
CLAP
CLAP
BECAUSE OF THE INHERITANCE YOU LEFT BEHIND, EVERY DAY OF MY LIFE HAS BEEN FUN.
YOU SAVED ALL THIS MONEY TO PLAY AROUND WITH, BUT NEVER GOT TO USE IT.
ARE YOU JEALOUS? I BET YOU'RE JEALOUS, HUH?
I'LL MAKE SURE TO SPEND IT ALL BEFORE I DIE, SO BE GRATEFUL!

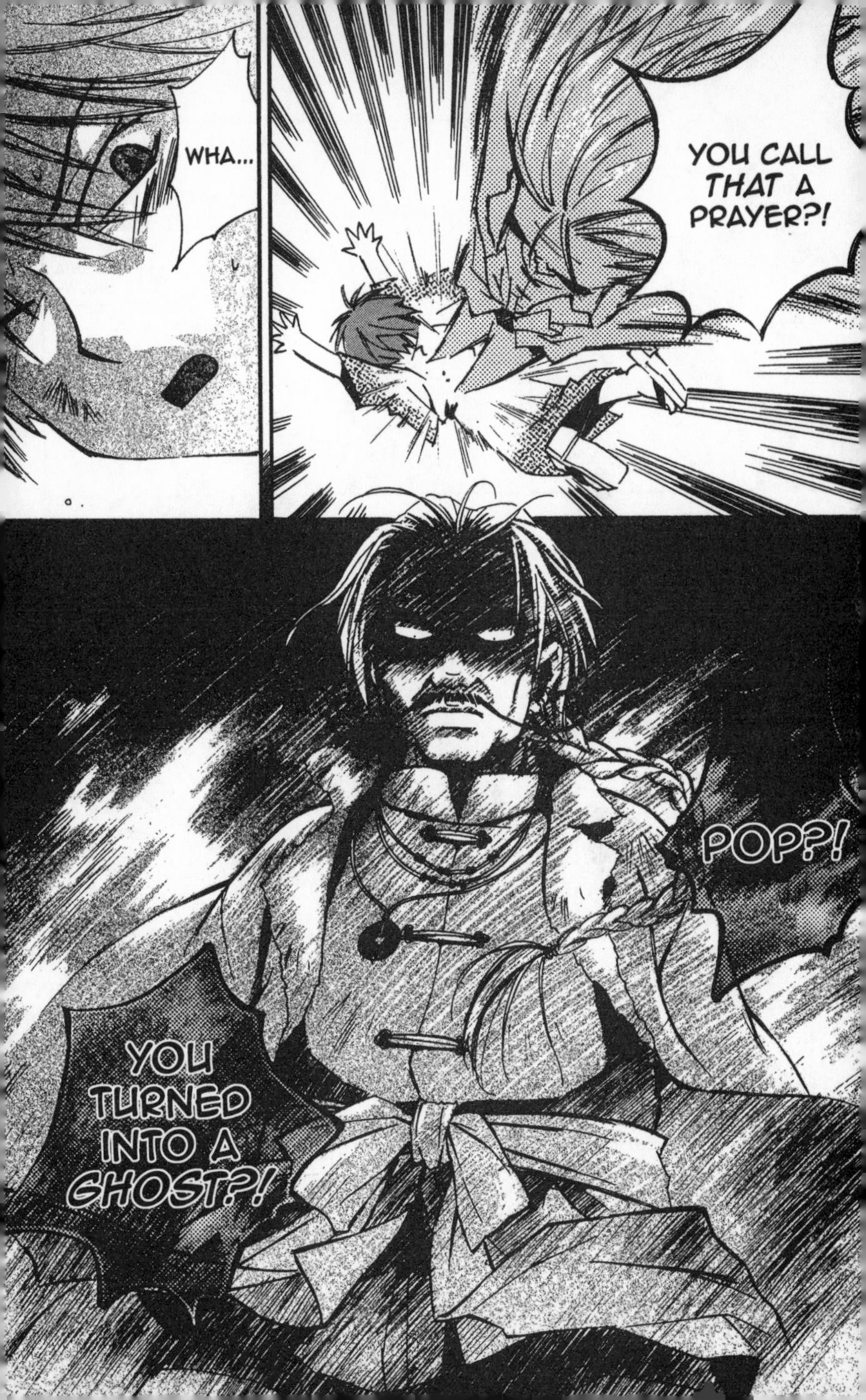
YOU CALL THAT A PRAYER?!
WHA...
POP?!
YOU TURNED INTO A GHOST?!

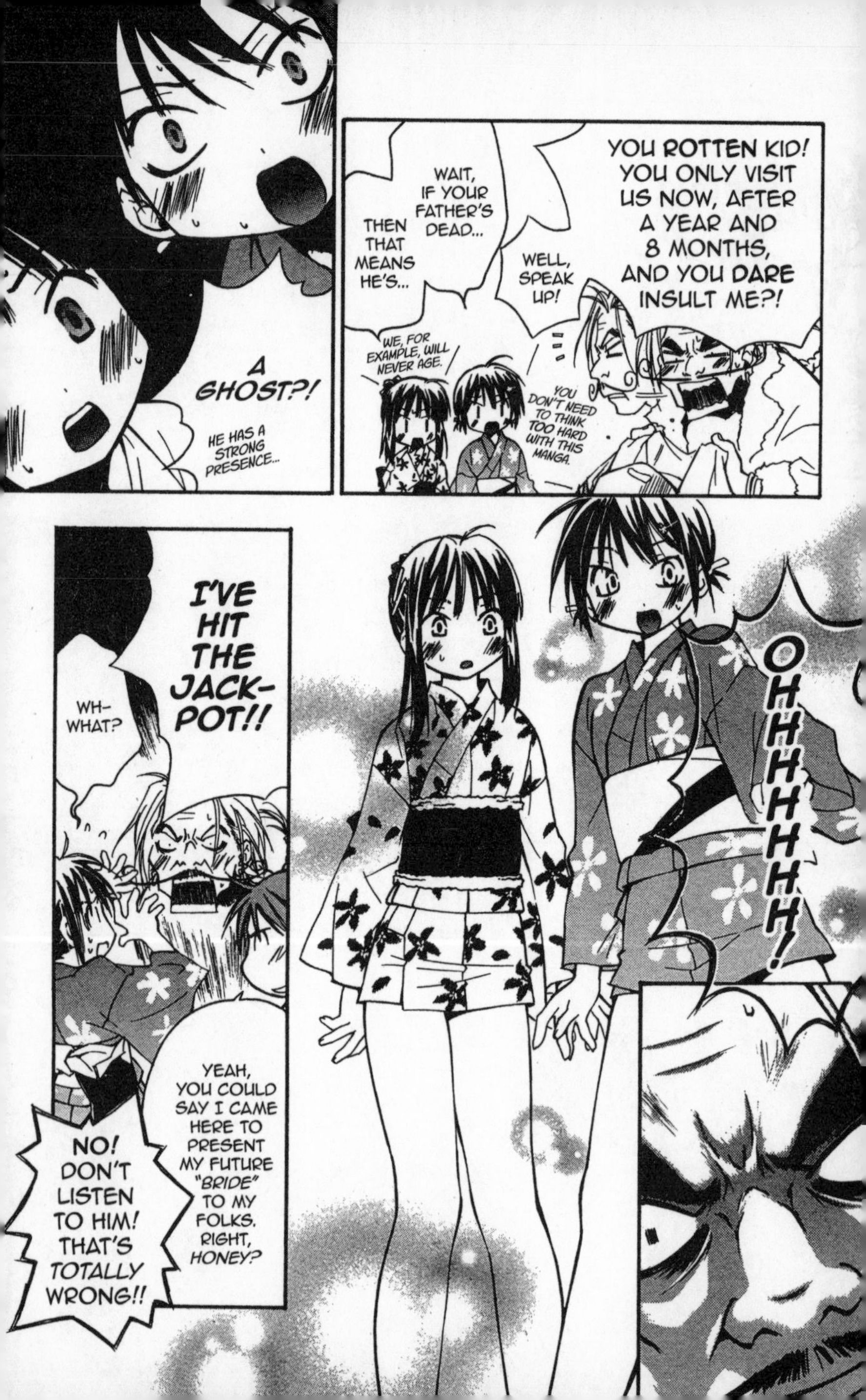
YOU ROTTEN KID! YOU ONLY VISIT US NOW, AFTER A YEAR AND 8 MONTHS, AND YOU DARE INSULT ME?!
WELL, SPEAK UP!
WAIT, IF YOUR FATHER'S DEAD...
THEN THAT MEANS HE'S...
YOU DON'T NEED TO THINK TOO HARD WITH THIS MANGA.
WE, FOR EXAMPLE, WILL NEVER AGE.
A GHOST?!
HE HAS A STRONG PRESENCE...
OHHHHHHHH!
I'VE HIT THE JACK-POT!!
WH-WHAT?
YEAH, YOU COULD SAY I CAME HERE TO PRESENT MY FUTURE "BRIDE" TO MY FOLKS. RIGHT, HONEY?
NO! DON'T LISTEN TO HIM! THAT'S TOTALLY WRONG!!

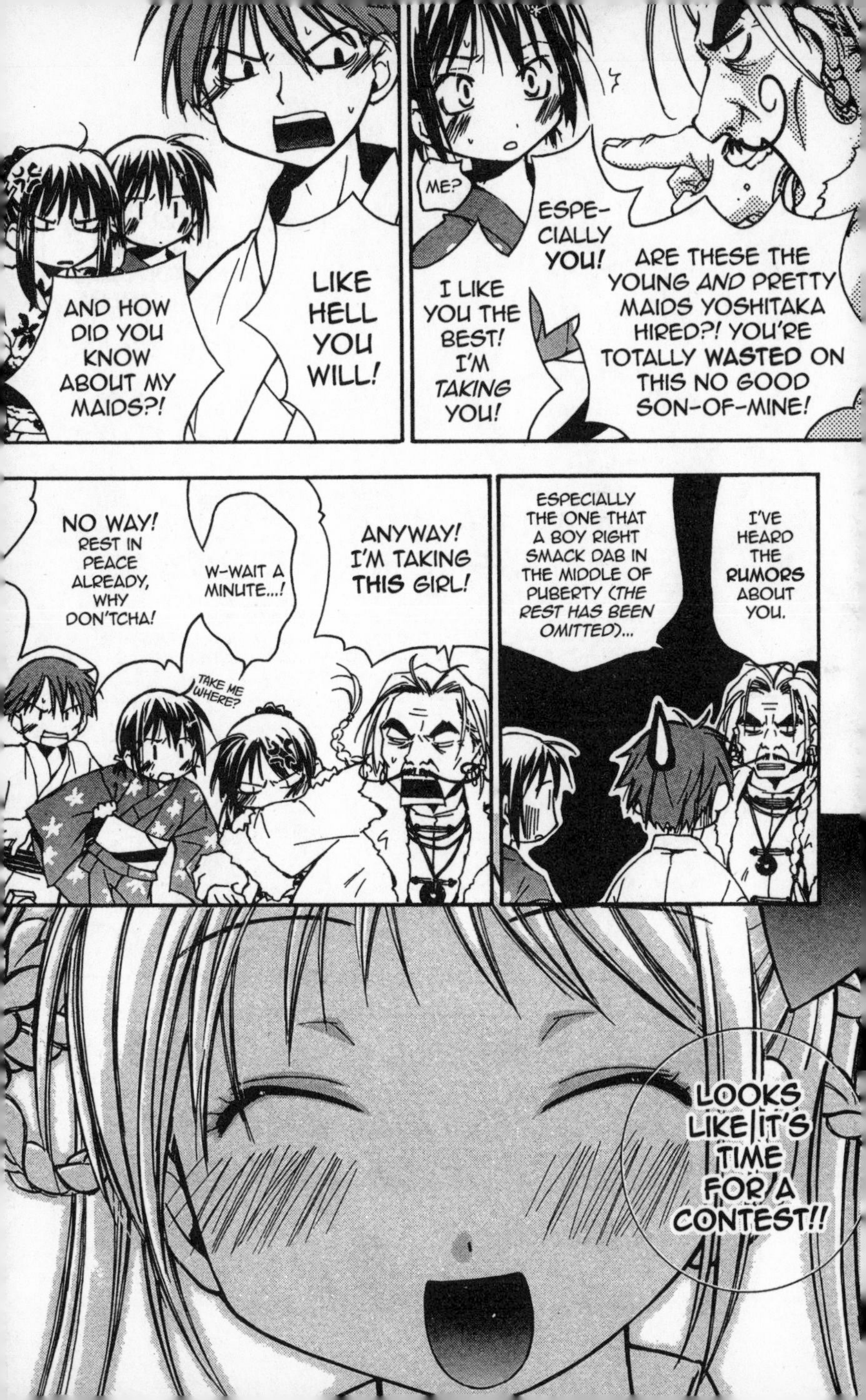
ARE THESE THE YOUNG AND PRETTY MAIDS YOSHITAKA HIRED?! YOU'RE TOTALLY WASTED ON THIS NO GOOD SON-OF-MINE!
ESPE-CIALLY YOU!
ME?
I LIKE YOU THE BEST! I'M TAKING YOU!
LIKE HELL YOU WILL!
AND HOW DID YOU KNOW ABOUT MY MAIDS?!
I'VE HEARD THE RUMORS ABOUT YOU.
ESPECIALLY THE ONE THAT A BOY RIGHT SMACK DAB IN THE MIDDLE OF PUBERTY (THE REST HAS BEEN OMITTED)...
ANYWAY! I'M TAKING THIS GIRL!
W-WAIT A MINUTE...!
TAKE ME WHERE?
NO WAY! REST IN PEACE ALREADY, WHY DON'TCHA!
LOOKS LIKE IT'S TIME FOR A CONTEST!!

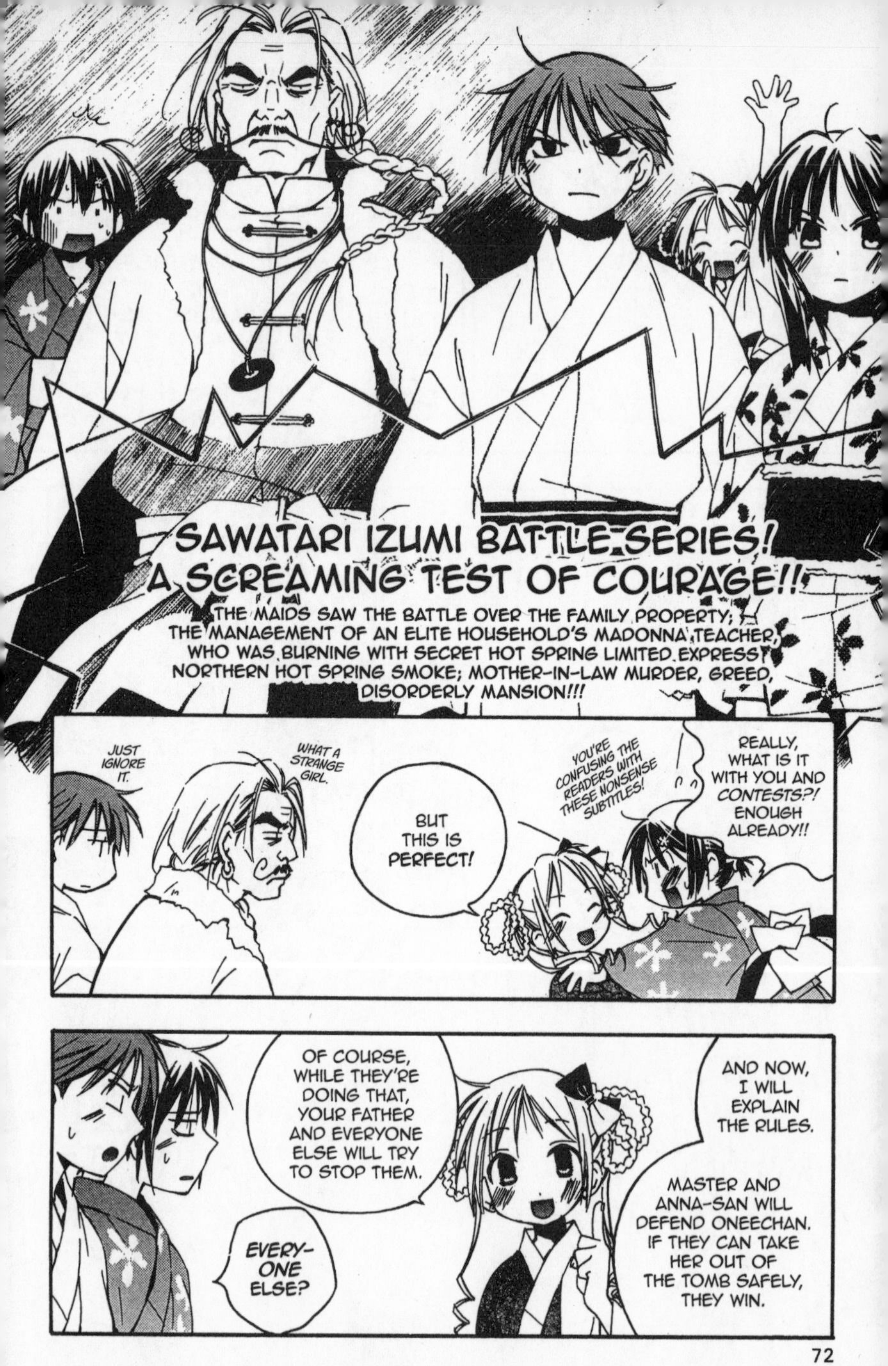
SAWATARI IZUMI BATTLE SERIES! A SCREAMING TEST OF COURAGE!!
THE MAIDS SAW THE BATTLE OVER THE FAMILY PROPERTY; THE MANAGEMENT OF AN ELITE HOUSEHOLD'S MADONNA TEACHER, WHO WAS BURNING WITH SECRET HOT SPRING LIMITED EXPRESS! NORTHERN HOT SPRING SMOKE; MOTHER-IN-LAW MURDER, GREED, DISORDERLY MANSION!!!
REALLY, WHAT IS IT WITH YOU AND CONTESTS?! ENOUGH ALREADY!!
YOU'RE CONFUSING THE READERS WITH THESE NONSENSE SUBTITLES!
BUT THIS IS PERFECT!
WHAT A STRANGE GIRL.
JUST IGNORE IT.
AND NOW, I WILL EXPLAIN THE RULES.
MASTER AND ANNA-SAN WILL DEFEND ONEECHAN. IF THEY CAN TAKE HER OUT OF THE TOMB SAFELY, THEY WIN.
OF COURSE, WHILE THEY'RE DOING THAT, YOUR FATHER AND EVERYONE ELSE WILL TRY TO STOP THEM.
EVERY-ONE ELSE?

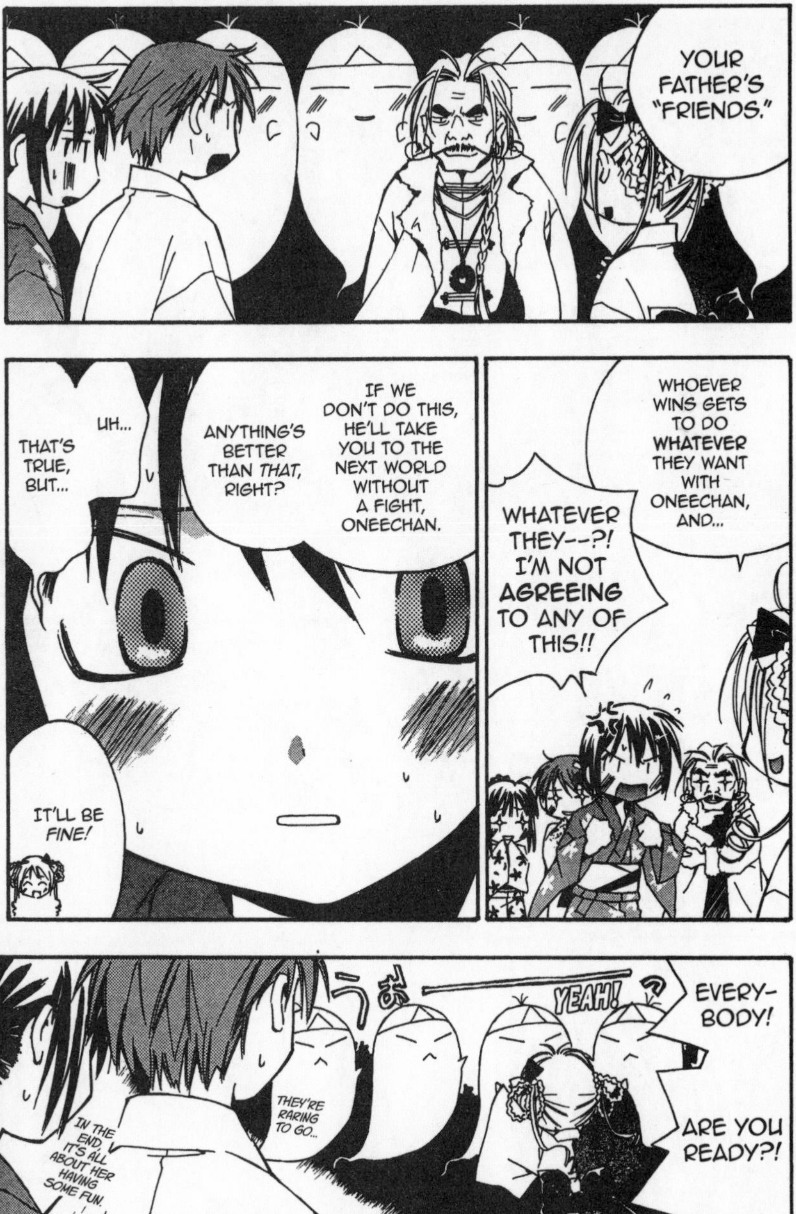
YOUR FATHER'S "FRIENDS."
WHOEVER WINS GETS TO DO WHATEVER THEY WANT WITH ONEECHAN, AND...
WHATEVER THEY--?! I'M NOT AGREEING TO ANY OF THIS!!
IF WE DON'T DO THIS, HE'LL TAKE YOU TO THE NEXT WORLD WITHOUT A FIGHT, ONEECHAN.
ANYTHING'S BETTER THAN *THAT*, RIGHT?
UH...
THAT'S TRUE, BUT...
IT'LL BE *FINE!*
EVERY-BODY!
ARE YOU READY?!
うお————
YEAH!
THEY'RE RARING TO GO...
IN THE END, IT'S ALL ABOUT HER HAVING SOME FUN.

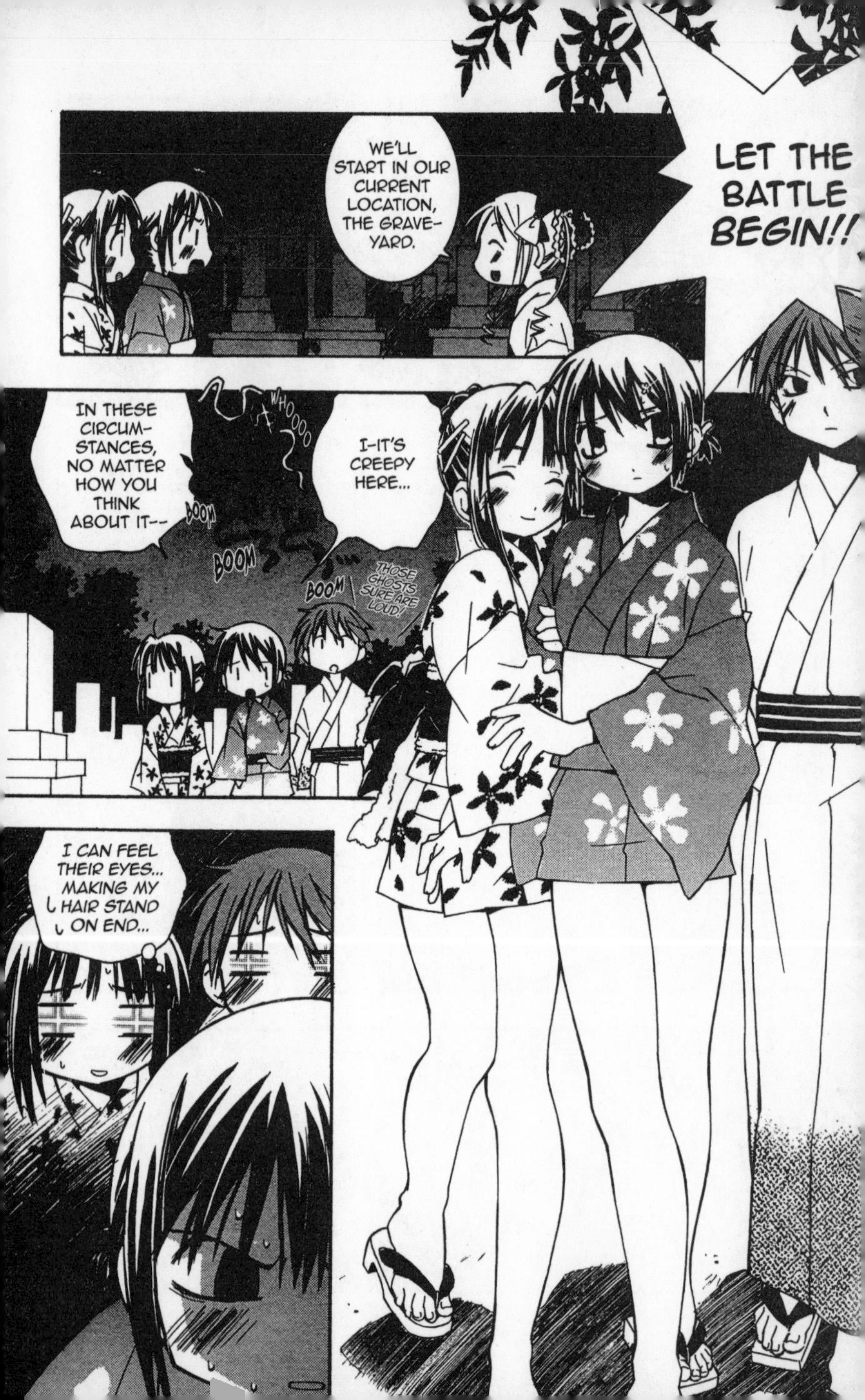
LET THE BATTLE BEGIN!!
WE'LL START IN OUR CURRENT LOCATION, THE GRAVE-YARD.
I-IT'S CREEPY HERE...
WHOOOO
IN THESE CIRCUM-STANCES, NO MATTER HOW YOU THINK ABOUT IT--
BOOM
BOOM
BOOM
THOSE GHOSTS SURE ARE LOUD!
I CAN FEEL THEIR EYES... MAKING MY HAIR STAND ON END...

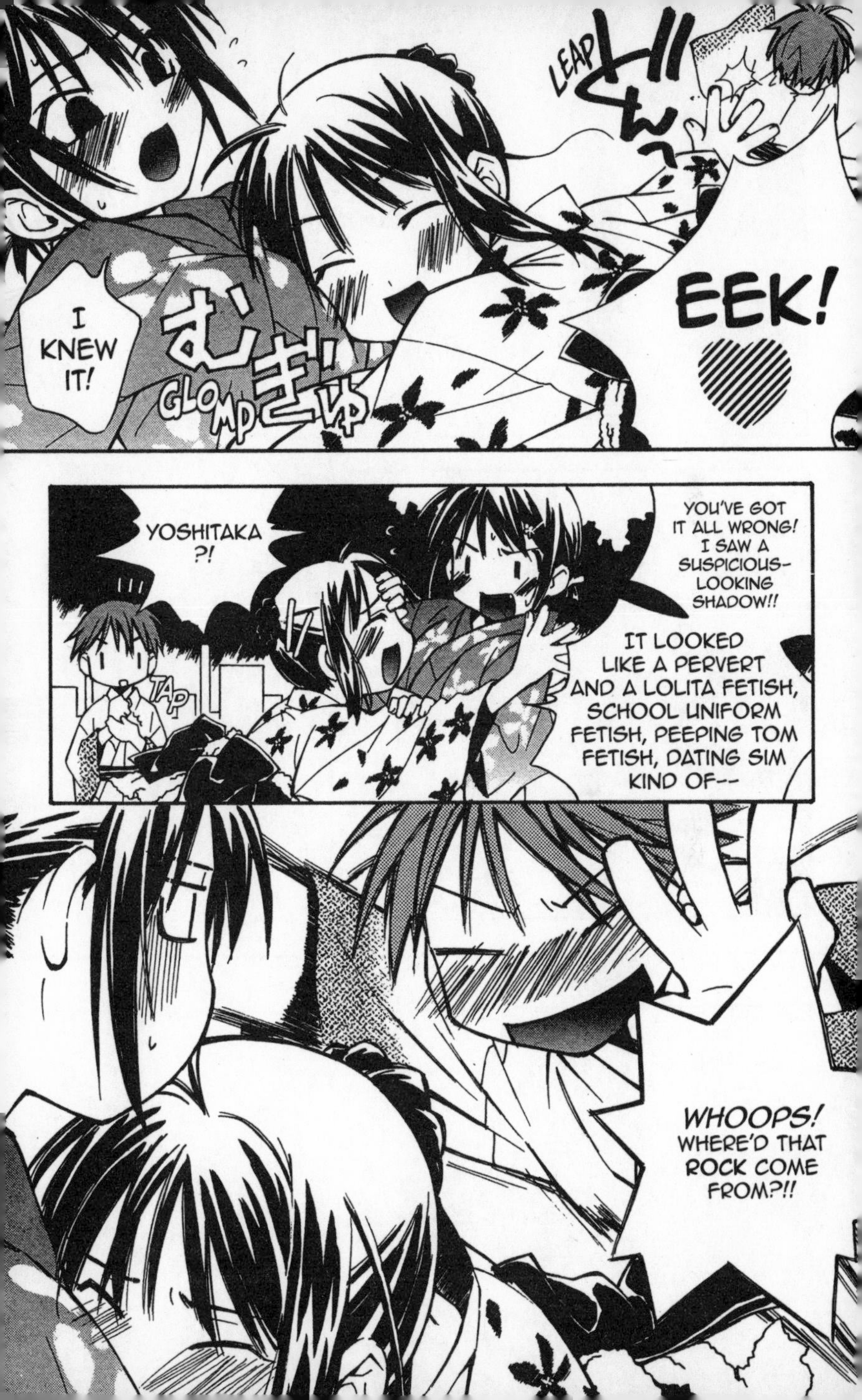
LEAP
EEK!
GLOMP
I KNEW IT!
YOU'VE GOT IT ALL WRONG! I SAW A SUSPICIOUS-LOOKING SHADOW!!
IT LOOKED LIKE A PERVERT AND A LOLITA FETISH, SCHOOL UNIFORM FETISH, PEEPING TOM FETISH, DATING SIM KIND OF--
YOSHITAKA ?!
TAP
WHOOPS! WHERE'D THAT ROCK COME FROM?!!

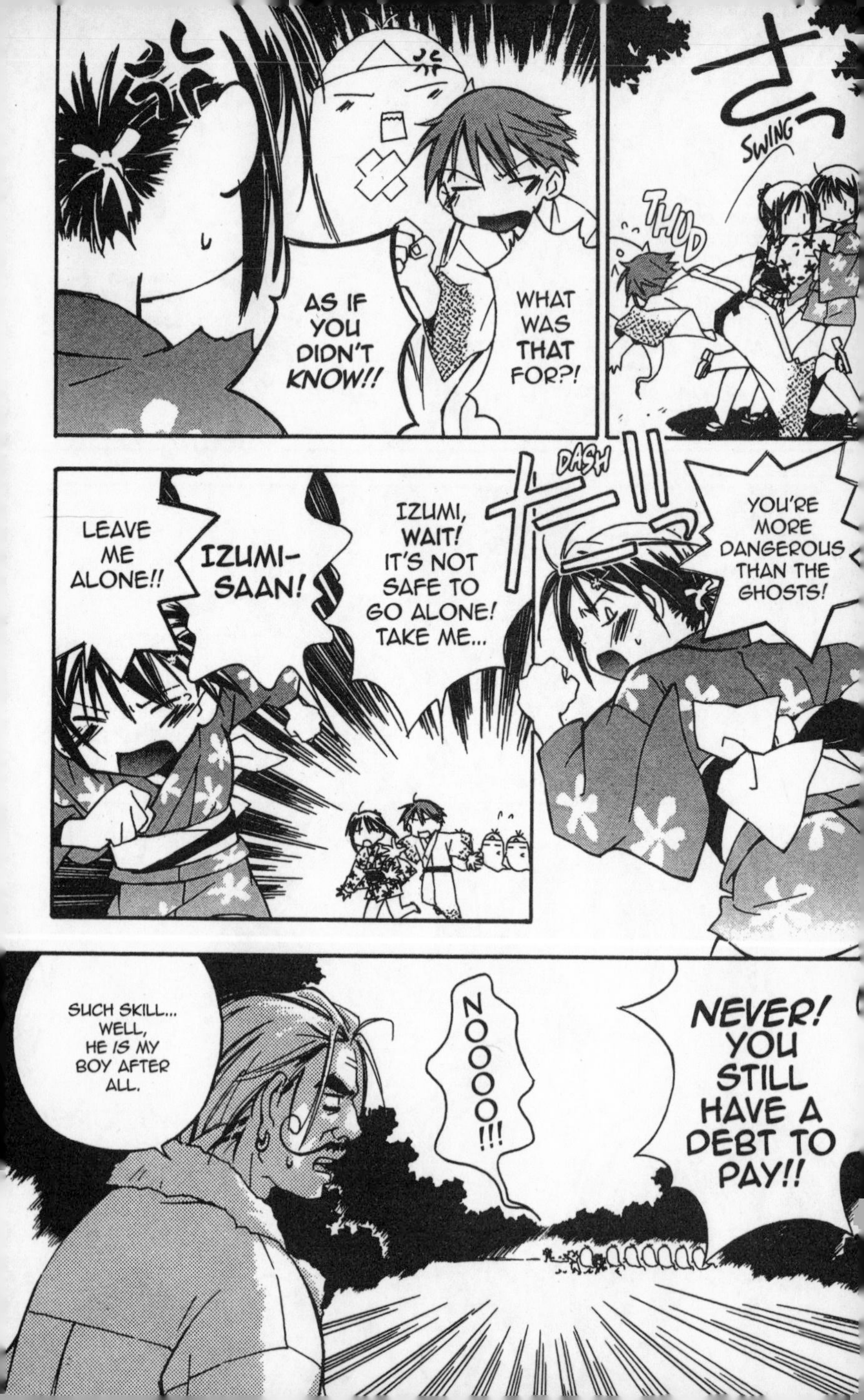
さっ
SWING
THUD
WHAT WAS THAT FOR?!
AS IF YOU DIDN'T KNOW!!
DASH
YOU'RE MORE DANGEROUS THAN THE GHOSTS!
IZUMI, WAIT! IT'S NOT SAFE TO GO ALONE! TAKE ME...
IZUMI-SAAN!
LEAVE ME ALONE!!
NEVER! YOU STILL HAVE A DEBT TO PAY!!
NOOOOO!!!
SUCH SKILL... WELL, HE IS MY BOY AFTER ALL.

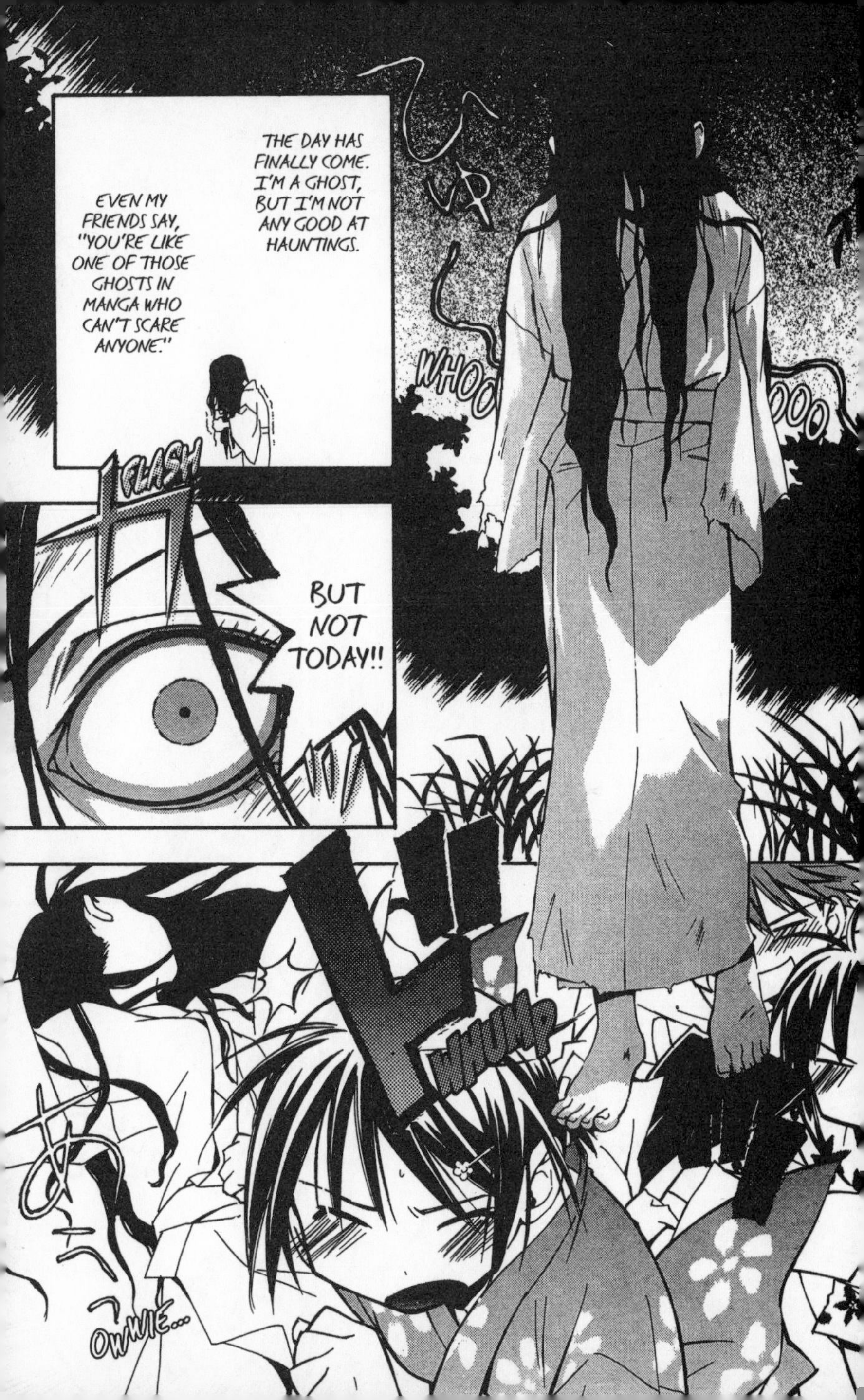
WHOOOOOOO
THE DAY HAS FINALLY COME. I'M A GHOST, BUT I'M NOT ANY GOOD AT HAUNTINGS.
EVEN MY FRIENDS SAY, "YOU'RE LIKE ONE OF THOSE GHOSTS IN MANGA WHO CAN'T SCARE ANYONE."
FLASH
BUT NOT TODAY!!
WHUMP
OWWIE...

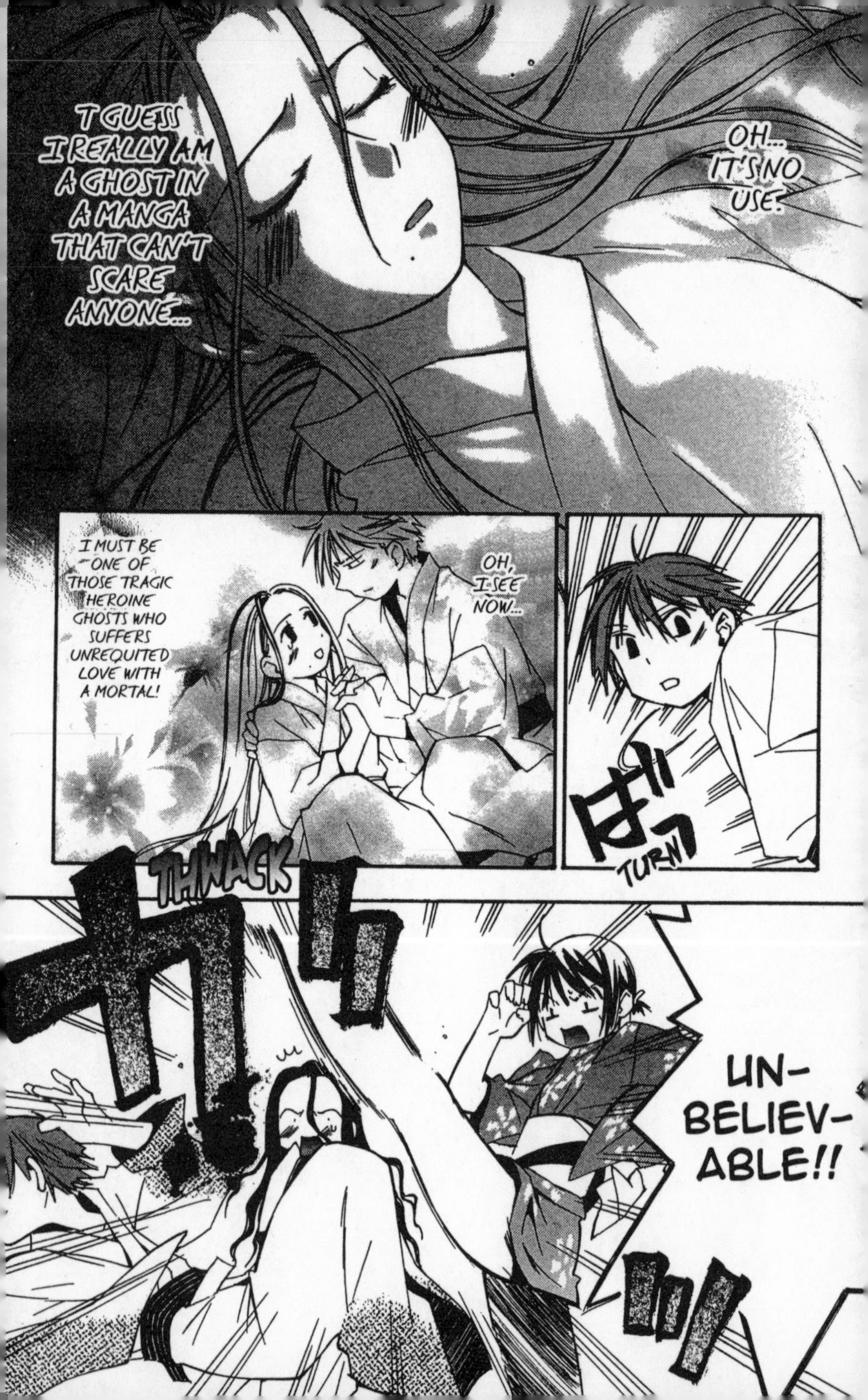
OH... IT'S NO USE.
I GUESS I REALLY AM A GHOST IN A MANGA THAT CAN'T SCARE ANYONE...
ぱっ
TURN
OH, I SEE NOW...
I MUST BE ONE OF THOSE TRAGIC HEROINE GHOSTS WHO SUFFERS UNREQUITED LOVE WITH A MORTAL!
ガッ
THWACK
UN-BELIEV-ABLE!!

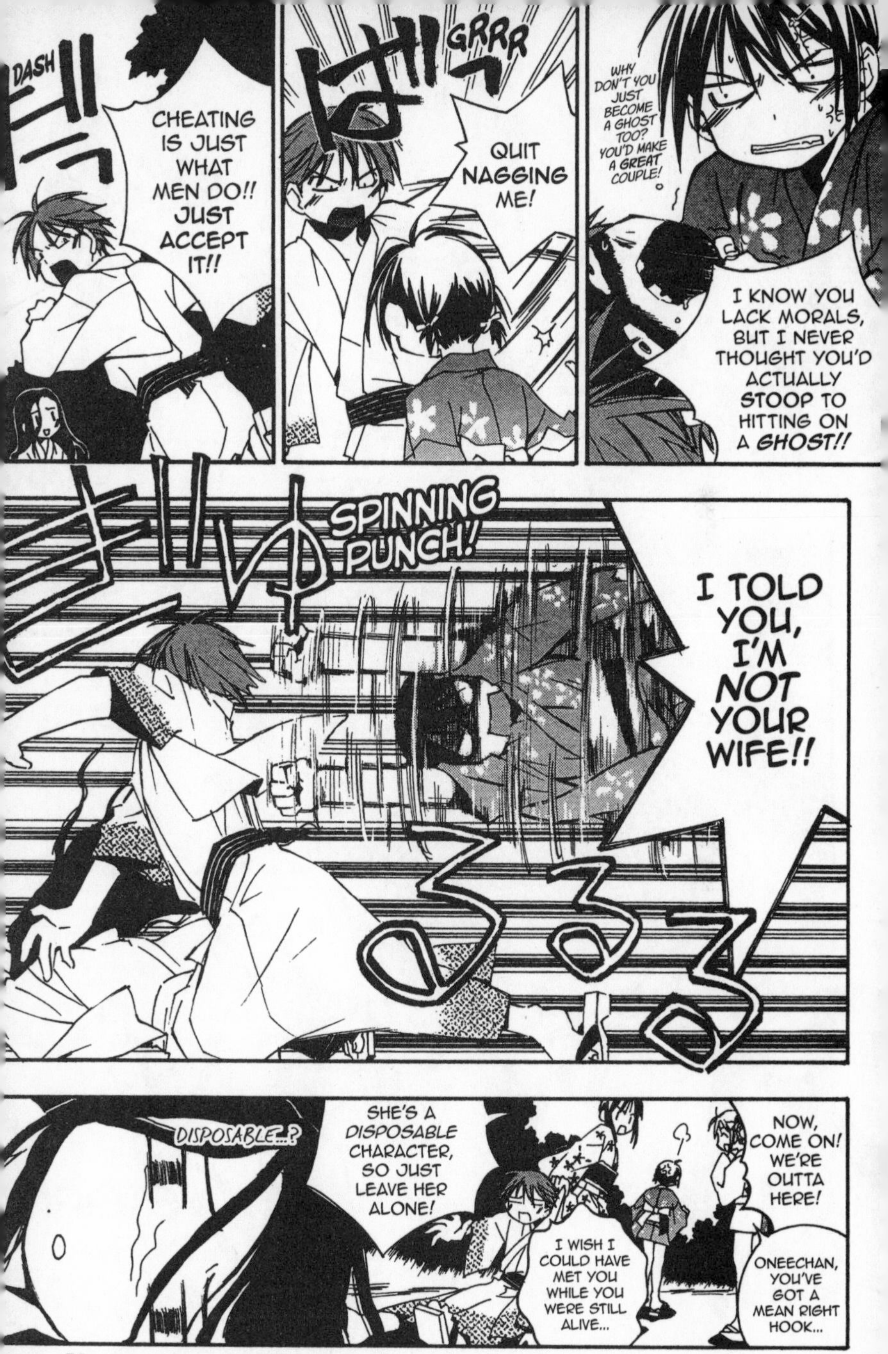
WHY DON'T YOU JUST BECOME A GHOST TOO? YOU'D MAKE A GREAT COUPLE!
I KNOW YOU LACK MORALS, BUT I NEVER THOUGHT YOU'D ACTUALLY STOOP TO HITTING ON A GHOST!!
GRRR
QUIT NAGGING ME!
DASH
CHEATING IS JUST WHAT MEN DO!! JUST ACCEPT IT!!
I TOLD YOU, I'M NOT YOUR WIFE!!
SPINNING PUNCH!
NOW, COME ON! WE'RE OUTTA HERE!
ONEECHAN, YOU'VE GOT A MEAN RIGHT HOOK...
SHE'S A DISPOSABLE CHARACTER, SO JUST LEAVE HER ALONE!
I WISH I COULD HAVE MET YOU WHILE YOU WERE STILL ALIVE...
DISPOSABLE...?

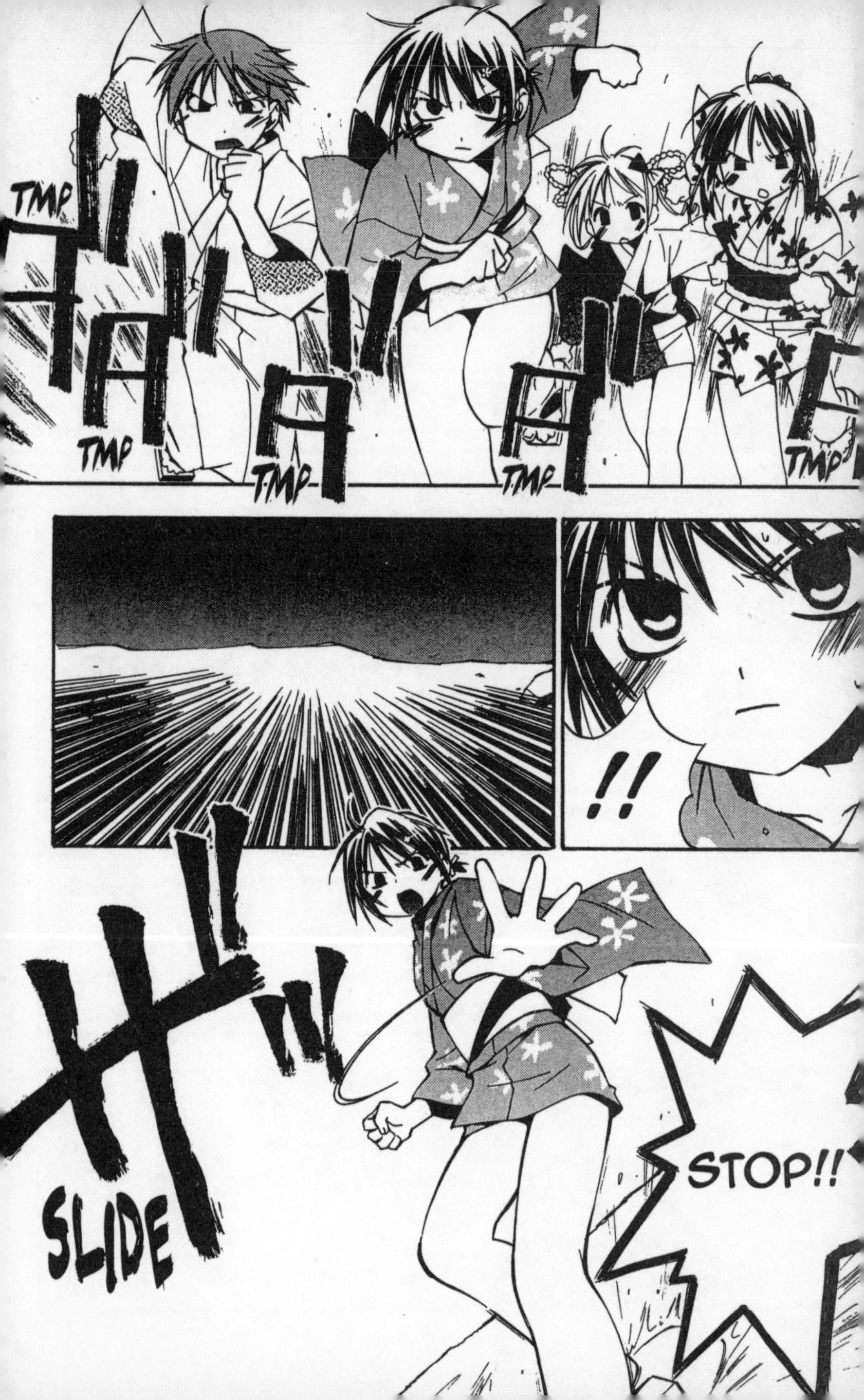
TMP
TMP
TMP
TMP
TMP
!!
STOP!!
SLIDE

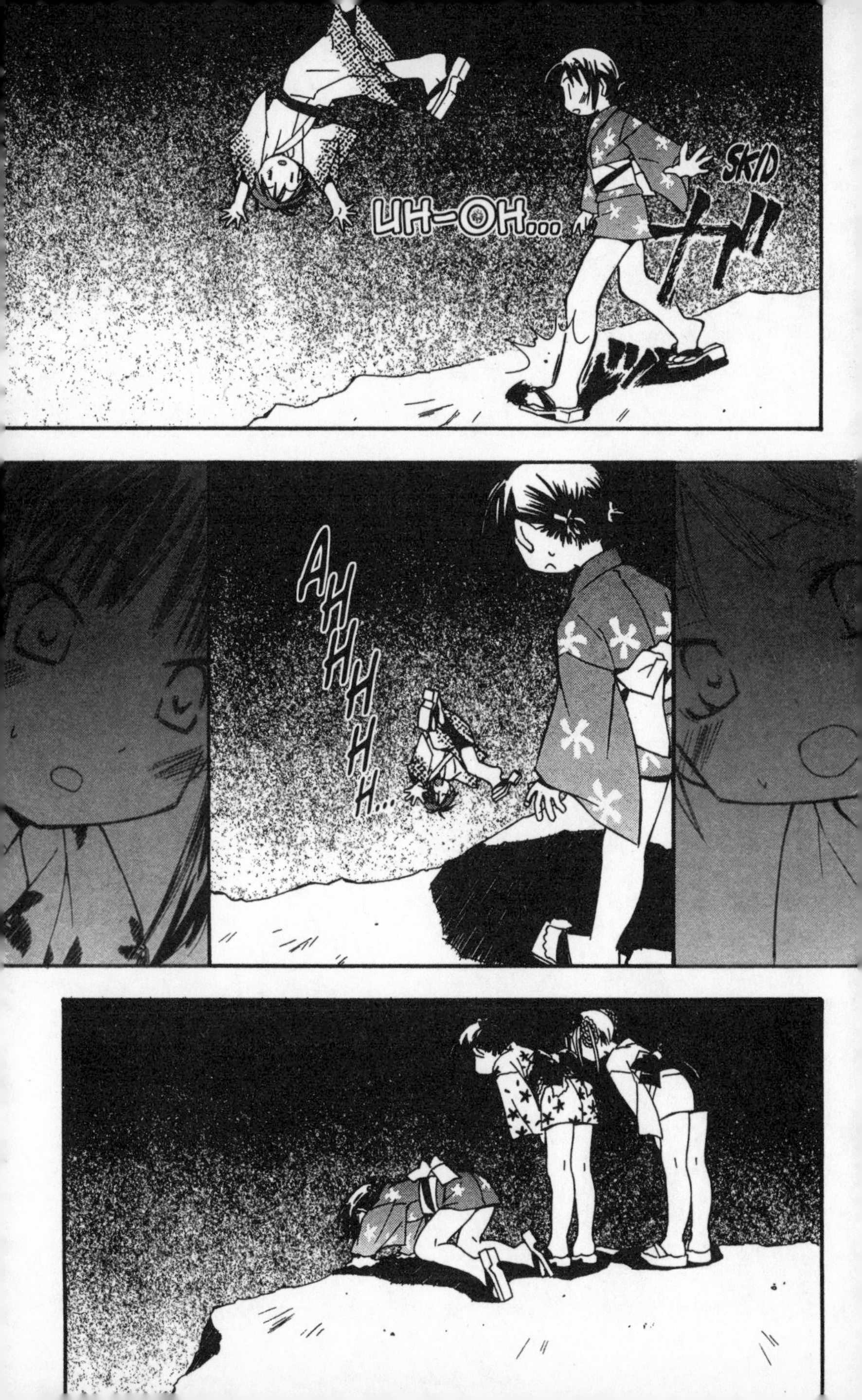
SKID
UH-OH...
AHHHHHH...

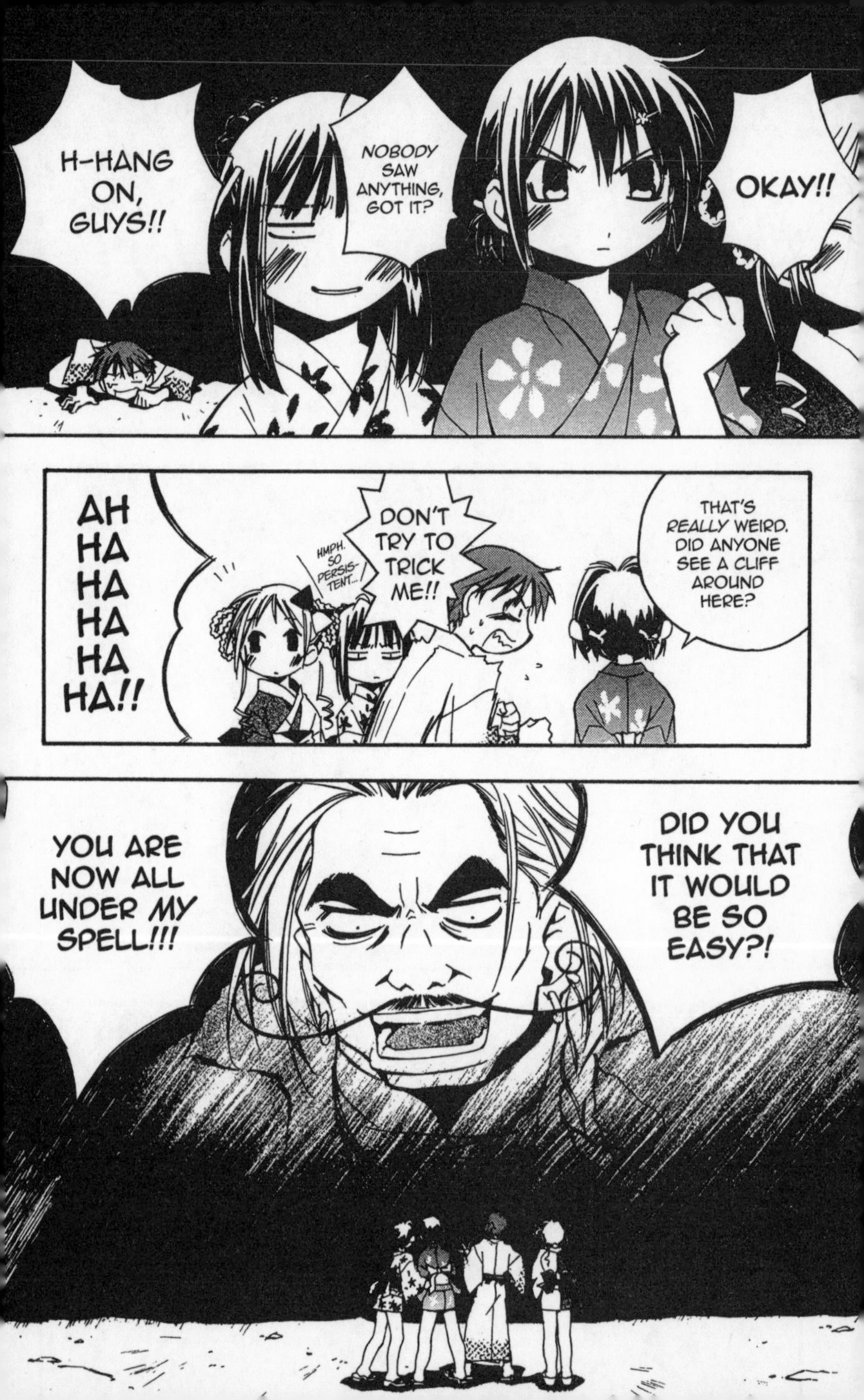
OKAY!!
NOBODY SAW ANYTHING, GOT IT?
H-HANG ON, GUYS!!
THAT'S *REALLY* WEIRD. DID ANYONE SEE A CLIFF AROUND HERE?
DON'T TRY TO TRICK ME!!
HMPH. SO PERSIS-TENT...
AH HA HA HA HA HA HA!!
DID YOU THINK THAT IT WOULD BE SO EASY?!
YOU ARE NOW ALL UNDER MY SPELL!!!

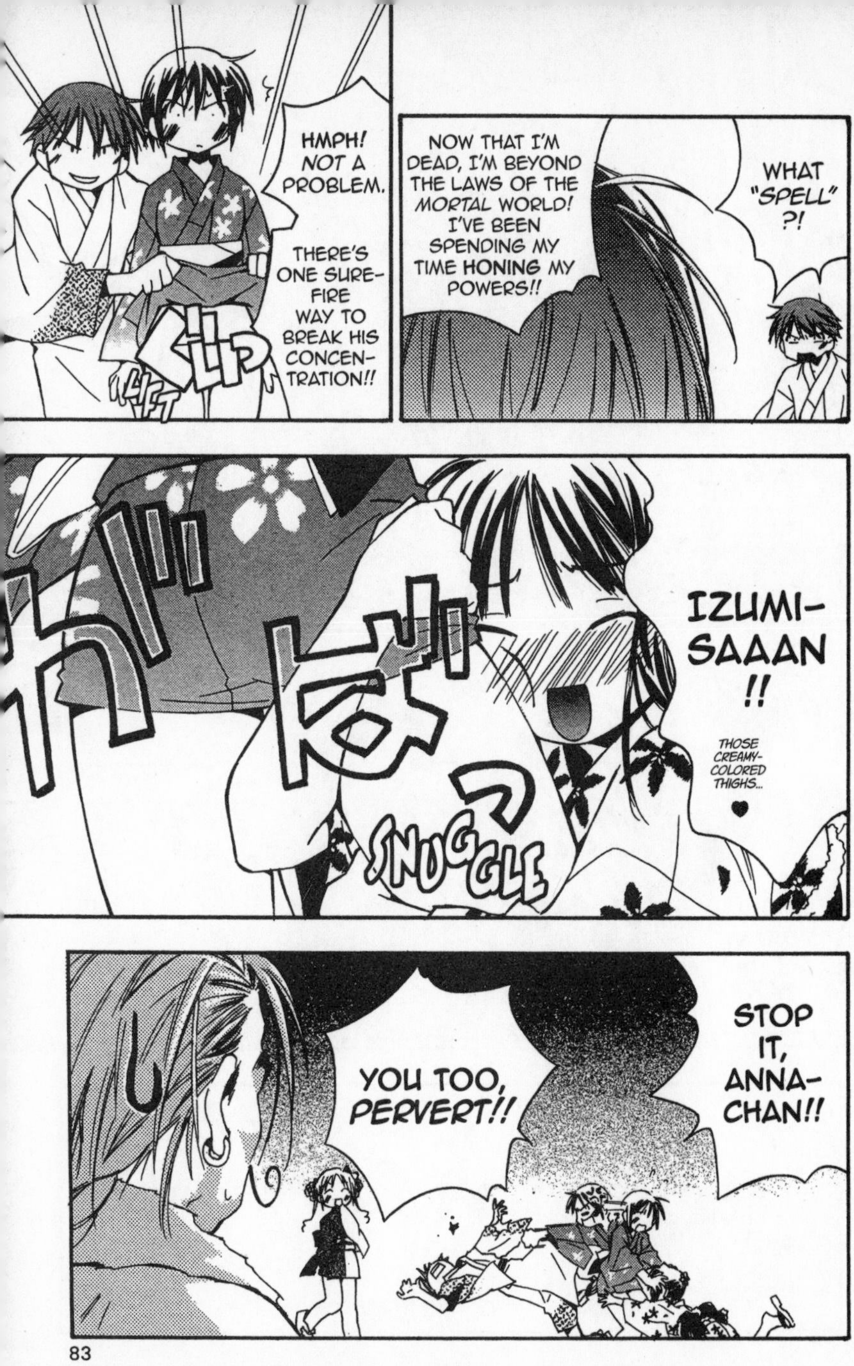
WHAT "SPELL" ?!
NOW THAT I'M DEAD, I'M BEYOND THE LAWS OF THE MORTAL WORLD! I'VE BEEN SPENDING MY TIME HONING MY POWERS!!
HMPH! NOT A PROBLEM.
THERE'S ONE SURE-FIRE WAY TO BREAK HIS CONCEN-TRATION!!
FLIP
LIFT
IZUMI-SAAAN !!
THOSE CREAMY-COLORED THIGHS... ♥
SNUGGLE
STOP IT, ANNA-CHAN!!
YOU TOO, PERVERT!!

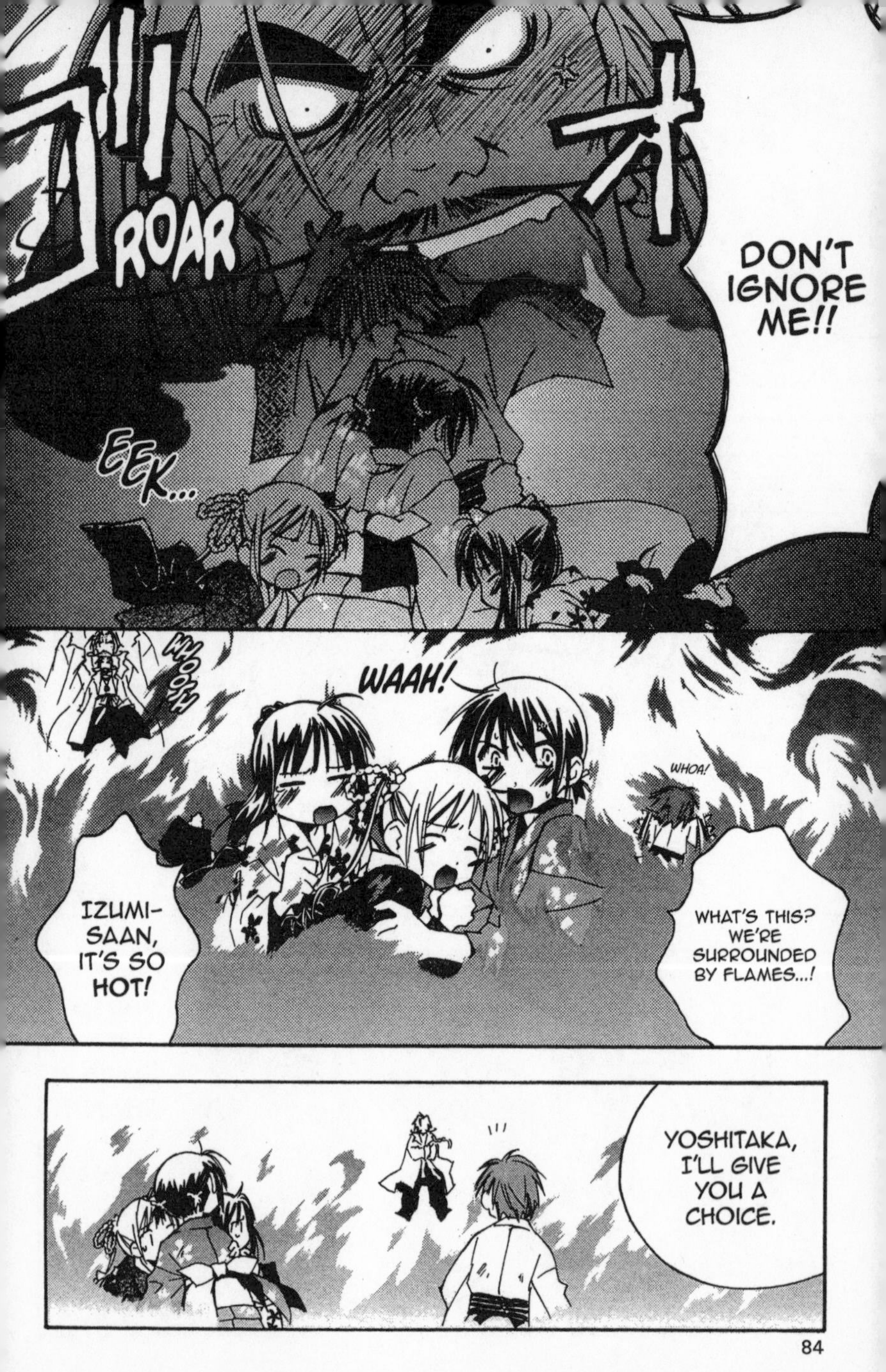
DON'T IGNORE ME!!
ROAR
EEK...
WHAT'S THIS? WE'RE SURROUNDED BY FLAMES...!
WHOA!
WAAH!
WHOOSH
IZUMI-SAAN, IT'S SO HOT!
YOSHITAKA, I'LL GIVE YOU A CHOICE.

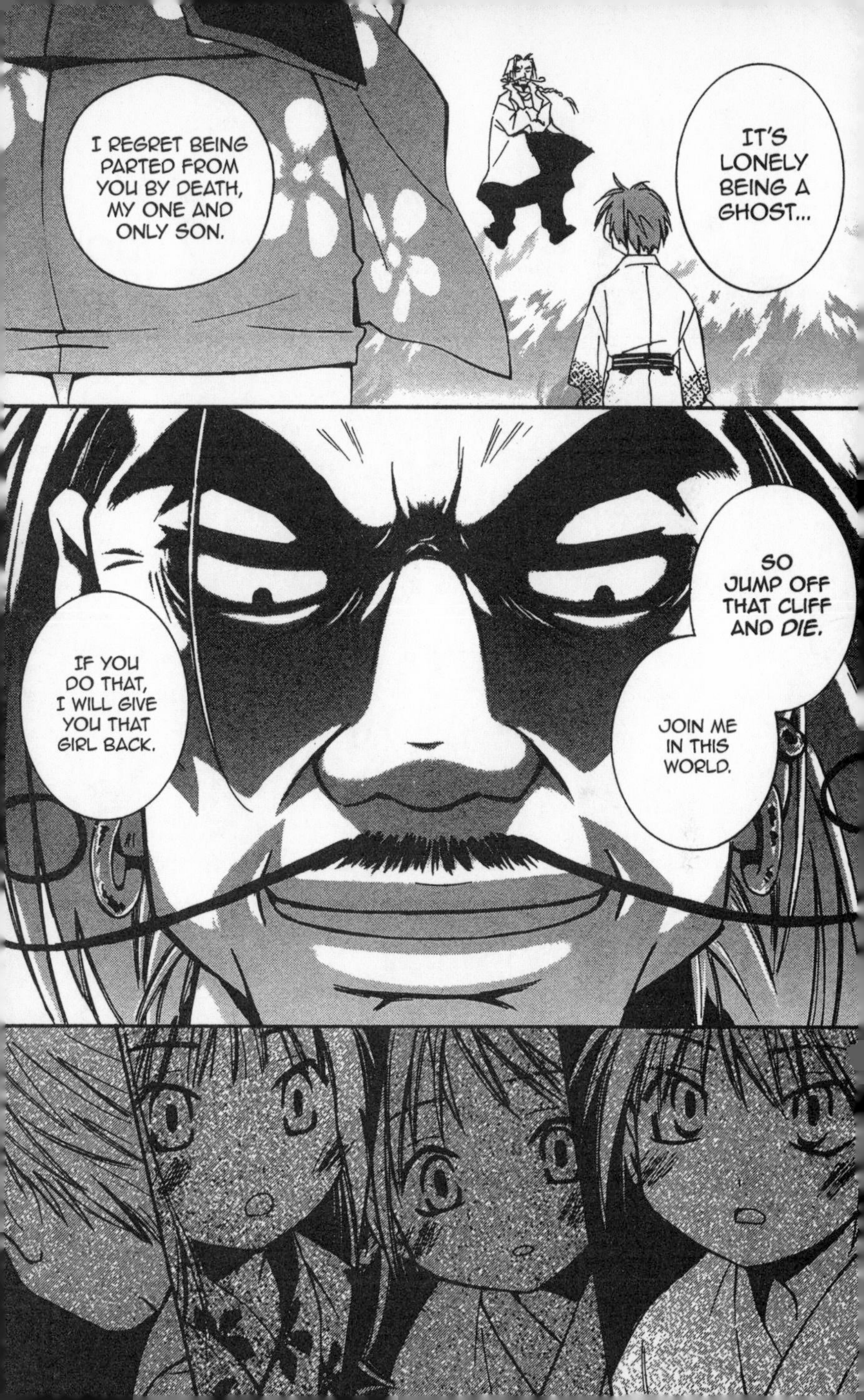
IT'S LONELY BEING A GHOST...
I REGRET BEING PARTED FROM YOU BY DEATH, MY ONE AND ONLY SON.
SO JUMP OFF THAT CLIFF AND *DIE.*
JOIN ME IN THIS WORLD.
IF YOU DO THAT, I WILL GIVE YOU THAT GIRL BACK.

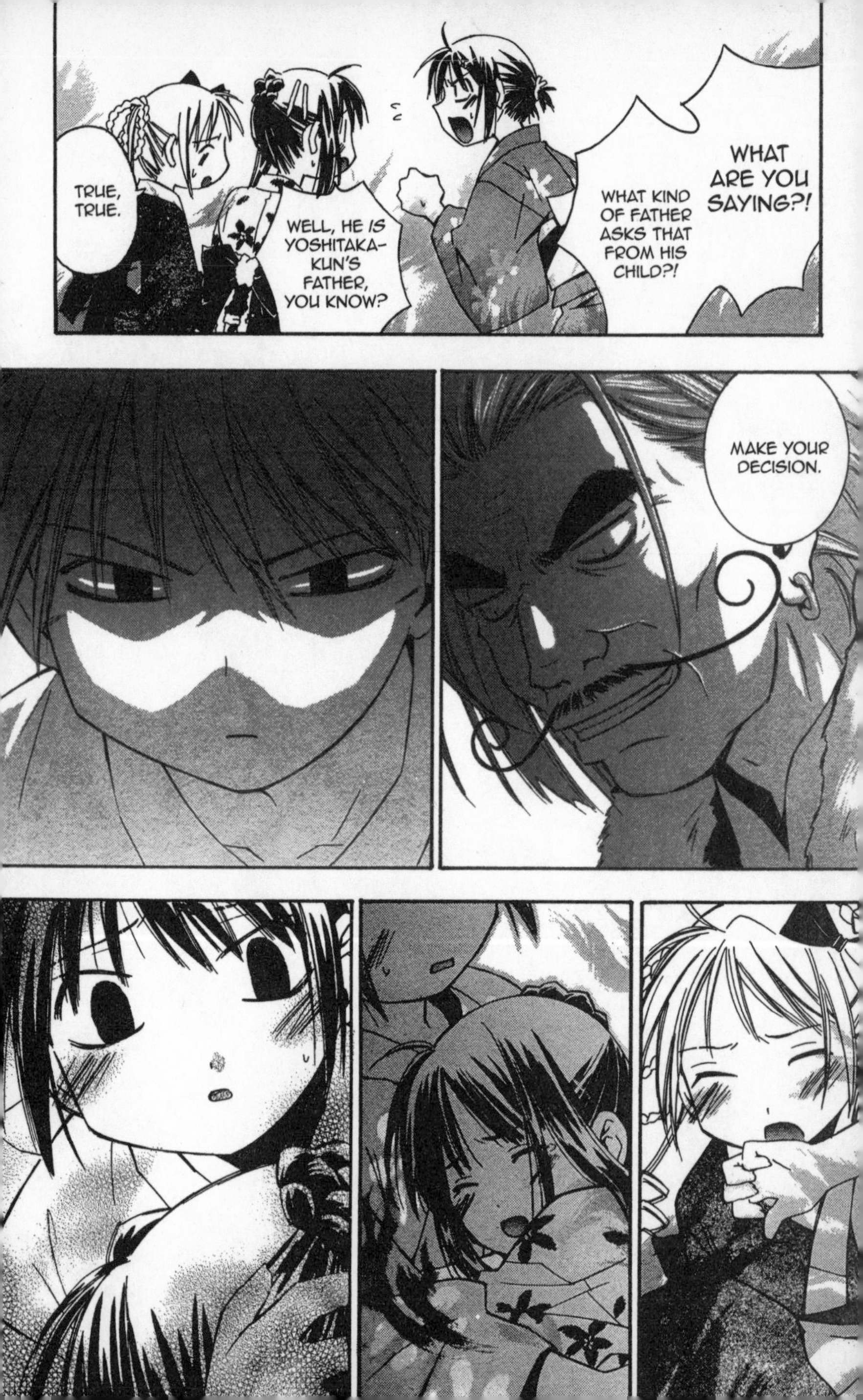
WHAT ARE YOU SAYING?!
WHAT KIND OF FATHER ASKS THAT FROM HIS CHILD?!
WELL, HE *IS* YOSHITAKA-KUN'S FATHER, YOU KNOW?
TRUE, TRUE.
MAKE YOUR DECISION.

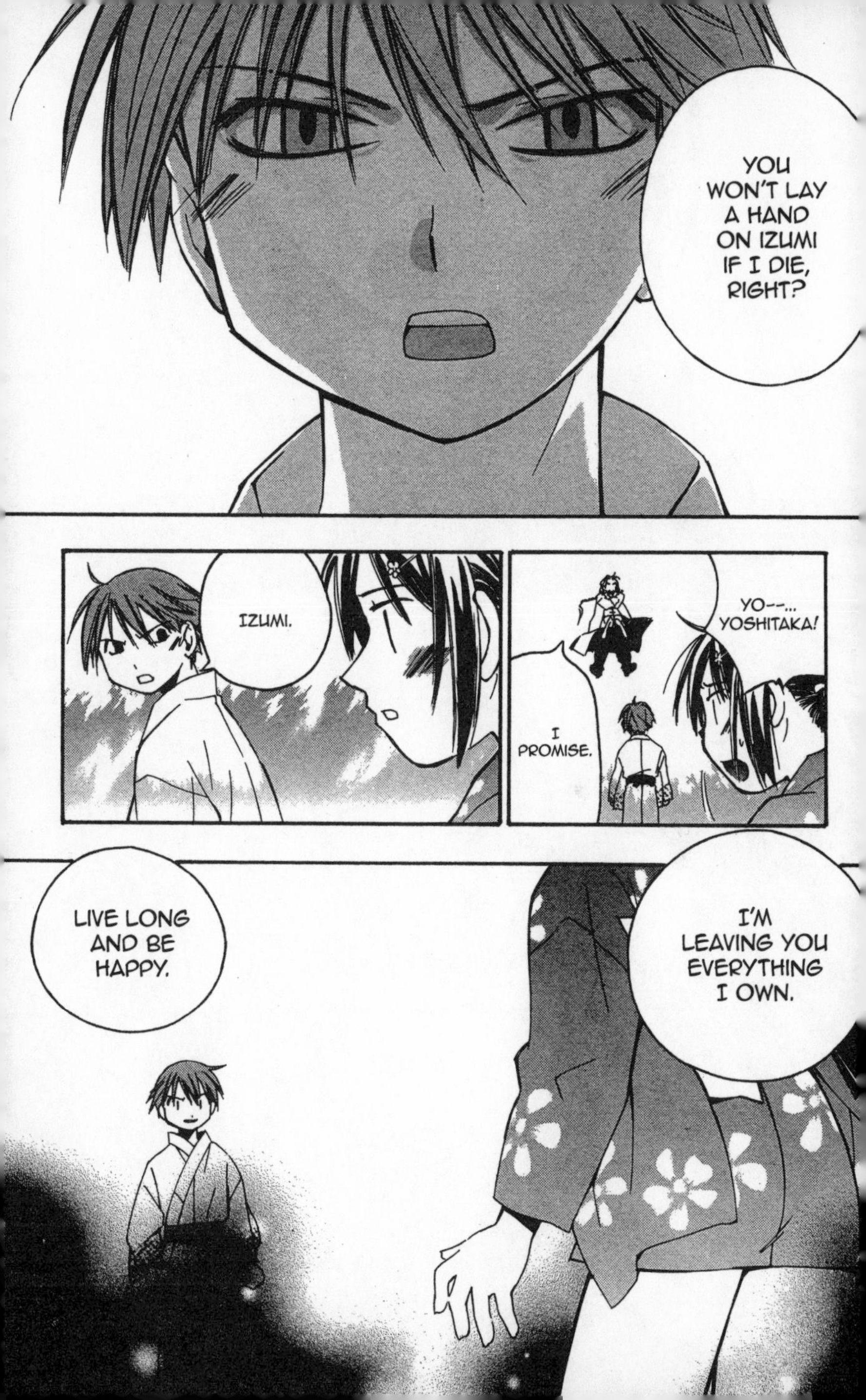
YOU WON'T LAY A HAND ON IZUMI IF I DIE, RIGHT?
YO--... YOSHITAKA!
I PROMISE.
IZUMI.
I'M LEAVING YOU EVERYTHING I OWN.
LIVE LONG AND BE HAPPY.

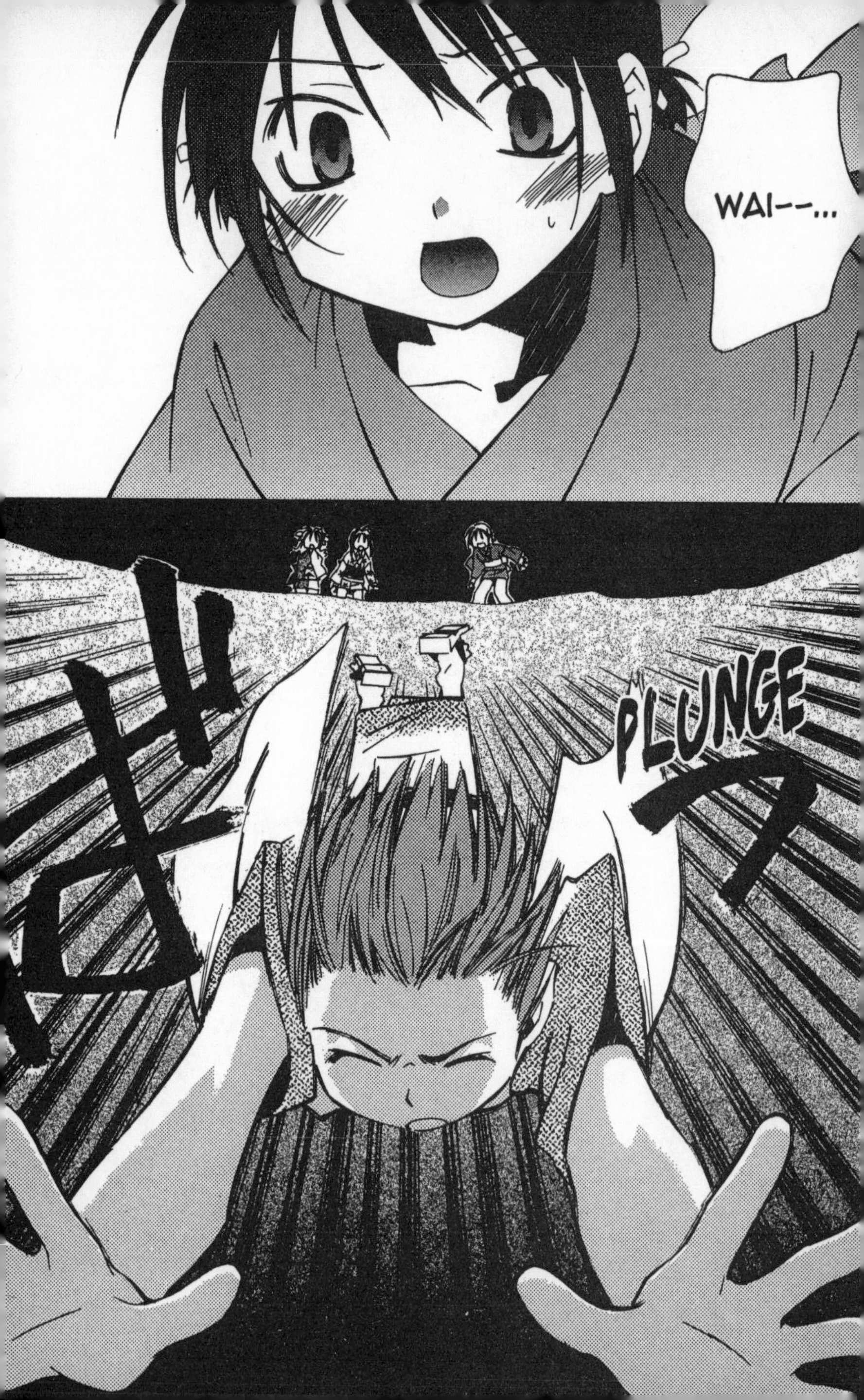
WAI--...
PLUNGE

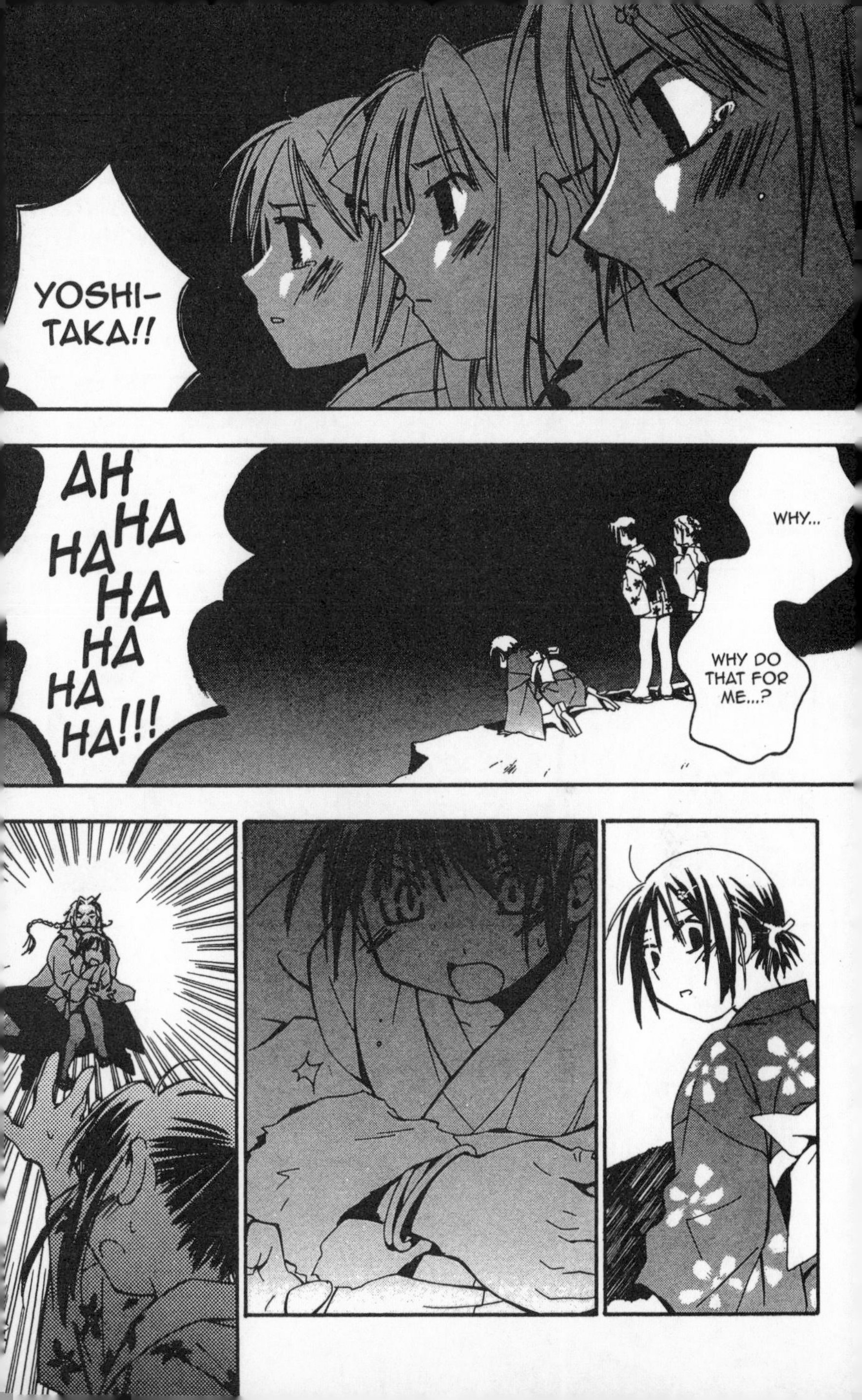
YOSHI-
TAKA!!
WHY...
WHY DO THAT FOR ME...?
AH HA HA HA HA HA HA HA!!!

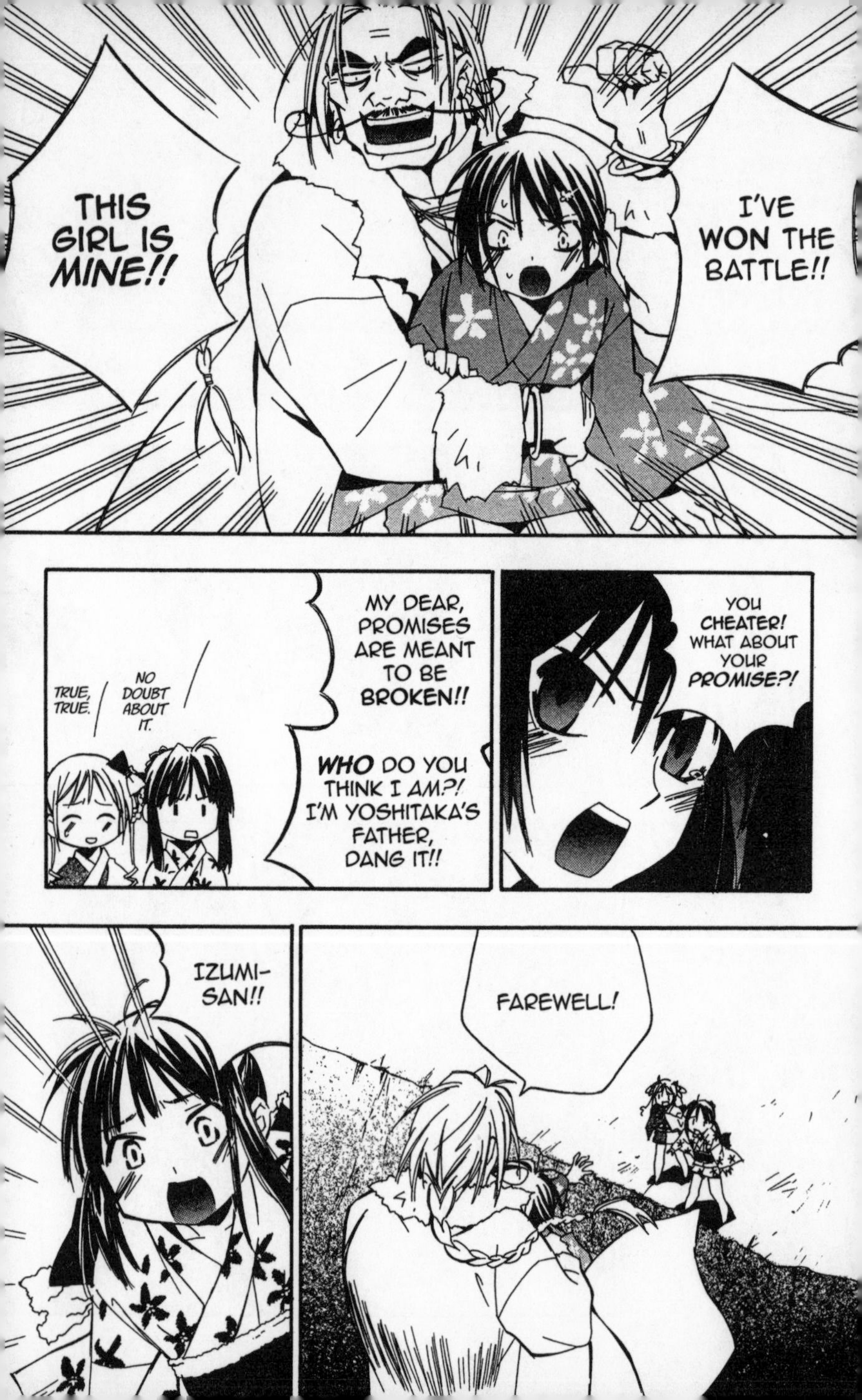
I'VE WON THE BATTLE!!
THIS GIRL IS MINE!!
YOU CHEATER! WHAT ABOUT YOUR PROMISE?!
MY DEAR, PROMISES ARE MEANT TO BE BROKEN!!
WHO DO YOU THINK I AM?! I'M YOSHITAKA'S FATHER, DANG IT!!
NO DOUBT ABOUT IT.
TRUE, TRUE.
FAREWELL!
IZUMI-SAN!!

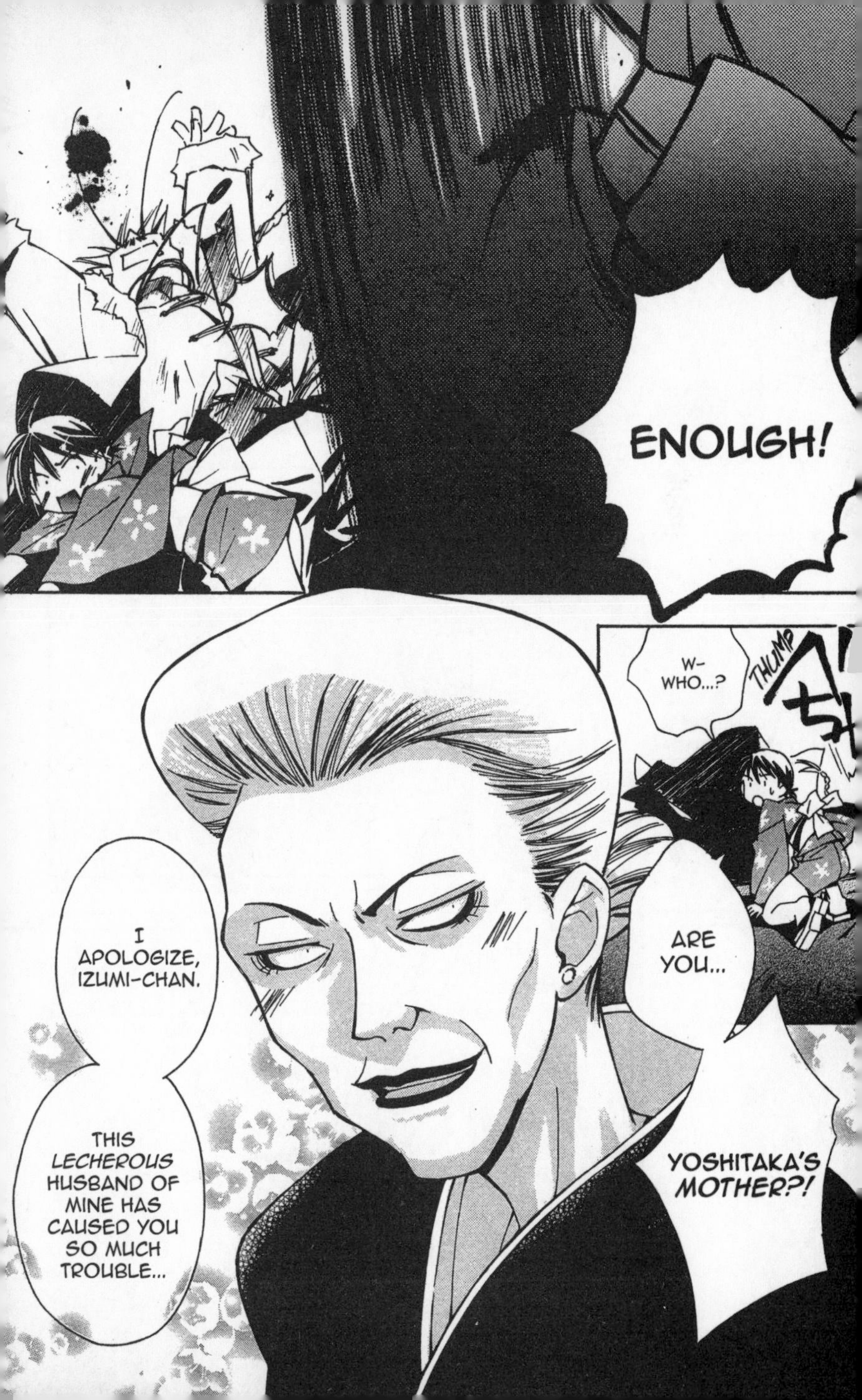
ENOUGH!
W-WHO...?
THUMP
ARE YOU...
YOSHITAKA'S MOTHER?!
I APOLOGIZE, IZUMI-CHAN.
THIS LECHEROUS HUSBAND OF MINE HAS CAUSED YOU SO MUCH TROUBLE...

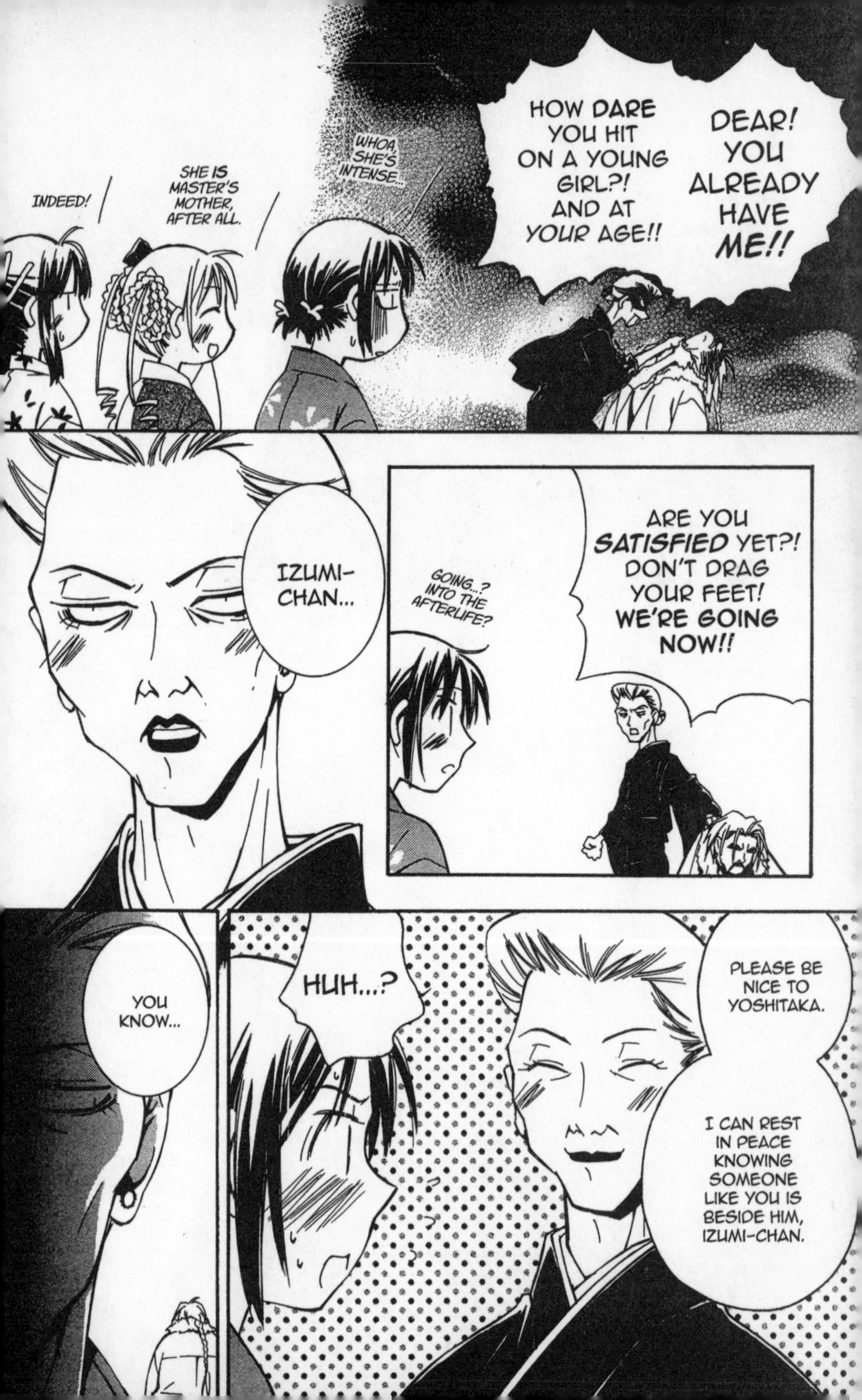
HOW DARE YOU HIT ON A YOUNG GIRL?! AND AT YOUR AGE!!
DEAR! YOU ALREADY HAVE ME!!
WHOA, SHE'S INTENSE...
SHE IS MASTER'S MOTHER, AFTER ALL.
INDEED!
ARE YOU SATISFIED YET?! DON'T DRAG YOUR FEET! WE'RE GOING NOW!!
GOING...? INTO THE AFTERLIFE?
IZUMI-CHAN...
PLEASE BE NICE TO YOSHITAKA.
I CAN REST IN PEACE KNOWING SOMEONE LIKE YOU IS BESIDE HIM, IZUMI-CHAN.
HUH...?
YOU KNOW...

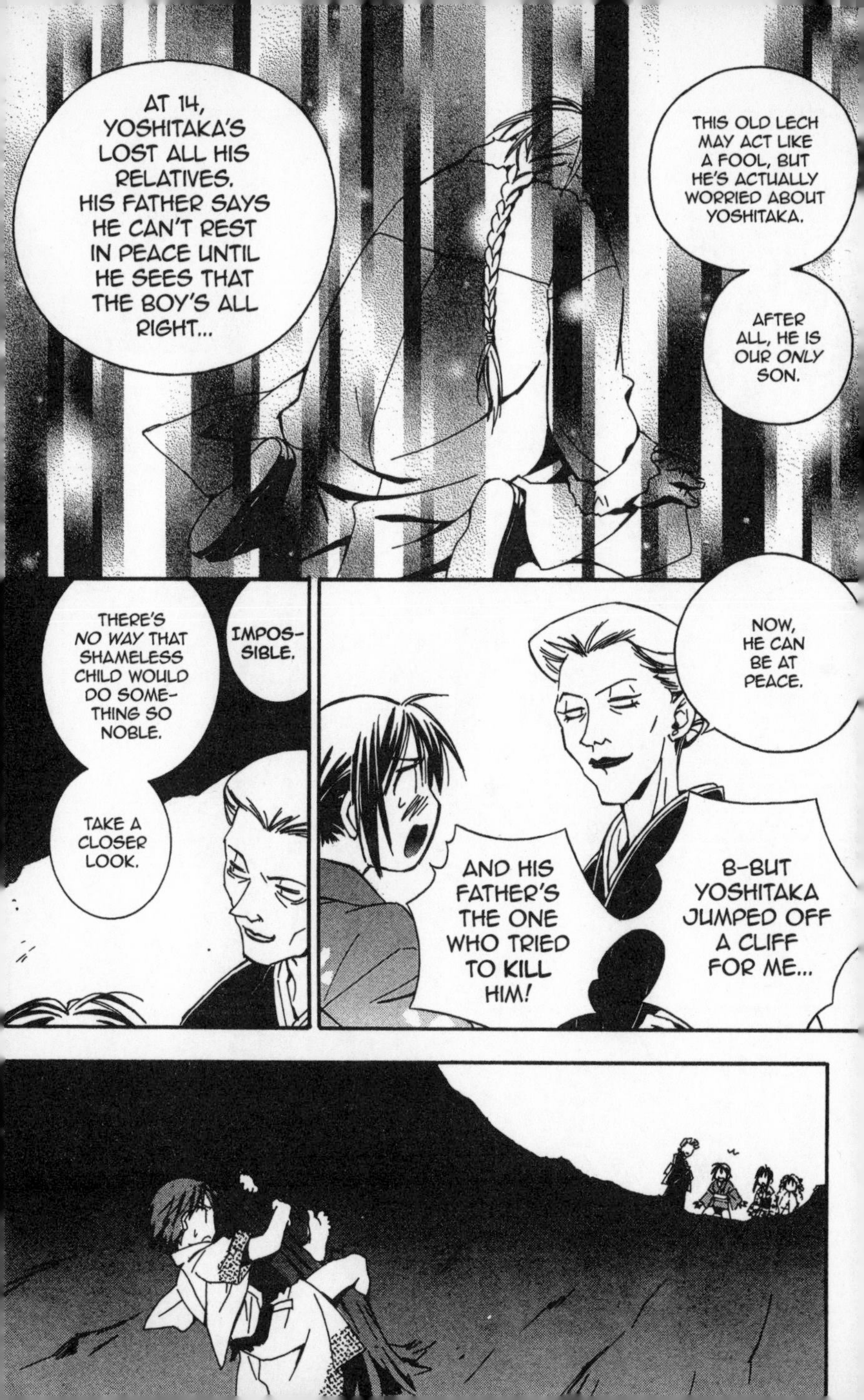
THIS OLD LECH MAY ACT LIKE A FOOL, BUT HE'S ACTUALLY WORRIED ABOUT YOSHITAKA.
AFTER ALL, HE IS OUR *ONLY* SON.
AT 14, YOSHITAKA'S LOST ALL HIS RELATIVES. HIS FATHER SAYS HE CAN'T REST IN PEACE UNTIL HE SEES THAT THE BOY'S ALL RIGHT...
NOW, HE CAN BE AT PEACE.
B-BUT YOSHITAKA JUMPED OFF A CLIFF FOR ME...
AND HIS FATHER'S THE ONE WHO TRIED TO **KILL** HIM!
IMPOSSIBLE.
THERE'S *NO WAY* THAT SHAMELESS CHILD WOULD DO SOMETHING SO NOBLE.
TAKE A CLOSER LOOK.

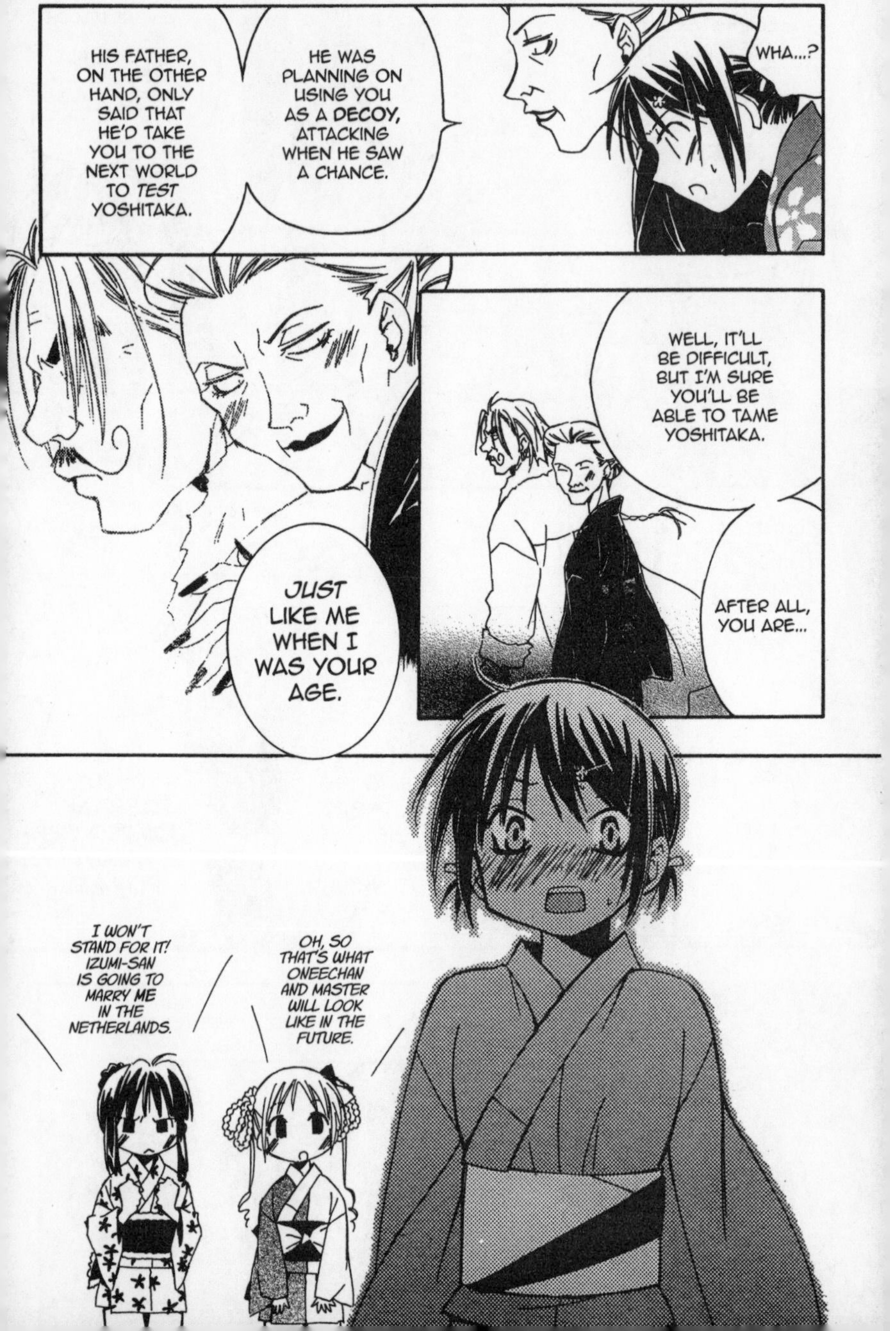
HIS FATHER, ON THE OTHER HAND, ONLY SAID THAT HE'D TAKE YOU TO THE NEXT WORLD TO *TEST* YOSHITAKA.
HE WAS PLANNING ON USING YOU AS A **DECOY**, ATTACKING WHEN HE SAW A CHANCE.
WHA...?
JUST LIKE ME WHEN I WAS YOUR AGE.
WELL, IT'LL BE DIFFICULT, BUT I'M SURE YOU'LL BE ABLE TO TAME YOSHITAKA.
AFTER ALL, YOU ARE...
I WON'T STAND FOR IT! IZUMI-SAN IS GOING TO MARRY **ME** IN THE NETHERLANDS.
OH, SO THAT'S WHAT ONEECHAN AND MASTER WILL LOOK LIKE IN THE FUTURE.

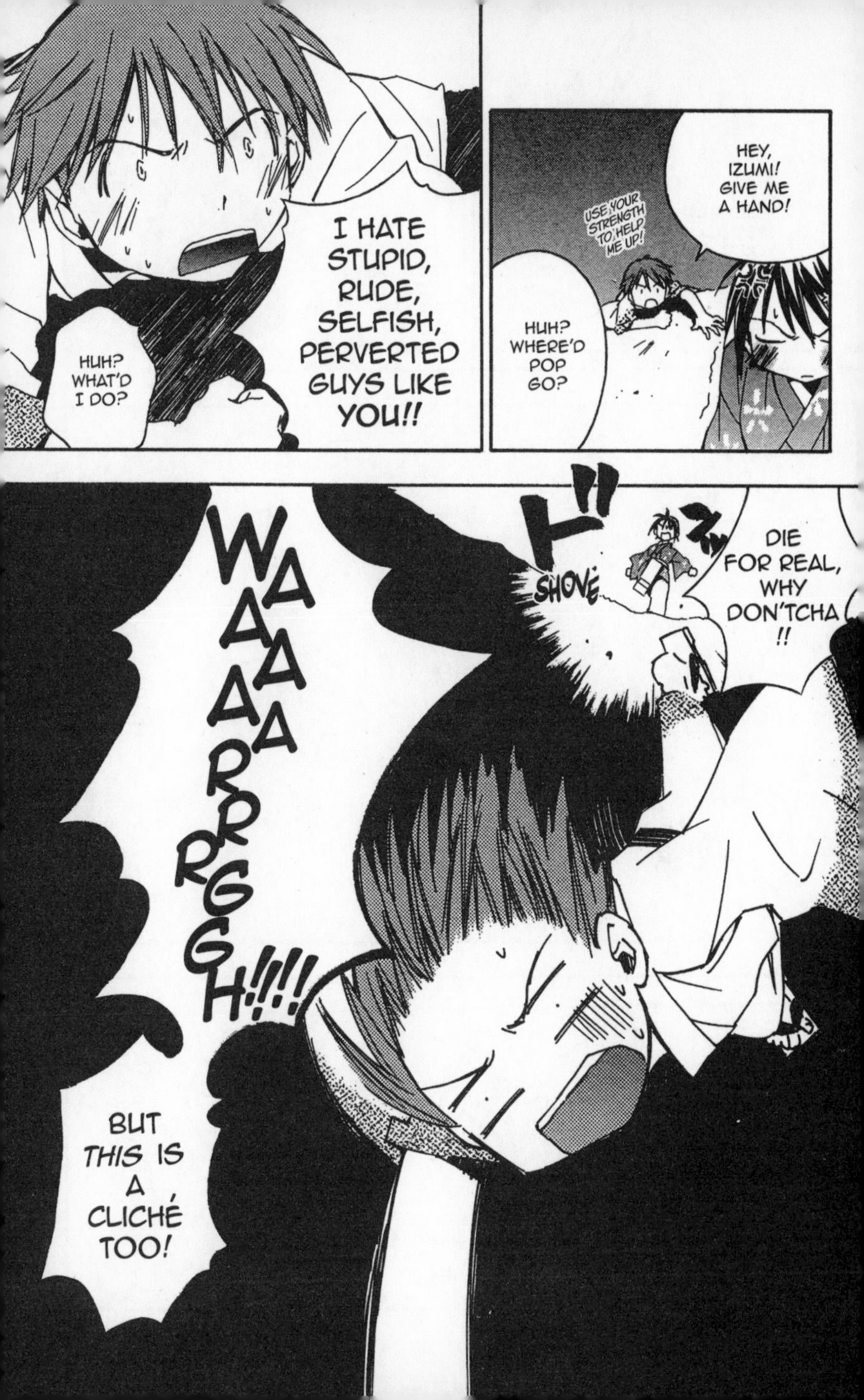
HEY, IZUMI! GIVE ME A HAND!
USE YOUR STRENGTH TO HELP ME UP!
HUH? WHERE'D POP GO?
I HATE STUPID, RUDE, SELFISH, PERVERTED GUYS LIKE YOU!!
HUH? WHAT'D I DO?
DIE FOR REAL, WHY DON'TCHA!!
SHOVE
WAAAAARRRGGH!!!!
BUT THIS IS A CLICHÉ TOO!

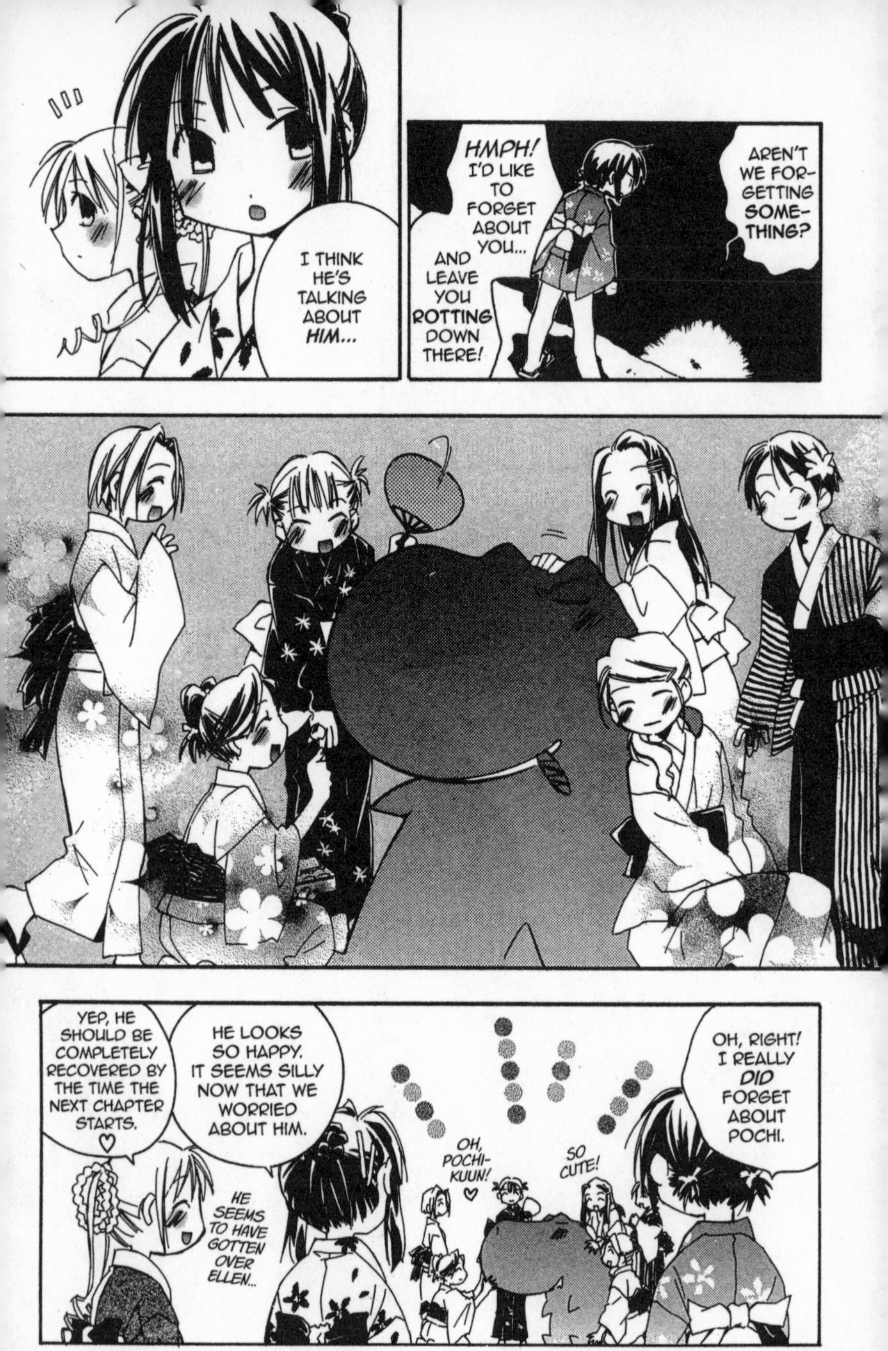
AREN'T WE FORGETTING SOMETHING?
HMPH! I'D LIKE TO FORGET ABOUT YOU...
AND LEAVE YOU ROTTING DOWN THERE!
I THINK HE'S TALKING ABOUT HIM...
OH, RIGHT! I REALLY DID FORGET ABOUT POCHI.
SO CUTE!
OH, POCHI-KUUN! ♡
HE LOOKS SO HAPPY. IT SEEMS SILLY NOW THAT WE WORRIED ABOUT HIM.
YEP, HE SHOULD BE COMPLETELY RECOVERED BY THE TIME THE NEXT CHAPTER STARTS. ♡
HE SEEMS TO HAVE GOTTEN OVER ELLEN...

SIDE STORY ● WE'LL HAVE POCHI EATING OUT OF OUR HANDS WITH THIS! ❤

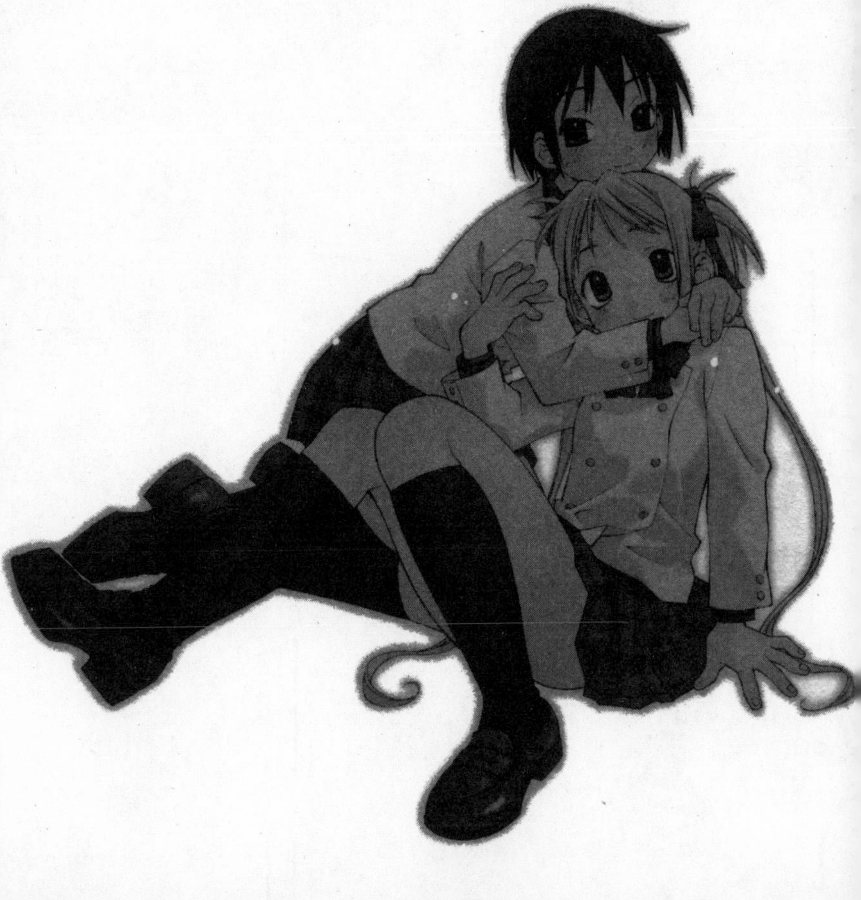

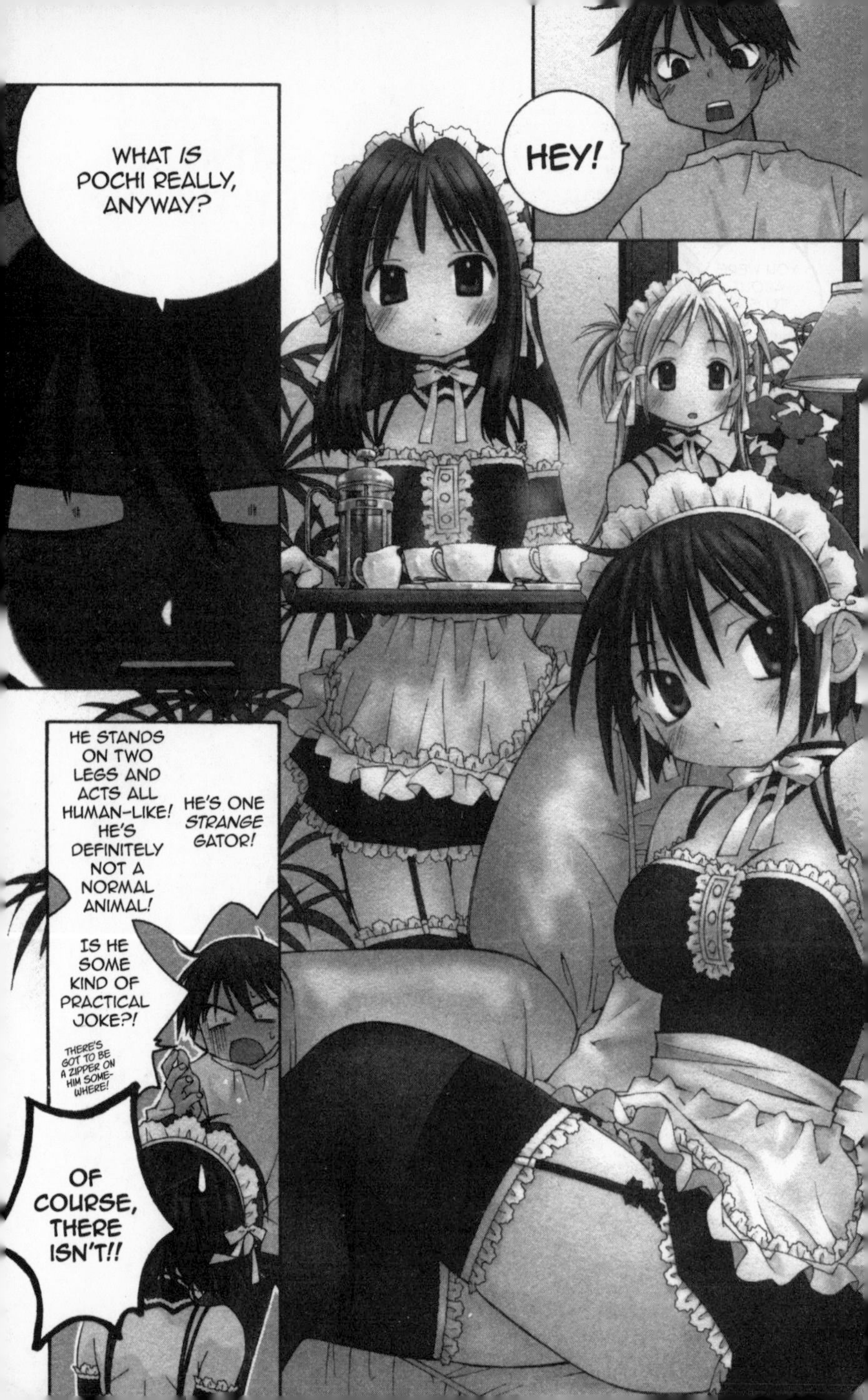
HEY!
WHAT *IS* POCHI REALLY, ANYWAY?
HE STANDS ON TWO LEGS AND ACTS ALL HUMAN-LIKE! HE'S DEFINITELY NOT A NORMAL ANIMAL!
HE'S ONE *STRANGE* GATOR!
IS HE SOME KIND OF PRACTICAL JOKE?!
THERE'S GOT TO BE A ZIPPER ON HIM SOME-WHERE!
OF COURSE, THERE ISN'T!!

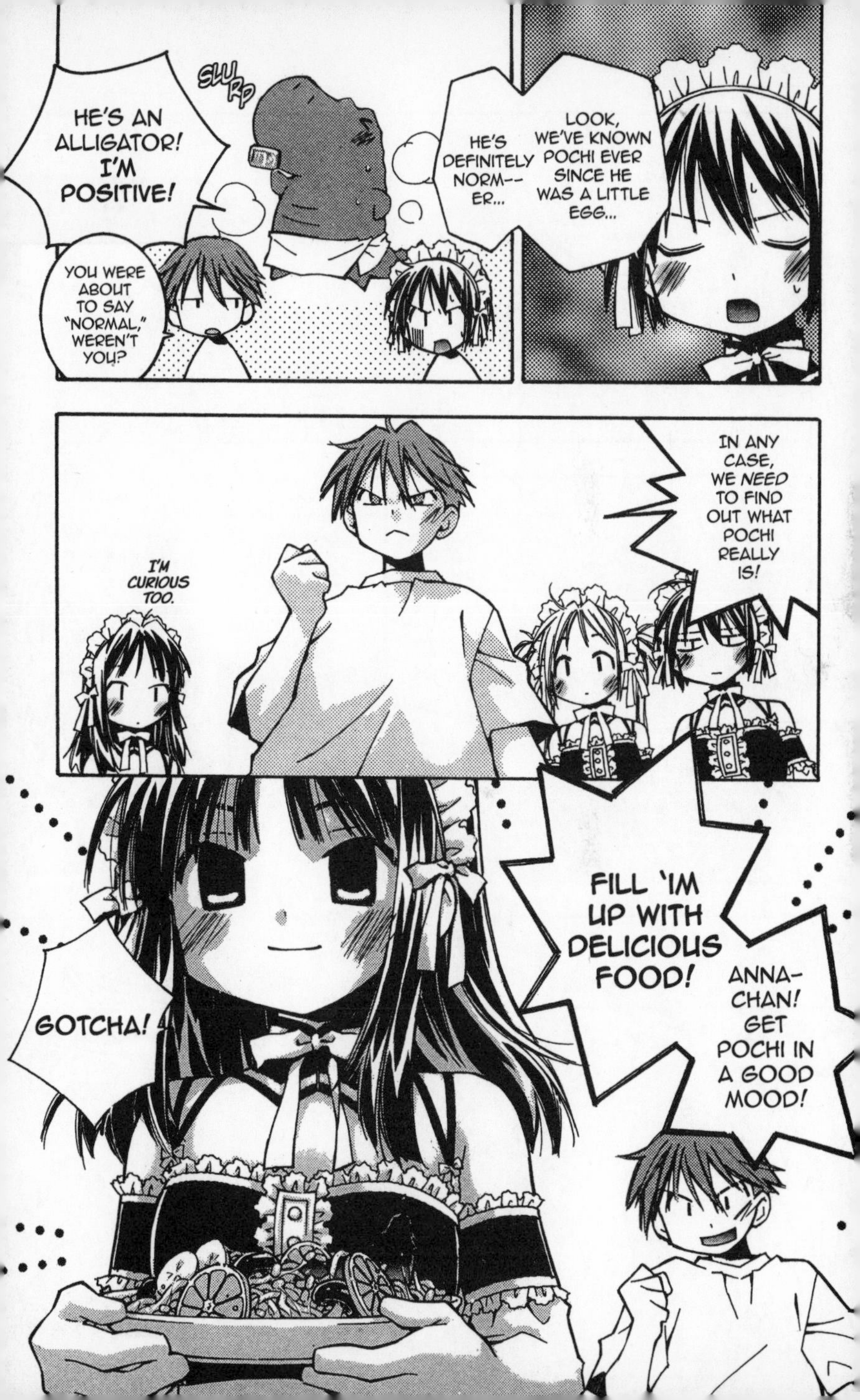
LOOK, WE'VE KNOWN POCHI EVER SINCE HE WAS A LITTLE EGG...
HE'S DEFINITELY NORM-- ER...
SLURP
HE'S AN ALLIGATOR! I'M POSITIVE!
YOU WERE ABOUT TO SAY "NORMAL," WEREN'T YOU?
IN ANY CASE, WE *NEED* TO FIND OUT WHAT POCHI REALLY IS!
I'M CURIOUS TOO.
ANNA-CHAN! GET POCHI IN A GOOD MOOD!
FILL 'IM UP WITH DELICIOUS FOOD!
GOTCHA!

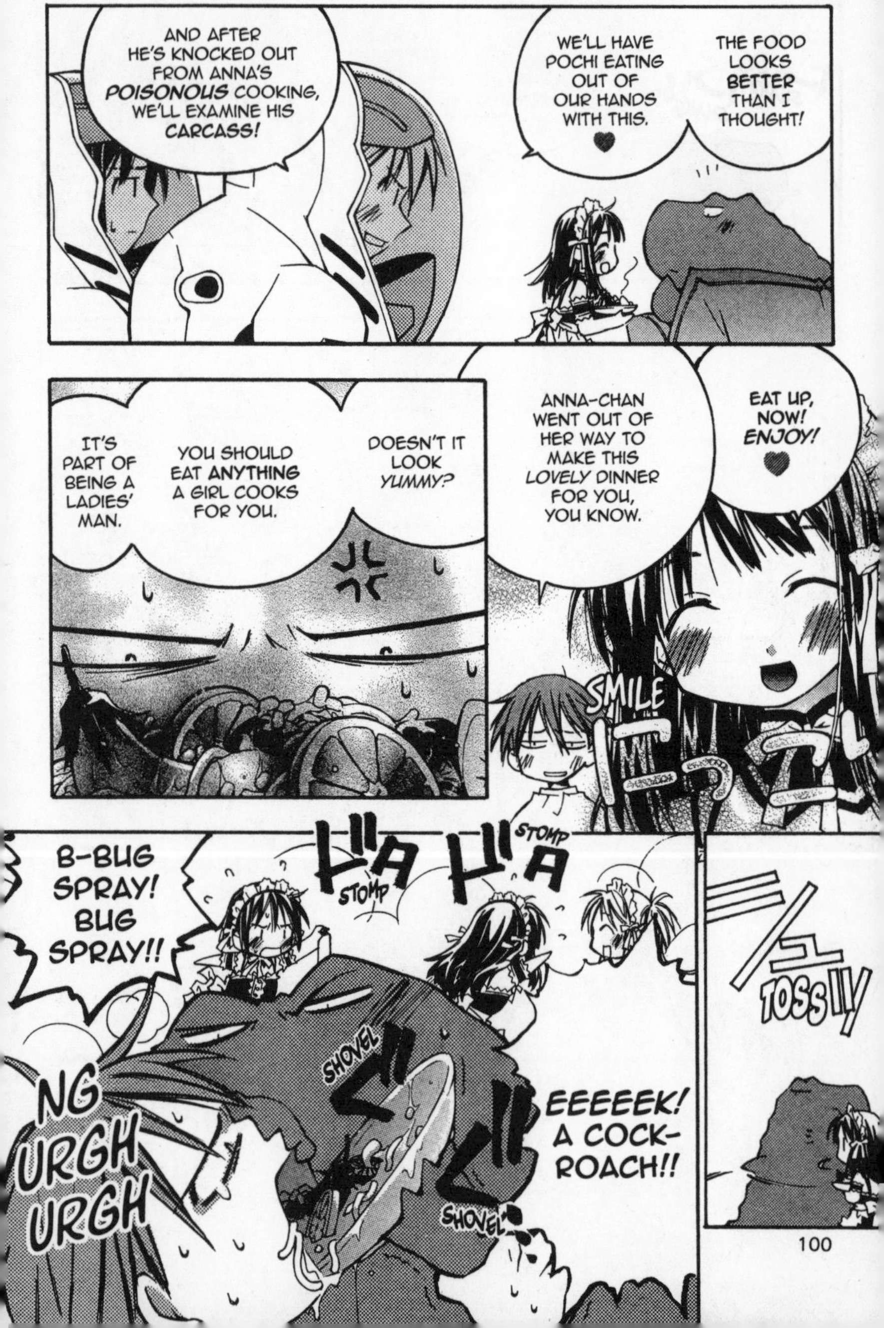
THE FOOD LOOKS BETTER THAN I THOUGHT!
WE'LL HAVE POCHI EATING OUT OF OUR HANDS WITH THIS. ♥
AND AFTER HE'S KNOCKED OUT FROM ANNA'S POISONOUS COOKING, WE'LL EXAMINE HIS CARCASS!
EAT UP, NOW! ENJOY! ♥
ANNA-CHAN WENT OUT OF HER WAY TO MAKE THIS LOVELY DINNER FOR YOU, YOU KNOW.
SMILE
DOESN'T IT LOOK YUMMY?
YOU SHOULD EAT ANYTHING A GIRL COOKS FOR YOU.
IT'S PART OF BEING A LADIES' MAN.
TOSS
STOMP
STOMP
B-BUG SPRAY! BUG SPRAY!!
EEEEEK! A COCK-ROACH!!
SHOVEL
SHOVEL
NG URGH URGH

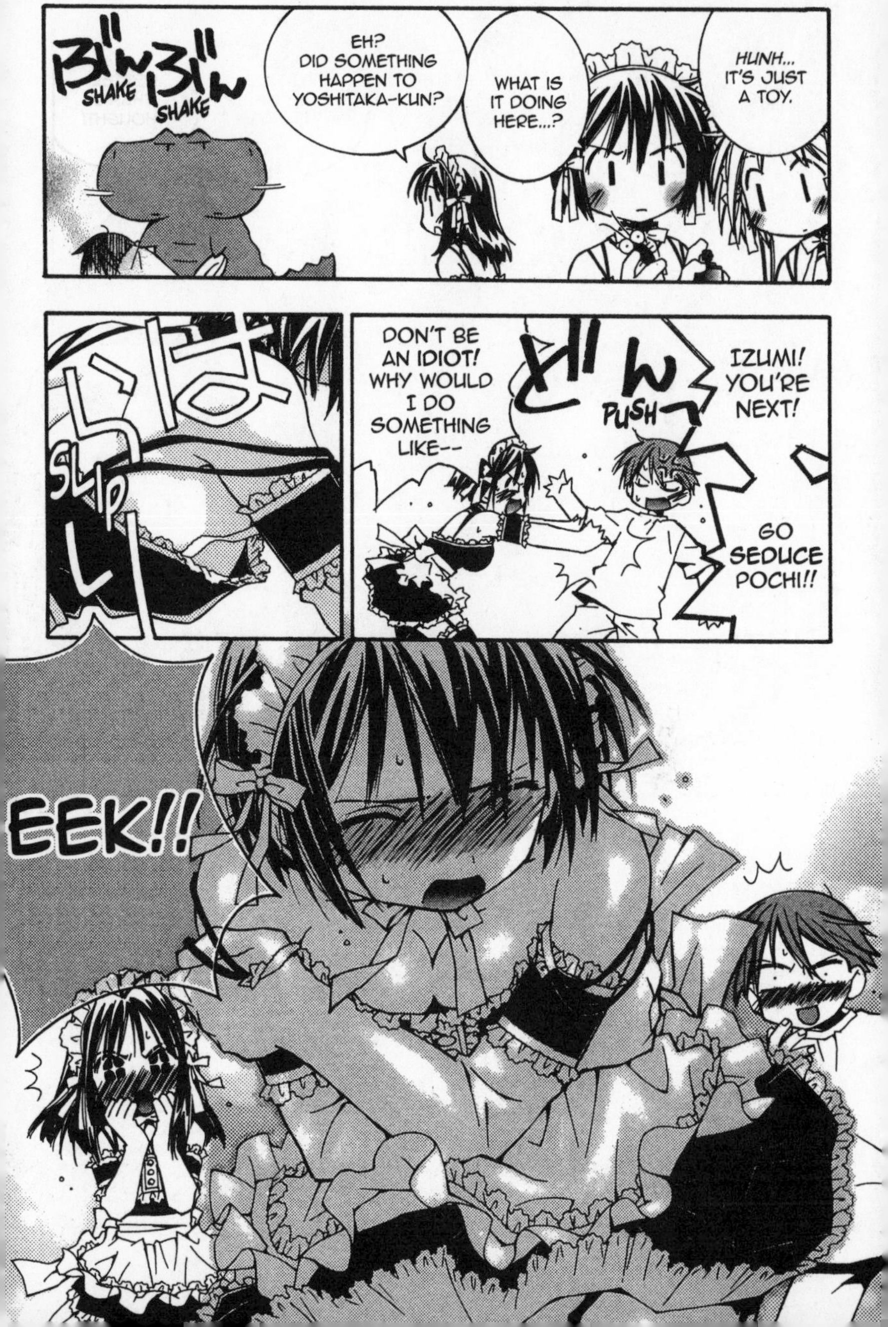
HUNH... IT'S JUST A TOY.
WHAT IS IT DOING HERE...?
EH? DID SOMETHING HAPPEN TO YOSHITAKA-KUN?
SHAKE SHAKE
IZUMI! YOU'RE NEXT!
GO SEDUCE POCHI!!
PUSH
DON'T BE AN IDIOT! WHY WOULD I DO SOMETHING LIKE--
SLIP
EEK!!

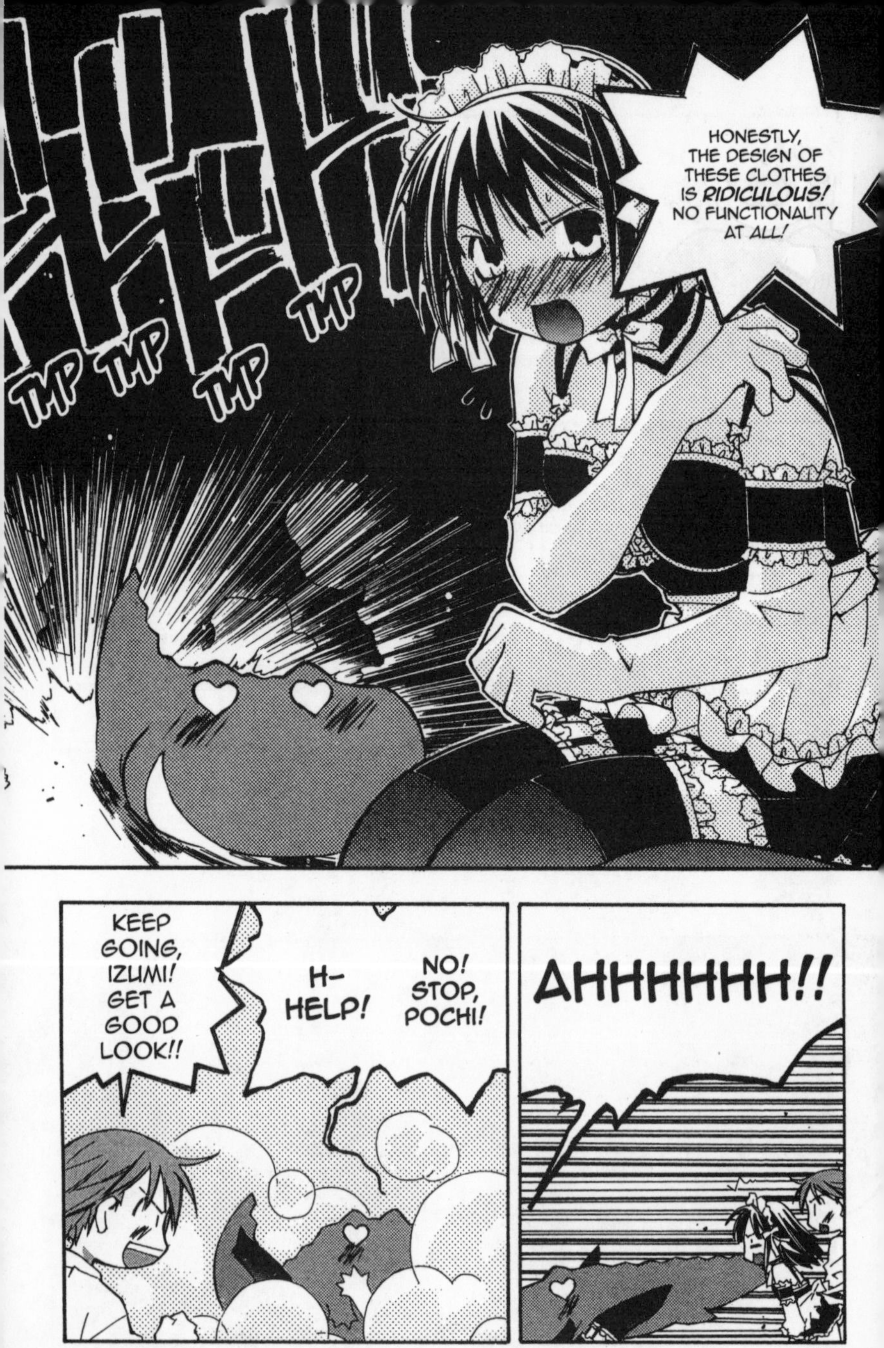
HONESTLY, THE DESIGN OF THESE CLOTHES IS ***RIDICULOUS!*** NO FUNCTIONALITY AT *ALL!*
TMP TMP TMP TMP
AHHHHHH!!
NO! STOP, POCHI!
H- HELP!
KEEP GOING, IZUMI! GET A GOOD LOOK!!

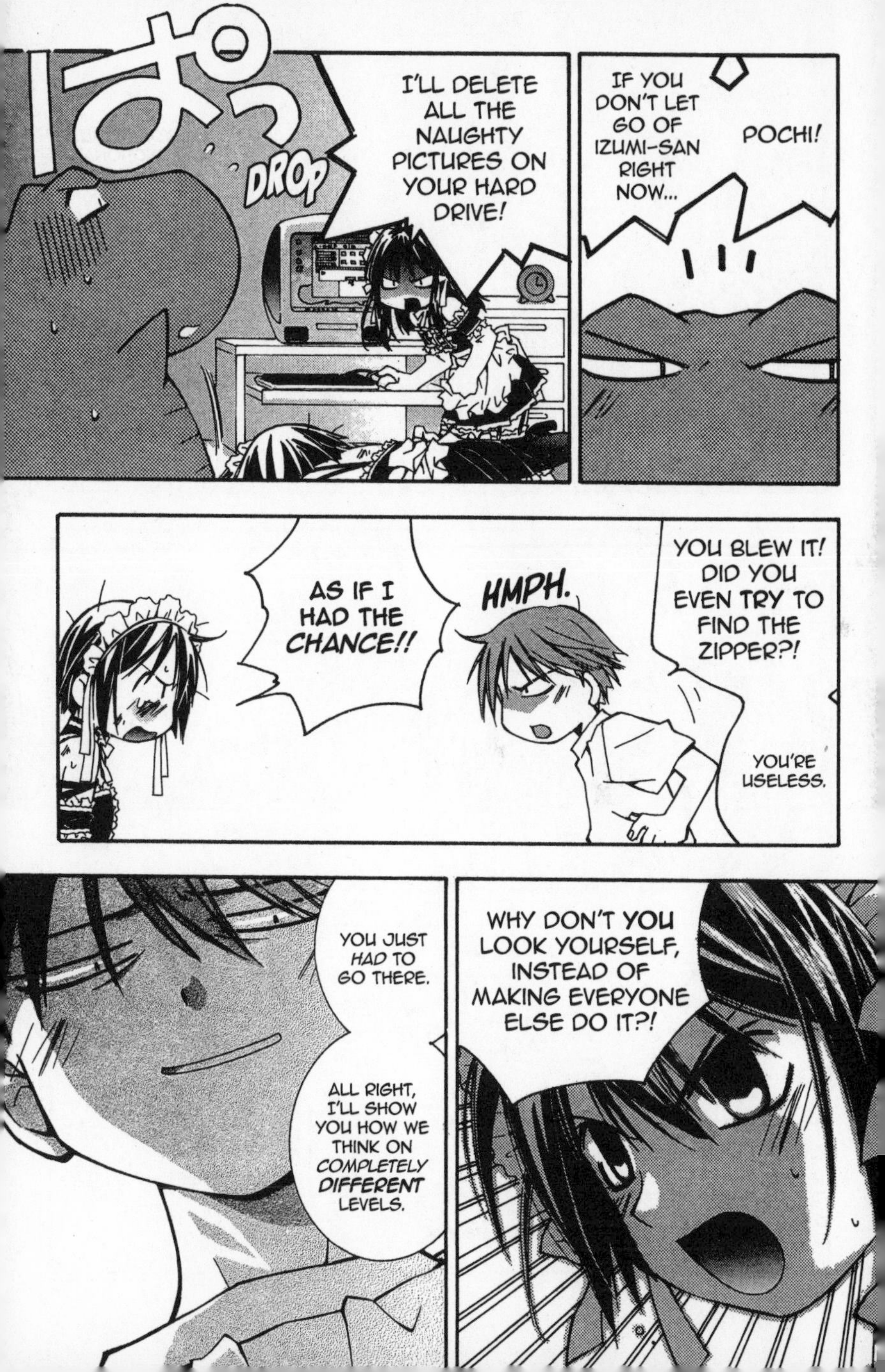
POCHI!
IF YOU DON'T LET GO OF IZUMI-SAN RIGHT NOW...
I'LL DELETE ALL THE NAUGHTY PICTURES ON YOUR HARD DRIVE!
ぱっ
DROP
YOU BLEW IT! DID YOU EVEN TRY TO FIND THE ZIPPER?!
YOU'RE USELESS.
HMPH.
AS IF I HAD THE CHANCE!!
WHY DON'T YOU LOOK YOURSELF, INSTEAD OF MAKING EVERYONE ELSE DO IT?!
YOU JUST HAD TO GO THERE.
ALL RIGHT, I'LL SHOW YOU HOW WE THINK ON COMPLETELY DIFFERENT LEVELS.

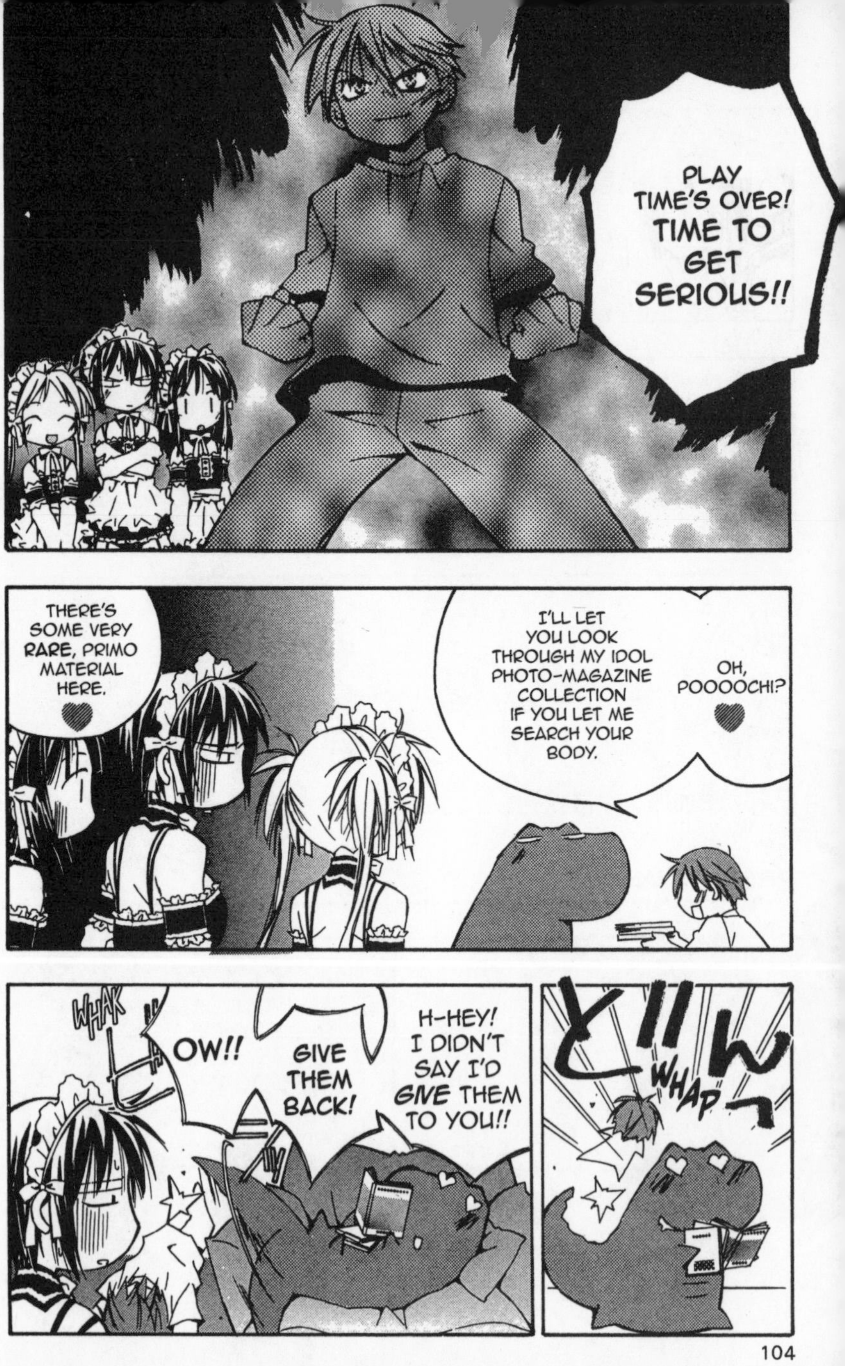
PLAY TIME'S OVER! TIME TO GET SERIOUS!!
OH, POOOOCHI?
I'LL LET YOU LOOK THROUGH MY IDOL PHOTO-MAGAZINE COLLECTION IF YOU LET ME SEARCH YOUR BODY.
THERE'S SOME VERY RARE, PRIMO MATERIAL HERE.
WHAP
H-HEY! I DIDN'T SAY I'D GIVE THEM TO YOU!!
GIVE THEM BACK!
OW!!
WHAK

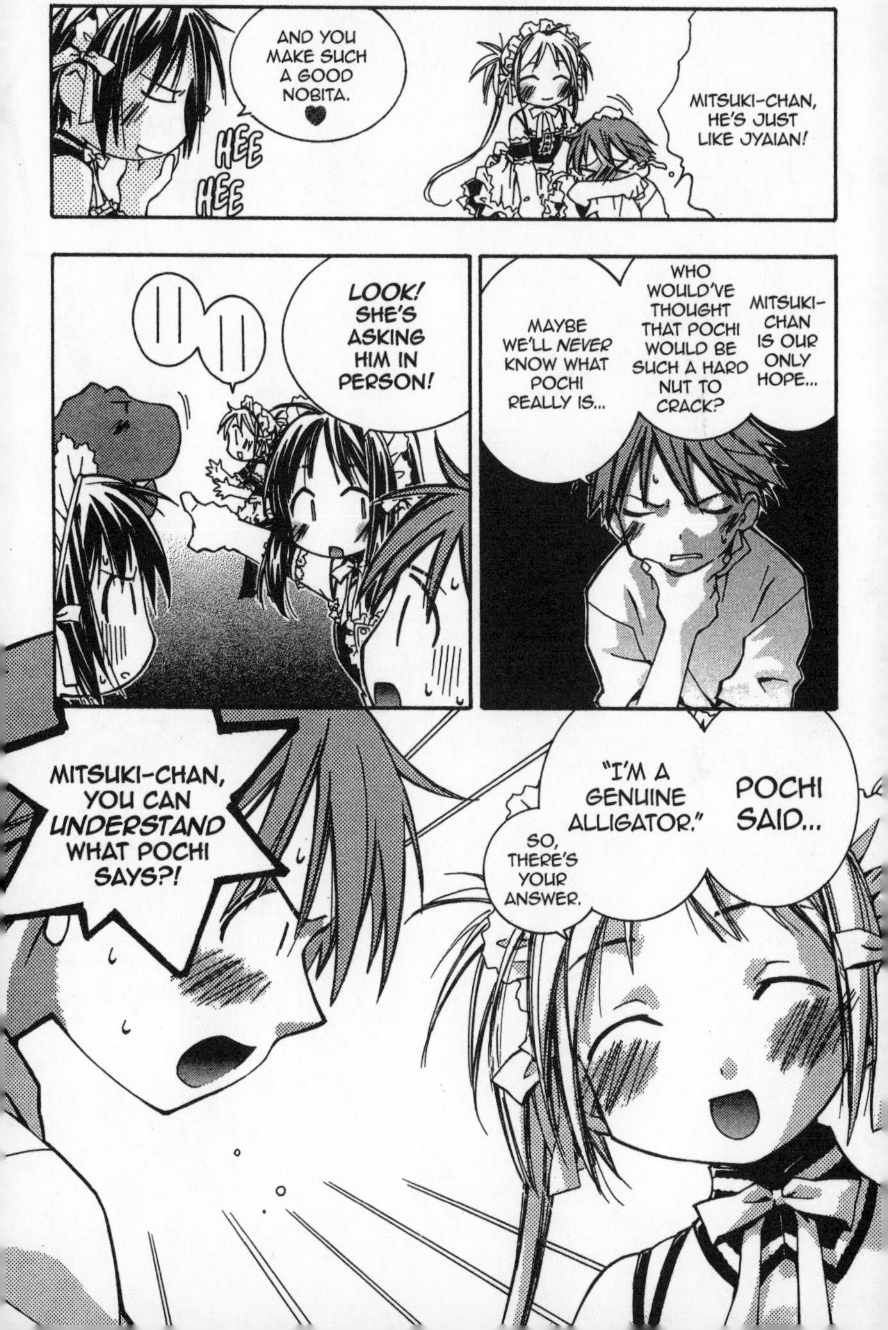
MITSUKI-CHAN, HE'S JUST LIKE JYAIAN!
AND YOU MAKE SUCH A GOOD NOBITA. ♥
HEE HEE
MITSUKI-CHAN IS OUR ONLY HOPE...
WHO WOULD'VE THOUGHT THAT POCHI WOULD BE SUCH A HARD NUT TO CRACK?
MAYBE WE'LL *NEVER* KNOW WHAT POCHI REALLY IS...
LOOK! SHE'S ASKING HIM IN PERSON!
!!
POCHI SAID...
"I'M A GENUINE ALLIGATOR."
SO, THERE'S YOUR ANSWER.
MITSUKI-CHAN, YOU CAN *UNDERSTAND* WHAT POCHI SAYS?!

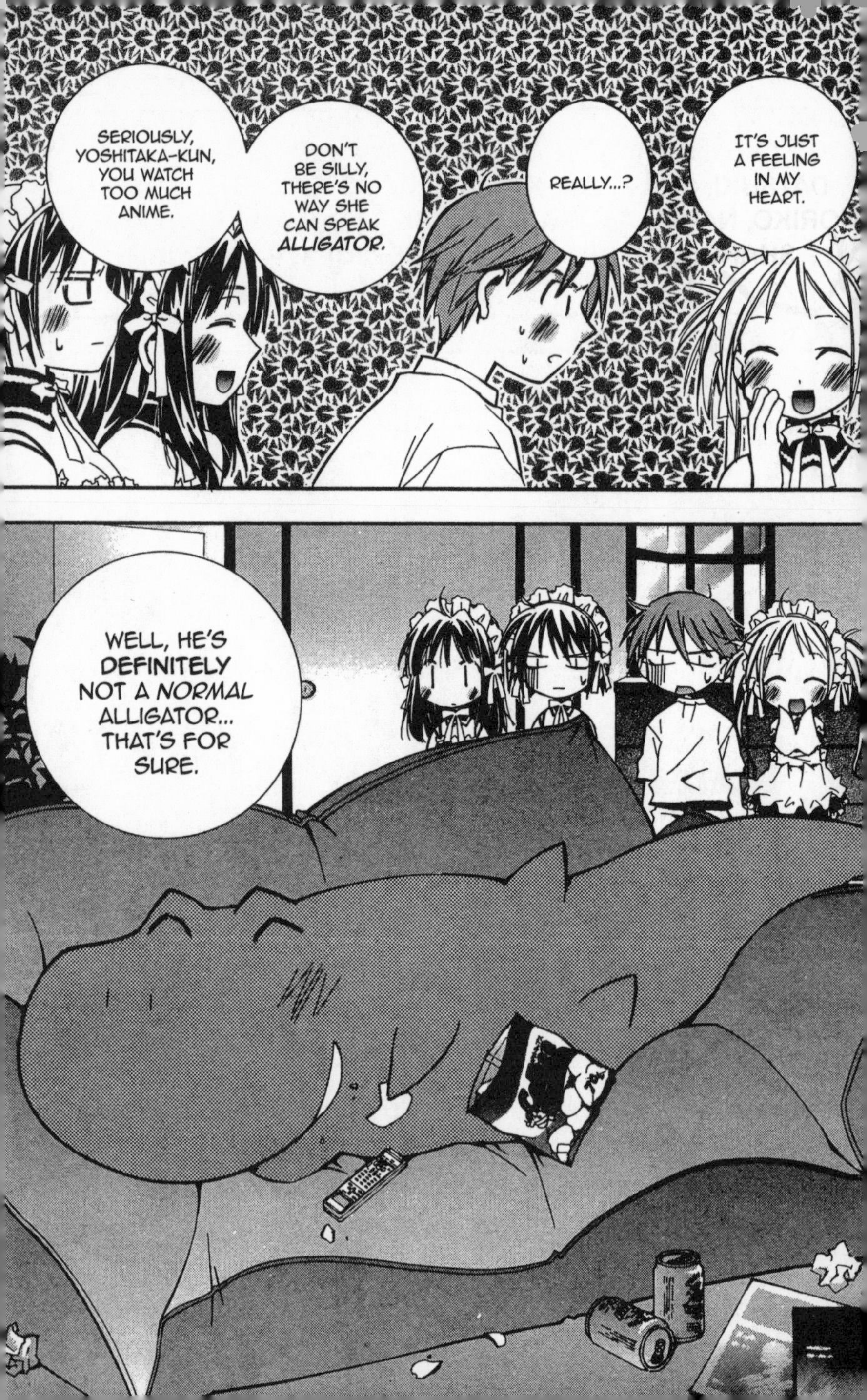
IT'S JUST A FEELING IN MY HEART.
REALLY...?
DON'T BE SILLY, THERE'S NO WAY SHE CAN SPEAK ALLIGATOR.
SERIOUSLY, YOSHITAKA-KUN, YOU WATCH TOO MUCH ANIME.
WELL, HE'S DEFINITELY NOT A NORMAL ALLIGATOR... THAT'S FOR SURE.

CHAPTER 7

CHISE, IZUMI, LUM, MISUZU, CORONA, IYO, FERDINAND, GIN, REI, MISA, KASUMI, HIROSURE, PAIKANA-SAN, SHIA, DATSUKI, SHAMPOO, KANATA, DAMA, CHOKO, LEIQUINNI, NORIKO, NADIA, ASUKA, TSUBASA, MAMI, MIA, RUMI, MINMAY, SHARON, YOSHINO, SCHIERKE, JULIA AND TWINKLE

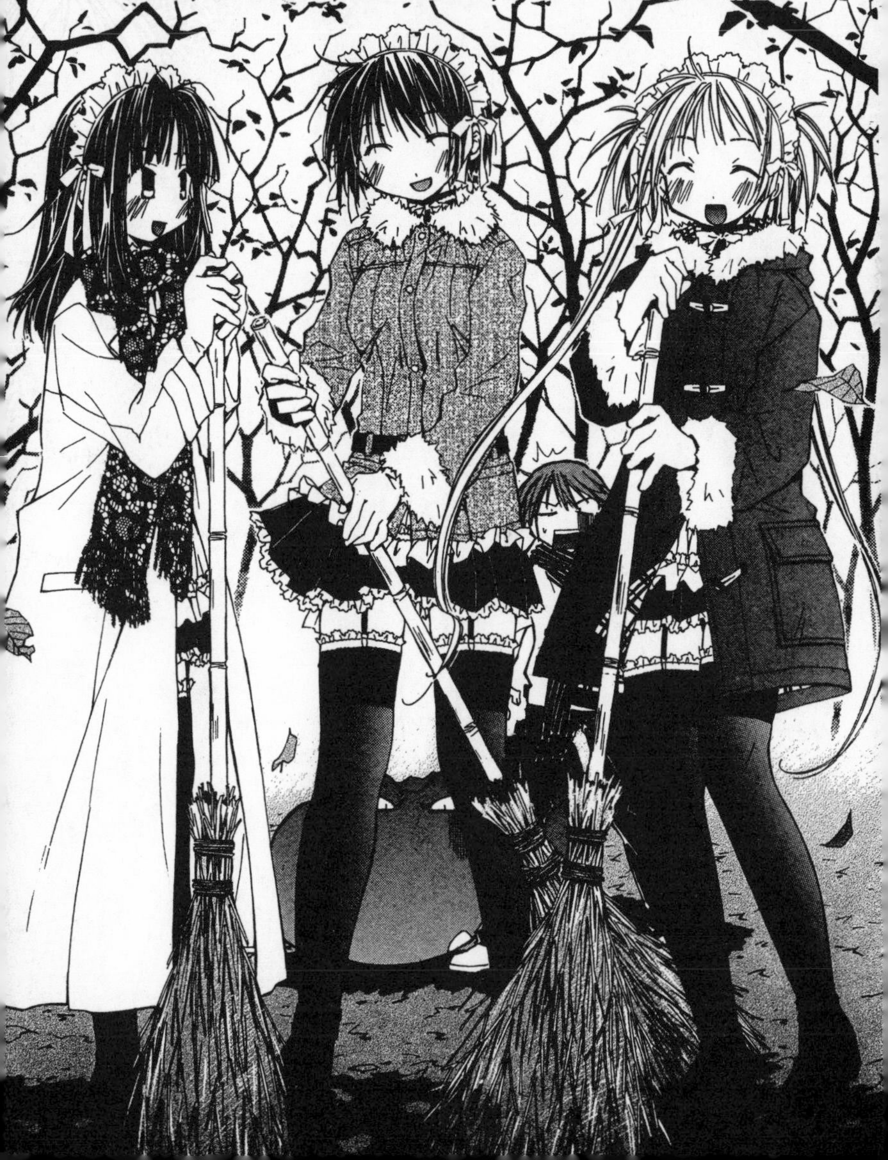

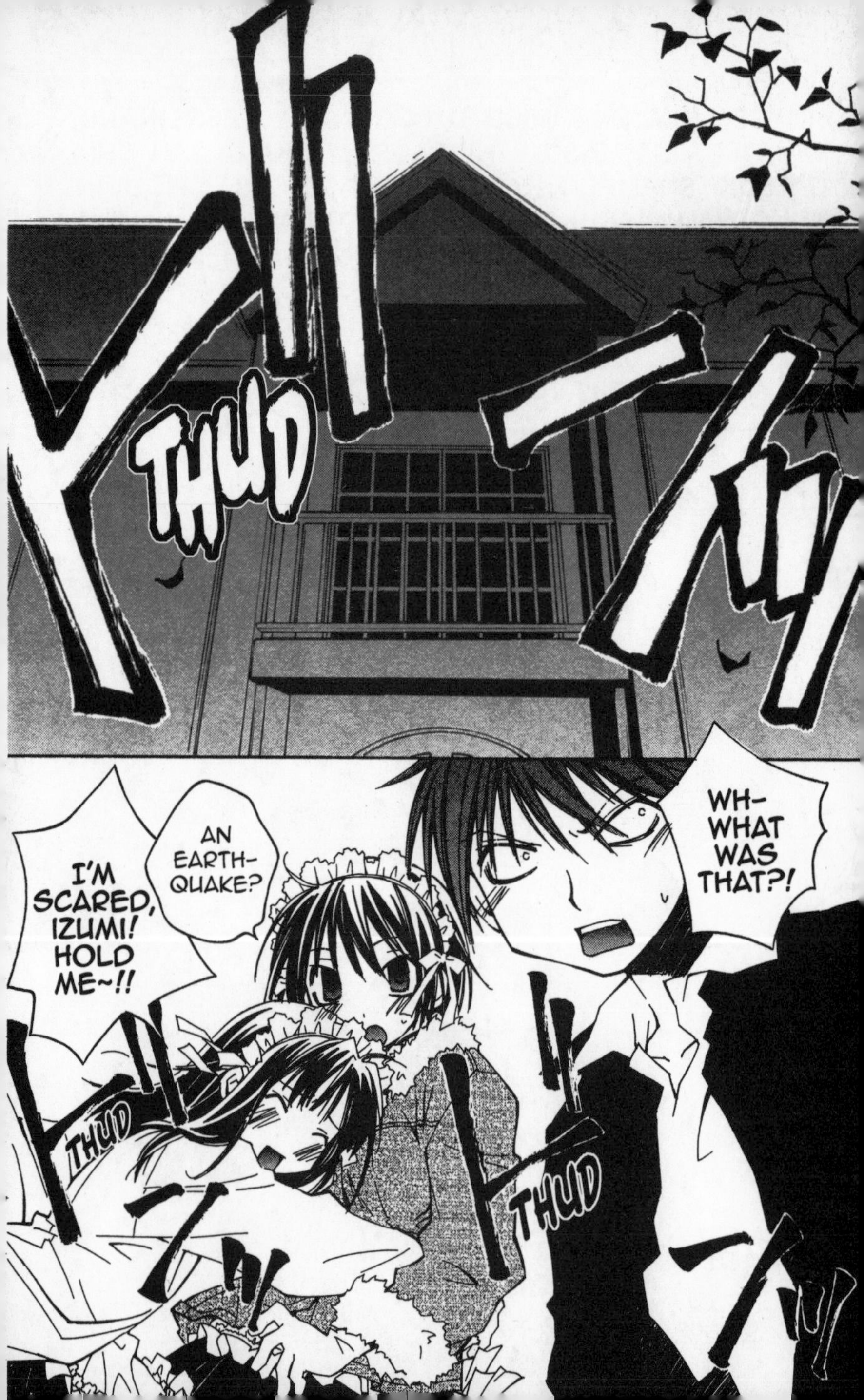
THUD
WH-WHAT WAS THAT?!
AN EARTH-QUAKE?
I'M SCARED, IZUMI! HOLD ME~!!
THUD
THUD

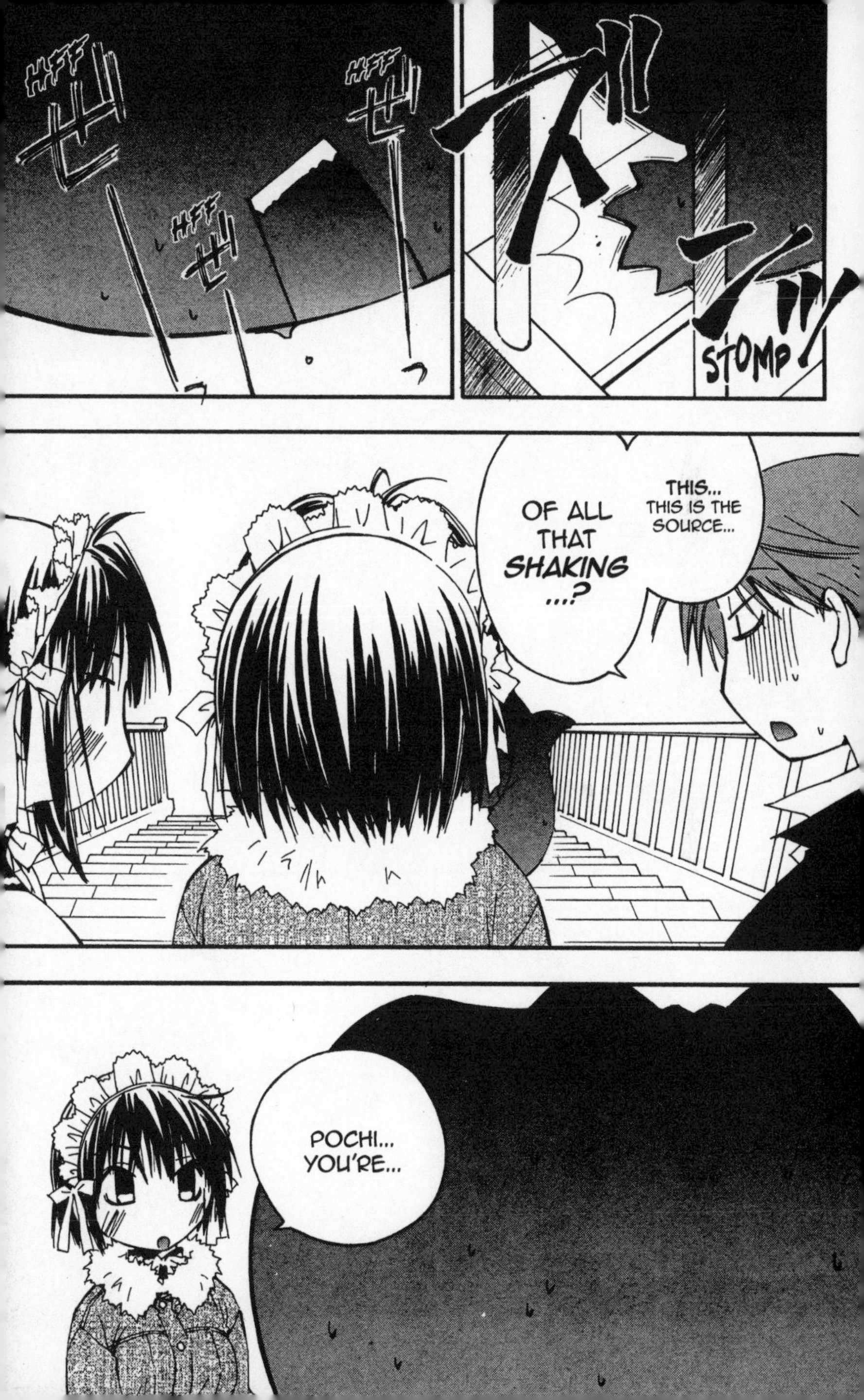
STOMP
HFF
HFF
HFF
THIS... THIS IS THE SOURCE... OF ALL THAT SHAKING ...?
POCHI... YOU'RE...

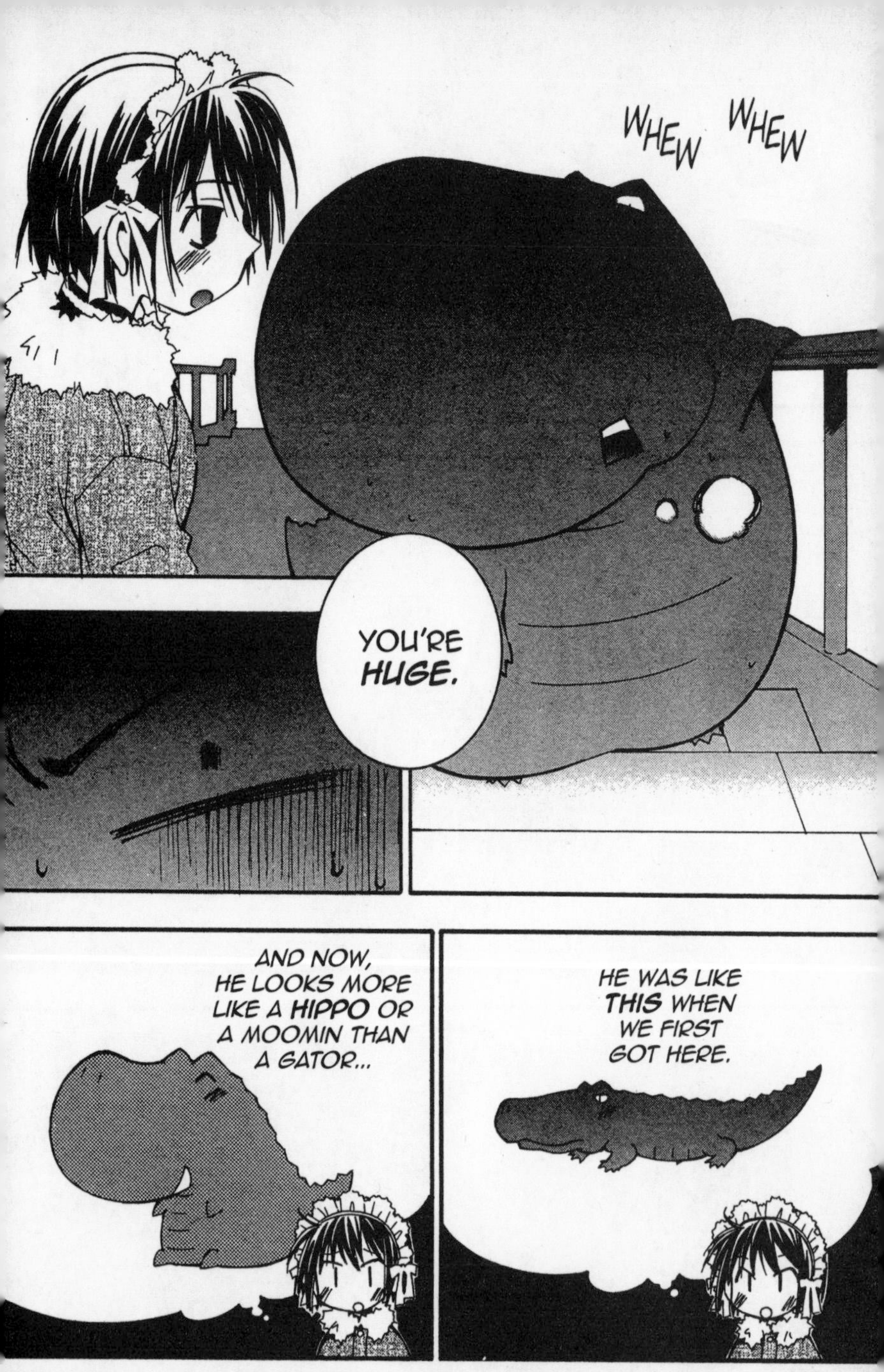
WHEW WHEW
YOU'RE HUGE.
HE WAS LIKE THIS WHEN WE FIRST GOT HERE.
AND NOW, HE LOOKS MORE LIKE A HIPPO OR A MOOMIN THAN A GATOR...

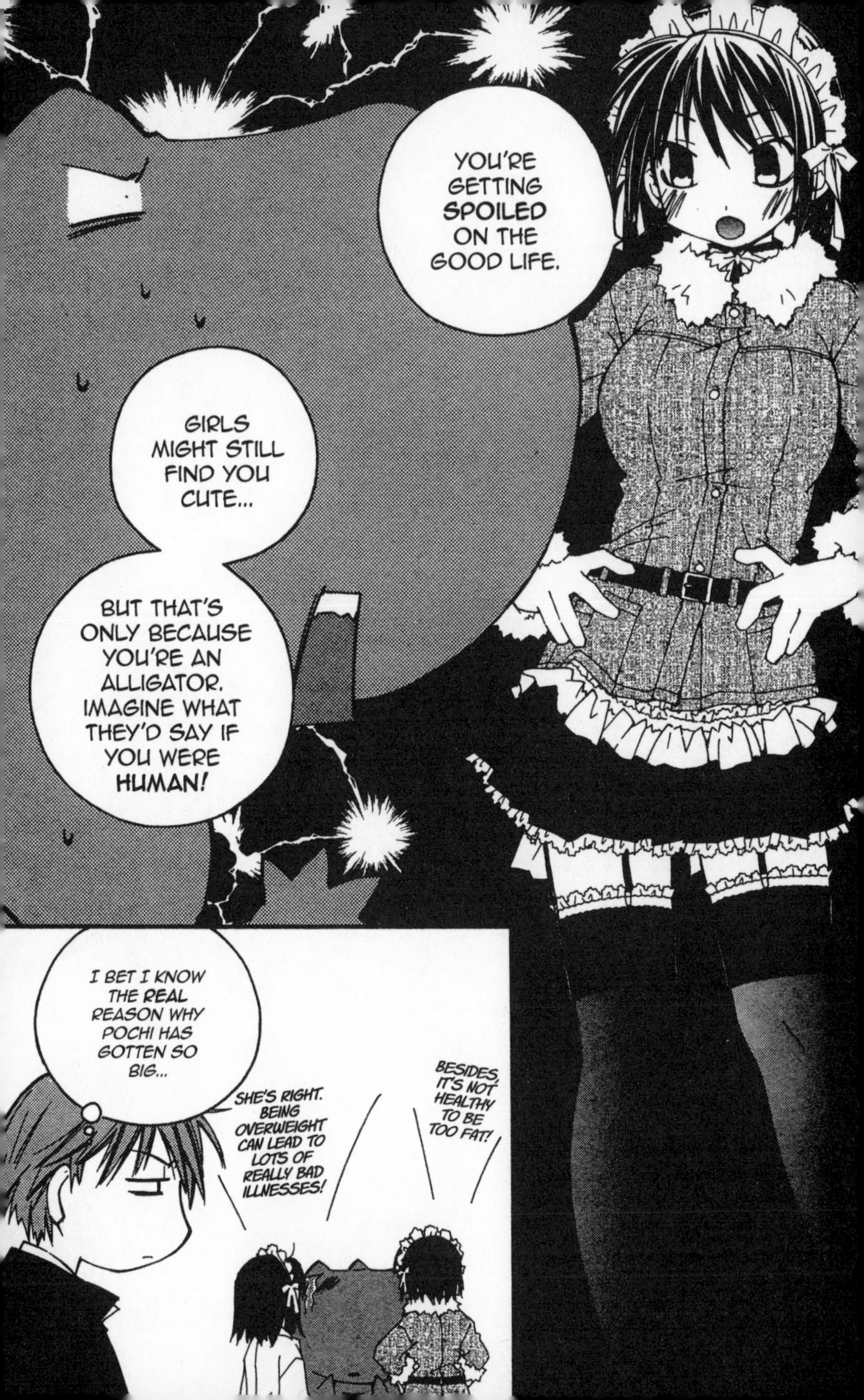
YOU'RE GETTING SPOILED ON THE GOOD LIFE.
GIRLS MIGHT STILL FIND YOU CUTE...
BUT THAT'S ONLY BECAUSE YOU'RE AN ALLIGATOR. IMAGINE WHAT THEY'D SAY IF YOU WERE HUMAN!
SHE'S RIGHT. BEING OVERWEIGHT CAN LEAD TO LOTS OF REALLY BAD ILLNESSES!
BESIDES, IT'S NOT HEALTHY TO BE TOO FAT!
I BET I KNOW THE REAL REASON WHY POCHI HAS GOTTEN SO BIG...

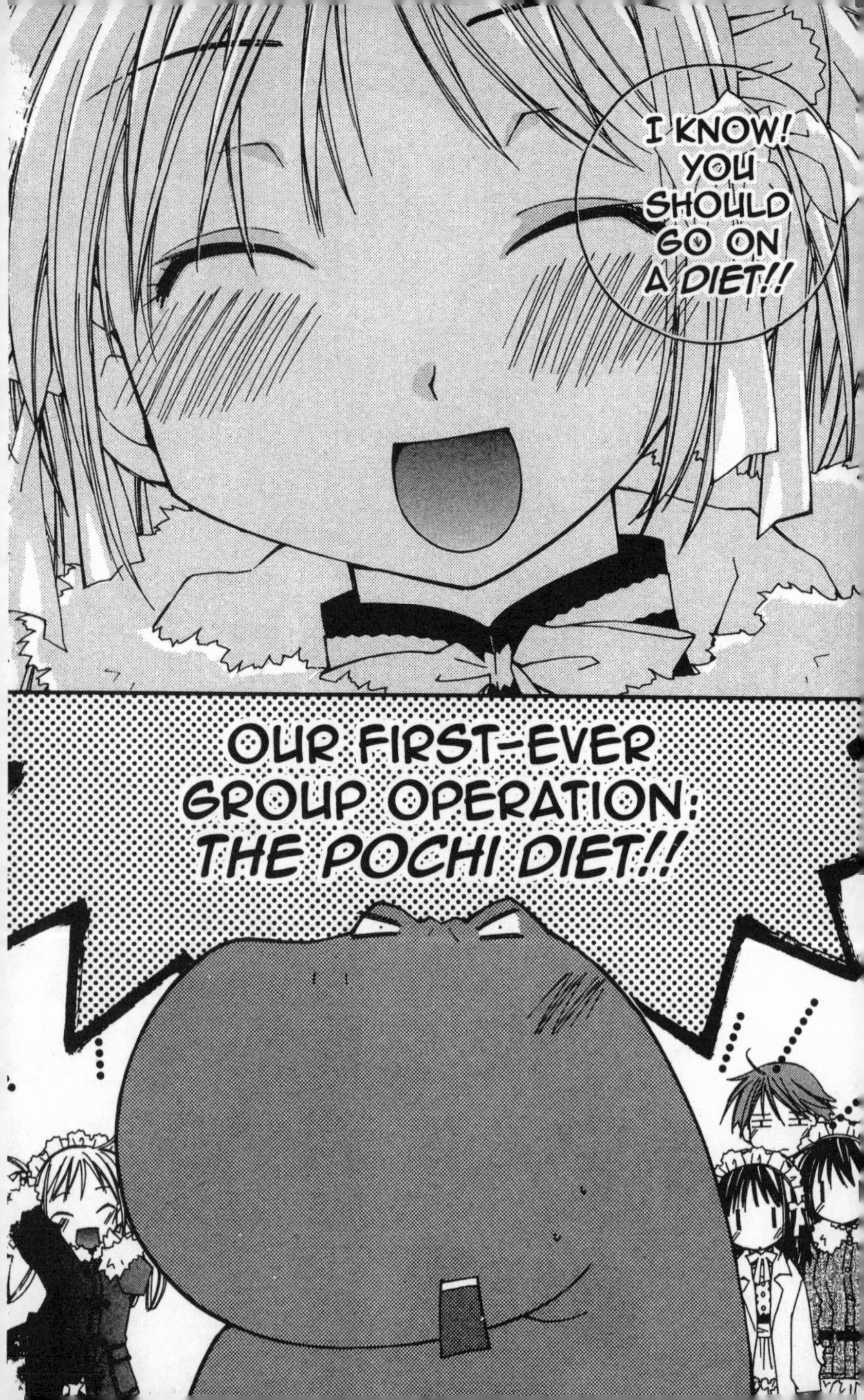
I KNOW! YOU SHOULD GO ON A DIET!!
OUR FIRST-EVER GROUP OPERATION: THE POCHI DIET!!

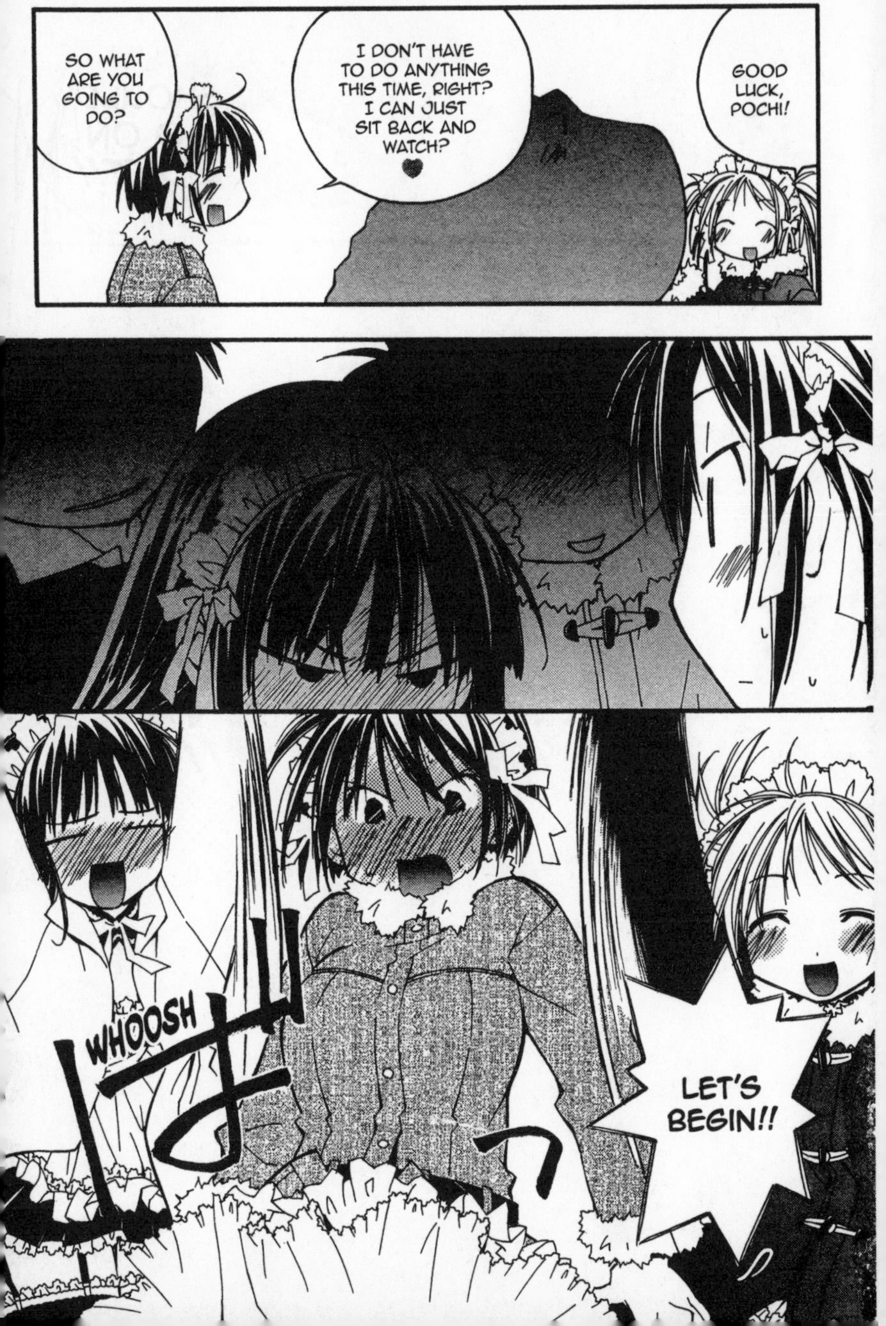
GOOD LUCK, POCHI!
I DON'T HAVE TO DO ANYTHING THIS TIME, RIGHT? I CAN JUST SIT BACK AND WATCH? ♥
SO WHAT ARE YOU GOING TO DO?
LET'S BEGIN!!
WHOOSH

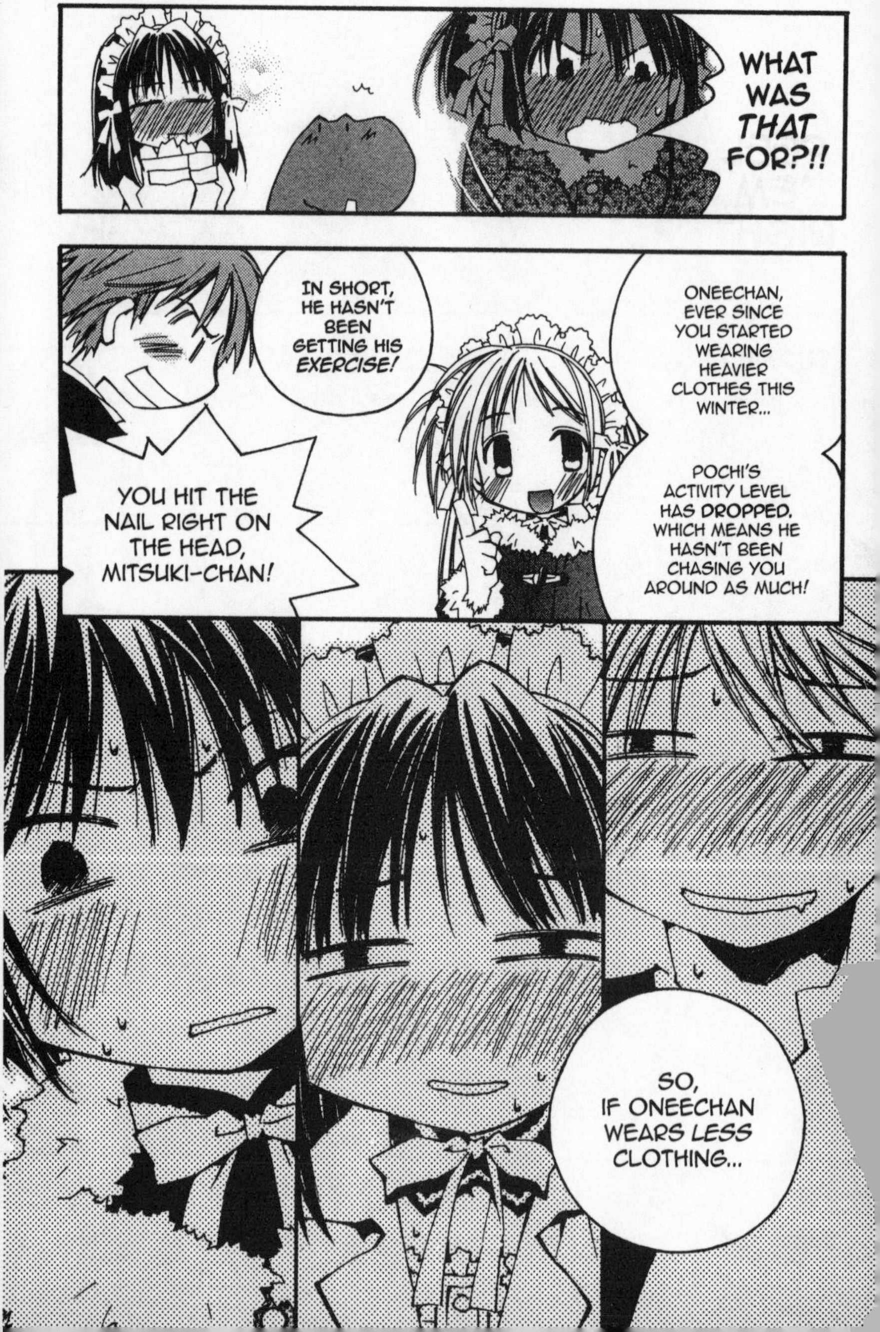
WHAT WAS THAT FOR?!!
ONEECHAN, EVER SINCE YOU STARTED WEARING HEAVIER CLOTHES THIS WINTER...
POCHI'S ACTIVITY LEVEL HAS DROPPED. WHICH MEANS HE HASN'T BEEN CHASING YOU AROUND AS MUCH!
IN SHORT, HE HASN'T BEEN GETTING HIS EXERCISE!
YOU HIT THE NAIL RIGHT ON THE HEAD, MITSUKI-CHAN!
SO, IF ONEECHAN WEARS LESS CLOTHING...

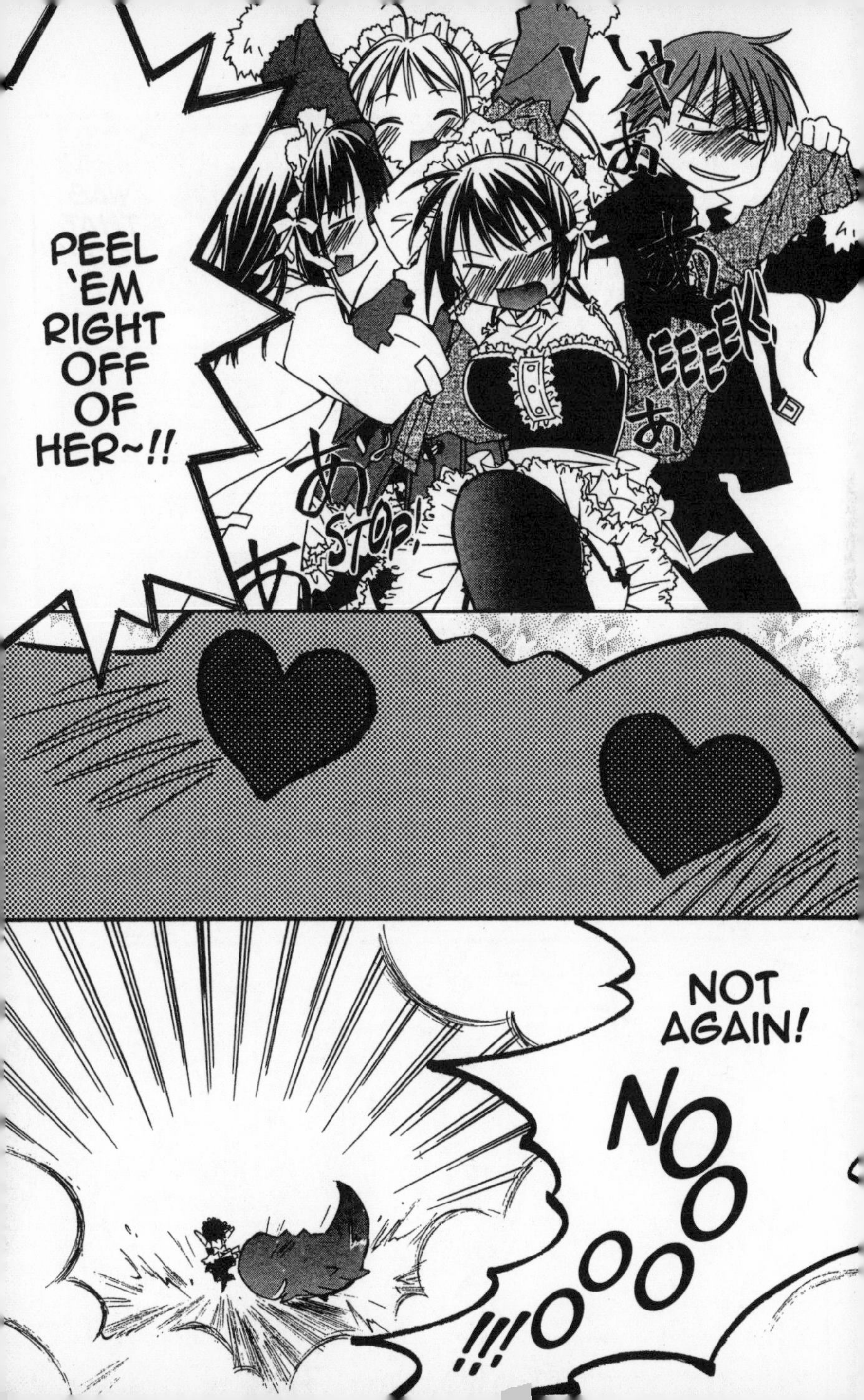
EEEEK!
PEEL 'EM RIGHT OFF OF HER~!!
STOP!
NOT AGAIN!
NOOOOOO!!!

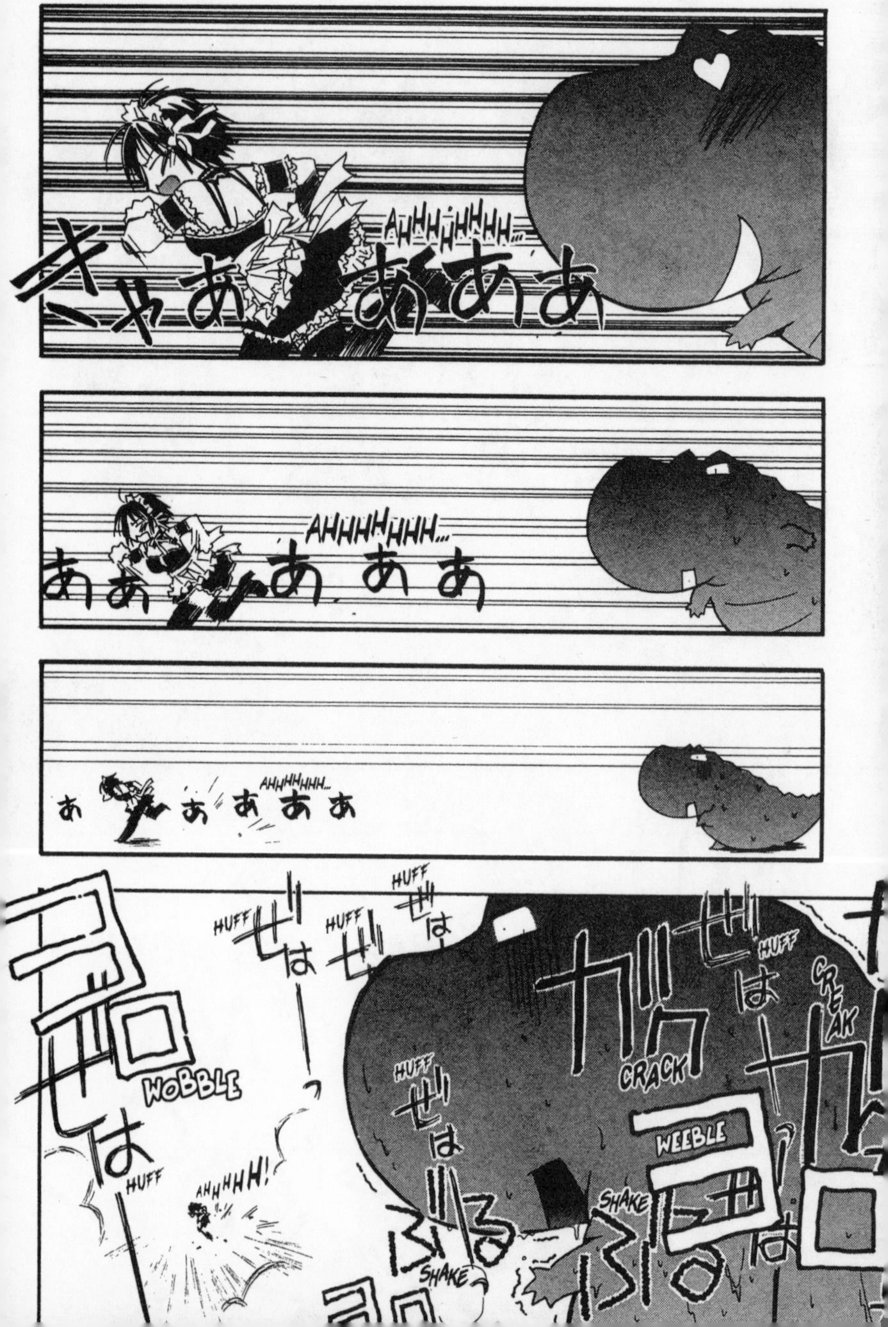

キャあ あああ
AHHHHHHHH...
ああ あああ
AHHHHHHH...
ああああああ
AHHHHHHHH...
CREAK
ガク
CRACK
ぜは
HUFF
ヨロ
WEEBLE
ぶる
SHAKE
ぜは
HUFF
ぶる
SHAKE
ぜは
HUFF
ぜは
HUFF
ヨロ
WOBBLE
ぜは
HUFF
AHHHHHH!

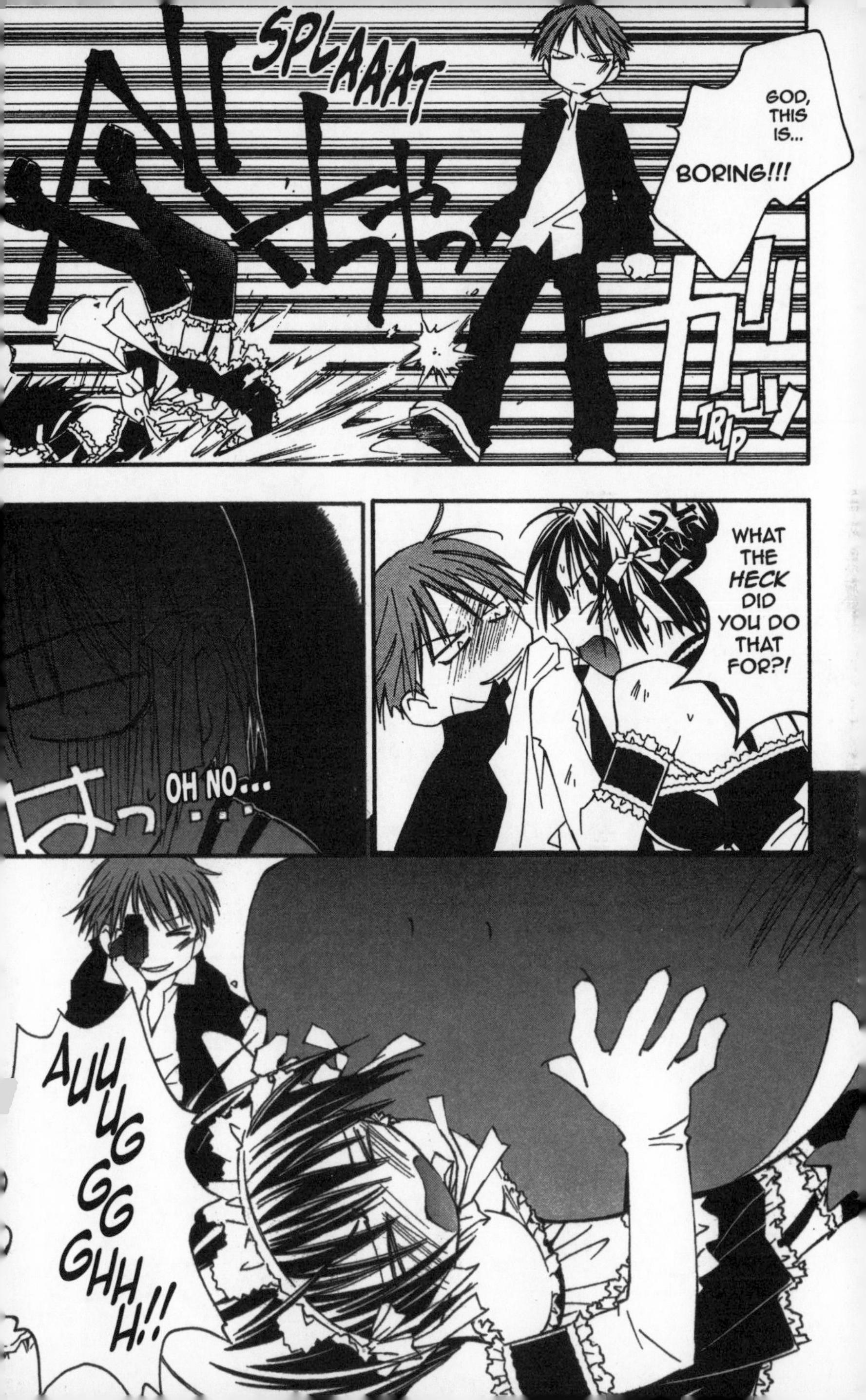
GOD, THIS IS... BORING!!!
TRIP
SPLAAAT
WHAT THE HECK DID YOU DO THAT FOR?!
OH NO...
AUUUGGGGHHHH!!

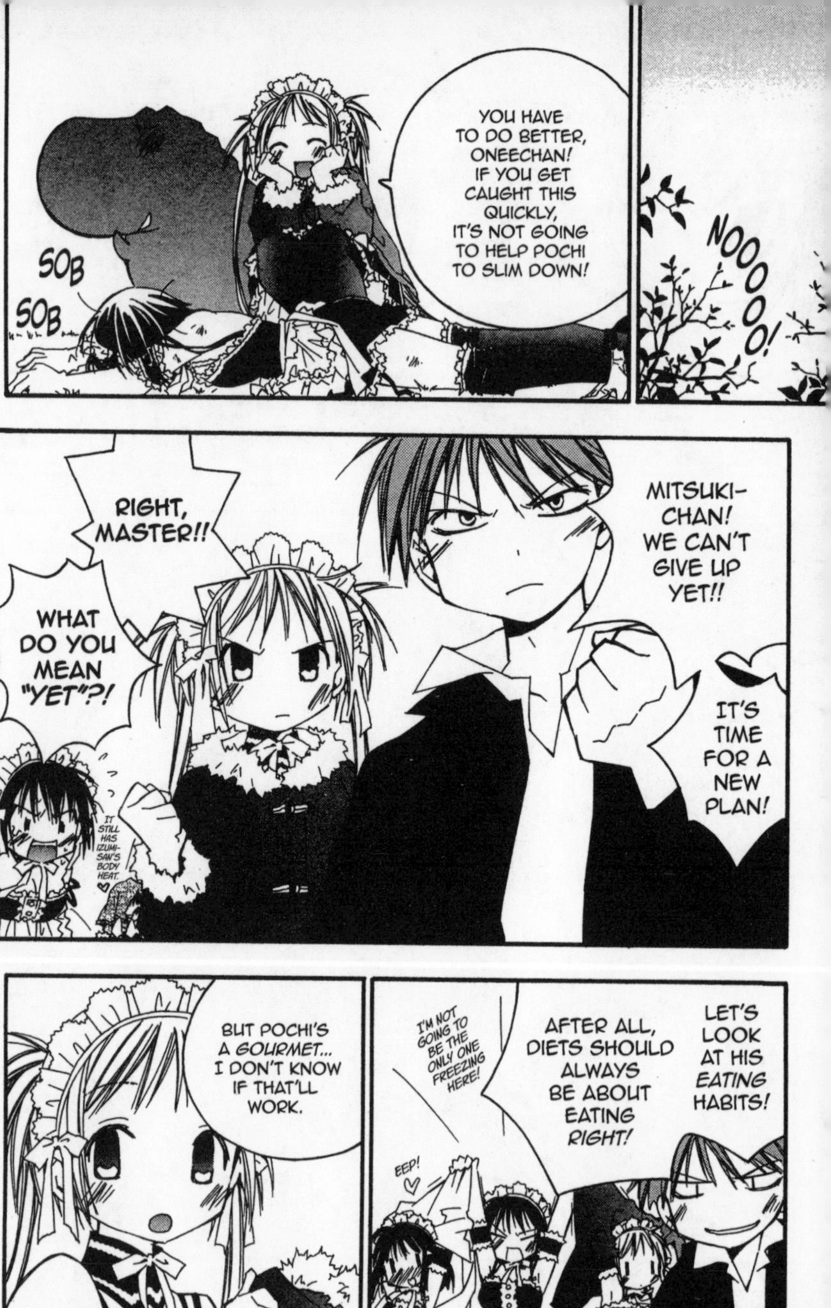
NOOOOO!
YOU HAVE TO DO BETTER, ONEECHAN! IF YOU GET CAUGHT THIS QUICKLY, IT'S NOT GOING TO HELP POCHI TO SLIM DOWN!
SOB
SOB
MITSUKI-CHAN! WE CAN'T GIVE UP YET!!
IT'S TIME FOR A NEW PLAN!
RIGHT, MASTER!!
WHAT DO YOU MEAN "YET"?!
IT STILL HAS IZUMI-SAN'S BODY HEAT.
LET'S LOOK AT HIS EATING HABITS!
AFTER ALL, DIETS SHOULD ALWAYS BE ABOUT EATING RIGHT!
I'M NOT GOING TO BE THE ONLY ONE FREEZING HERE!
EEP!
BUT POCHI'S A GOURMET... I DON'T KNOW IF THAT'LL WORK.

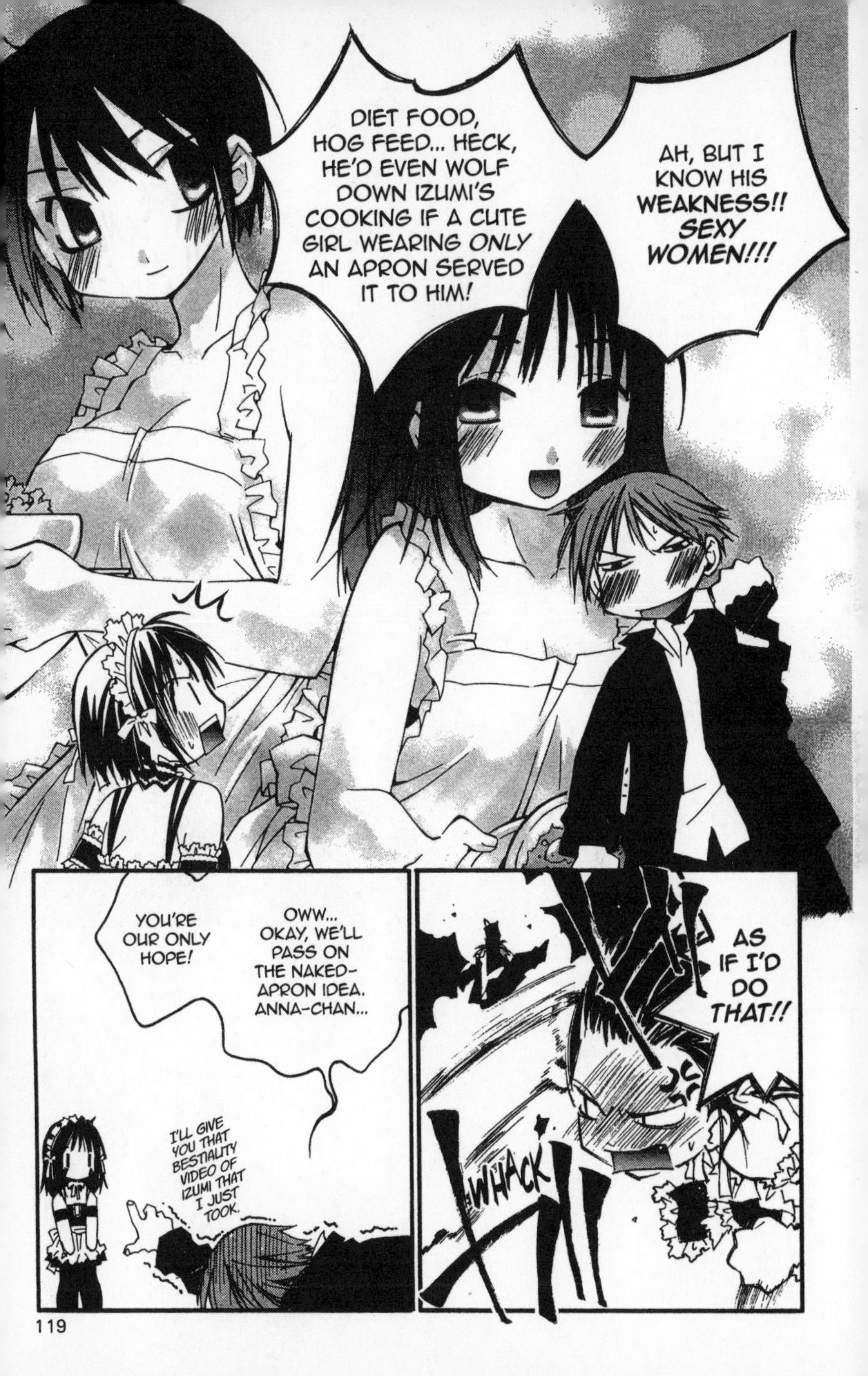
AH, BUT I KNOW HIS WEAKNESS!! SEXY WOMEN!!!
DIET FOOD, HOG FEED... HECK, HE'D EVEN WOLF DOWN IZUMI'S COOKING IF A CUTE GIRL WEARING ONLY AN APRON SERVED IT TO HIM!
AS IF I'D DO THAT!!
WHACK
OWW... OKAY, WE'LL PASS ON THE NAKED-APRON IDEA. ANNA-CHAN...
YOU'RE OUR ONLY HOPE!
I'LL GIVE YOU THAT BESTIALITY VIDEO OF IZUMI THAT I JUST TOOK.

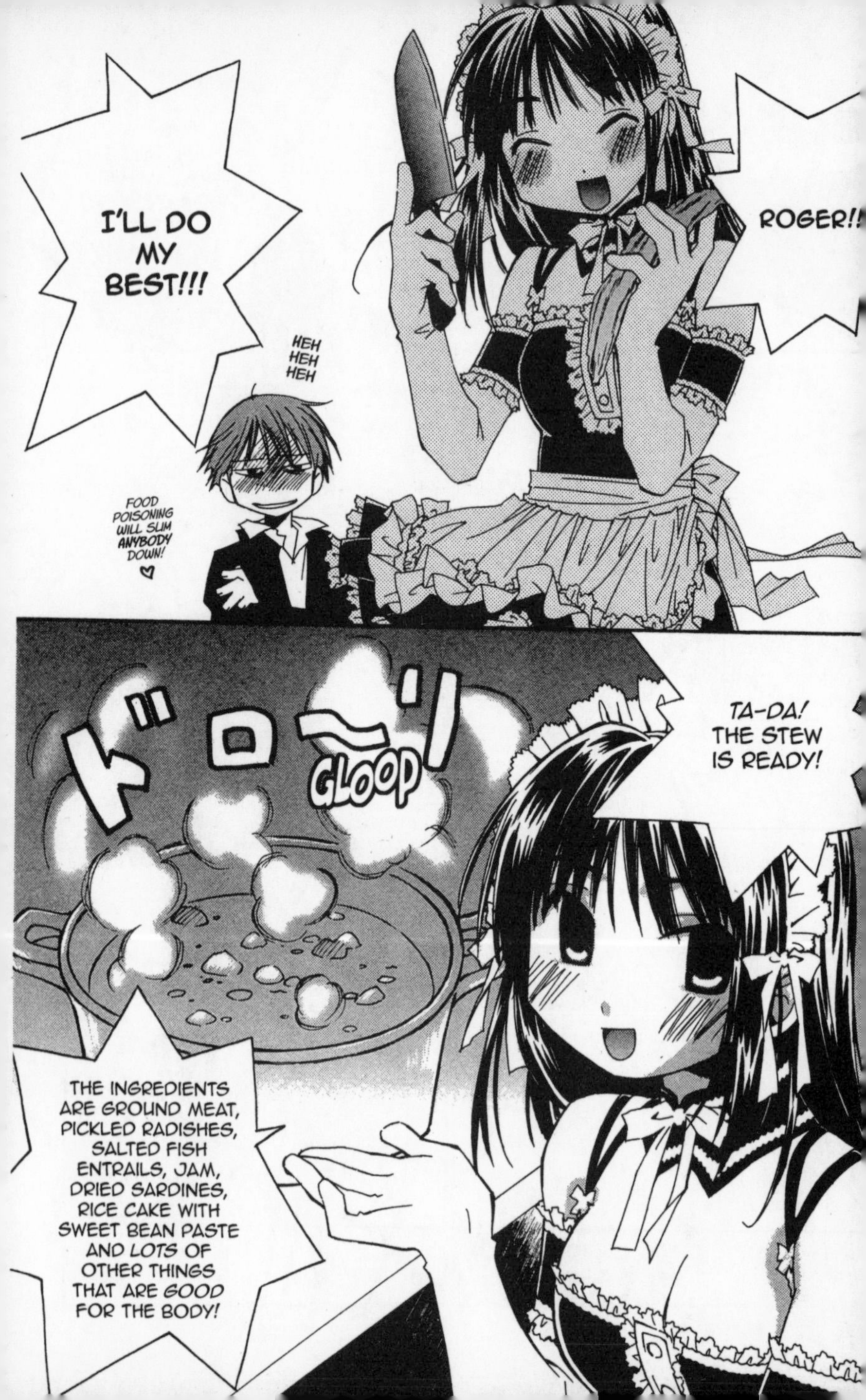
ROGER!!
I'LL DO MY BEST!!!
HEH HEH HEH
FOOD POISONING WILL SLIM ANYBODY DOWN! ♡
TA-DA! THE STEW IS READY!
ドロ～リ
GLOOP
THE INGREDIENTS ARE GROUND MEAT, PICKLED RADISHES, SALTED FISH ENTRAILS, JAM, DRIED SARDINES, RICE CAKE WITH SWEET BEAN PASTE AND *LOTS* OF OTHER THINGS THAT ARE *GOOD* FOR THE BODY!

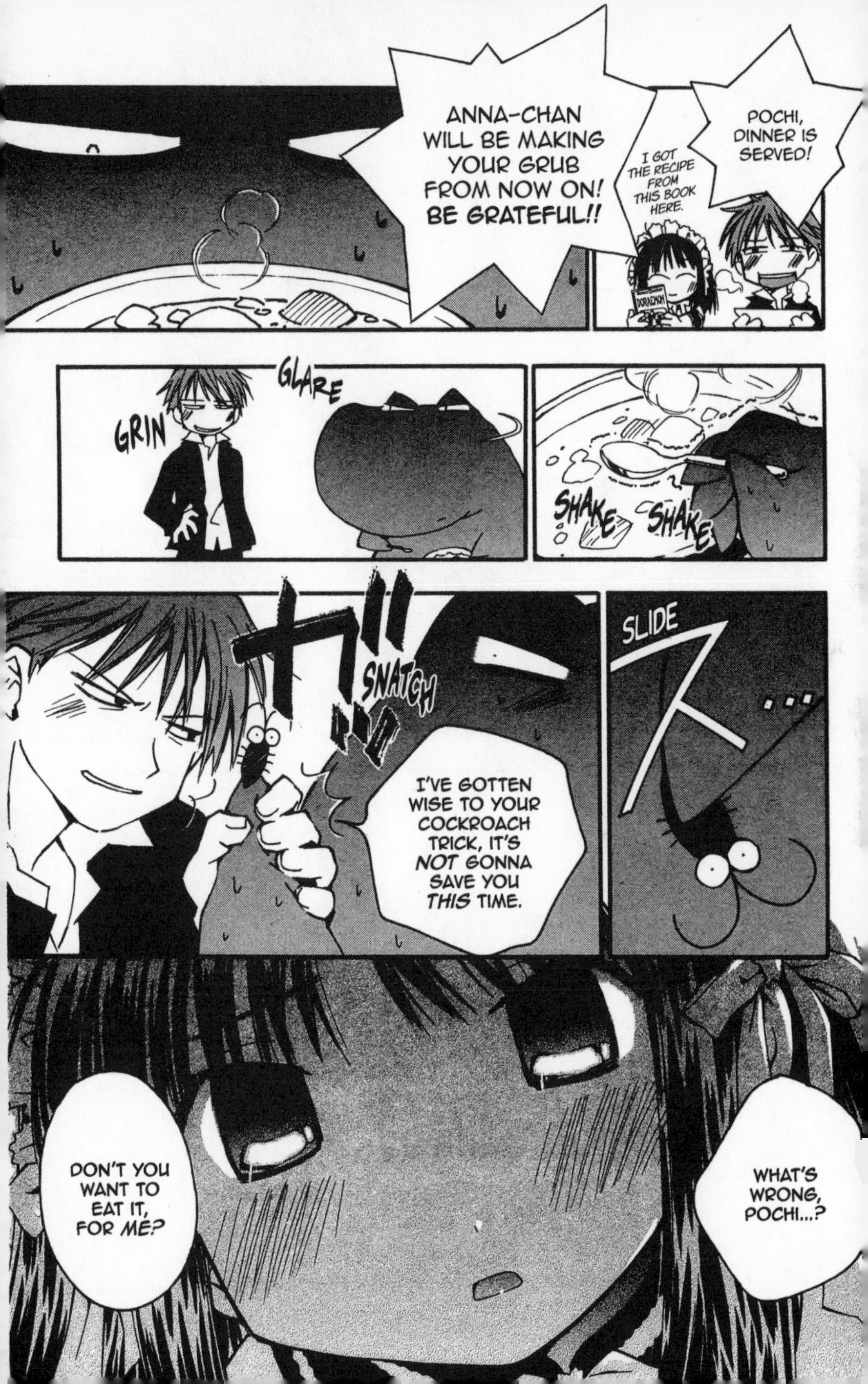

POCHI, DINNER IS SERVED!
I GOT THE RECIPE FROM THIS BOOK HERE.
ANNA-CHAN WILL BE MAKING YOUR GRUB FROM NOW ON! BE GRATEFUL!!
SHAKE
SHAKE
GLARE
GRIN
SLIDE
...
SNATCH
I'VE GOTTEN WISE TO YOUR COCKROACH TRICK, IT'S *NOT* GONNA SAVE YOU *THIS* TIME.
WHAT'S WRONG, POCHI...?
DON'T YOU WANT TO EAT IT, FOR *ME*?

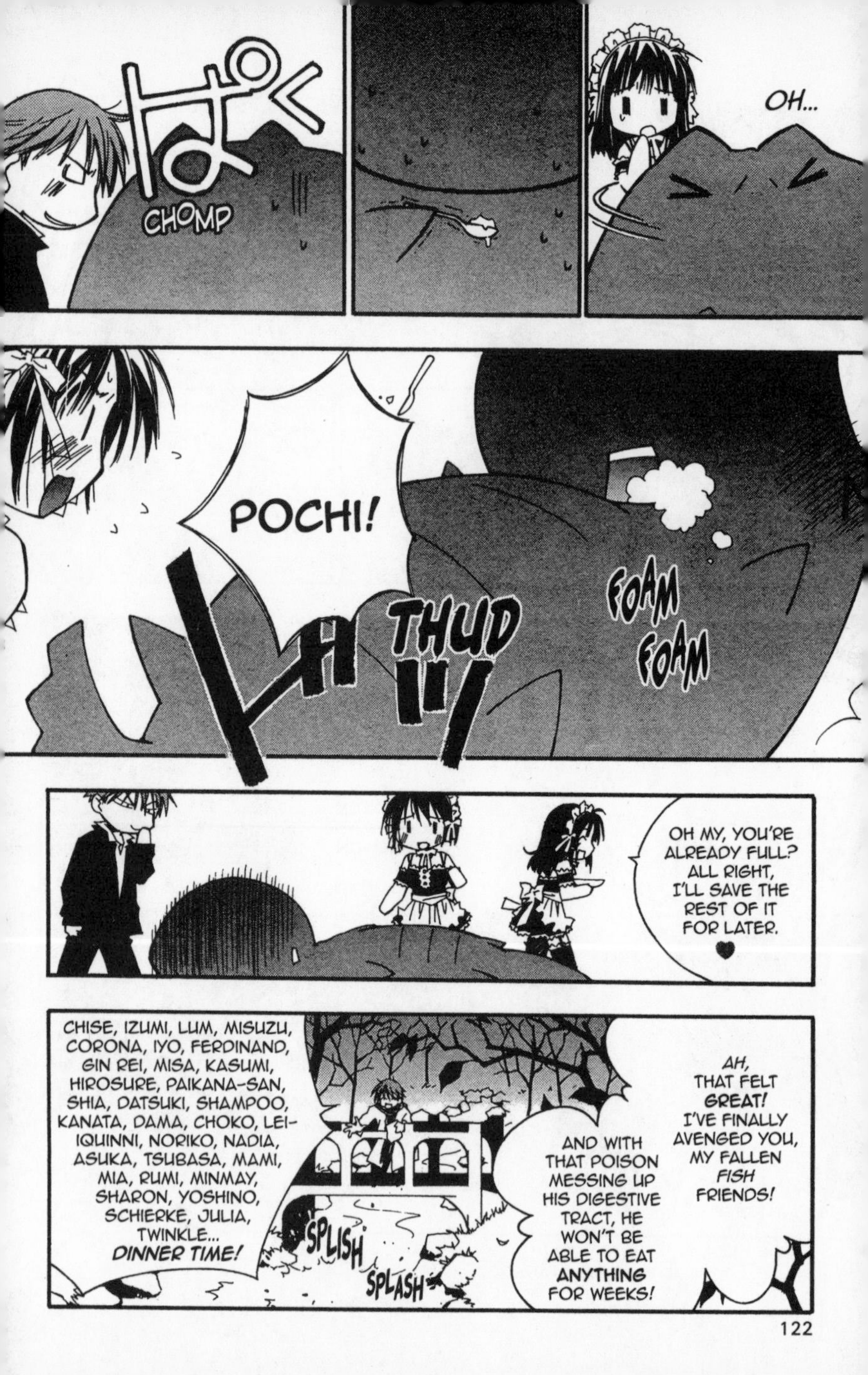
OH...
CHOMP
POCHI!
THUD
FOAM FOAM
OH MY, YOU'RE ALREADY FULL? ALL RIGHT, I'LL SAVE THE REST OF IT FOR LATER. ♥
AH, THAT FELT **GREAT!** I'VE FINALLY AVENGED YOU, MY FALLEN *FISH* FRIENDS!
AND WITH THAT POISON MESSING UP HIS DIGESTIVE TRACT, HE WON'T BE ABLE TO EAT **ANYTHING** FOR WEEKS!
SPLISH
SPLASH
CHISE, IZUMI, LUM, MISUZU, CORONA, IYO, FERDINAND, GIN REI, MISA, KASUMI, HIROSURE, PAIKANA-SAN, SHIA, DATSUKI, SHAMPOO, KANATA, DAMA, CHOKO, LEI-IQUINNI, NORIKO, NADIA, ASUKA, TSUBASA, MAMI, MIA, RUMI, MINMAY, SHARON, YOSHINO, SCHIERKE, JULIA, TWINKLE... *DINNER TIME!*

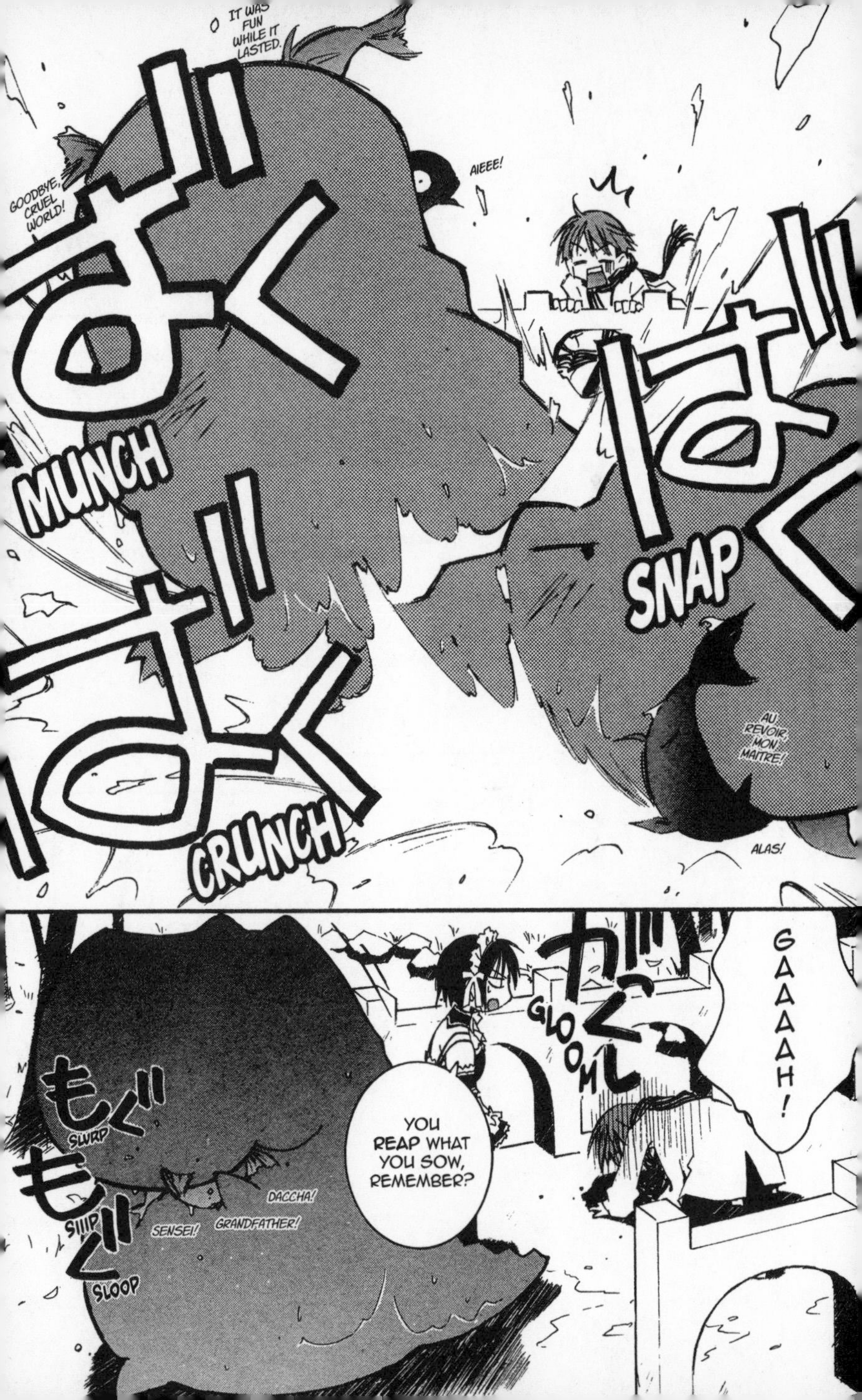
AIEEE!
SNAP
AU REVOIR, MON MAITRE!
ALAS!
IT WAS FUN WHILE IT LASTED.
GOODBYE, CRUEL WORLD!
MUNCH
CRUNCH
GAAAAH!
GLOOM
YOU REAP WHAT YOU SOW, REMEMBER?
DACCHA!
GRANDFATHER!
SENSEI!
SLURP
SLIIP
SLOOP

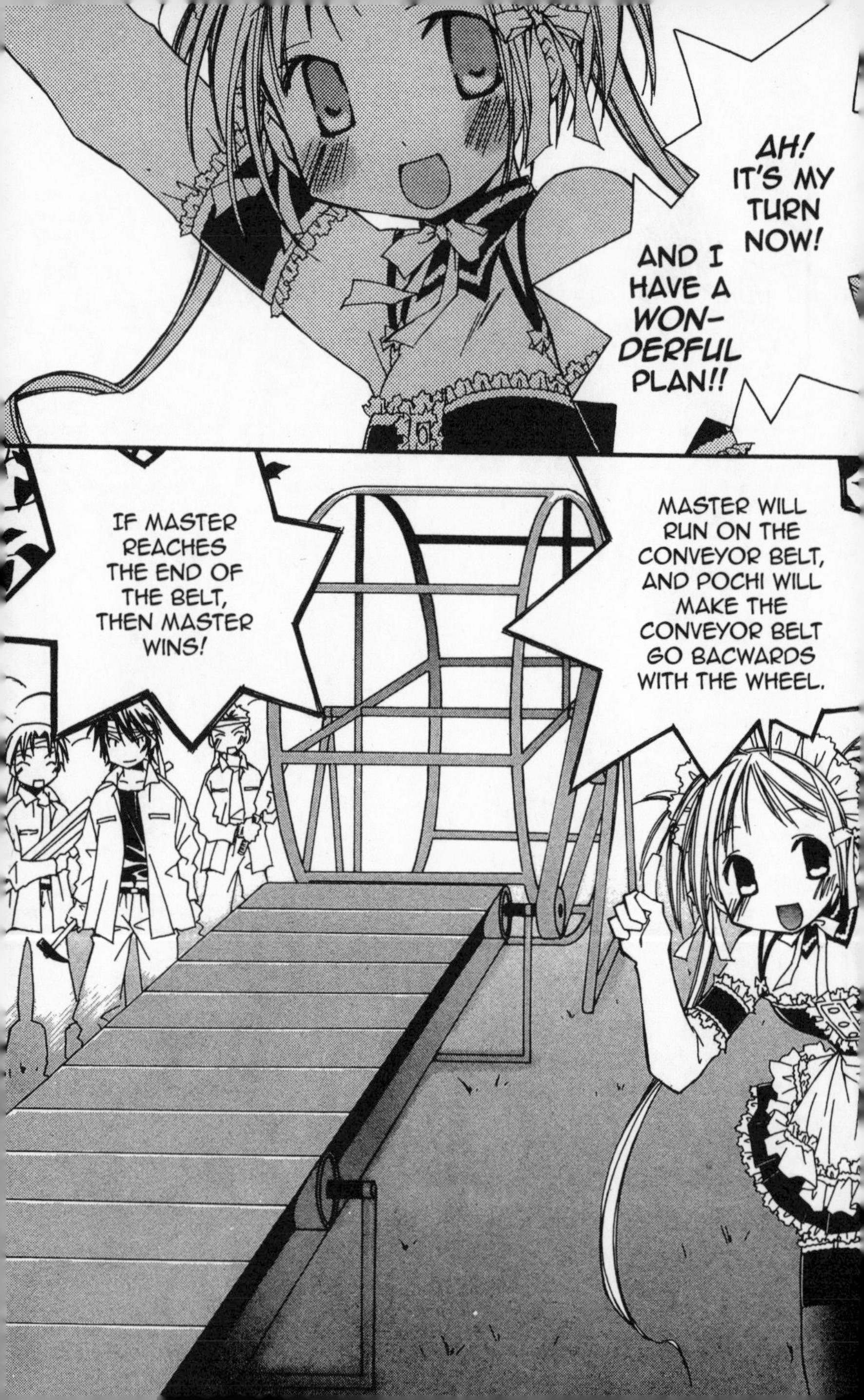
AH! IT'S MY TURN NOW!
AND I HAVE A WON-DERFUL PLAN!!
MASTER WILL RUN ON THE CONVEYOR BELT, AND POCHI WILL MAKE THE CONVEYOR BELT GO BACWARDS WITH THE WHEEL.
IF MASTER REACHES THE END OF THE BELT, THEN MASTER WINS!

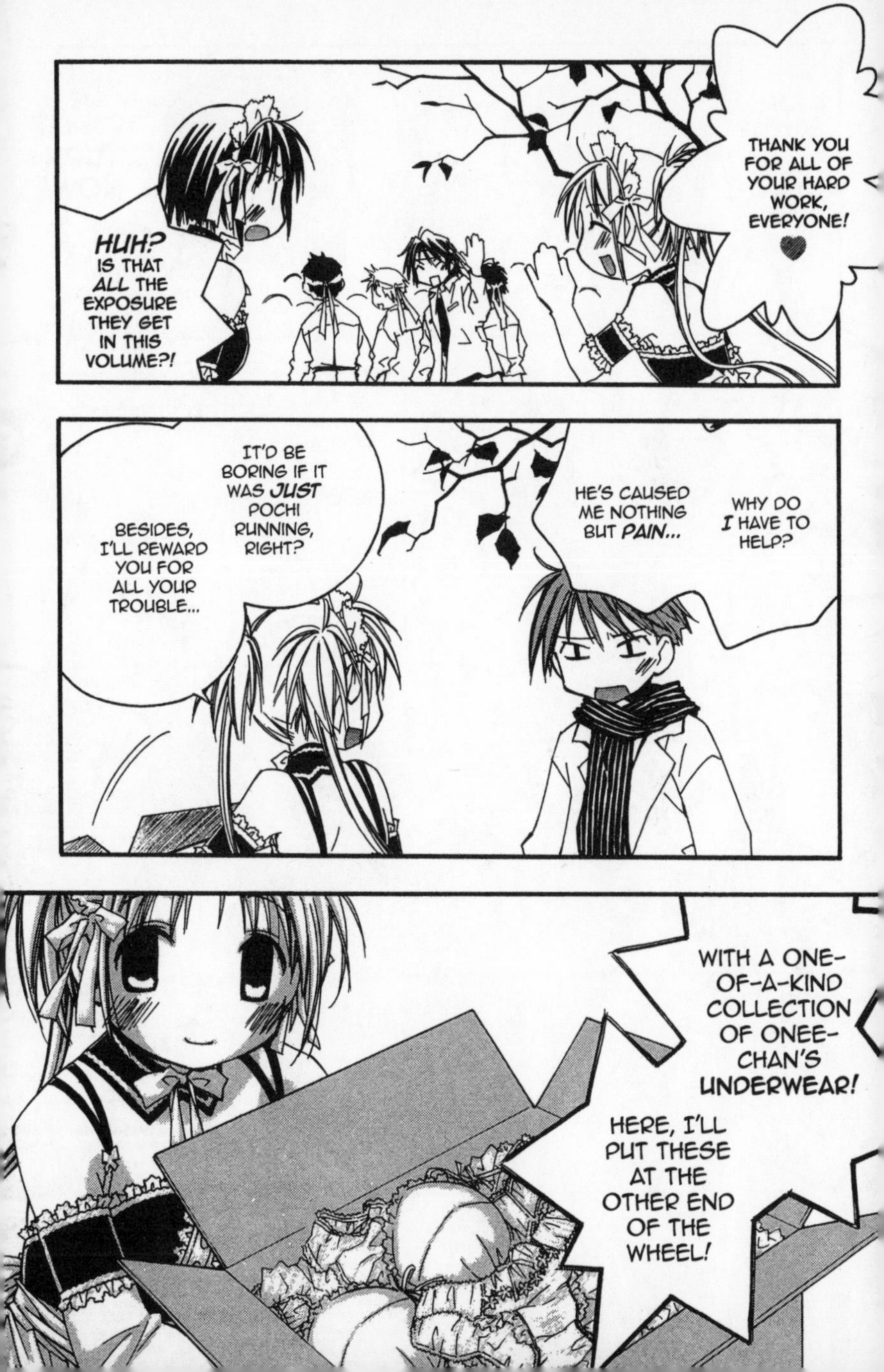
THANK YOU FOR ALL OF YOUR HARD WORK, EVERYONE!
HUH? IS THAT ALL THE EXPOSURE THEY GET IN THIS VOLUME?!
WHY DO I HAVE TO HELP?
HE'S CAUSED ME NOTHING BUT PAIN...
IT'D BE BORING IF IT WAS JUST POCHI RUNNING, RIGHT?
BESIDES, I'LL REWARD YOU FOR ALL YOUR TROUBLE...
WITH A ONE-OF-A-KIND COLLECTION OF ONEE-CHAN'S UNDERWEAR!
HERE, I'LL PUT THESE AT THE OTHER END OF THE WHEEL!

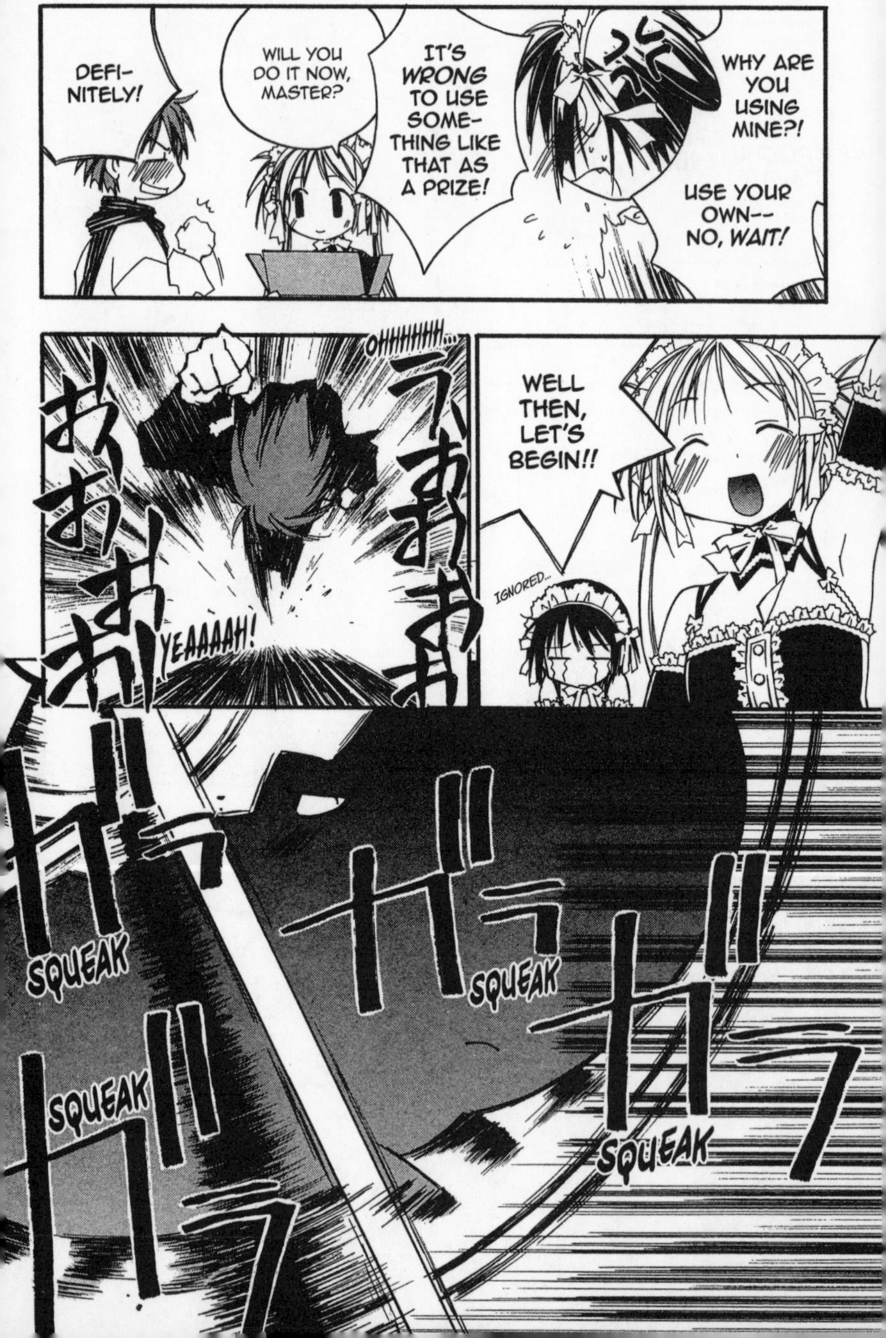
WHY ARE YOU USING MINE?!
USE YOUR OWN-- NO, WAIT!
IT'S *WRONG* TO USE SOME-THING LIKE THAT AS A PRIZE!
WILL YOU DO IT NOW, MASTER?
DEFI-NITELY!
WELL THEN, LET'S BEGIN!!
IGNORED...
OHHHHHHH...
YEAAAAH!
SQUEAK
SQUEAK
SQUEAK
SQUEAK

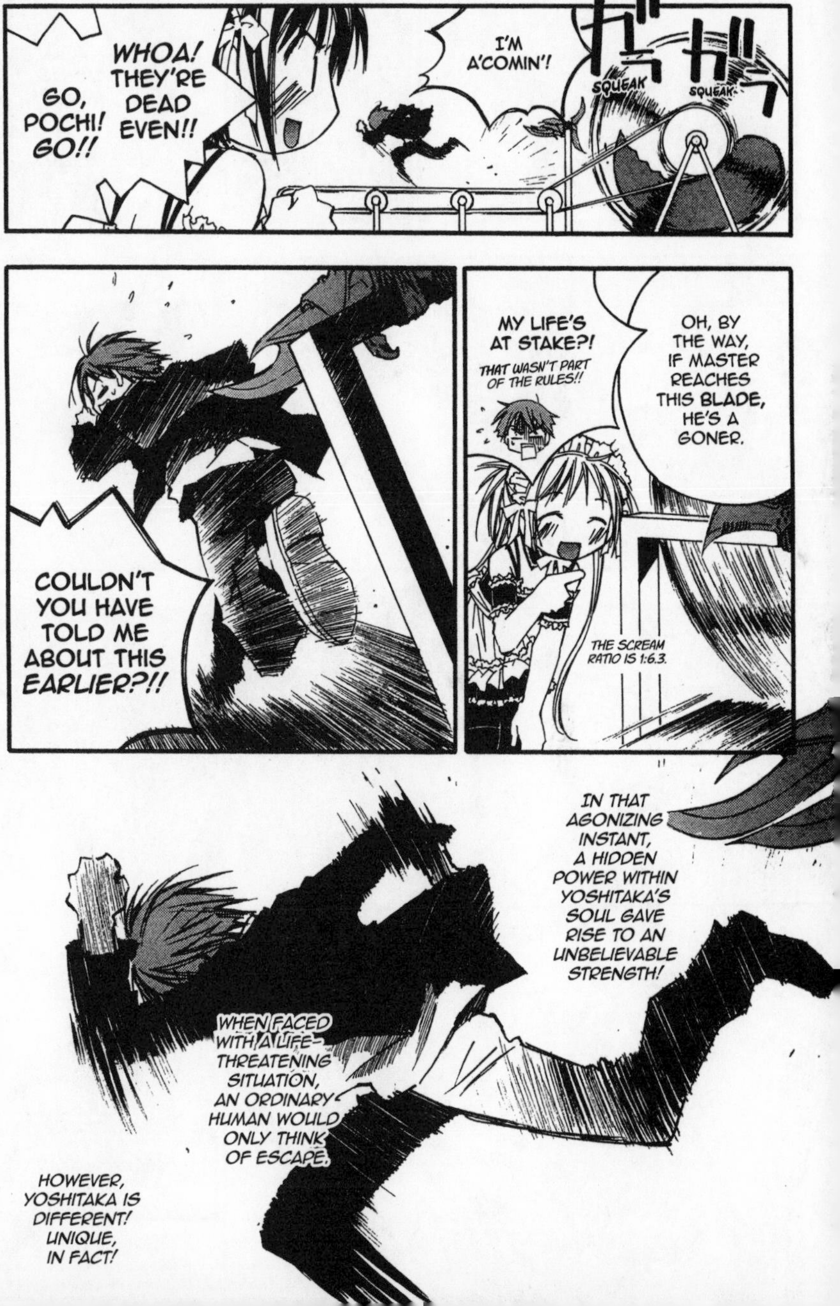
SQUEAK
SQUEAK
I'M A'COMIN'!
WHOA! THEY'RE DEAD EVEN!!
GO, POCHI! GO!!
OH, BY THE WAY, IF MASTER REACHES THIS BLADE, HE'S A GONER.
MY LIFE'S AT STAKE?!
THAT WASN'T PART OF THE RULES!!
THE SCREAM RATIO IS 1:6.3.
COULDN'T YOU HAVE TOLD ME ABOUT THIS EARLIER?!!
IN THAT AGONIZING INSTANT, A HIDDEN POWER WITHIN YOSHITAKA'S SOUL GAVE RISE TO AN UNBELIEVABLE STRENGTH!
WHEN FACED WITH A LIFE-THREATENING SITUATION, AN ORDINARY HUMAN WOULD ONLY THINK OF ESCAPE.
HOWEVER, YOSHITAKA IS DIFFERENT! UNIQUE, IN FACT!

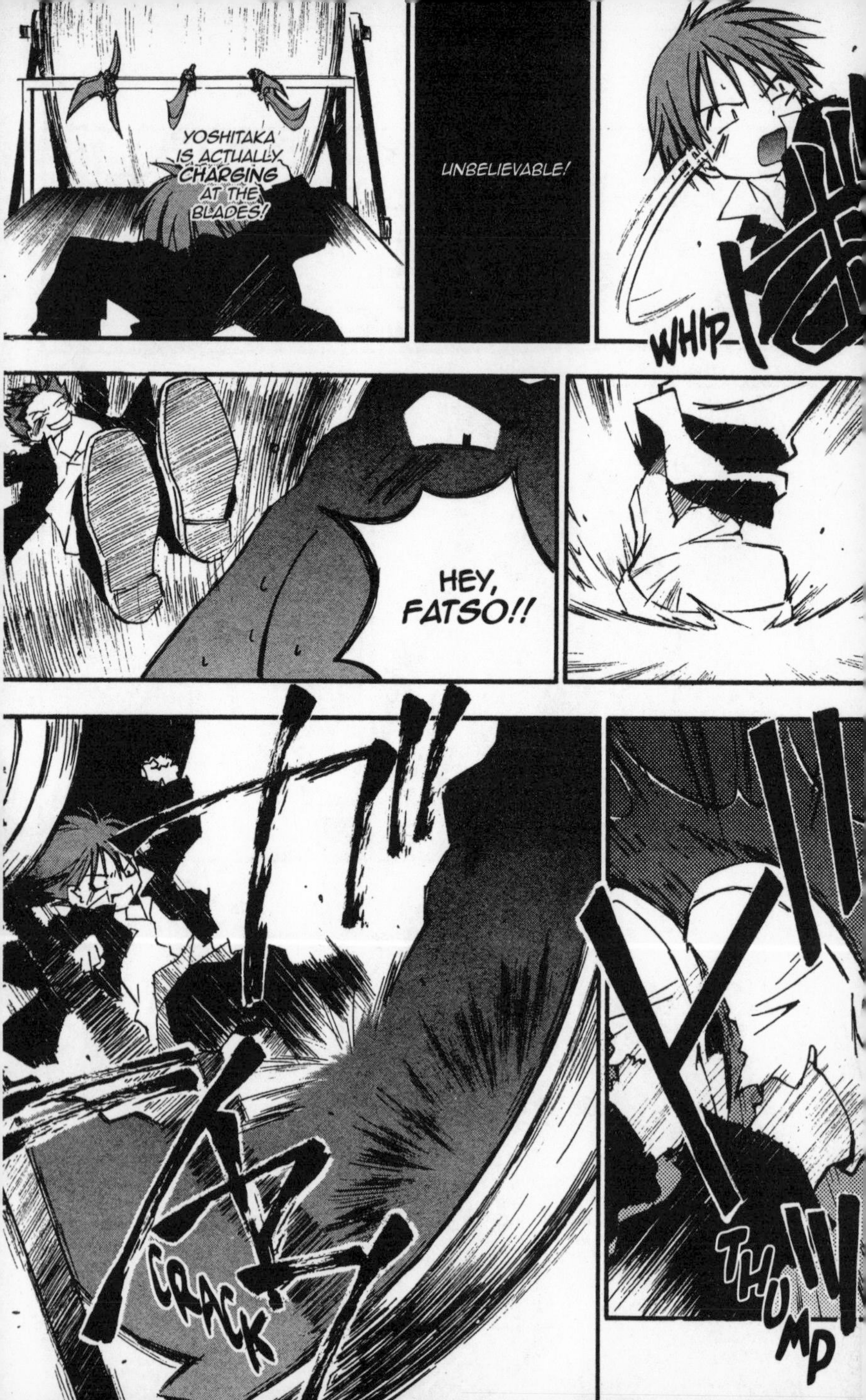
WHIP
UNBELIEVABLE!
YOSHITAKA IS ACTUALLY CHARGING AT THE BLADES!
HEY, FATSO!!
THUMP
CRACK

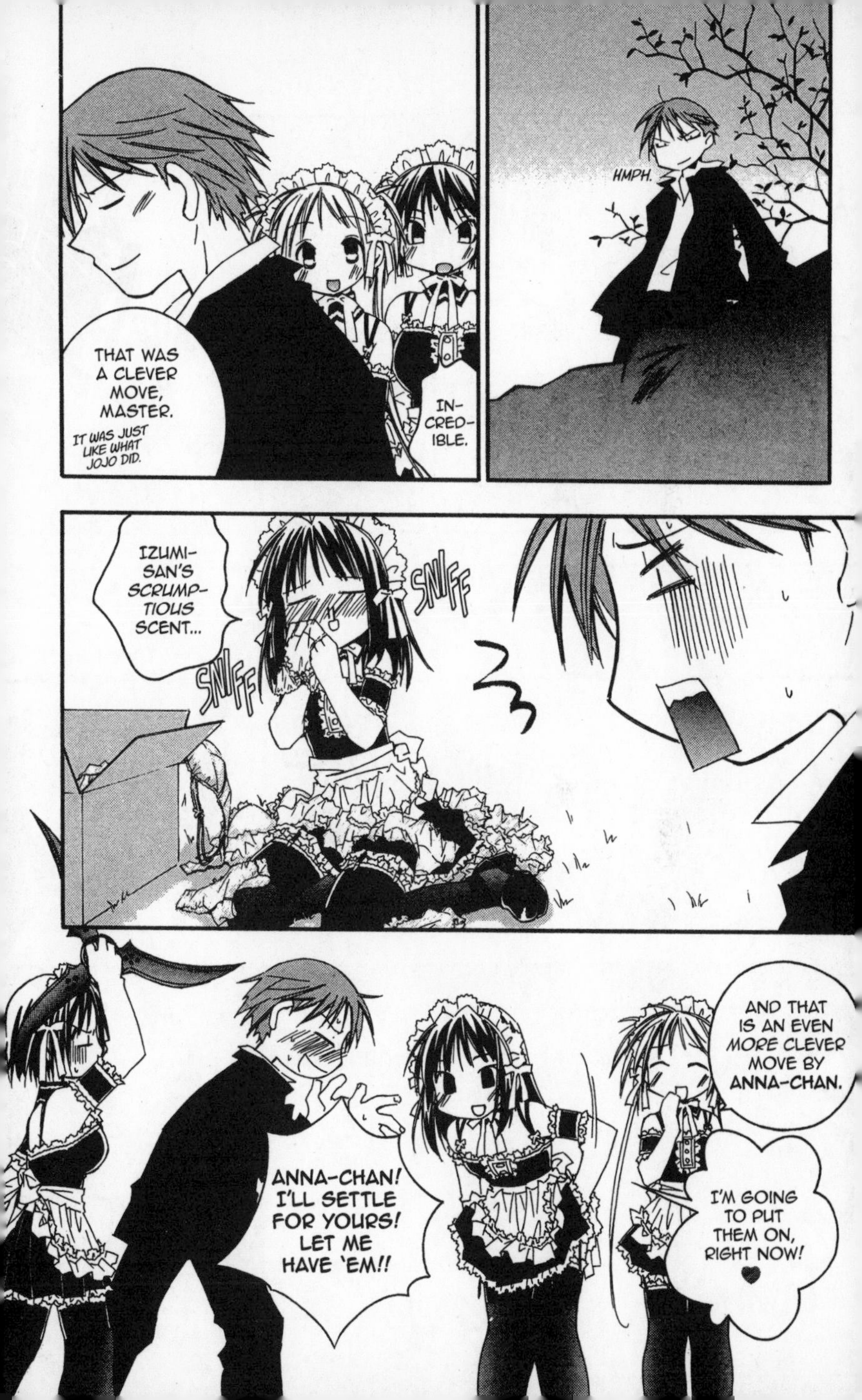
HMPH.
THAT WAS A CLEVER MOVE, MASTER.
IT WAS JUST LIKE WHAT JOJO DID.
INCREDIBLE.
SNIFFF
IZUMI-SAN'S SCRUMPTIOUS SCENT...
SNIFFF
AND THAT IS AN EVEN MORE CLEVER MOVE BY ANNA-CHAN.
I'M GOING TO PUT THEM ON, RIGHT NOW! ♥
ANNA-CHAN! I'LL SETTLE FOR YOURS! LET ME HAVE 'EM!!

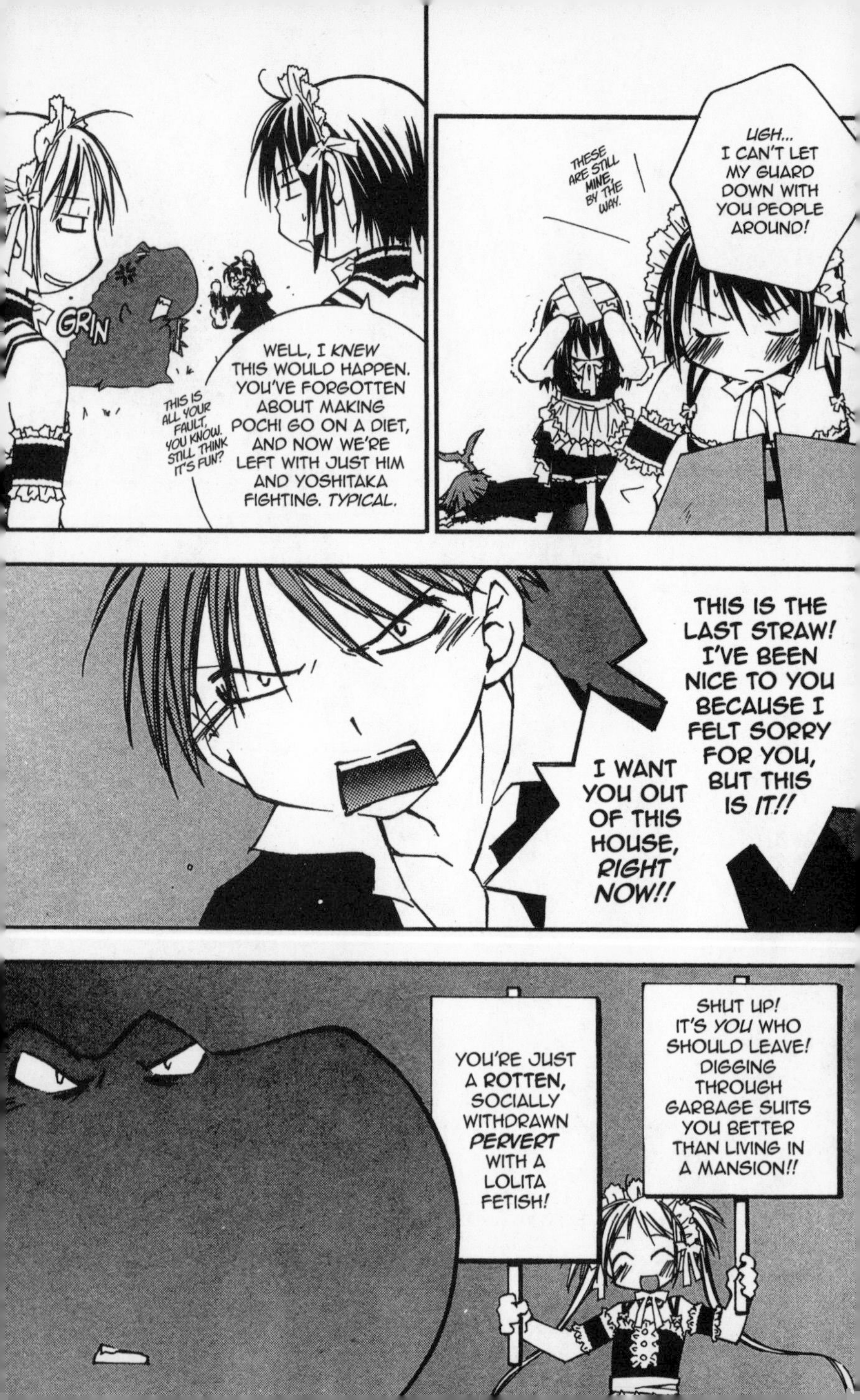
UGH... I CAN'T LET MY GUARD DOWN WITH YOU PEOPLE AROUND!
THESE ARE STILL MINE, BY THE WAY.
GRIN
WELL, I *KNEW* THIS WOULD HAPPEN. YOU'VE FORGOTTEN ABOUT MAKING POCHI GO ON A DIET, AND NOW WE'RE LEFT WITH JUST HIM AND YOSHITAKA FIGHTING. *TYPICAL*.
THIS IS ALL YOUR FAULT, YOU KNOW. STILL THINK IT'S FUN?
THIS IS THE LAST STRAW! I'VE BEEN NICE TO YOU BECAUSE I FELT SORRY FOR YOU, BUT THIS IS *IT*!!
I WANT YOU OUT OF THIS HOUSE, *RIGHT NOW*!!
SHUT UP! IT'S *YOU* WHO SHOULD LEAVE! DIGGING THROUGH GARBAGE SUITS YOU BETTER THAN LIVING IN A MANSION!!
YOU'RE JUST A **ROTTEN**, SOCIALLY WITHDRAWN ***PERVERT*** WITH A LOLITA FETISH!

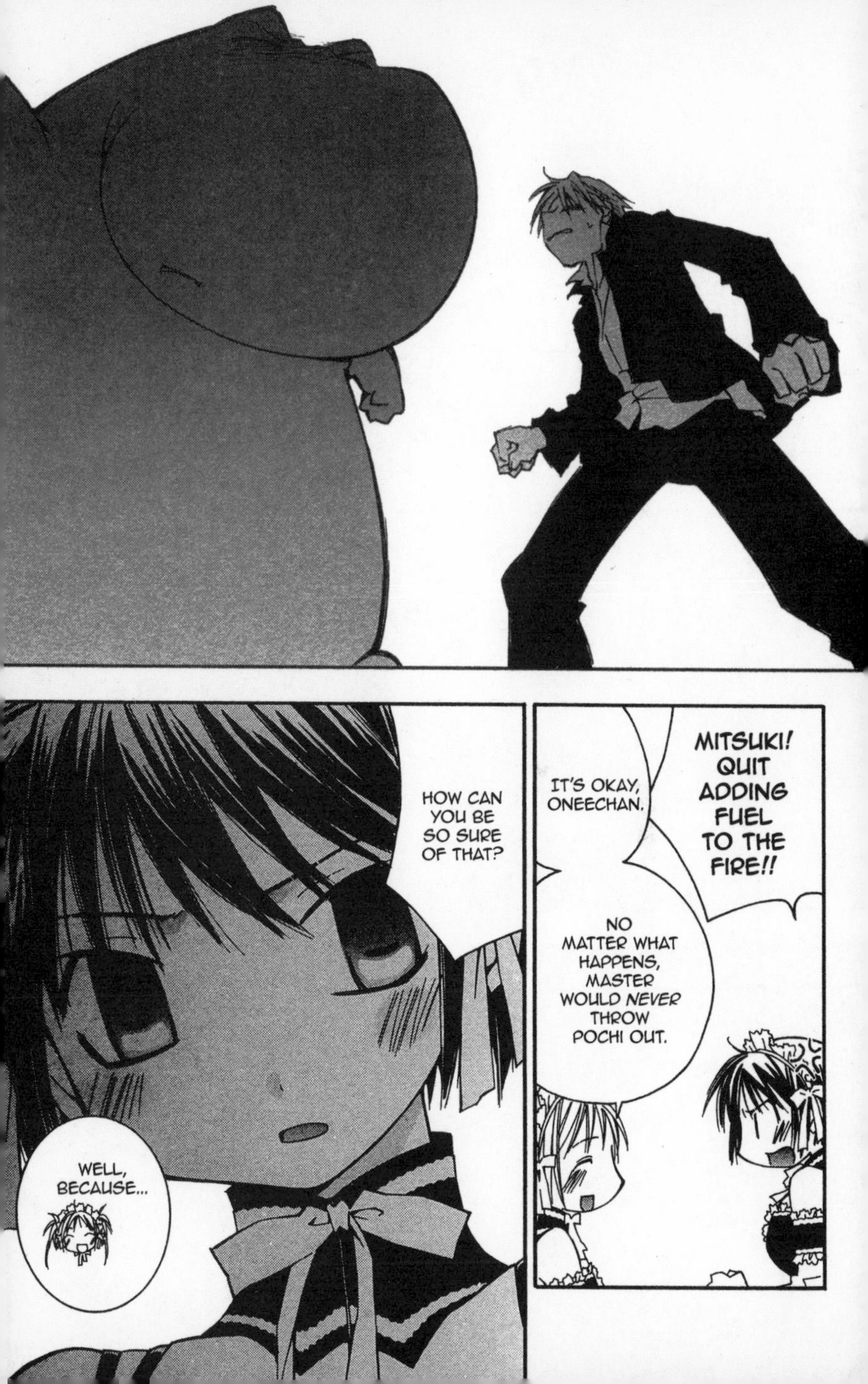
MITSUKI! QUIT ADDING FUEL TO THE FIRE!!
IT'S OKAY, ONEECHAN.
NO MATTER WHAT HAPPENS, MASTER WOULD *NEVER* THROW POCHI OUT.
HOW CAN YOU BE SO SURE OF THAT?
WELL, BECAUSE...

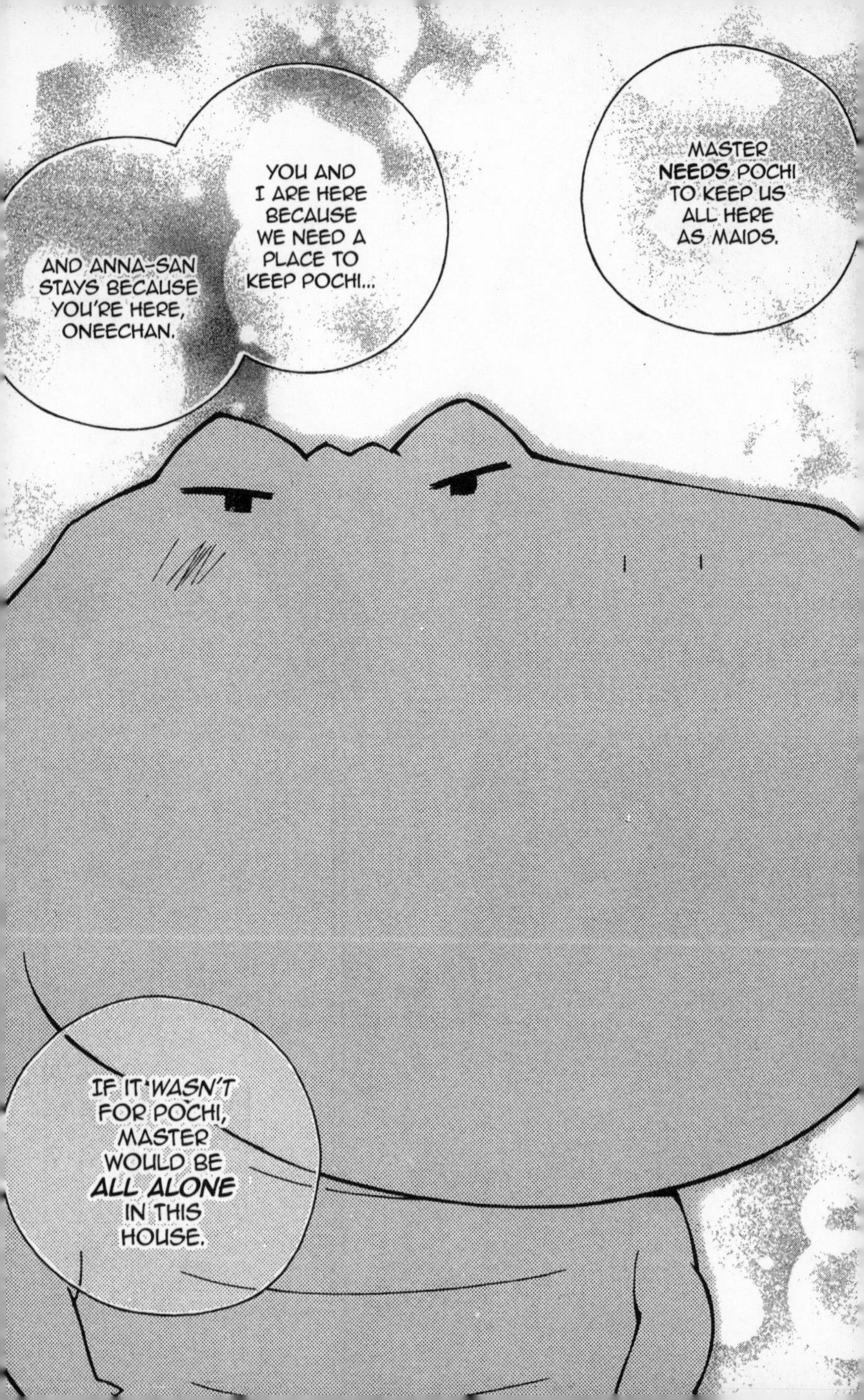
MASTER NEEDS POCHI TO KEEP US ALL HERE AS MAIDS.
YOU AND I ARE HERE BECAUSE WE NEED A PLACE TO KEEP POCHI...
AND ANNA-SAN STAYS BECAUSE YOU'RE HERE, ONEECHAN.
IF IT WASN'T FOR POCHI, MASTER WOULD BE ALL ALONE IN THIS HOUSE.

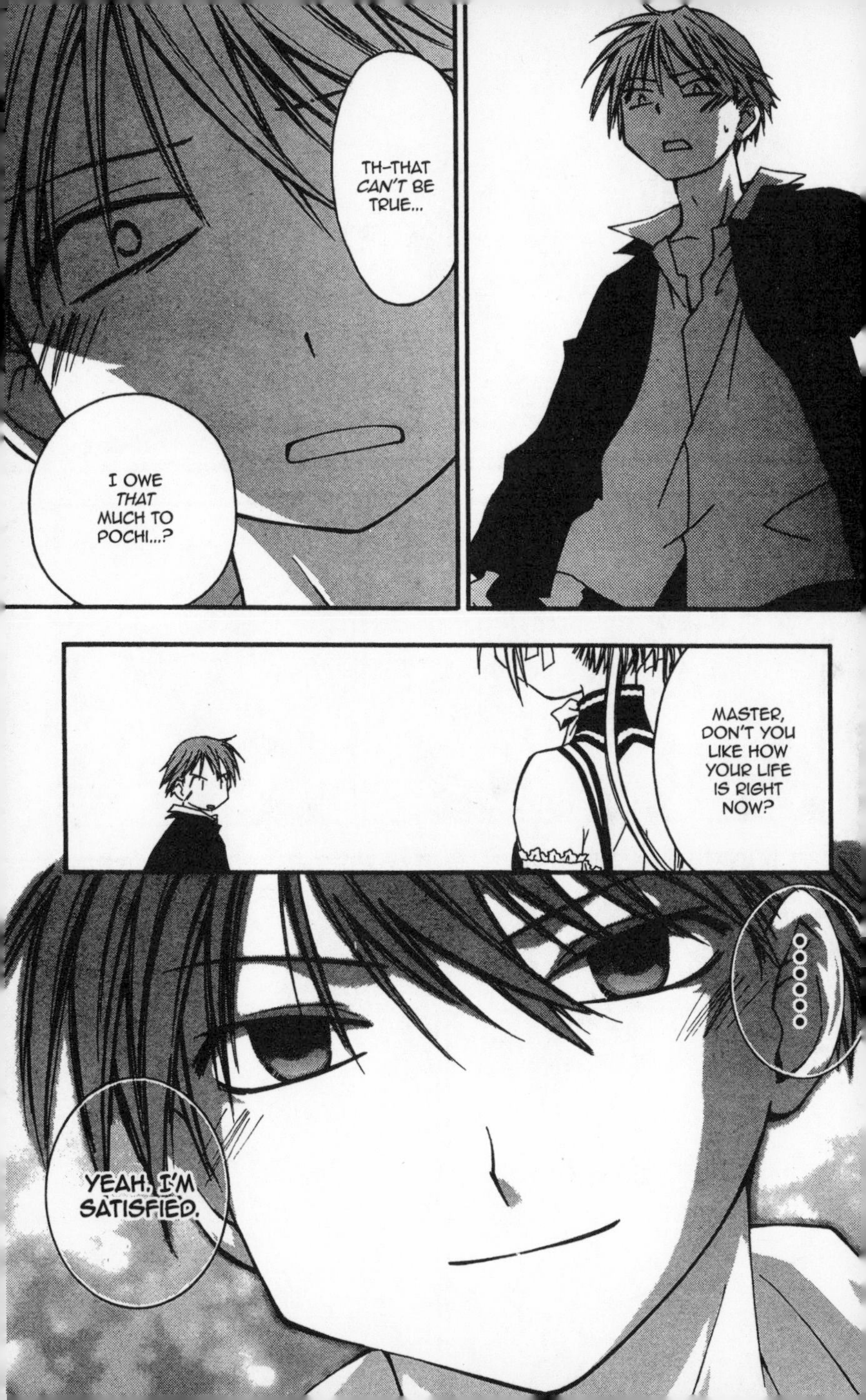
TH-THAT *CAN'T* BE TRUE...
I OWE *THAT* MUCH TO POCHI...?
MASTER, DON'T YOU LIKE HOW YOUR LIFE IS RIGHT NOW?
......
YEAH. I'M SATISFIED.

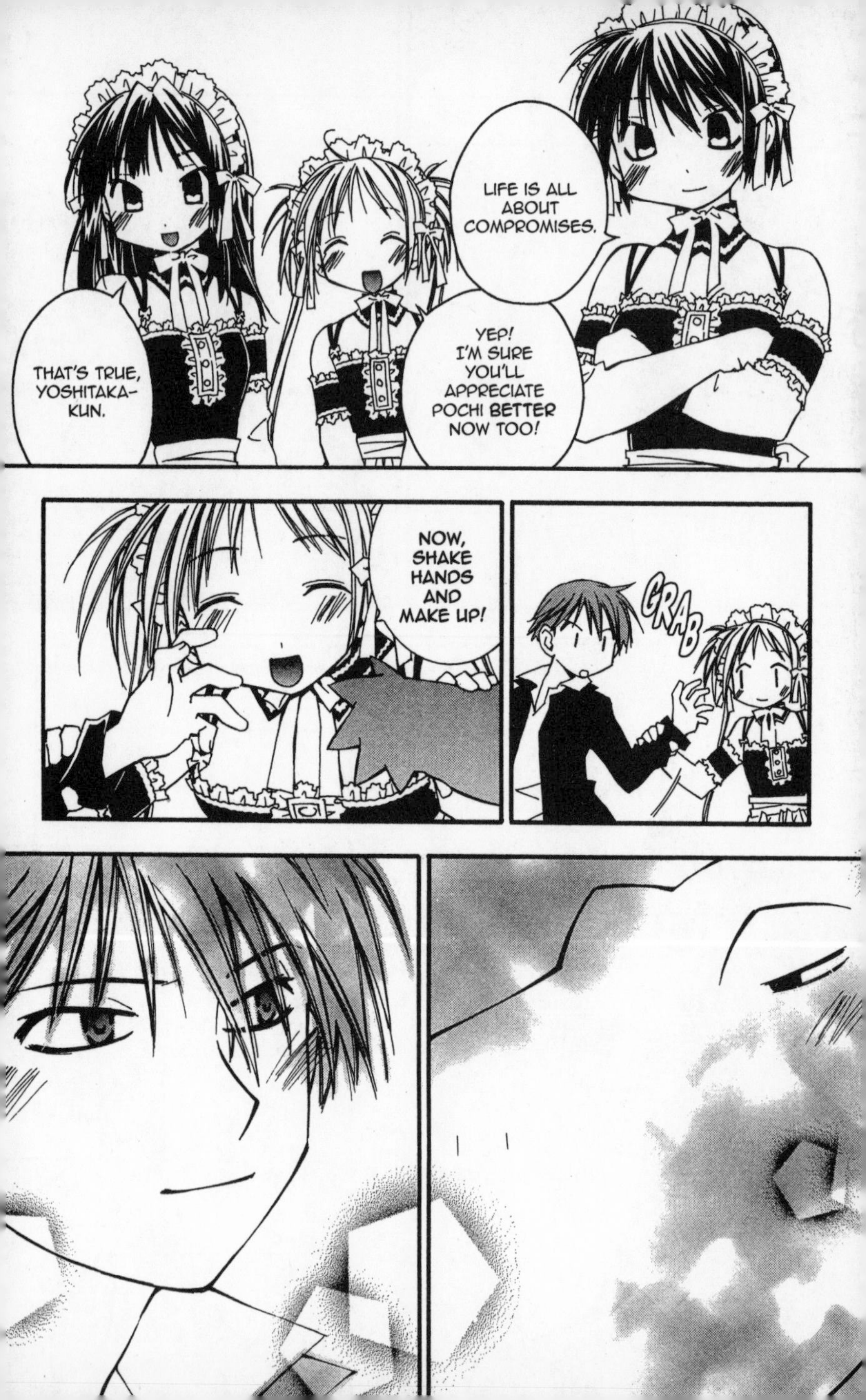
LIFE IS ALL ABOUT COMPROMISES.
YEP! I'M SURE YOU'LL APPRECIATE POCHI BETTER NOW TOO!
THAT'S TRUE, YOSHITAKA-KUN.
GRAB
NOW, SHAKE HANDS AND MAKE UP!

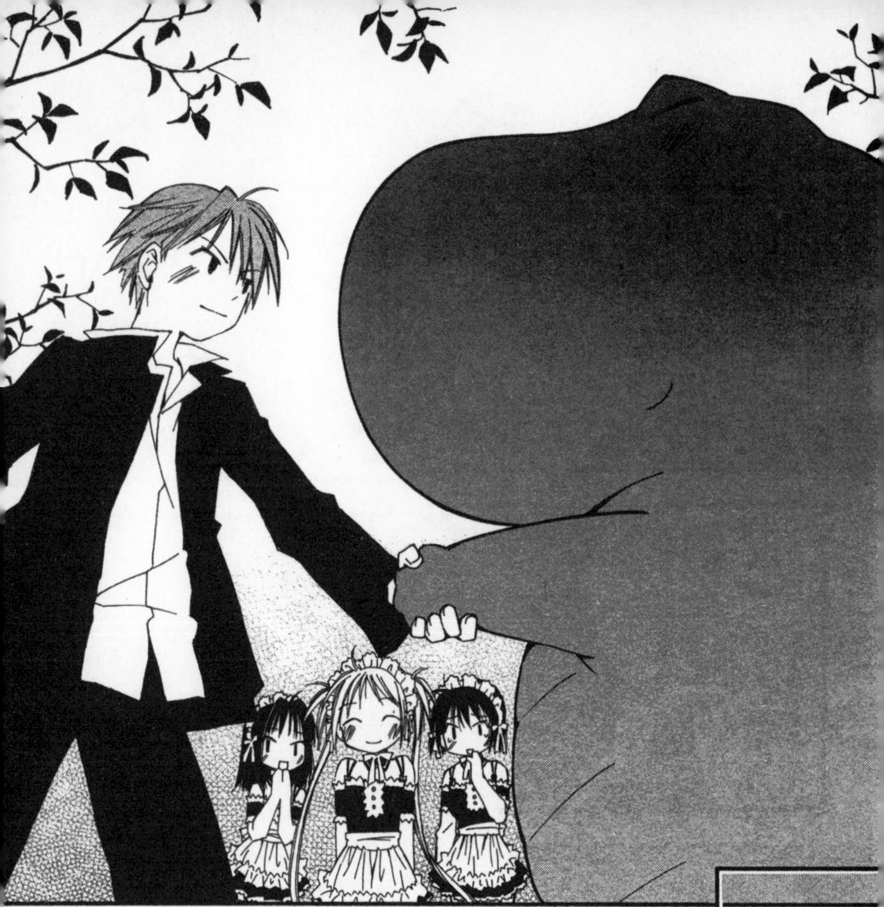
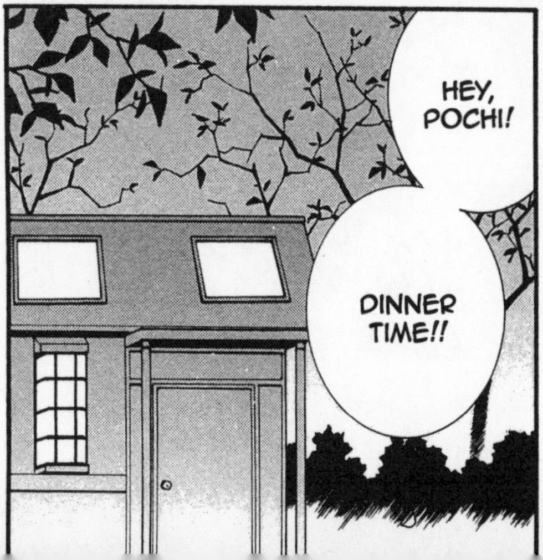
HEY, POCHI!
DINNER TIME!!

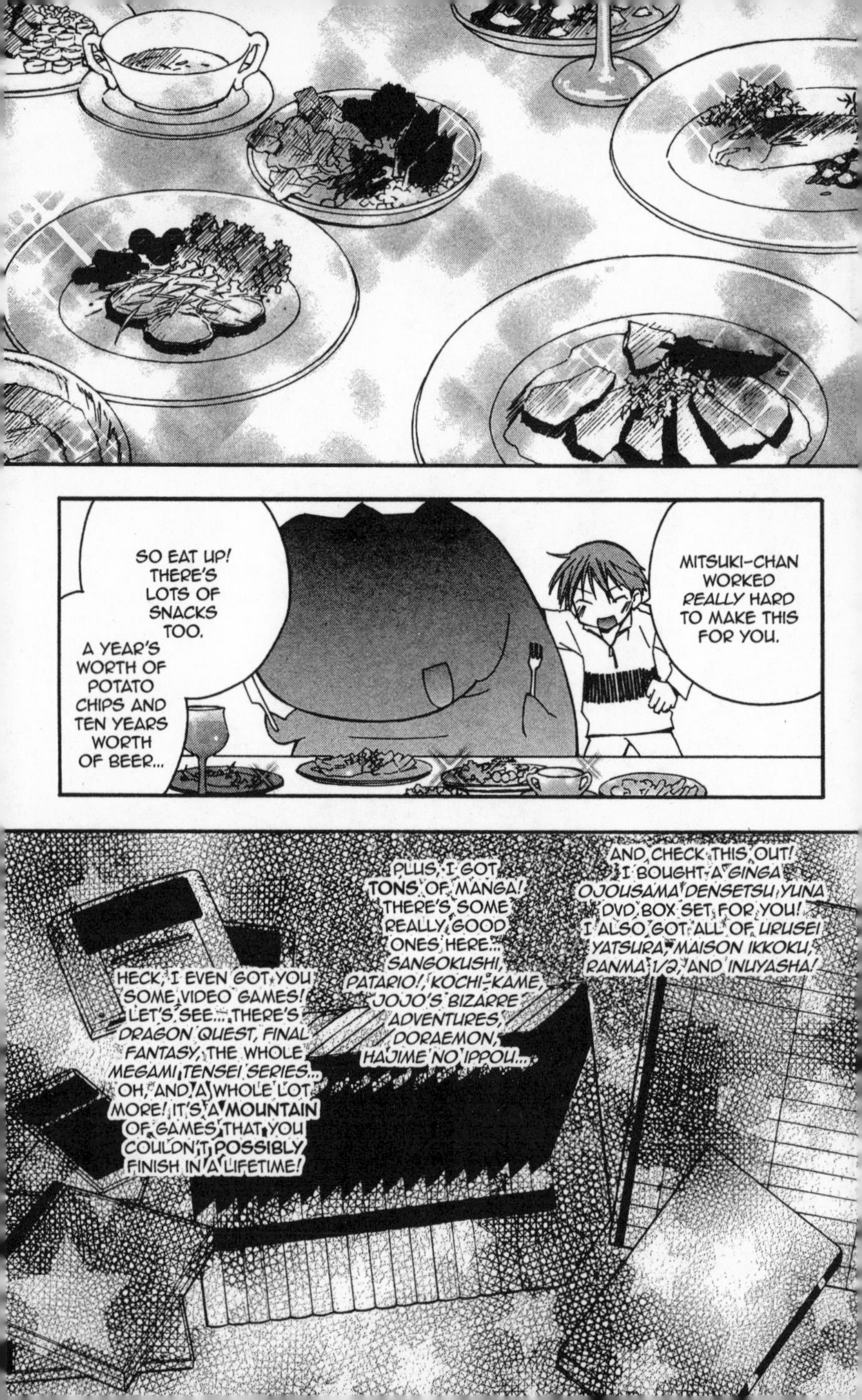
MITSUKI-CHAN WORKED REALLY HARD TO MAKE THIS FOR YOU.
SO EAT UP! THERE'S LOTS OF SNACKS TOO.
A YEAR'S WORTH OF POTATO CHIPS AND TEN YEARS WORTH OF BEER...
AND CHECK THIS OUT! I BOUGHT A GINGA OJOUSAMA DENSETSU YUNA DVD BOX SET FOR YOU! I ALSO GOT ALL OF URUSEI YATSURA, MAISON IKKOKU, RANMA 1/2, AND INUYASHA!
PLUS, I GOT TONS OF MANGA! THERE'S SOME REALLY GOOD ONES HERE... SANGOKUSHI, PATARIO!, KOCHI-KAME, JOJO'S BIZARRE ADVENTURES, DORAEMON, HAJIME NO IPPOU...
HECK, I EVEN GOT YOU SOME VIDEO GAMES! LET'S SEE... THERE'S DRAGON QUEST, FINAL FANTASY, THE WHOLE MEGAMI TENSEI SERIES... OH, AND A WHOLE LOT MORE! IT'S A MOUNTAIN OF GAMES THAT YOU COULDN'T POSSIBLY FINISH IN A LIFETIME!

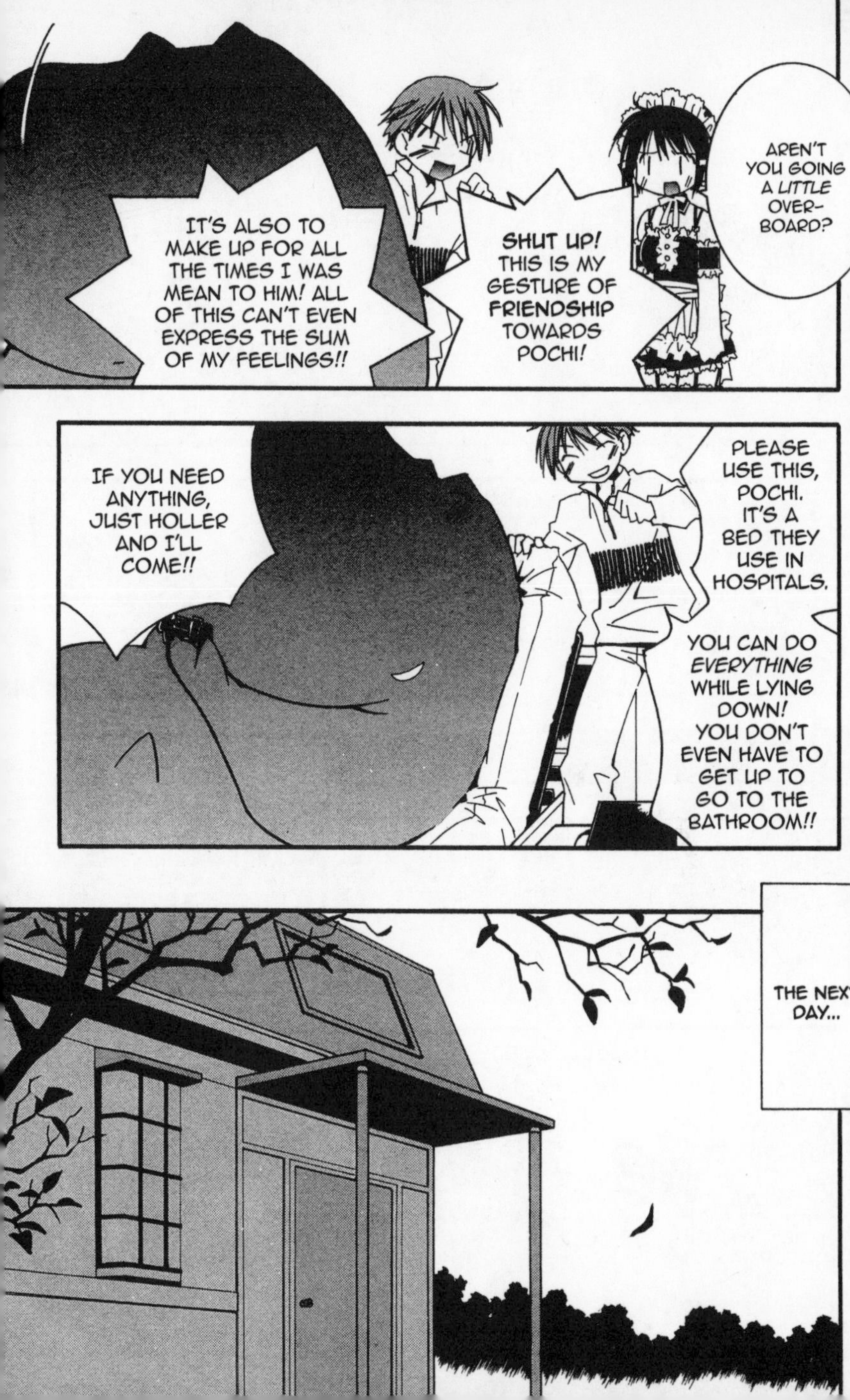
AREN'T YOU GOING A *LITTLE* OVER-BOARD?
SHUT UP! THIS IS MY GESTURE OF FRIENDSHIP TOWARDS POCHI!
IT'S ALSO TO MAKE UP FOR ALL THE TIMES I WAS MEAN TO HIM! ALL OF THIS CAN'T EVEN EXPRESS THE SUM OF MY FEELINGS!!
PLEASE USE THIS, POCHI. IT'S A BED THEY USE IN HOSPITALS.
YOU CAN DO *EVERYTHING* WHILE LYING DOWN! YOU DON'T EVEN HAVE TO GET UP TO GO TO THE BATHROOM!!
IF YOU NEED ANYTHING, JUST HOLLER AND I'LL COME!!
THE NEXT DAY...

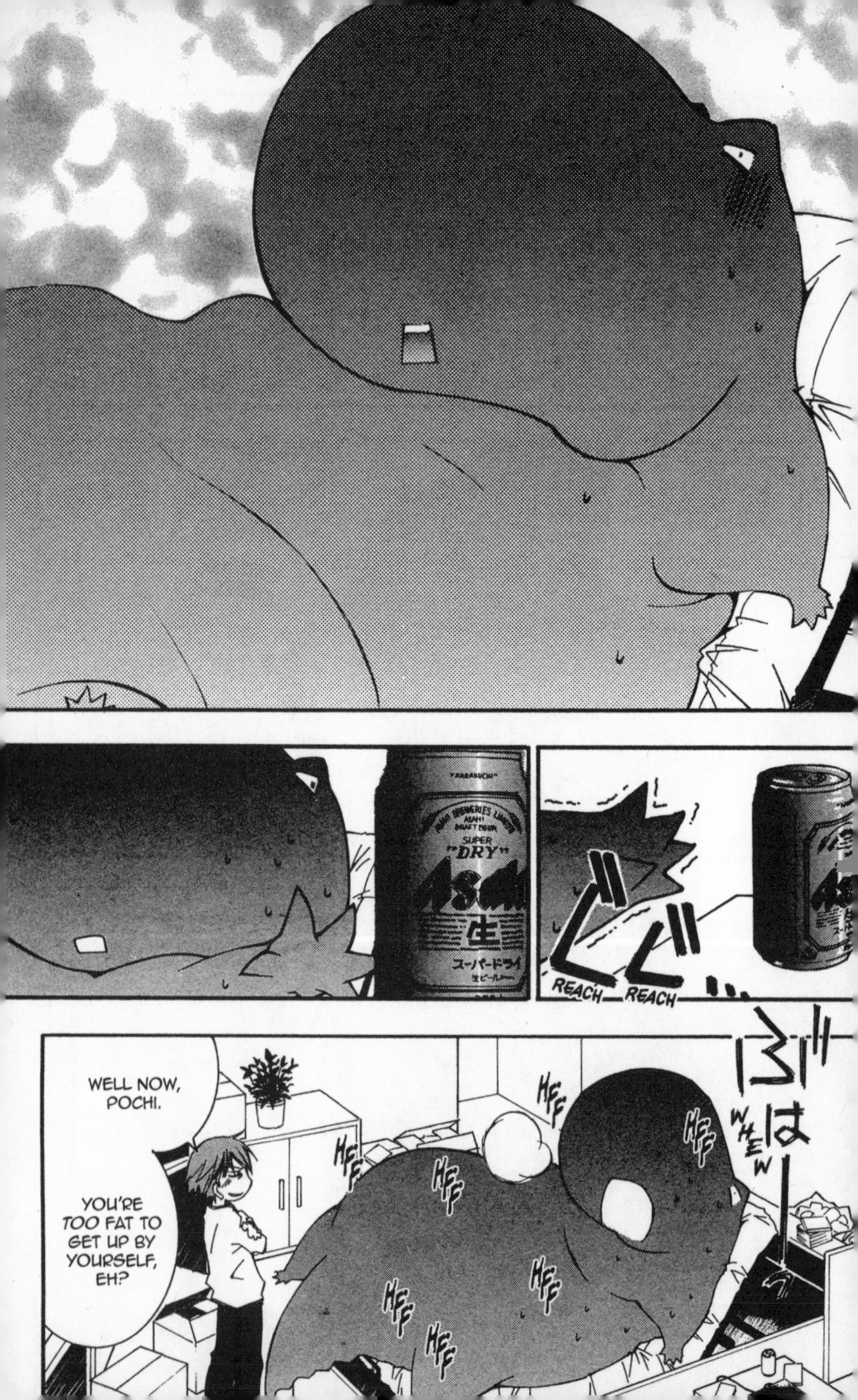
ぐぐ…
REACH REACH
SUPER
"DRY"
スーパードライ
ぶはー
WHEW
HFF HFF HFF HFF HFF HFF HFF
WELL NOW, POCHI.
YOU'RE *TOO* FAT TO GET UP BY YOURSELF, EH?

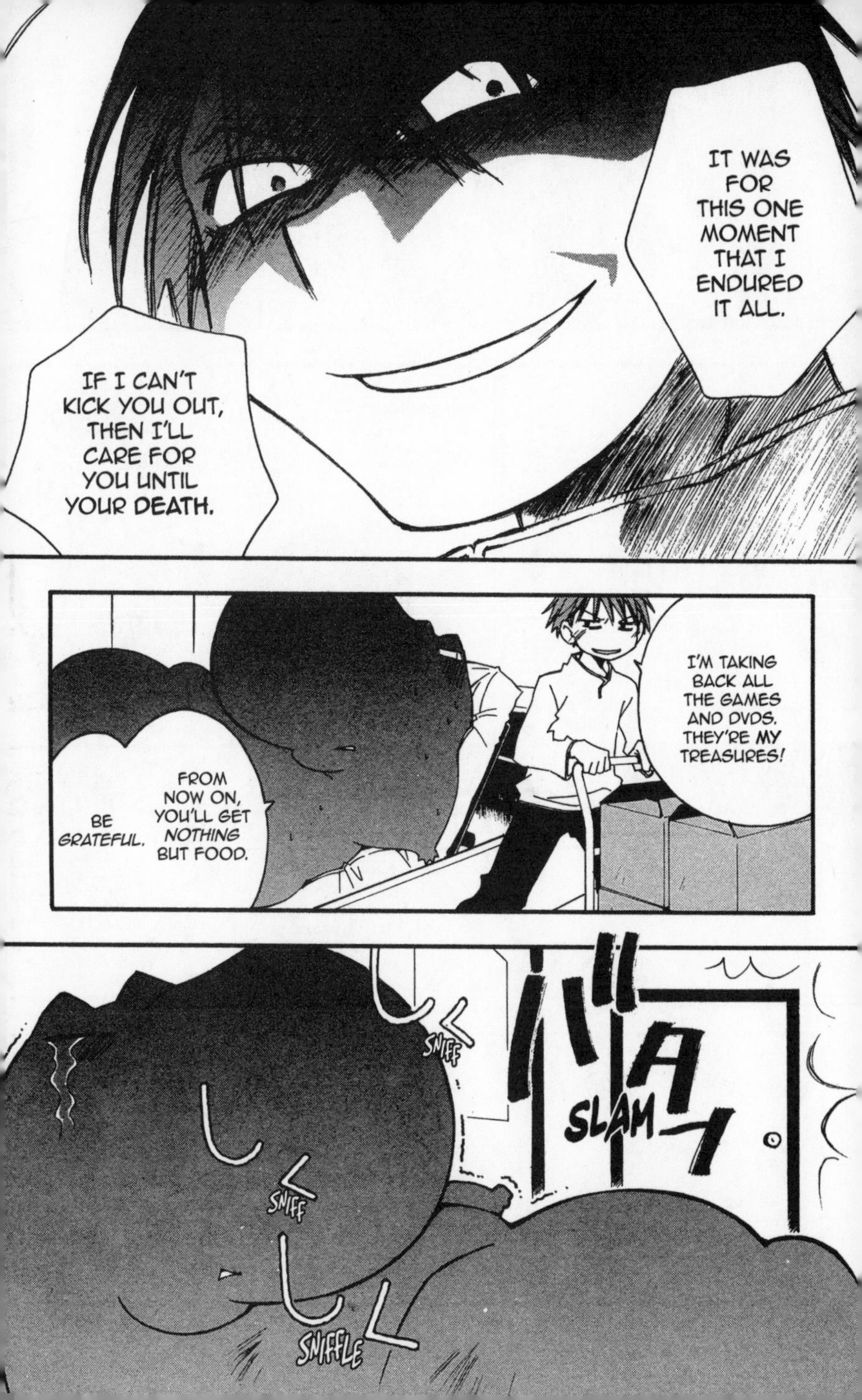

IT WAS FOR THIS ONE MOMENT THAT I ENDURED IT ALL.
IF I CAN'T KICK YOU OUT, THEN I'LL CARE FOR YOU UNTIL YOUR DEATH.
I'M TAKING BACK ALL THE GAMES AND DVDS. THEY'RE MY TREASURES!
FROM NOW ON, YOU'LL GET NOTHING BUT FOOD.
BE GRATEFUL.
SLAM
SNIFF
SNIFF
SNIFFLE

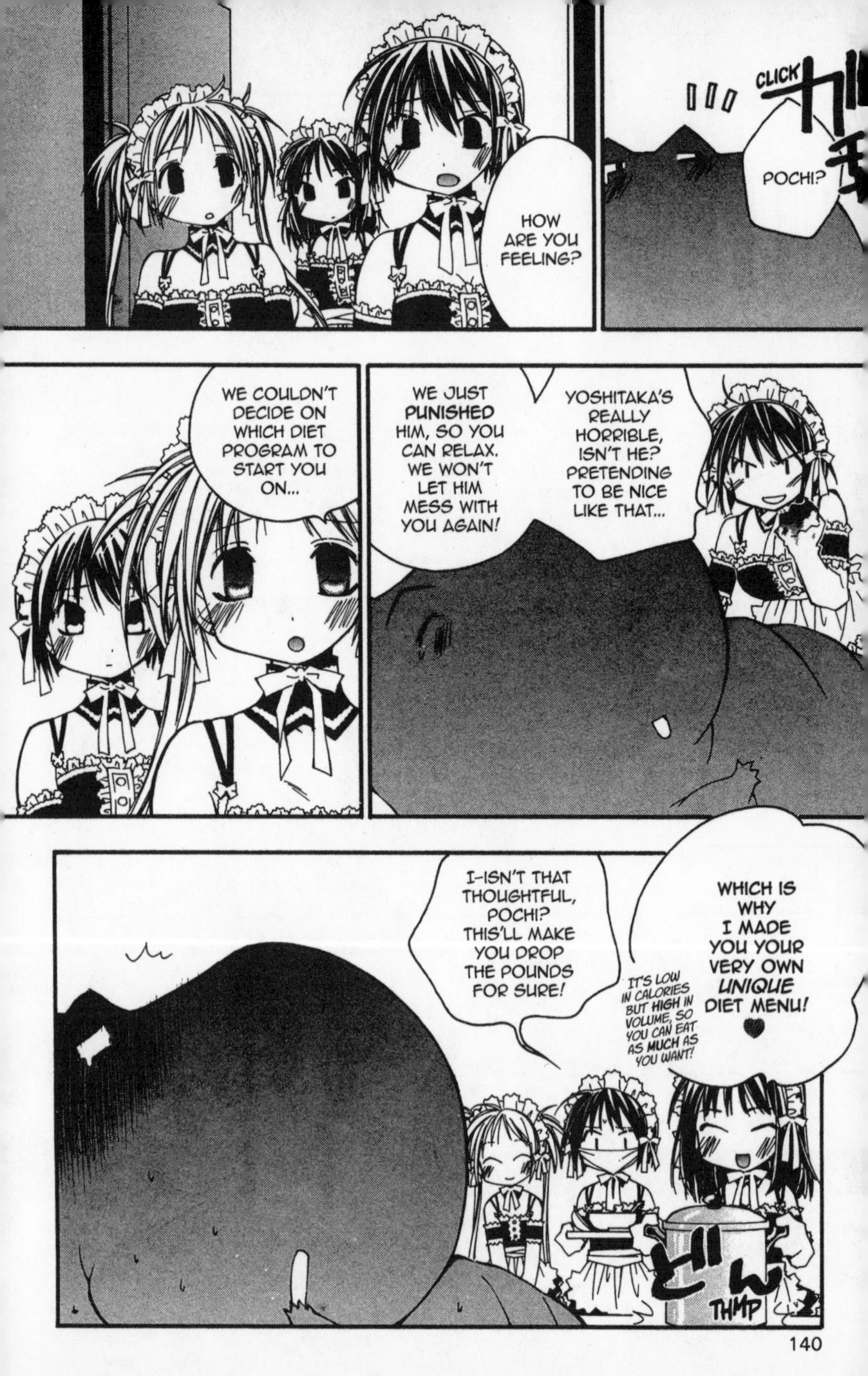
CLICK
POCHI?
HOW ARE YOU FEELING?
YOSHITAKA'S REALLY HORRIBLE, ISN'T HE? PRETENDING TO BE NICE LIKE THAT...
WE JUST PUNISHED HIM, SO YOU CAN RELAX. WE WON'T LET HIM MESS WITH YOU AGAIN!
WE COULDN'T DECIDE ON WHICH DIET PROGRAM TO START YOU ON...
WHICH IS WHY I MADE YOU YOUR VERY OWN UNIQUE DIET MENU! ♥
IT'S LOW IN CALORIES BUT HIGH IN VOLUME, SO YOU CAN EAT AS MUCH AS YOU WANT!
I-ISN'T THAT THOUGHTFUL, POCHI? THIS'LL MAKE YOU DROP THE POUNDS FOR SURE!
THMP

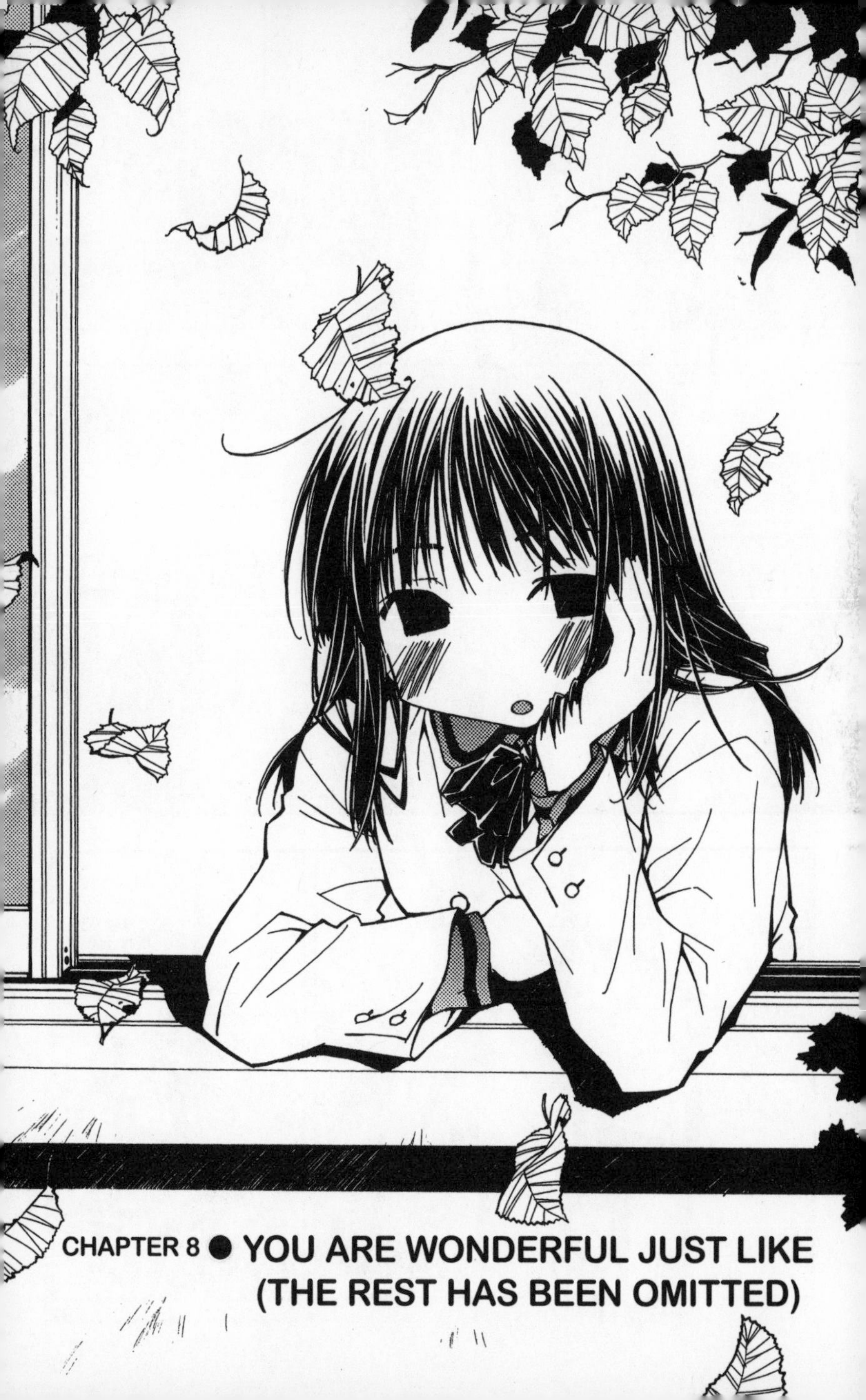

CHAPTER 8 ● YOU ARE WONDERFUL JUST LIKE (THE REST HAS BEEN OMITTED)

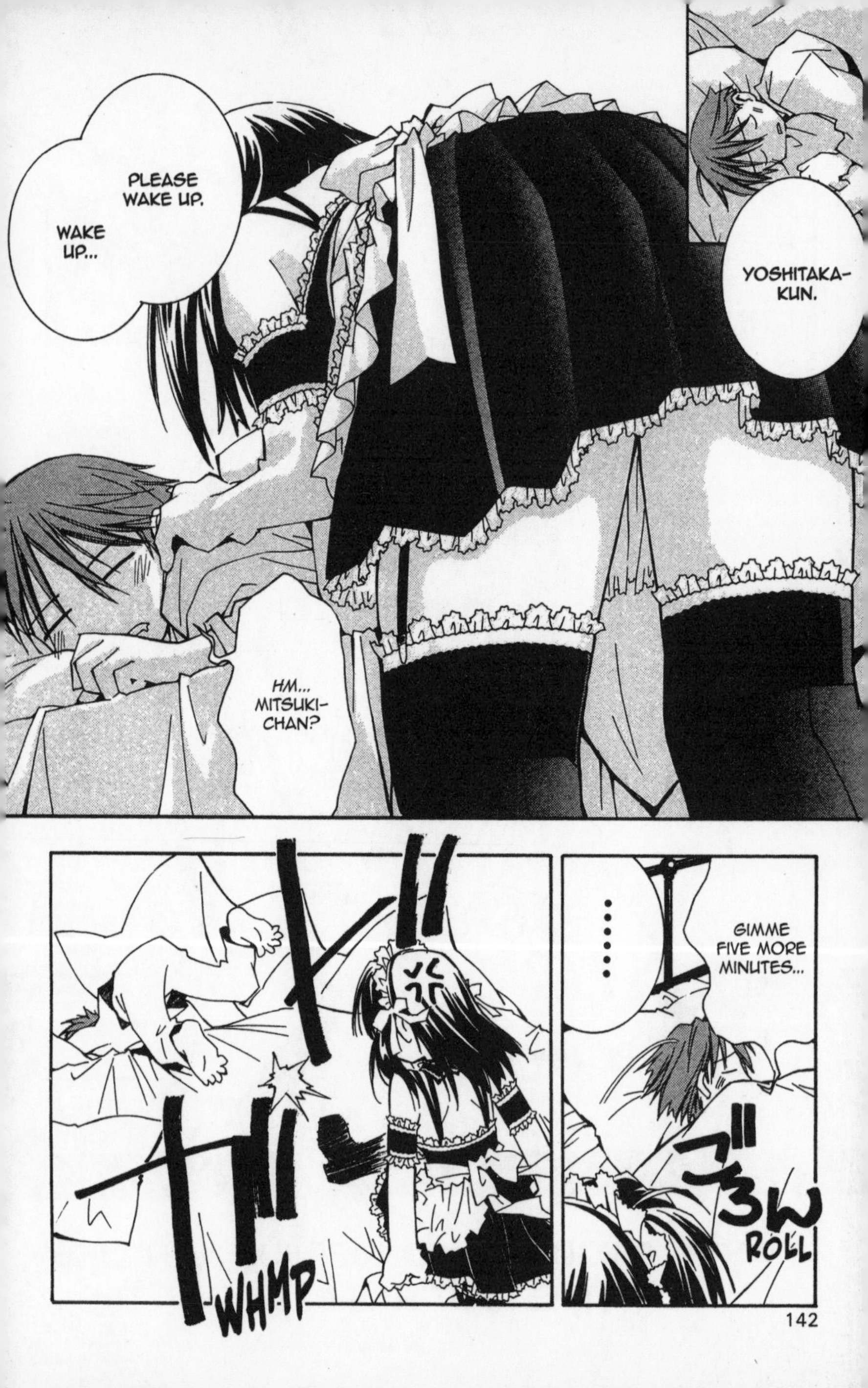
YOSHITAKA-KUN.
PLEASE WAKE UP.
WAKE UP...
HM... MITSUKI-CHAN?
GIMME FIVE MORE MINUTES...
......
ごろ
ROLL
WHMP

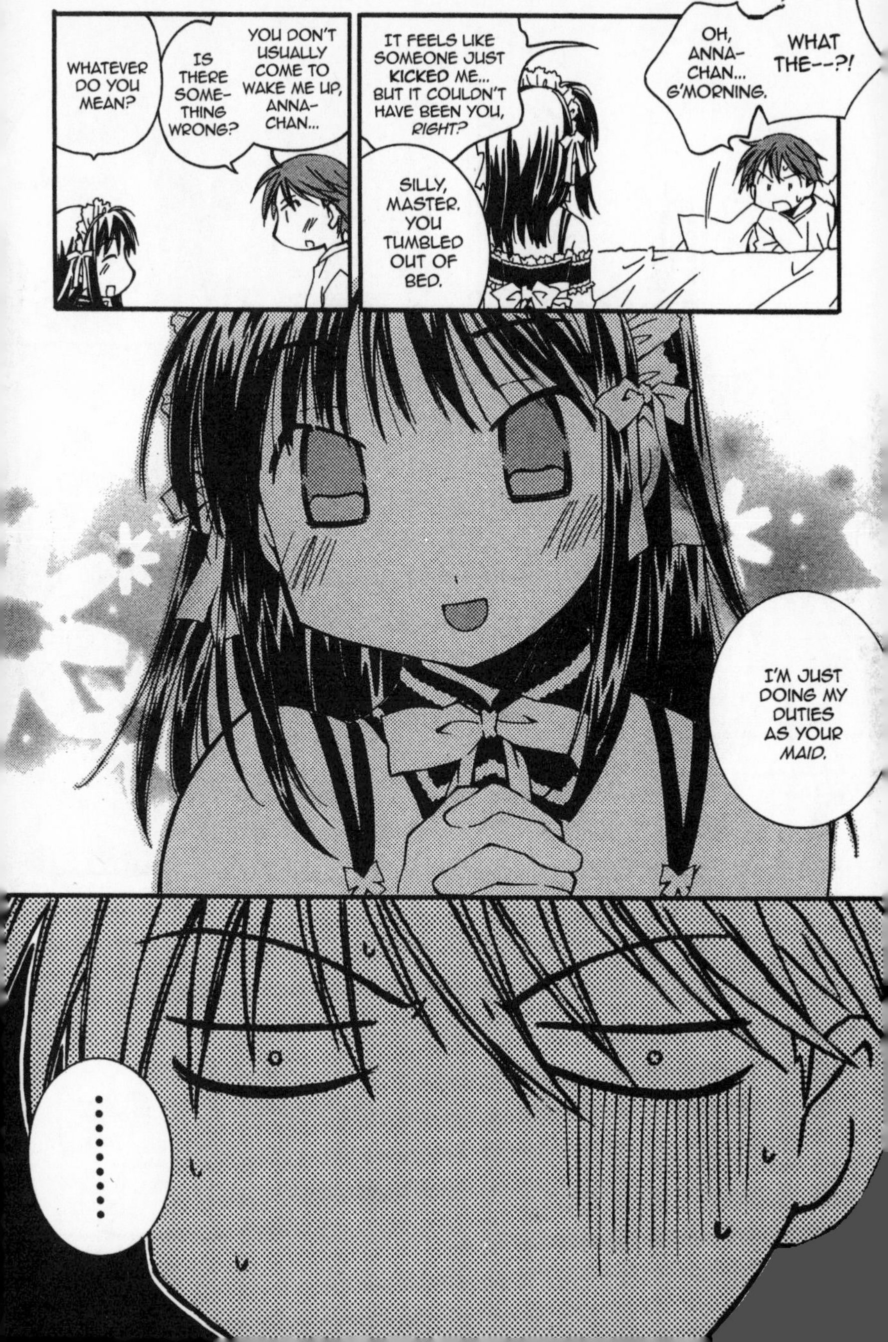
WHAT THE--?!
OH, ANNA-CHAN... G'MORNING.
IT FEELS LIKE SOMEONE JUST **KICKED** ME... BUT IT COULDN'T HAVE BEEN YOU, *RIGHT?*
SILLY, MASTER. YOU TUMBLED OUT OF BED.
YOU DON'T USUALLY COME TO WAKE ME UP, ANNA-CHAN...
IS THERE SOME-THING WRONG?
WHATEVER DO YOU MEAN?
I'M JUST DOING MY DUTIES AS YOUR *MAID.*
....

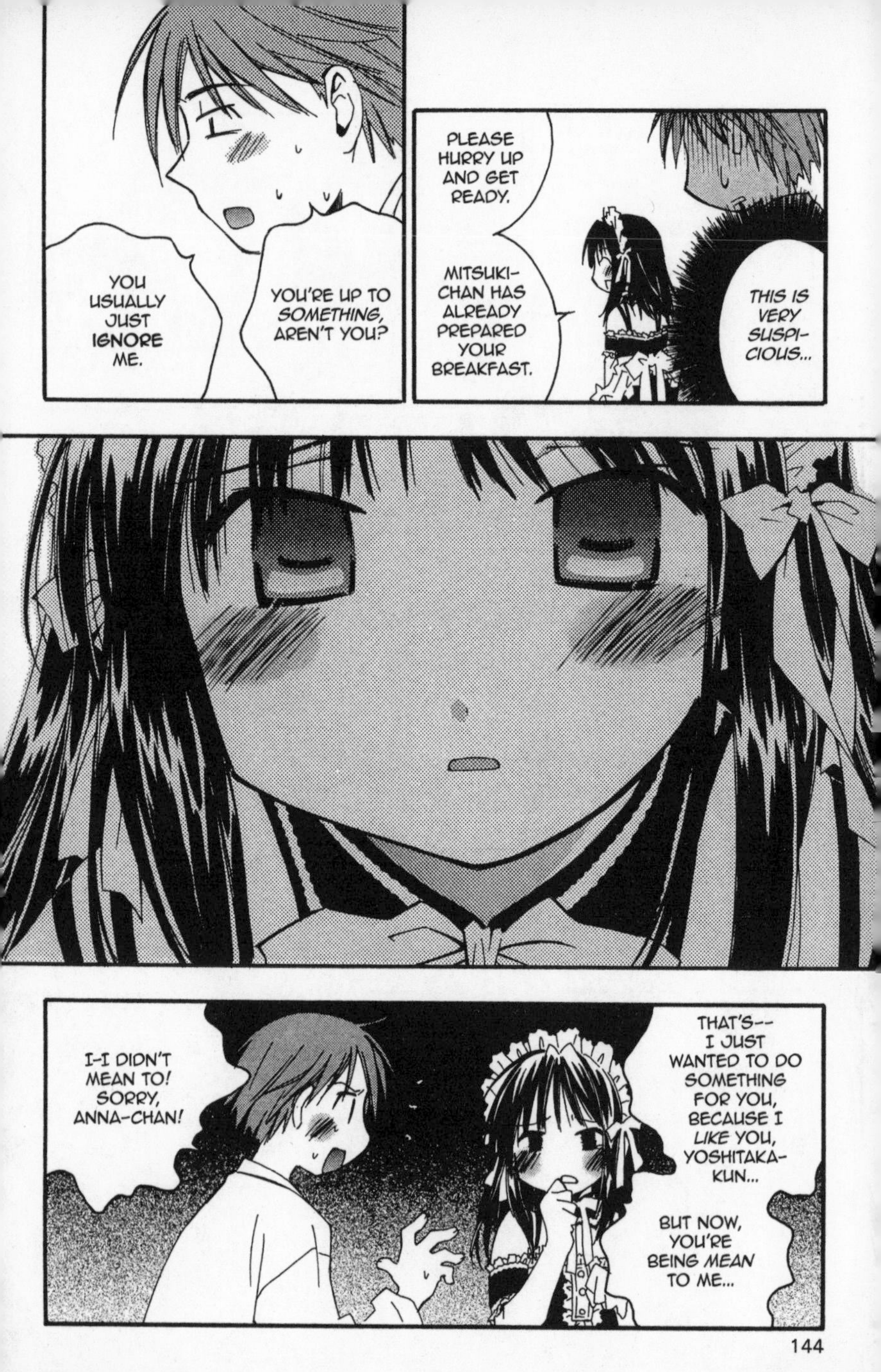
PLEASE HURRY UP AND GET READY.
MITSUKI-CHAN HAS ALREADY PREPARED YOUR BREAKFAST.
THIS IS VERY SUSPICIOUS...
YOU'RE UP TO SOMETHING, AREN'T YOU?
YOU USUALLY JUST IGNORE ME.
THAT'S-- I JUST WANTED TO DO SOMETHING FOR YOU, BECAUSE I LIKE YOU, YOSHITAKA-KUN...
BUT NOW, YOU'RE BEING MEAN TO ME...
I-I DIDN'T MEAN TO! SORRY, ANNA-CHAN!

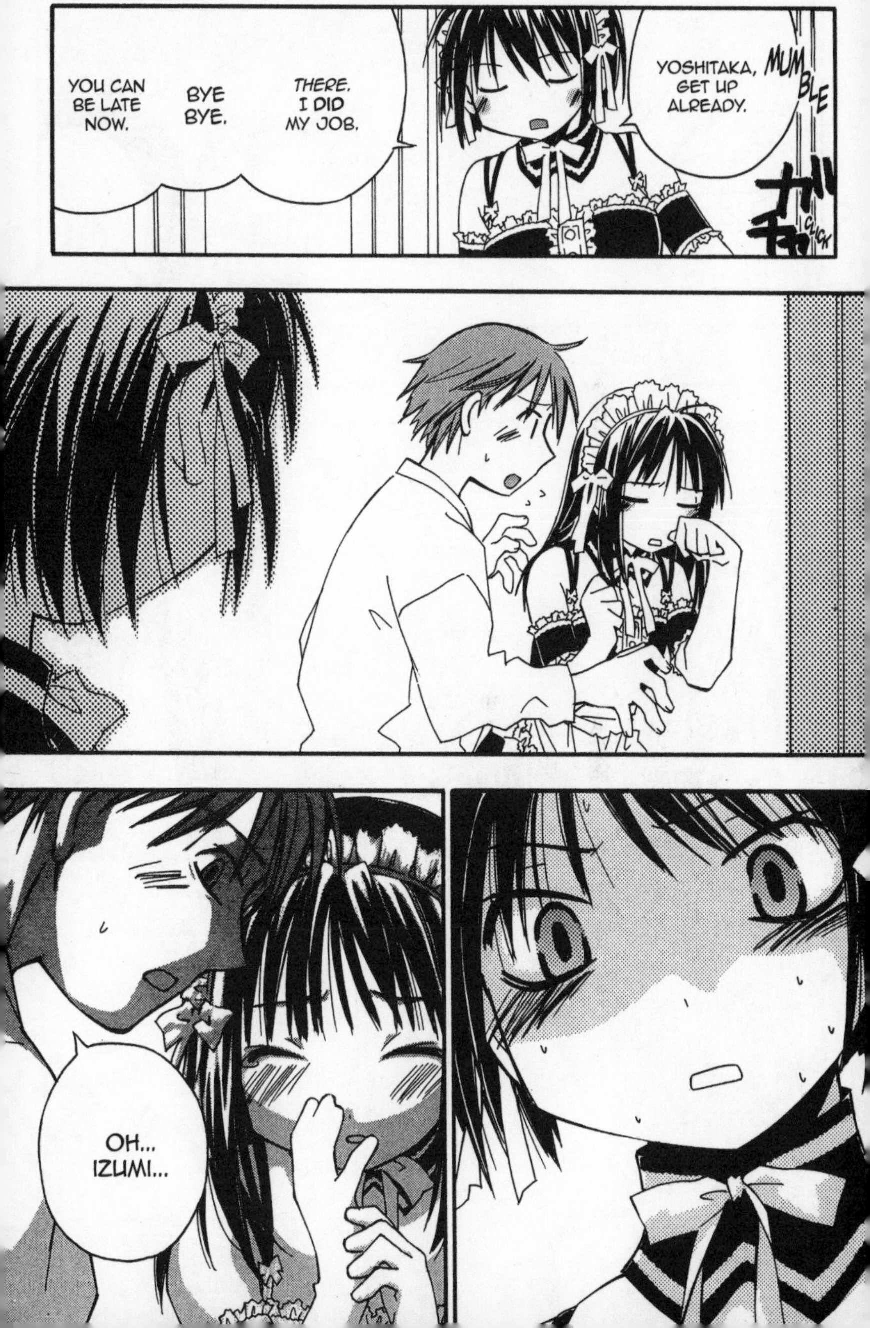
MUMBLE
YOSHITAKA, GET UP ALREADY.
CLICK
THERE. I DID MY JOB.
BYE BYE.
YOU CAN BE LATE NOW.
OH... IZUMI...

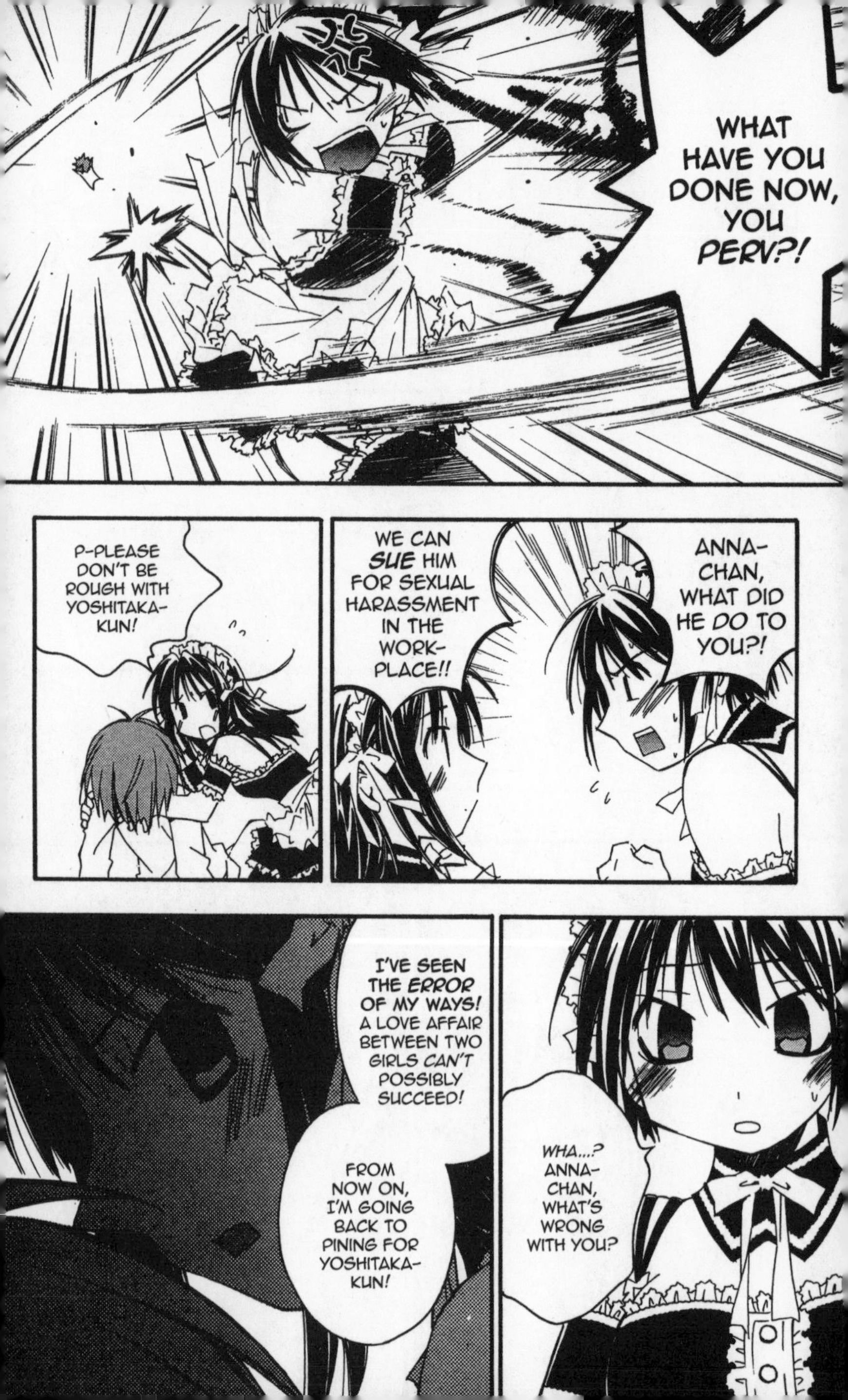
WHAT HAVE YOU DONE NOW, YOU *PERV?!*
ANNA-CHAN, WHAT DID HE *DO* TO YOU?!
WE CAN ***SUE*** HIM FOR SEXUAL HARASSMENT IN THE WORK-PLACE!!
P-PLEASE DON'T BE ROUGH WITH YOSHITAKA-KUN!
WHA...? ANNA-CHAN, WHAT'S WRONG WITH YOU?
I'VE SEEN THE *ERROR* OF MY WAYS! A LOVE AFFAIR BETWEEN TWO GIRLS *CAN'T* POSSIBLY SUCCEED!
FROM NOW ON, I'M GOING BACK TO PINING FOR YOSHITAKA-KUN!

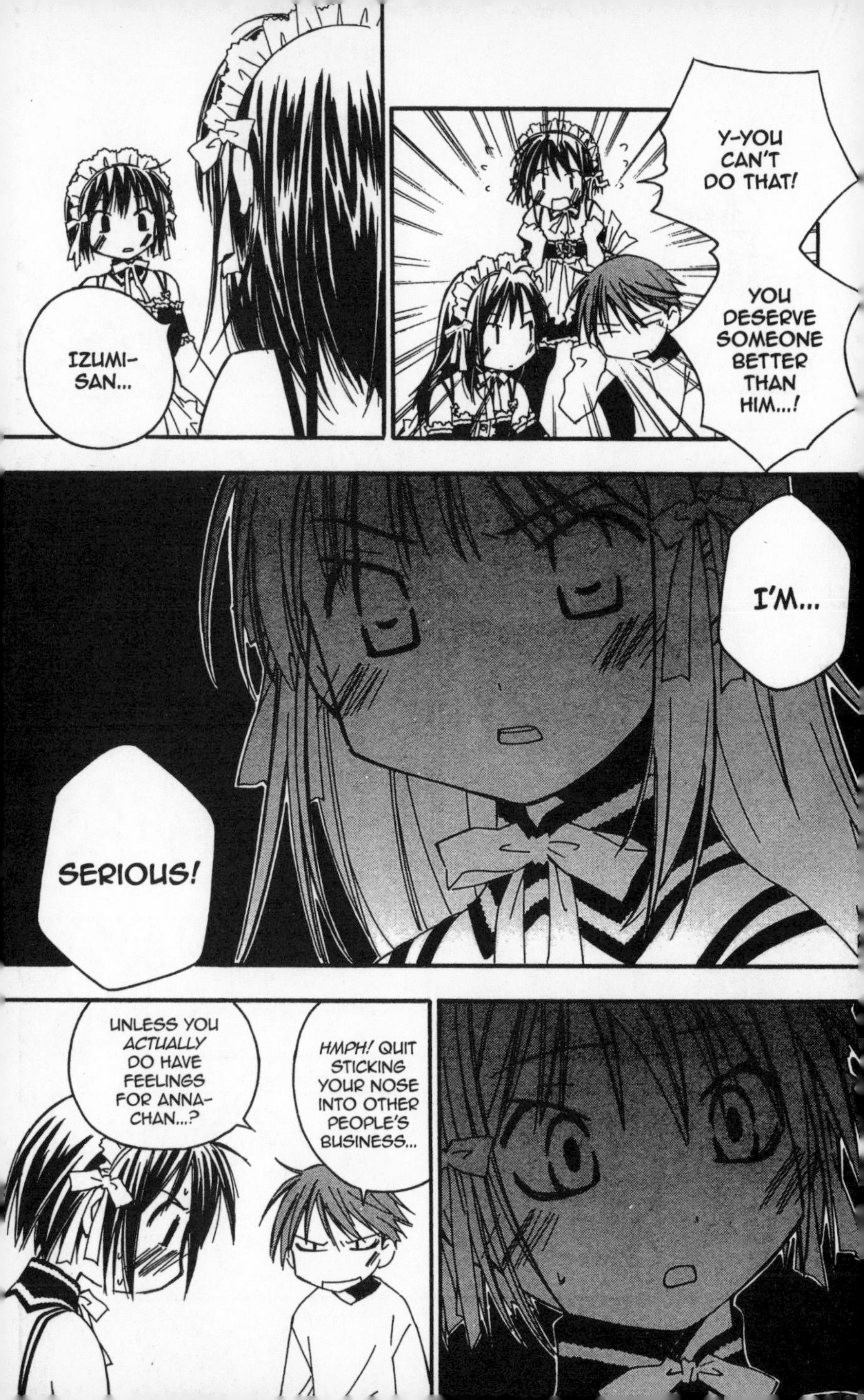
Y-YOU CAN'T DO THAT!
YOU DESERVE SOMEONE BETTER THAN HIM...!
IZUMI-SAN...
I'M...
SERIOUS!
HMPH! QUIT STICKING YOUR NOSE INTO OTHER PEOPLE'S BUSINESS...
UNLESS YOU *ACTUALLY* DO HAVE FEELINGS FOR ANNA-CHAN...?

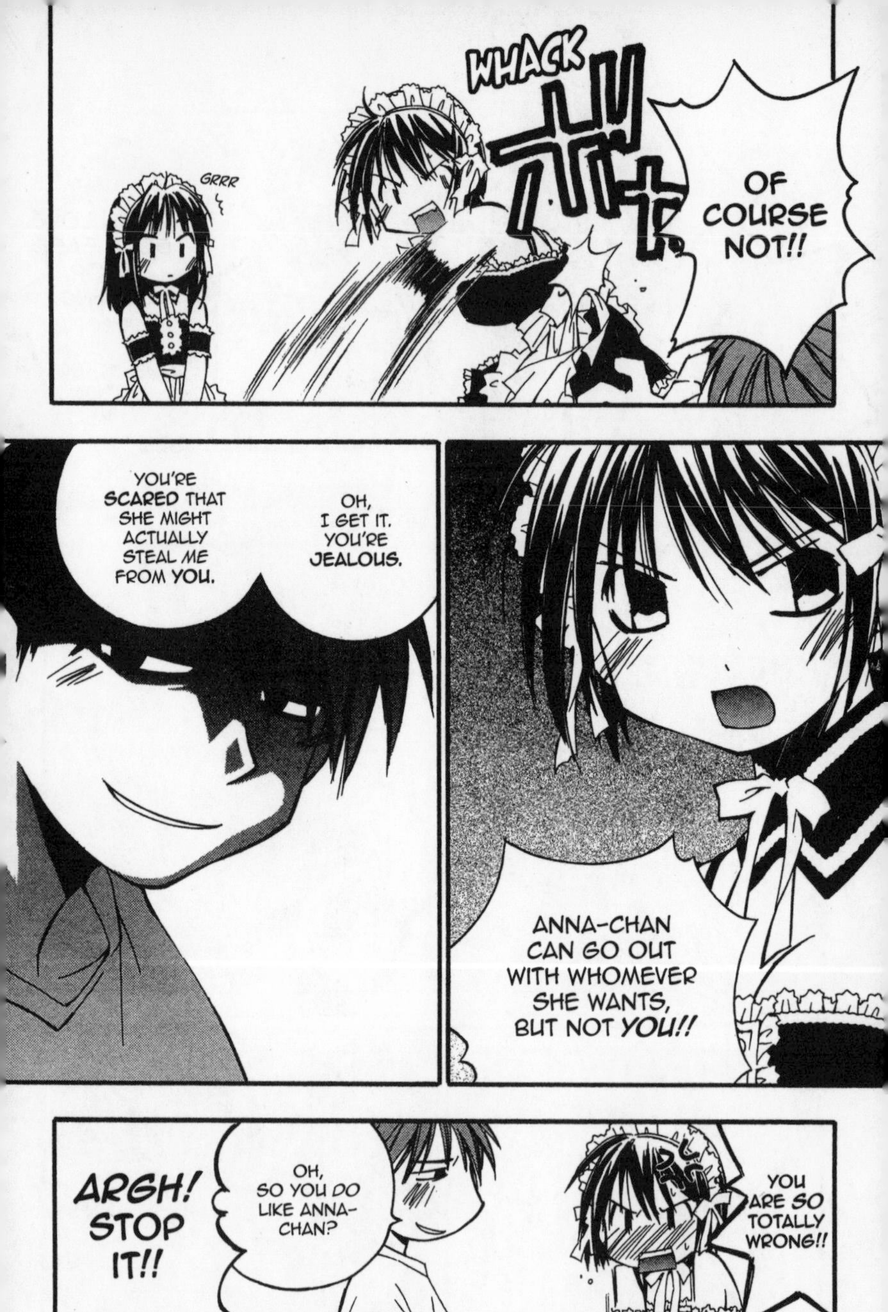
OF COURSE NOT!!
WHACK
GRRR
ANNA-CHAN CAN GO OUT WITH WHOMEVER SHE WANTS, BUT NOT YOU!!
OH, I GET IT. YOU'RE JEALOUS.
YOU'RE SCARED THAT SHE MIGHT ACTUALLY STEAL ME FROM YOU.
YOU ARE SO TOTALLY WRONG!!
OH, SO YOU DO LIKE ANNA-CHAN?
ARGH! STOP IT!!

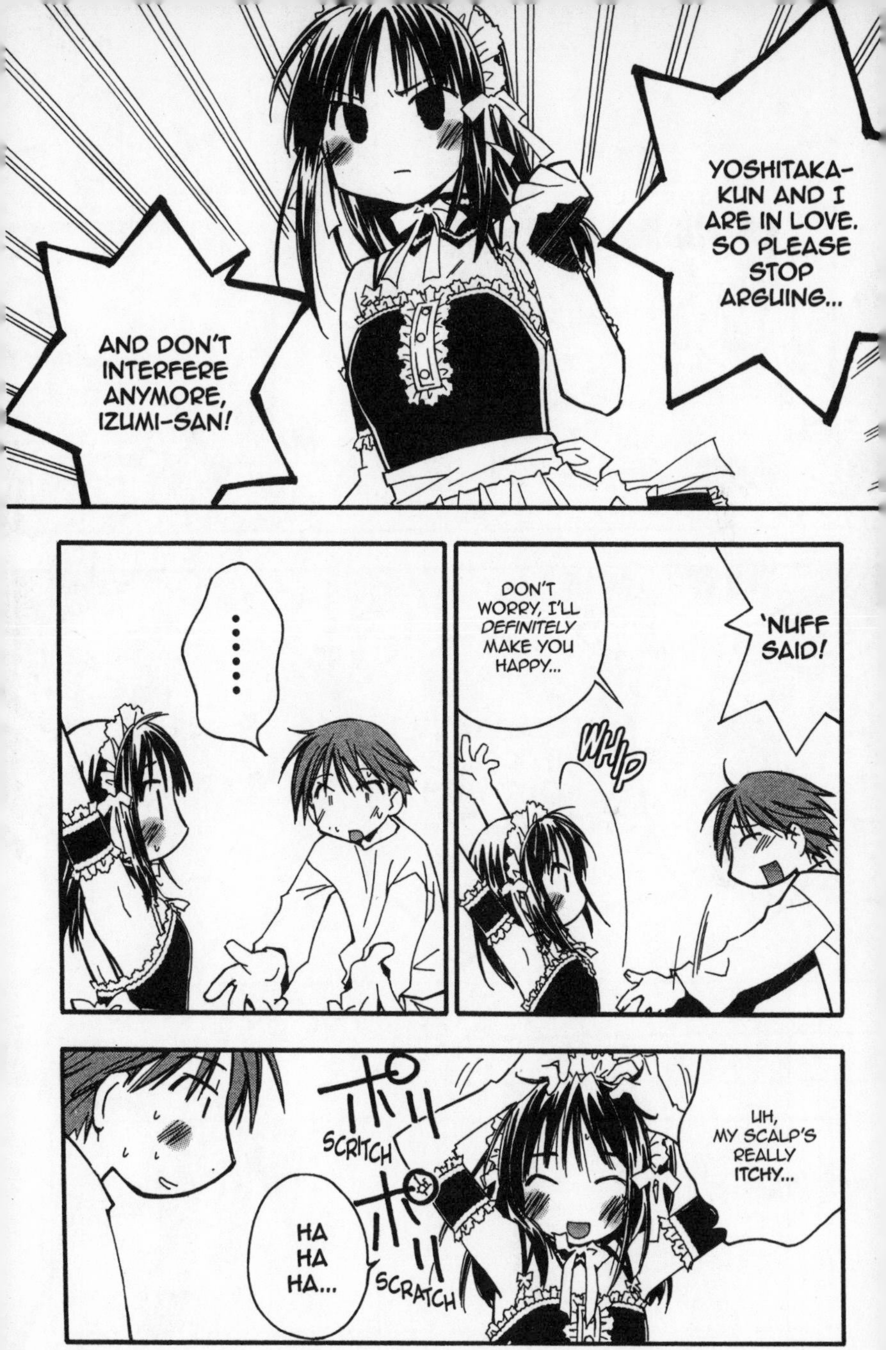
YOSHITAKA-KUN AND I ARE IN LOVE. SO PLEASE STOP ARGUING...
AND DON'T INTERFERE ANYMORE, IZUMI-SAN!
'NUFF SAID!
DON'T WORRY, I'LL DEFINITELY MAKE YOU HAPPY...
WHIP
......
UH, MY SCALP'S REALLY ITCHY...
SCRITCH
SCRATCH
HA HA HA...

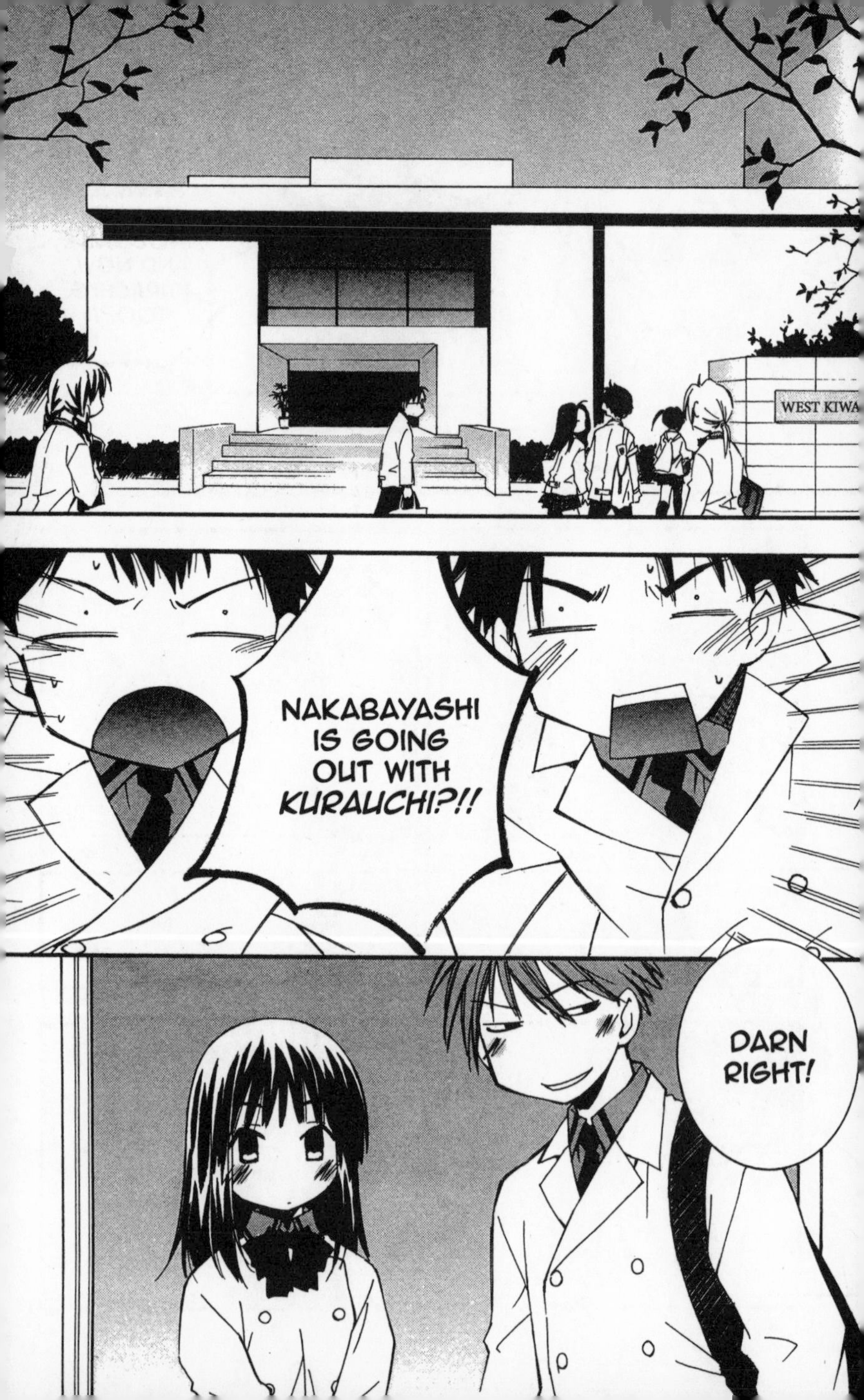
WEST KIWA
NAKABAYASHI IS GOING OUT WITH KURAUCHI?!!
DARN RIGHT!

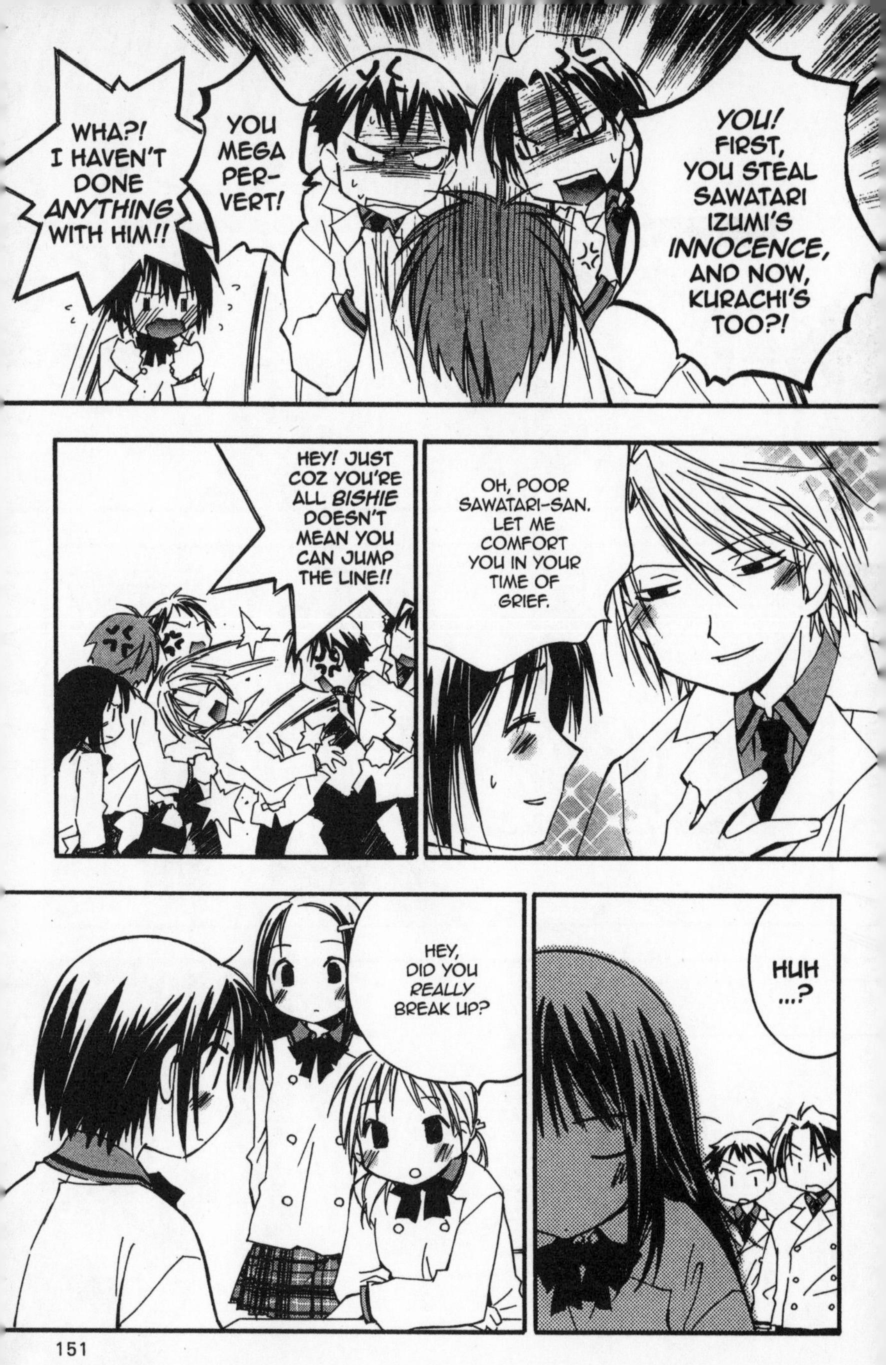
YOU! FIRST, YOU STEAL SAWATARI IZUMI'S INNOCENCE, AND NOW, KURACHI'S TOO?!
YOU MEGA PER-VERT!
WHA?! I HAVEN'T DONE ANYTHING WITH HIM!!
OH, POOR SAWATARI-SAN. LET ME COMFORT YOU IN YOUR TIME OF GRIEF.
HEY! JUST COZ YOU'RE ALL BISHIE DOESN'T MEAN YOU CAN JUMP THE LINE!!
HUH ...?
HEY, DID YOU REALLY BREAK UP?

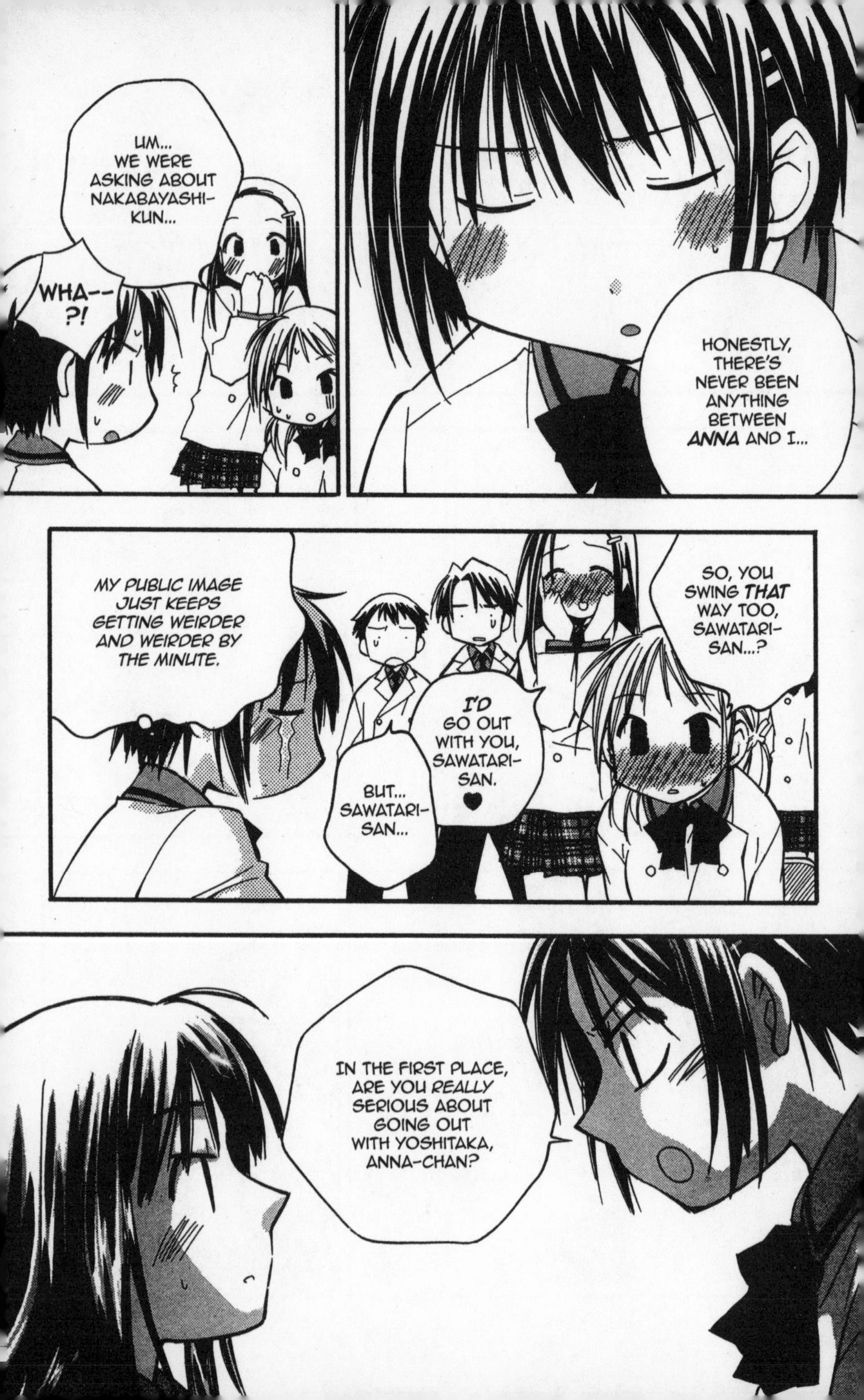
HONESTLY, THERE'S NEVER BEEN ANYTHING BETWEEN ANNA AND I...
UM... WE WERE ASKING ABOUT NAKABAYASHI-KUN...
WHA--?!
SO, YOU SWING THAT WAY TOO, SAWATARI-SAN...?
I'D GO OUT WITH YOU, SAWATARI-SAN. ♥
BUT... SAWATARI-SAN...
MY PUBLIC IMAGE JUST KEEPS GETTING WEIRDER AND WEIRDER BY THE MINUTE.
IN THE FIRST PLACE, ARE YOU REALLY SERIOUS ABOUT GOING OUT WITH YOSHITAKA, ANNA-CHAN?

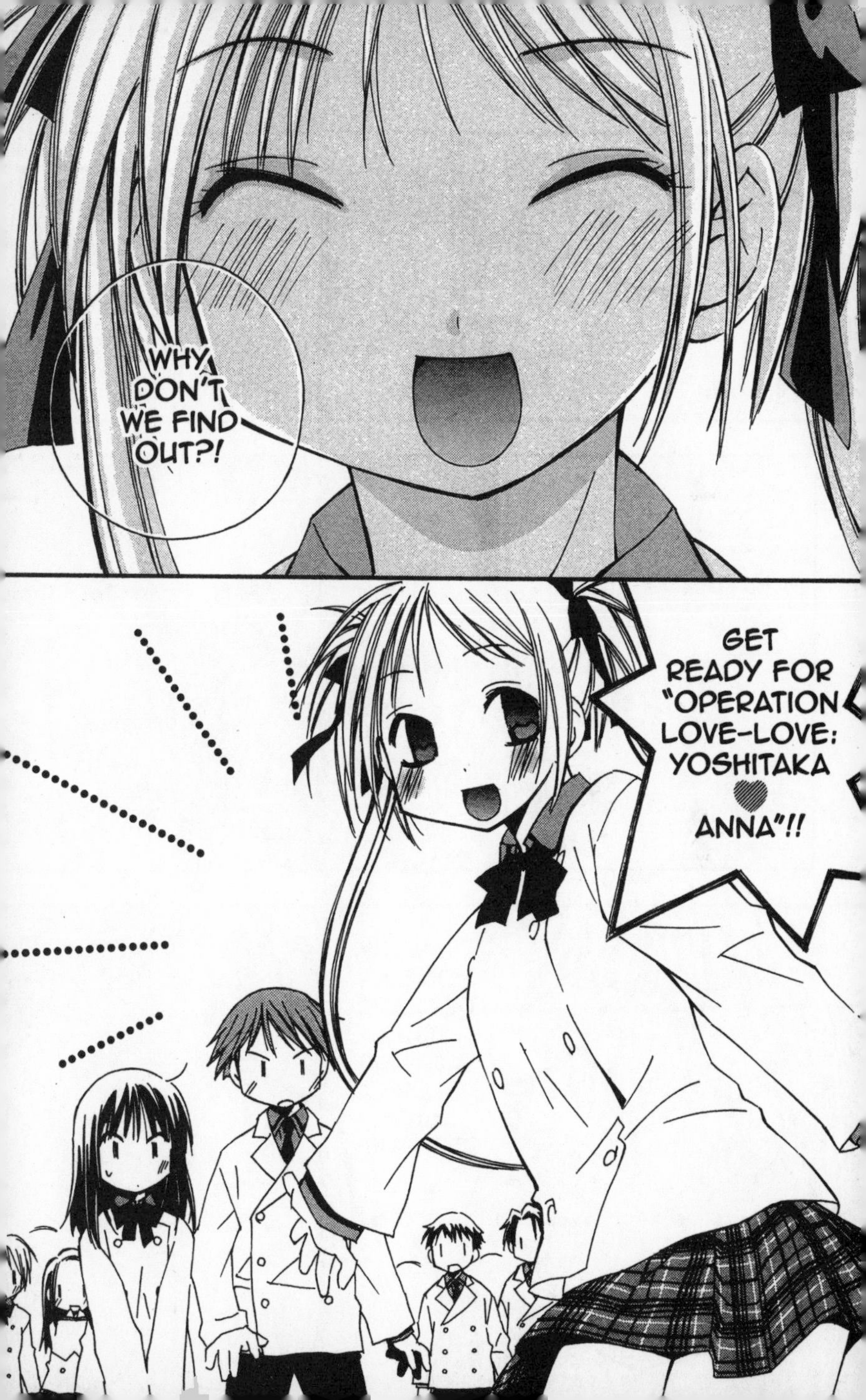
WHY DON'T WE FIND OUT?!
GET READY FOR "OPERATION LOVE-LOVE: YOSHITAKA ♥ ANNA"!!

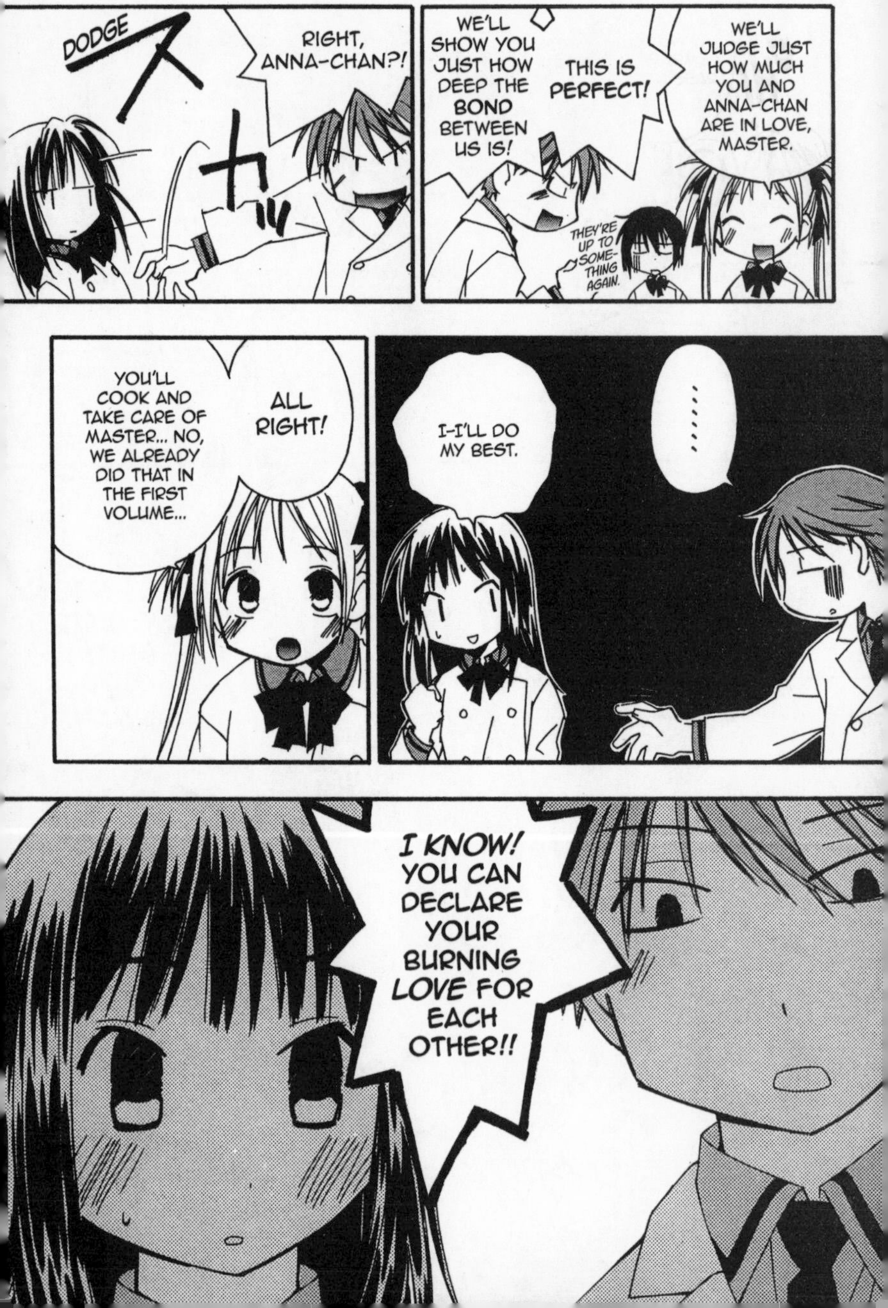
WE'LL JUDGE JUST HOW MUCH YOU AND ANNA-CHAN ARE IN LOVE, MASTER.
THIS IS PERFECT!
WE'LL SHOW YOU JUST HOW DEEP THE BOND BETWEEN US IS!
THEY'RE UP TO SOME-THING AGAIN.
RIGHT, ANNA-CHAN?!
DODGE
......
I-I'LL DO MY BEST.
ALL RIGHT!
YOU'LL COOK AND TAKE CARE OF MASTER... NO, WE ALREADY DID THAT IN THE FIRST VOLUME...
I KNOW! YOU CAN DECLARE YOUR BURNING LOVE FOR EACH OTHER!!

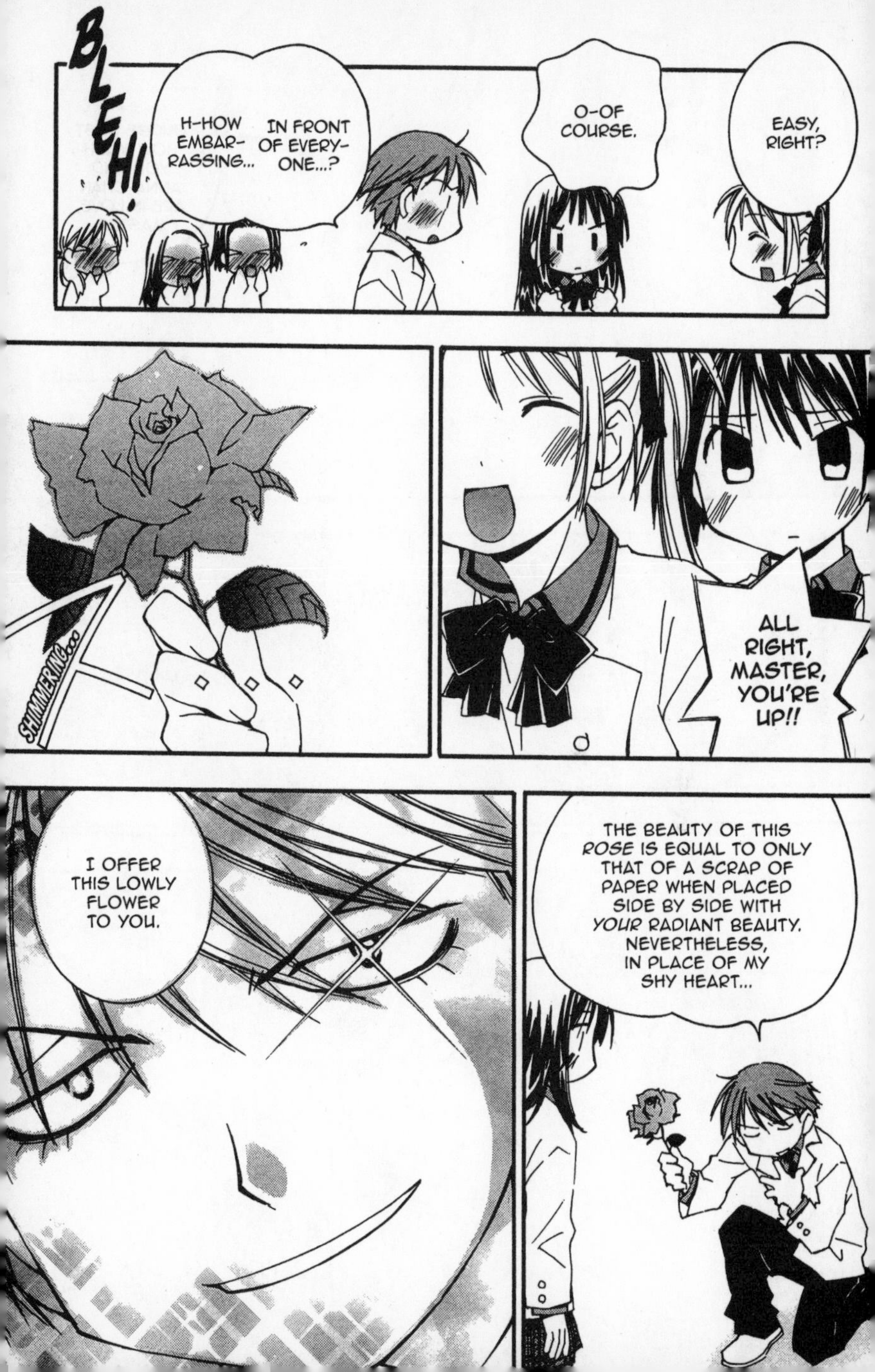
EASY, RIGHT?
O-OF COURSE.
H-HOW EMBARRASSING... IN FRONT OF EVERYONE...?
BLEH!
ALL RIGHT, MASTER, YOU'RE UP!!
SHIMMERING...
THE BEAUTY OF THIS ROSE IS EQUAL TO ONLY THAT OF A SCRAP OF PAPER WHEN PLACED SIDE BY SIDE WITH YOUR RADIANT BEAUTY. NEVERTHELESS, IN PLACE OF MY SHY HEART...
I OFFER THIS LOWLY FLOWER TO YOU.

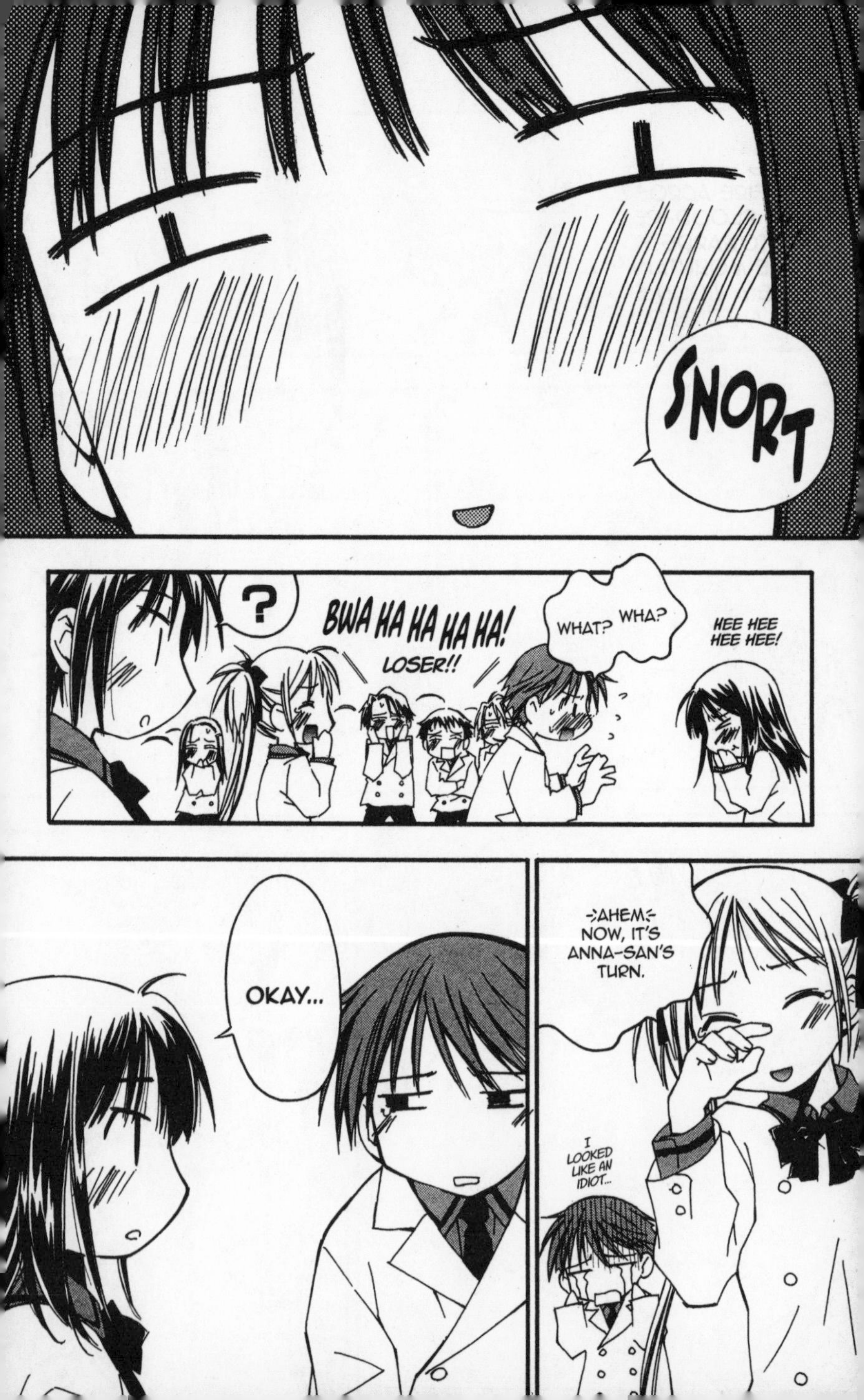
SNORT
HEE HEE HEE HEE!
WHAT? WHA?
BWA HA HA HA HA!
LOSER!!
?
-AHEM- NOW, IT'S ANNA-SAN'S TURN.
I LOOKED LIKE AN IDIOT...
OKAY...

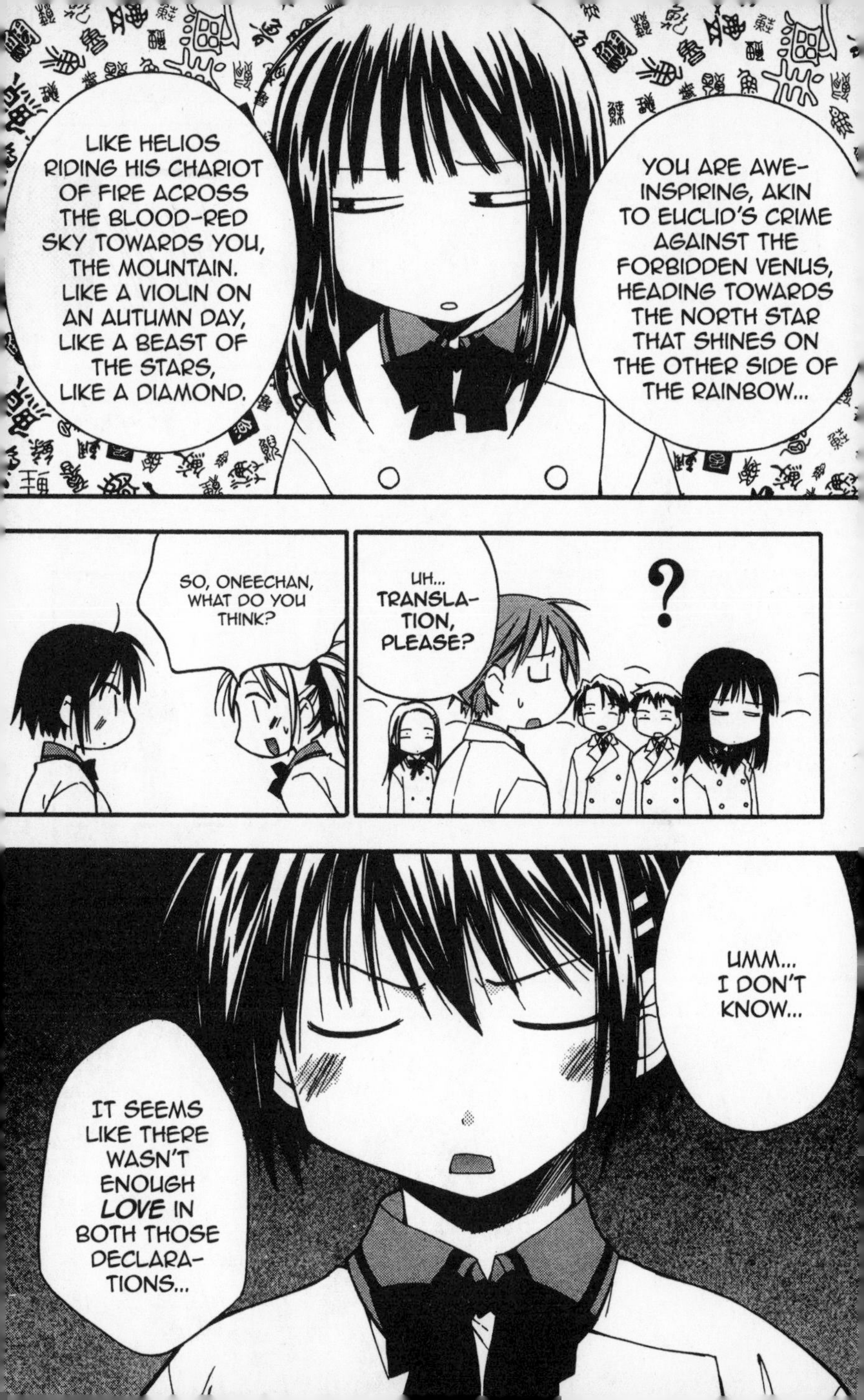
YOU ARE AWE-INSPIRING, AKIN TO EUCLID'S CRIME AGAINST THE FORBIDDEN VENUS, HEADING TOWARDS THE NORTH STAR THAT SHINES ON THE OTHER SIDE OF THE RAINBOW...
LIKE HELIOS RIDING HIS CHARIOT OF FIRE ACROSS THE BLOOD-RED SKY TOWARDS YOU, THE MOUNTAIN. LIKE A VIOLIN ON AN AUTUMN DAY, LIKE A BEAST OF THE STARS, LIKE A DIAMOND.
?
UH... TRANSLA-TION, PLEASE?
SO, ONEECHAN, WHAT DO YOU THINK?
UMM... I DON'T KNOW...
IT SEEMS LIKE THERE WASN'T ENOUGH *LOVE* IN BOTH THOSE DECLARA-TIONS...

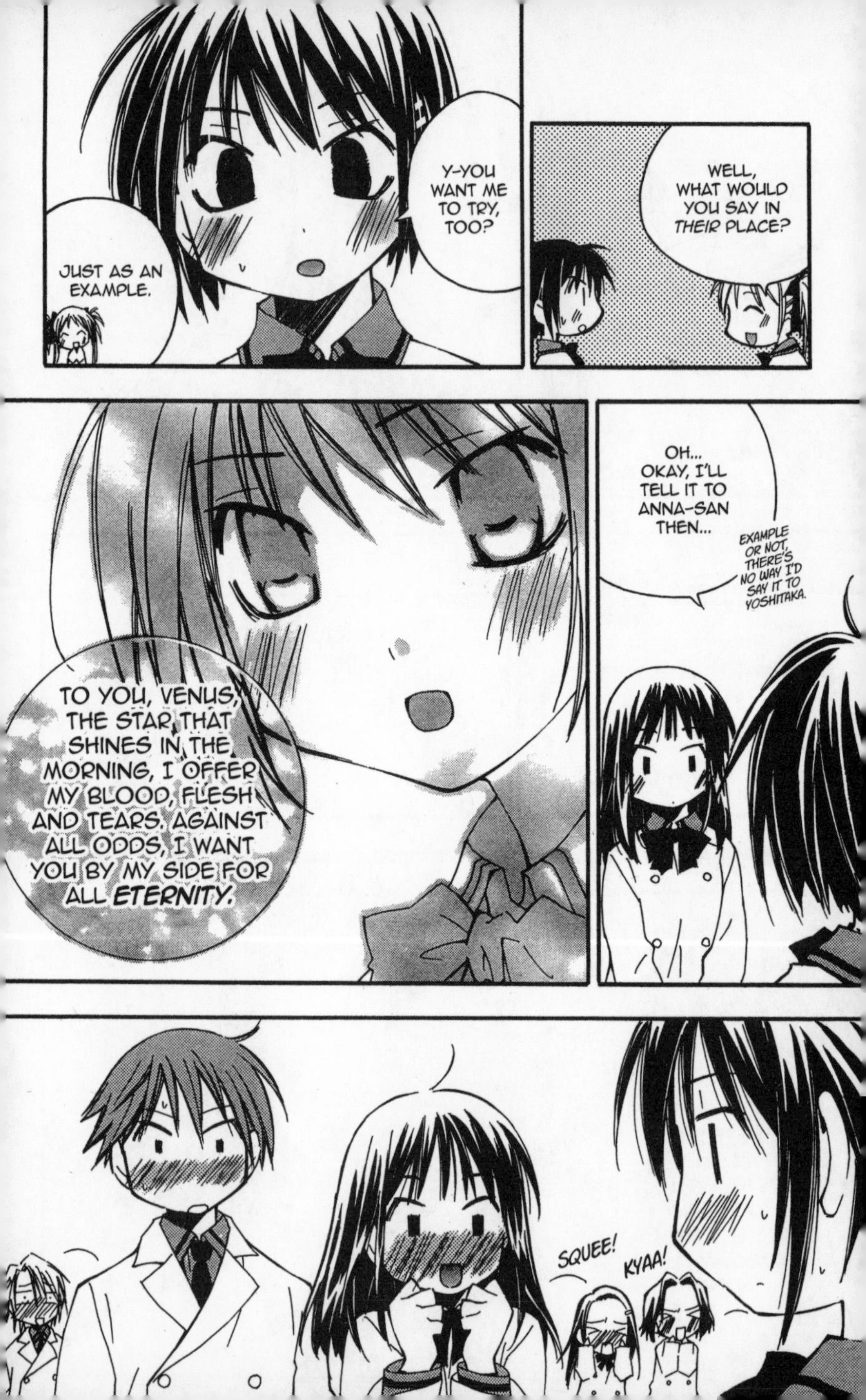
WELL, WHAT WOULD YOU SAY IN *THEIR* PLACE?
Y-YOU WANT ME TO TRY, TOO?
JUST AS AN EXAMPLE.
OH... OKAY, I'LL TELL IT TO ANNA-SAN THEN...
EXAMPLE OR NOT, THERE'S NO WAY I'D SAY IT TO YOSHITAKA.
TO YOU, VENUS, THE STAR THAT SHINES IN THE MORNING, I OFFER MY BLOOD, FLESH AND TEARS. AGAINST ALL ODDS, I WANT YOU BY MY SIDE FOR ALL *ETERNITY.*
KYAA!
SQUEE!

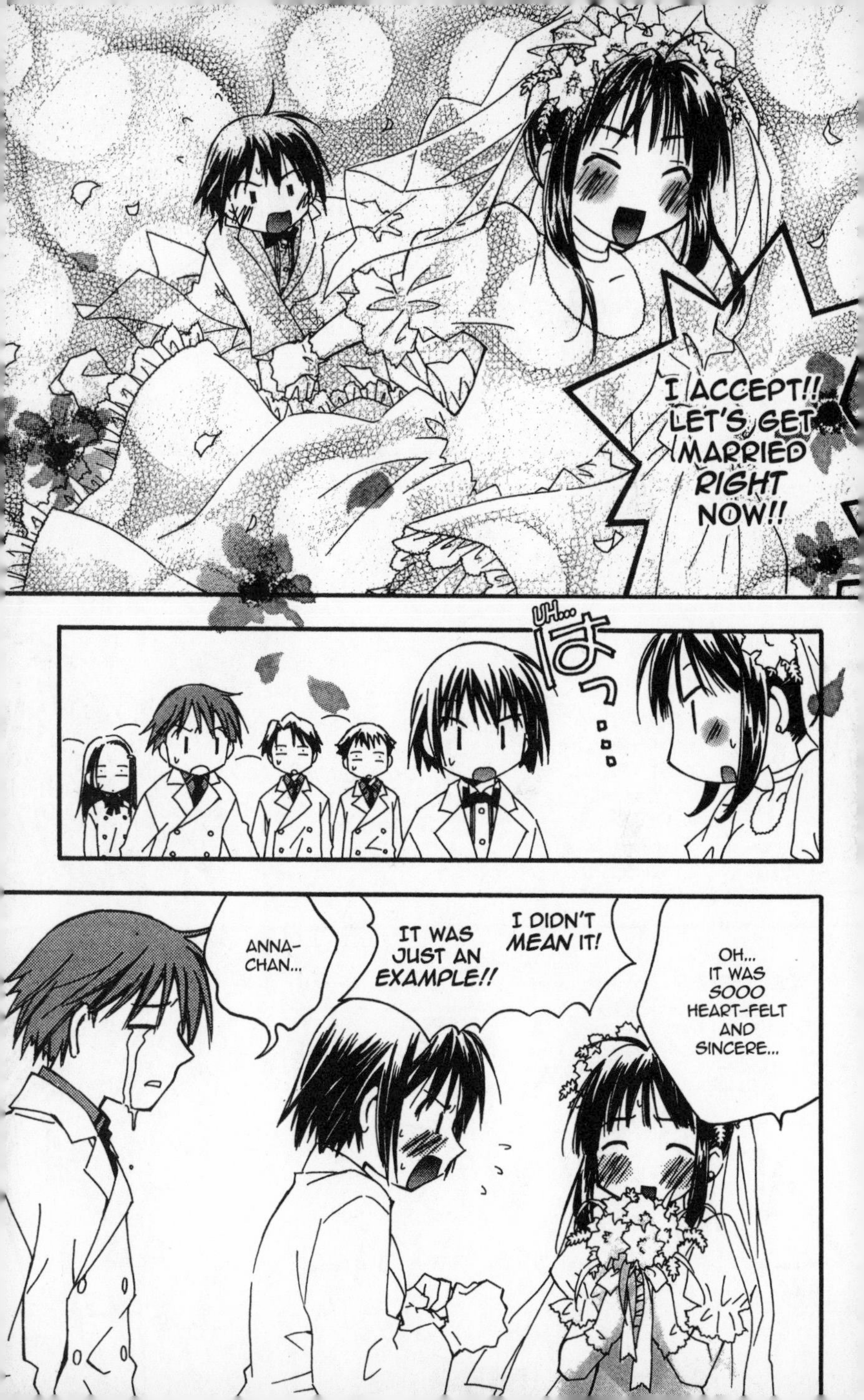
I ACCEPT!! LET'S GET MARRIED RIGHT NOW!!
UH... はっ...
OH... IT WAS SOOO HEART-FELT AND SINCERE...
I DIDN'T MEAN IT!
IT WAS JUST AN EXAMPLE!!
ANNA-CHAN...

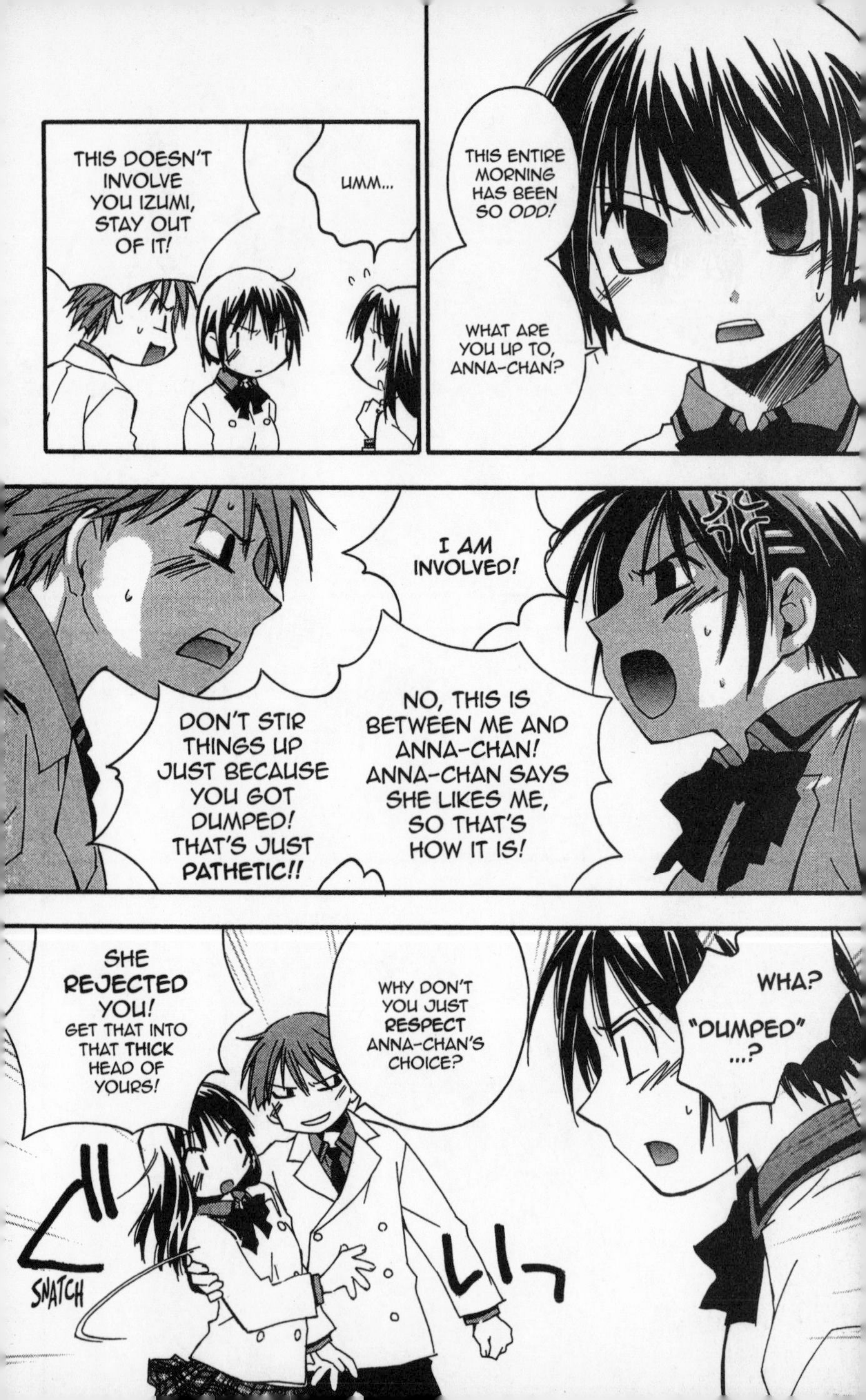
THIS ENTIRE MORNING HAS BEEN SO *ODD!*
WHAT ARE YOU UP TO, ANNA-CHAN?
UMM...
THIS DOESN'T INVOLVE YOU IZUMI, STAY OUT OF IT!
I *AM* INVOLVED!
NO, THIS IS BETWEEN ME AND ANNA-CHAN! ANNA-CHAN SAYS SHE LIKES ME, SO THAT'S HOW IT IS!
DON'T STIR THINGS UP JUST BECAUSE YOU GOT DUMPED! THAT'S JUST **PATHETIC!!**
WHA? "DUMPED" ...?
WHY DON'T YOU JUST **RESPECT** ANNA-CHAN'S CHOICE?
SHE **REJECTED** YOU! GET THAT INTO THAT **THICK** HEAD OF YOURS!
SNATCH

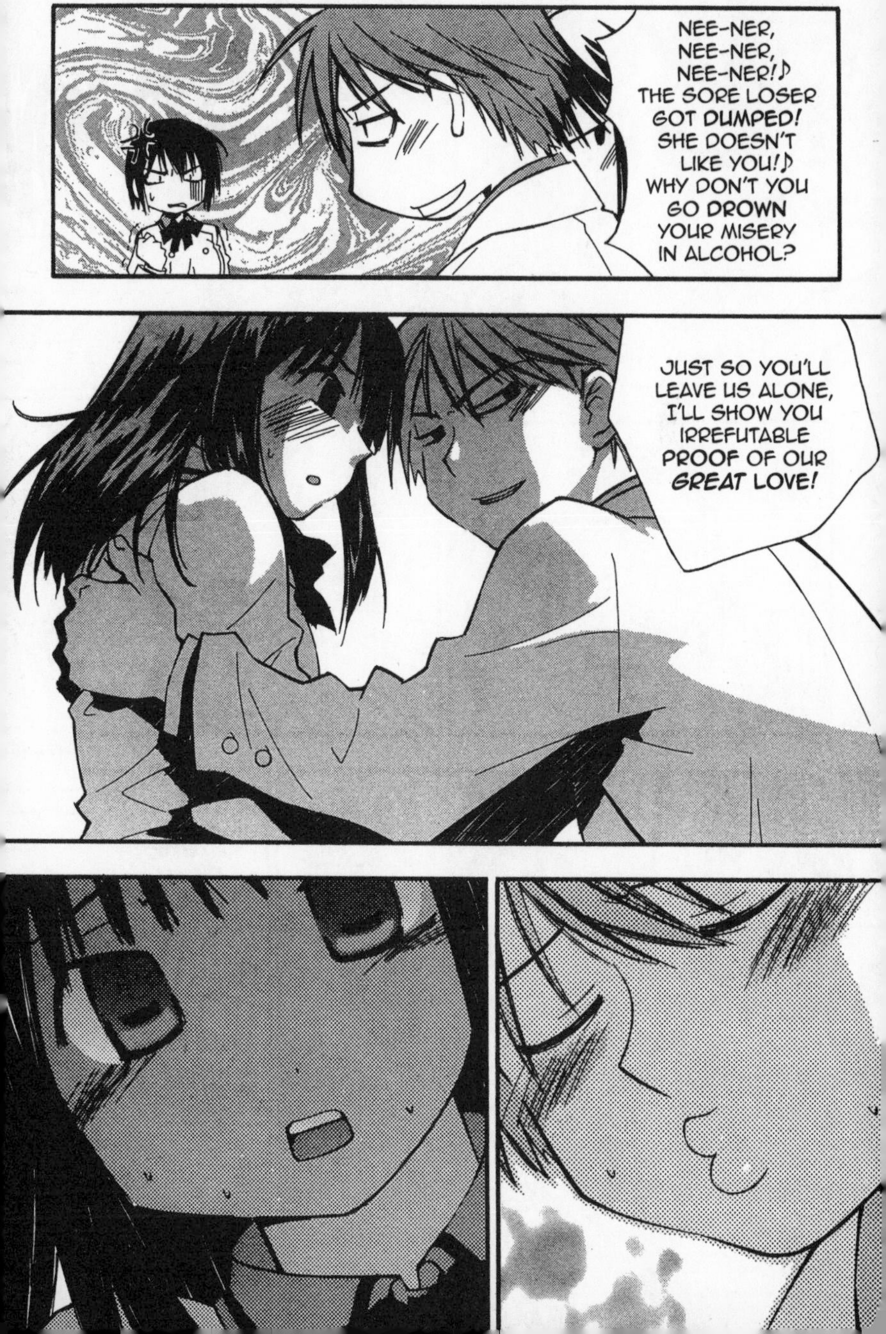
NEE-NER, NEE-NER, NEE-NER!♪ THE SORE LOSER GOT DUMPED! SHE DOESN'T LIKE YOU!♪ WHY DON'T YOU GO DROWN YOUR MISERY IN ALCOHOL?
JUST SO YOU'LL LEAVE US ALONE, I'LL SHOW YOU IRREFUTABLE PROOF OF OUR GREAT LOVE!

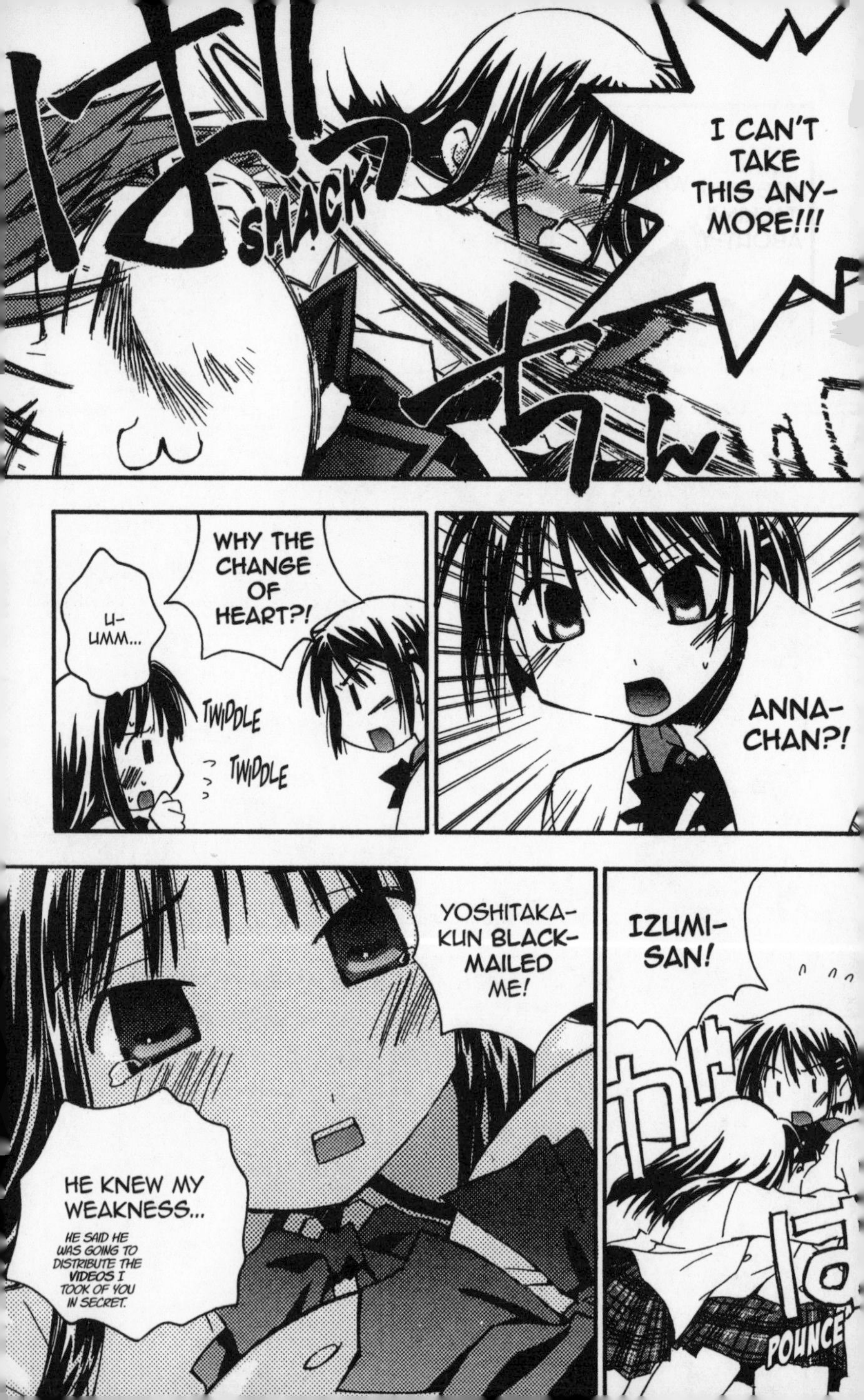
I CAN'T TAKE THIS ANY-MORE!!!
SHACK
ANNA-CHAN?!
WHY THE CHANGE OF HEART?!
U-UMM...
TWIDDLE
TWIDDLE
IZUMI-SAN!
POUNCE
YOSHITAKA-KUN BLACK-MAILED ME!
HE KNEW MY WEAKNESS...
HE SAID HE WAS GOING TO DISTRIBUTE THE VIDEOS I TOOK OF YOU IN SECRET.

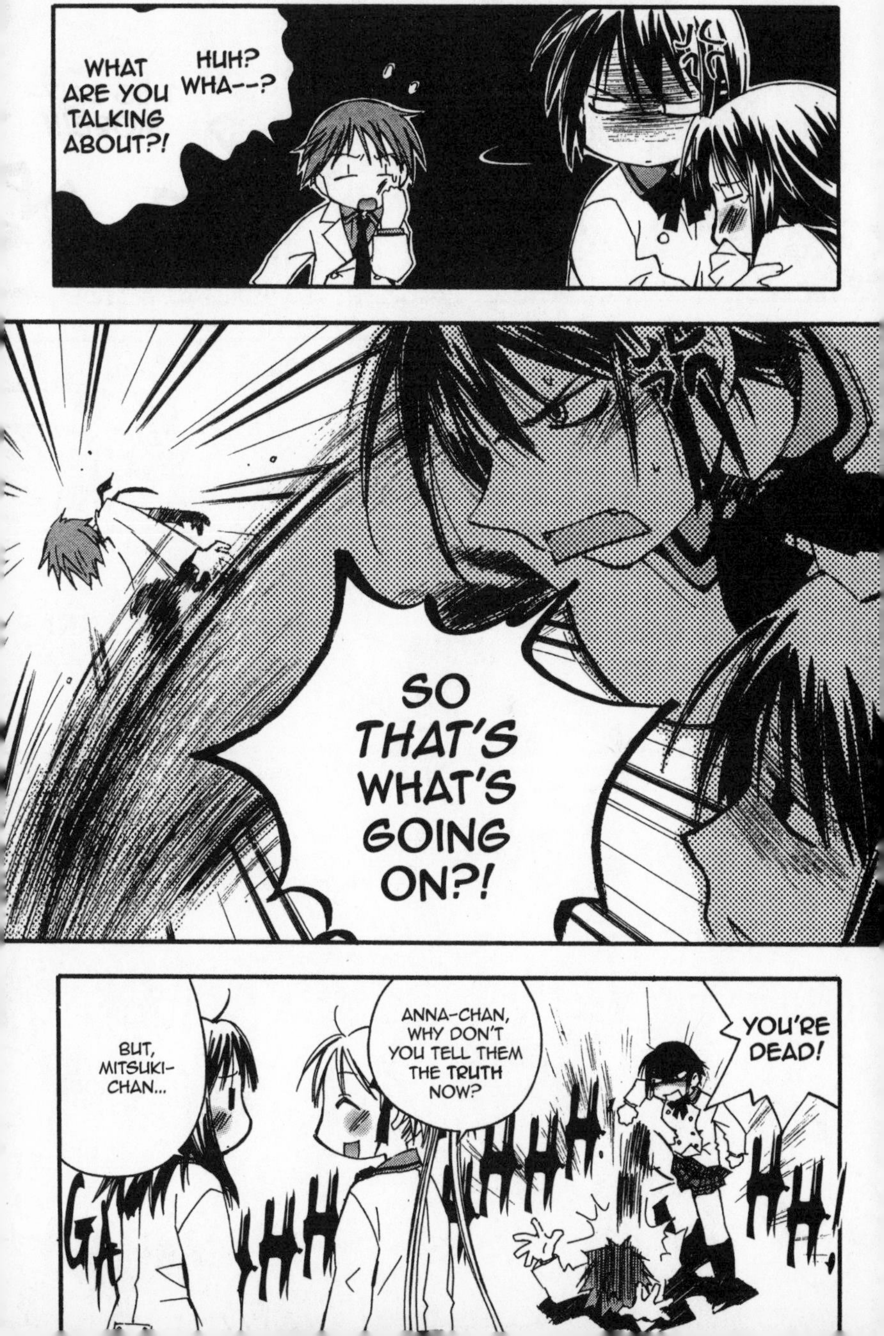
HUH? WHA--?
WHAT ARE YOU TALKING ABOUT?!
SO THAT'S WHAT'S GOING ON?!
YOU'RE DEAD!
ANNA-CHAN, WHY DON'T YOU TELL THEM THE TRUTH NOW?
BUT, MITSUKI-CHAN...

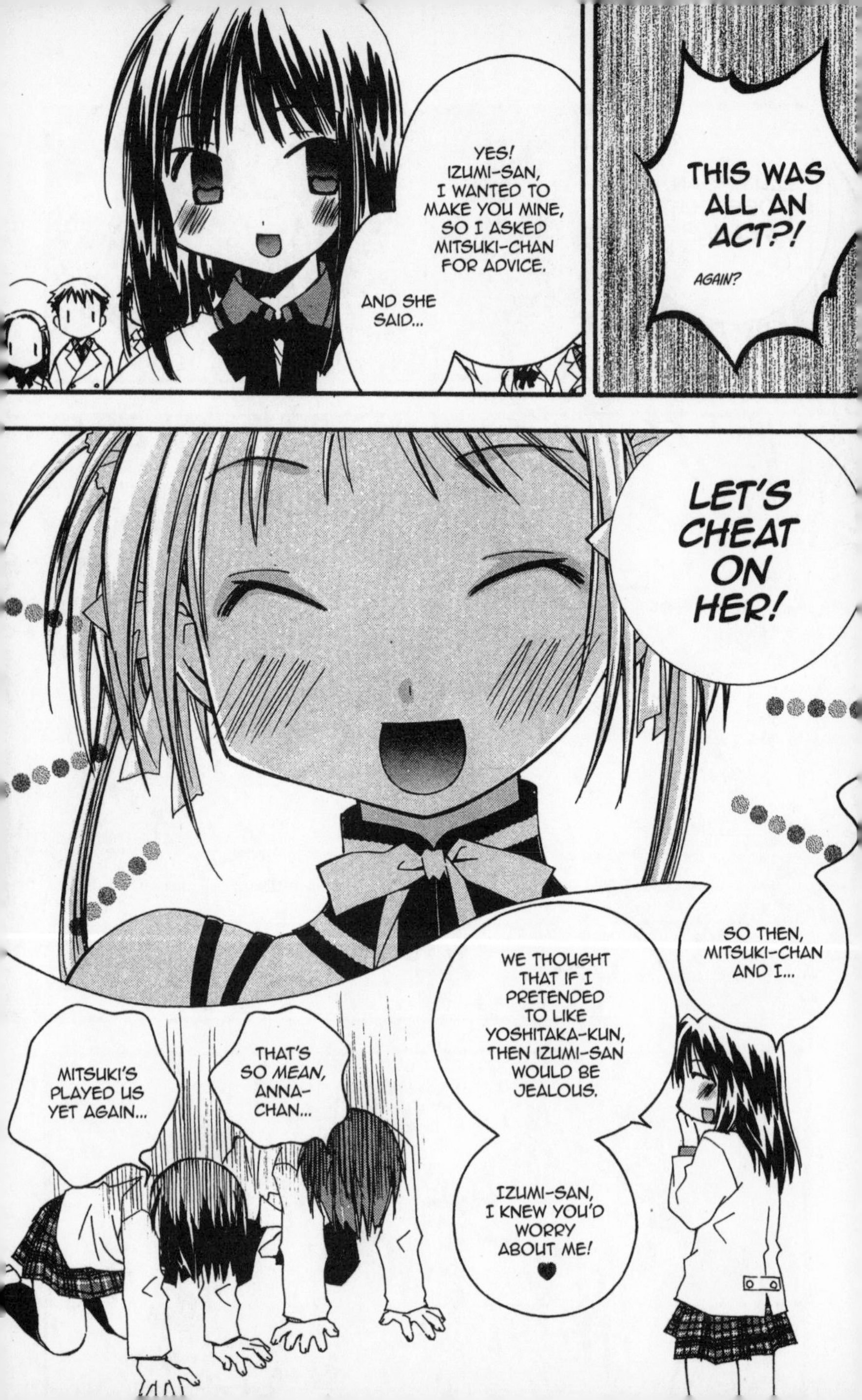
THIS WAS ALL AN ACT?!
AGAIN?
YES! IZUMI-SAN, I WANTED TO MAKE YOU MINE, SO I ASKED MITSUKI-CHAN FOR ADVICE.
AND SHE SAID...
LET'S CHEAT ON HER!
SO THEN, MITSUKI-CHAN AND I...
WE THOUGHT THAT IF I PRETENDED TO LIKE YOSHITAKA-KUN, THEN IZUMI-SAN WOULD BE JEALOUS.
IZUMI-SAN, I KNEW YOU'D WORRY ABOUT ME! ♥
THAT'S SO MEAN, ANNA-CHAN...
MITSUKI'S PLAYED US YET AGAIN...

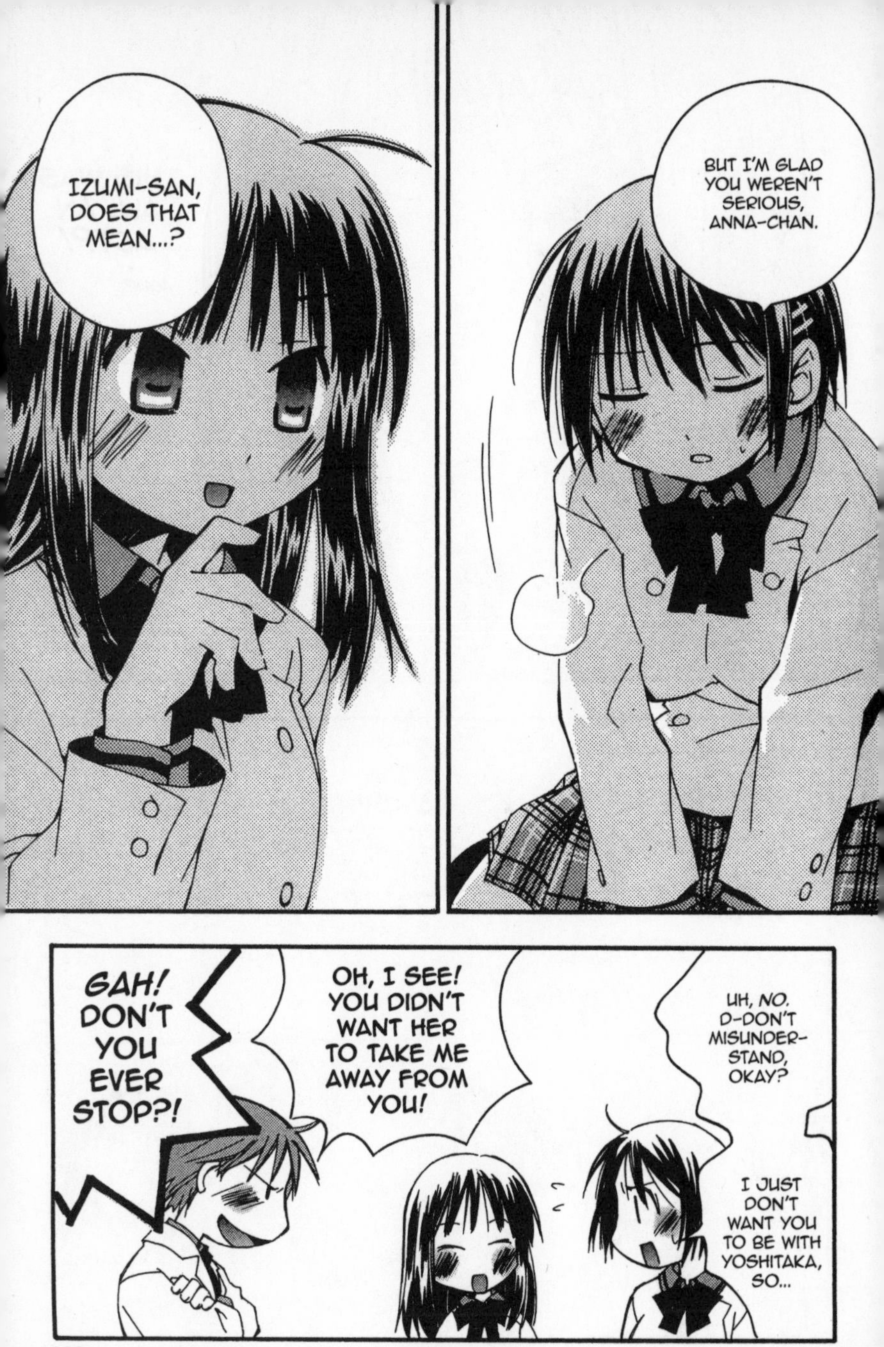
BUT I'M GLAD YOU WEREN'T SERIOUS, ANNA-CHAN.
IZUMI-SAN, DOES THAT MEAN...?
UH, NO. D-DON'T MISUNDER-STAND, OKAY?
I JUST DON'T WANT YOU TO BE WITH YOSHITAKA, SO...
OH, I SEE! YOU DIDN'T WANT HER TO TAKE ME AWAY FROM YOU!
GAH! DON'T YOU EVER STOP?!

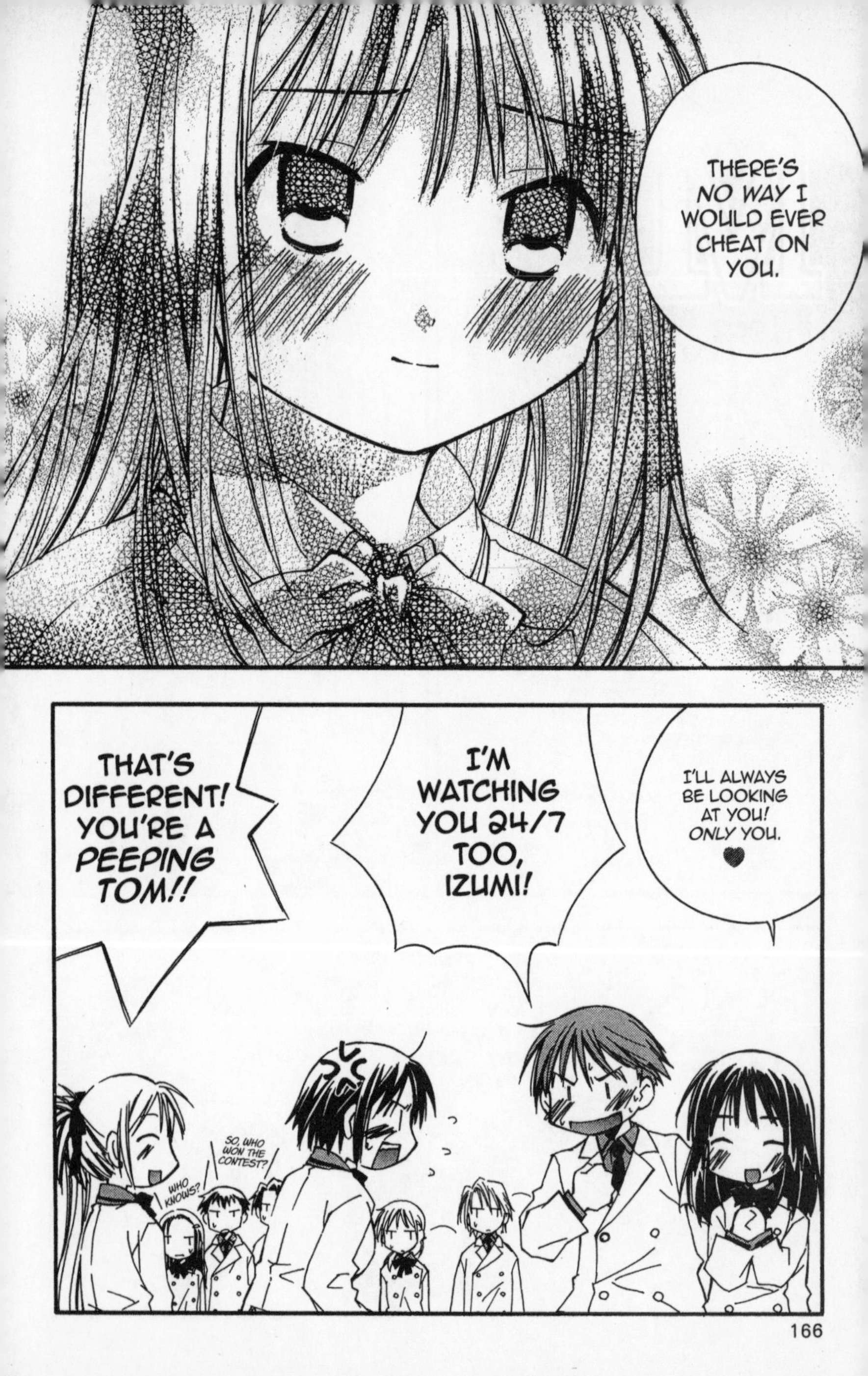
THERE'S NO WAY I WOULD EVER CHEAT ON YOU.
I'LL ALWAYS BE LOOKING AT YOU! ONLY YOU. ♥
I'M WATCHING YOU 24/7 TOO, IZUMI!
THAT'S DIFFERENT! YOU'RE A PEEPING TOM!!
SO, WHO WON THE CONTEST?
WHO KNOWS?

THIS IS MY MASTER

SUB-PLOT COLLECTION ①

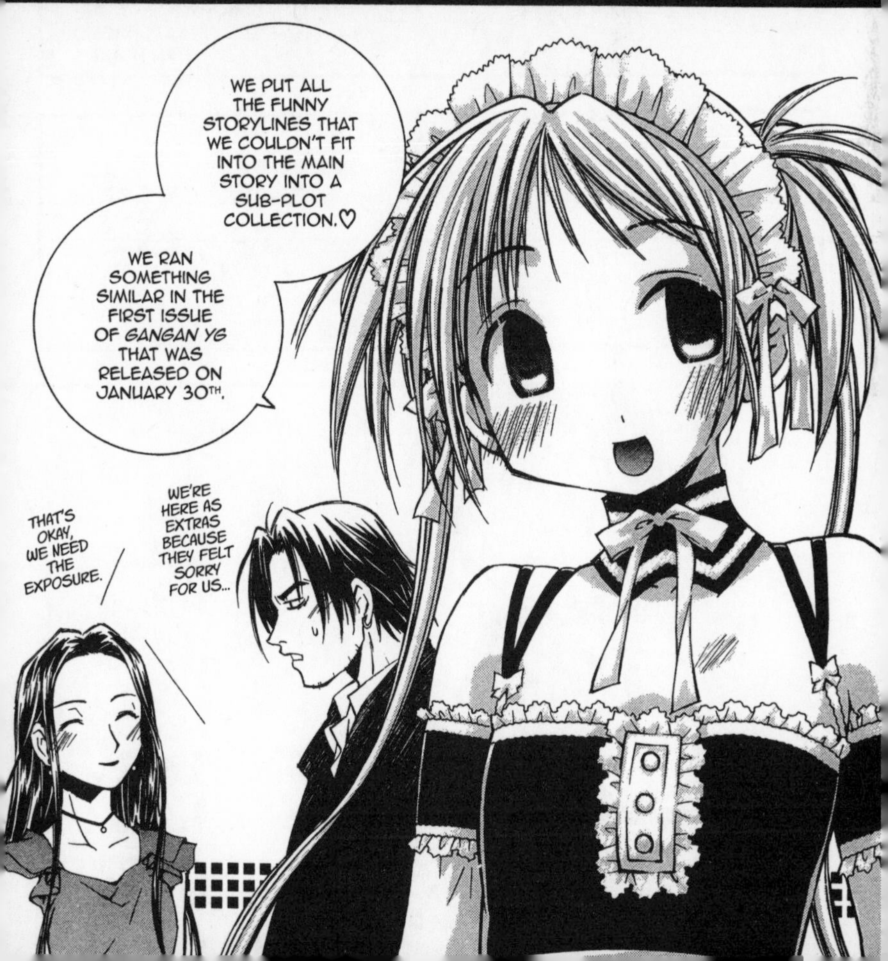

WE PUT ALL THE FUNNY STORYLINES THAT WE COULDN'T FIT INTO THE MAIN STORY INTO A SUB-PLOT COLLECTION.♡
WE RAN SOMETHING SIMILAR IN THE FIRST ISSUE OF *GANGAN YG* THAT WAS RELEASED ON JANUARY 30TH.
WE'RE HERE AS EXTRAS BECAUSE THEY FELT SORRY FOR US...
THAT'S OKAY, WE NEED THE EXPOSURE.

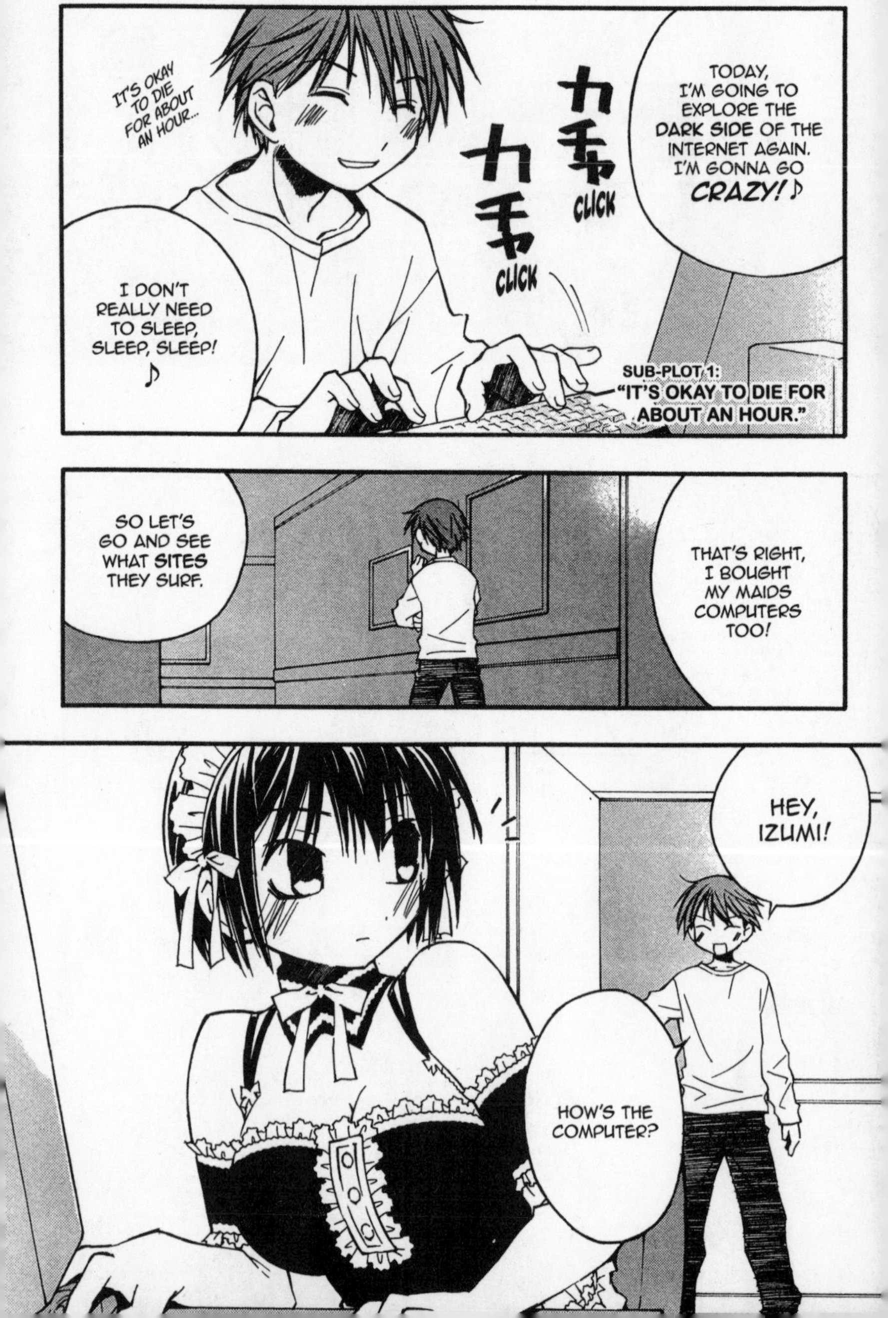
TODAY, I'M GOING TO EXPLORE THE DARK SIDE OF THE INTERNET AGAIN. I'M GONNA GO CRAZY! ♪
カチ CLICK
カチ CLICK
IT'S OKAY TO DIE FOR ABOUT AN HOUR...
I DON'T REALLY NEED TO SLEEP, SLEEP, SLEEP! ♪
SUB-PLOT 1: "IT'S OKAY TO DIE FOR ABOUT AN HOUR."
THAT'S RIGHT, I BOUGHT MY MAIDS COMPUTERS TOO!
SO LET'S GO AND SEE WHAT SITES THEY SURF.
HEY, IZUMI!
HOW'S THE COMPUTER?

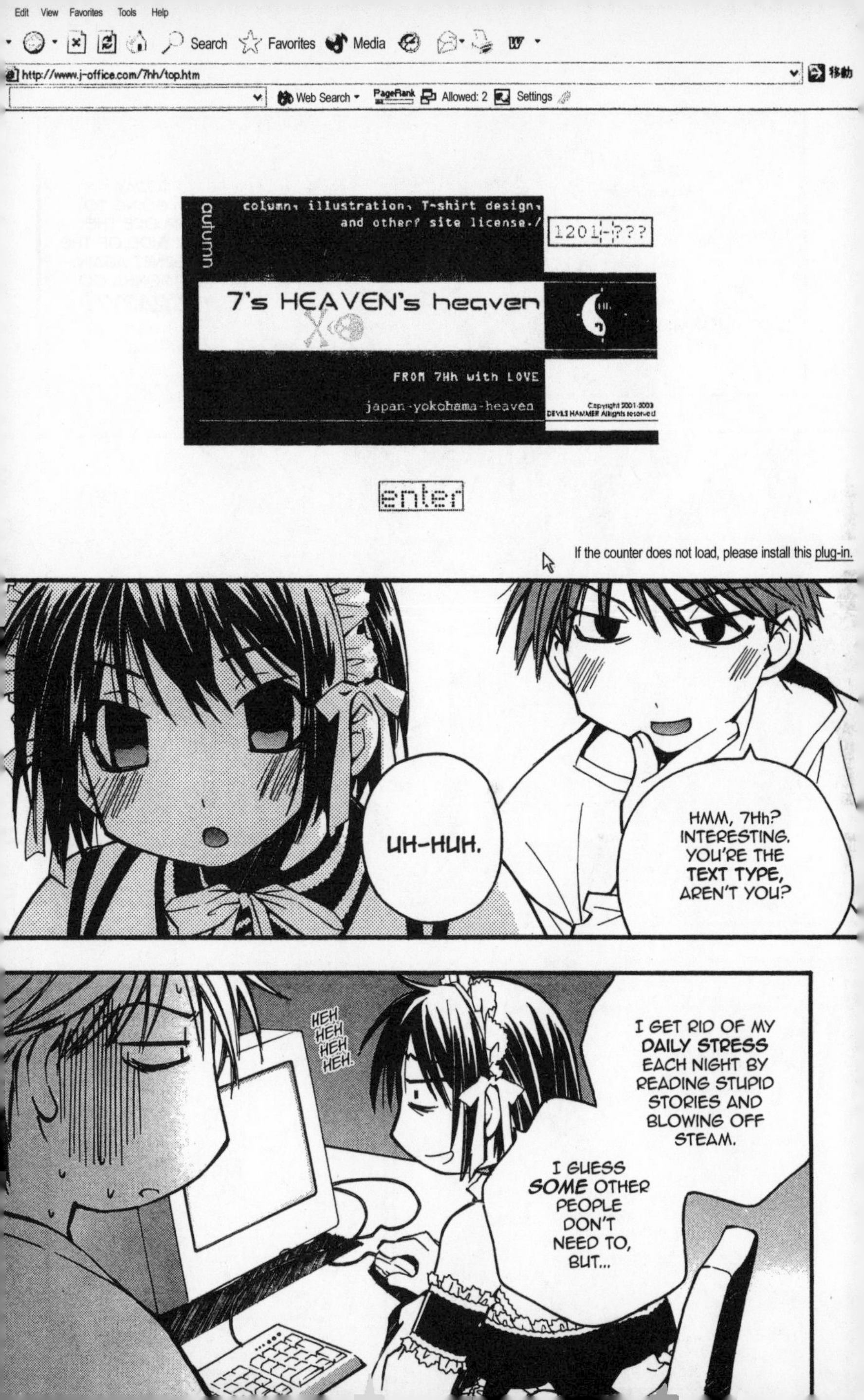
Edit View Favorites Tools Help
Search Favorites Media
http://www.j-office.com/7hh/top.htm
移動
Web Search PageRank Allowed: 2 Settings
autumn
column, illustration, T-shirt design, and other? site license./
1201-???
7's HEAVEN's heaven
FROM 7Hh with LOVE
japan-yokohama-heaven
Copyright 2001-2003 DEVILS HAMMER Allrights reserved
enter
If the counter does not load, please install this plug-in.
HMM, 7Hh? INTERESTING. YOU'RE THE TEXT TYPE, AREN'T YOU?
UH-HUH.
I GET RID OF MY DAILY STRESS EACH NIGHT BY READING STUPID STORIES AND BLOWING OFF STEAM.
HEH HEH HEH HEH.
I GUESS SOME OTHER PEOPLE DON'T NEED TO, BUT...

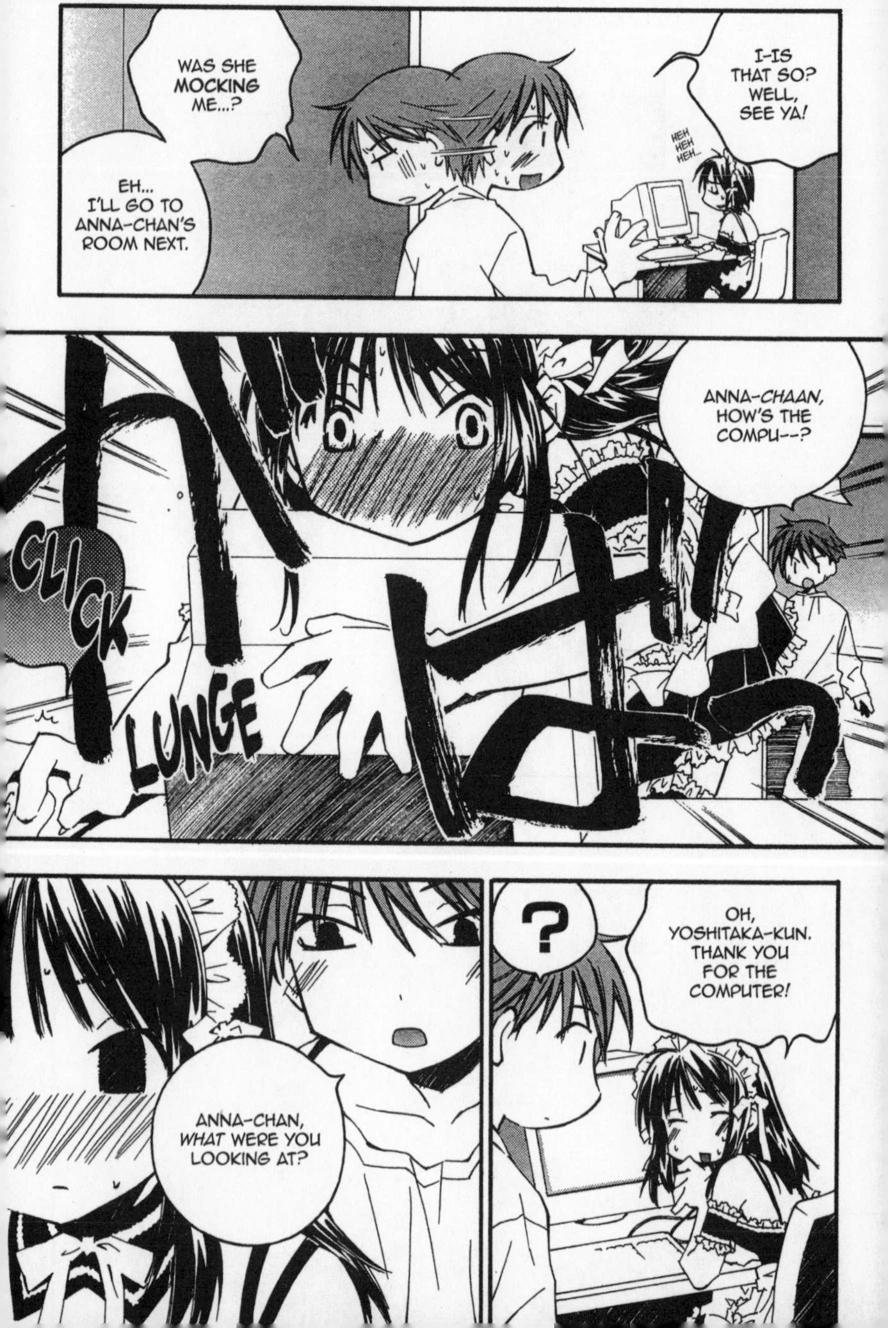
I-IS THAT SO? WELL, SEE YA!
HEH HEH HEH...
WAS SHE MOCKING ME...?
EH... I'LL GO TO ANNA-CHAN'S ROOM NEXT.
ANNA-*CHAAN*, HOW'S THE COMPU--?
CLICK
LUNGE
?
OH, YOSHITAKA-KUN. THANK YOU FOR THE COMPUTER!
ANNA-CHAN, *WHAT* WERE YOU LOOKING AT?

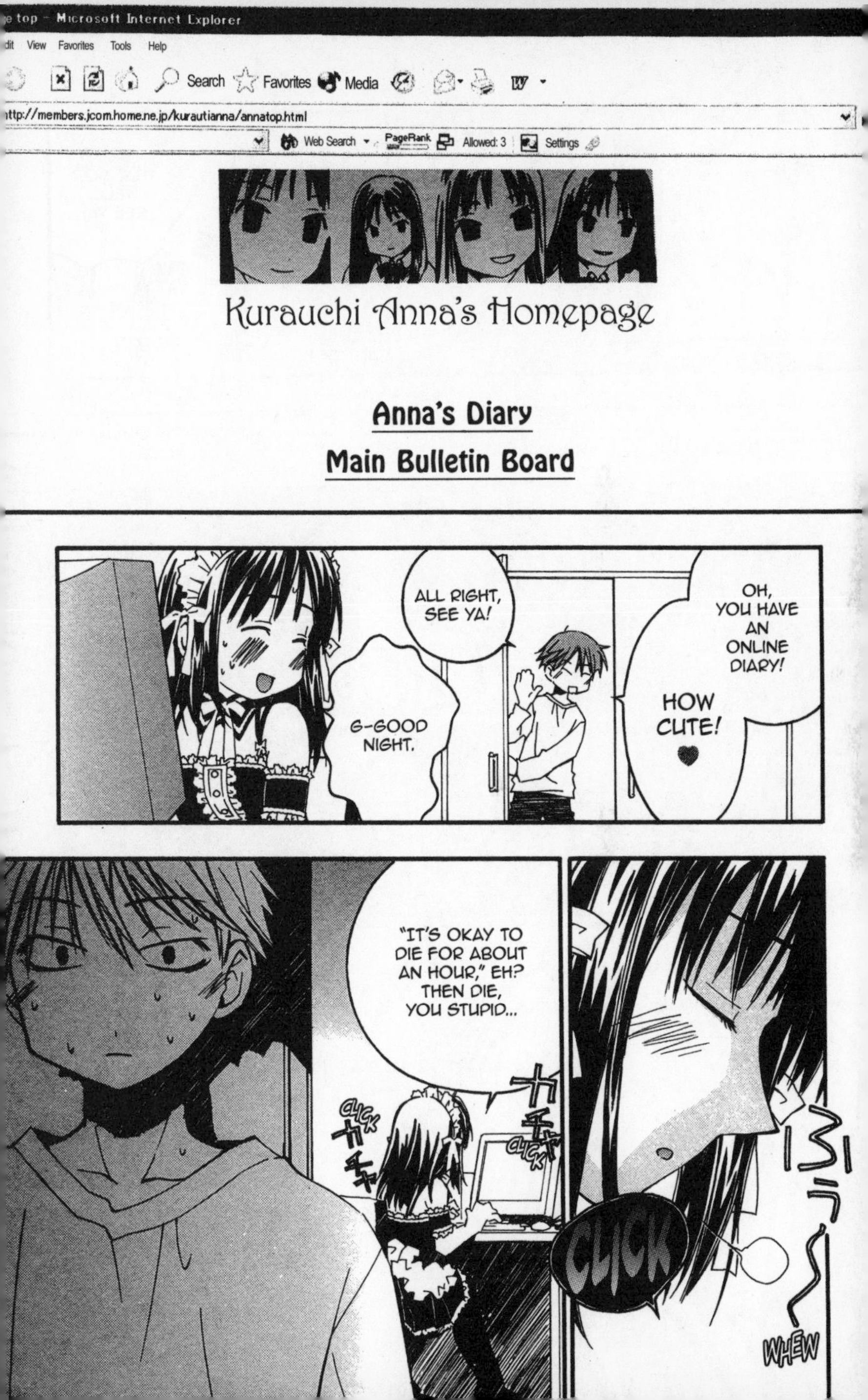
e top - Microsoft Internet Explorer
dit View Favorites Tools Help
Search Favorites Media
http://members.jcom.home.ne.jp/kurautianna/annatop.html
Web Search PageRank Allowed: 3 Settings
Kurauchi Anna's Homepage
Anna's Diary
Main Bulletin Board
OH, YOU HAVE AN ONLINE DIARY!
HOW CUTE! ♥
ALL RIGHT, SEE YA!
G-GOOD NIGHT.
CLICK
WHEW
"IT'S OKAY TO DIE FOR ABOUT AN HOUR," EH? THEN DIE, YOU STUPID...
CLICK
CLICK

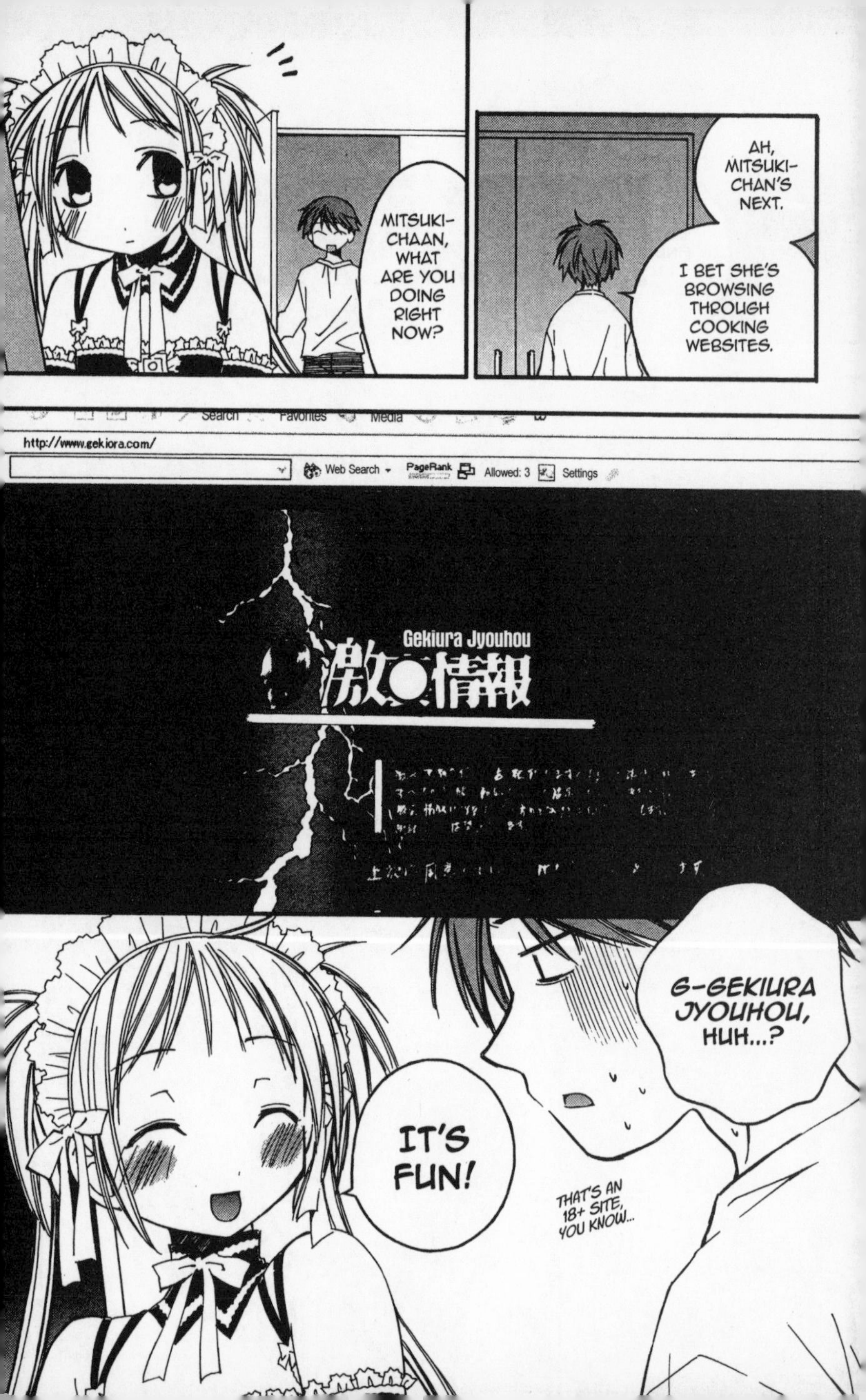
AH, MITSUKI-CHAN'S NEXT.
I BET SHE'S BROWSING THROUGH COOKING WEBSITES.
MITSUKI-CHAAN, WHAT ARE YOU DOING RIGHT NOW?
Search Favorites Media
http://www.gekiora.com/
Web Search PageRank Allowed: 3 Settings
Gekiura Jyouhou
激○情報
G-GEKIURA JYOUHOU, HUH...?
IT'S FUN!
THAT'S AN 18+ SITE, YOU KNOW...

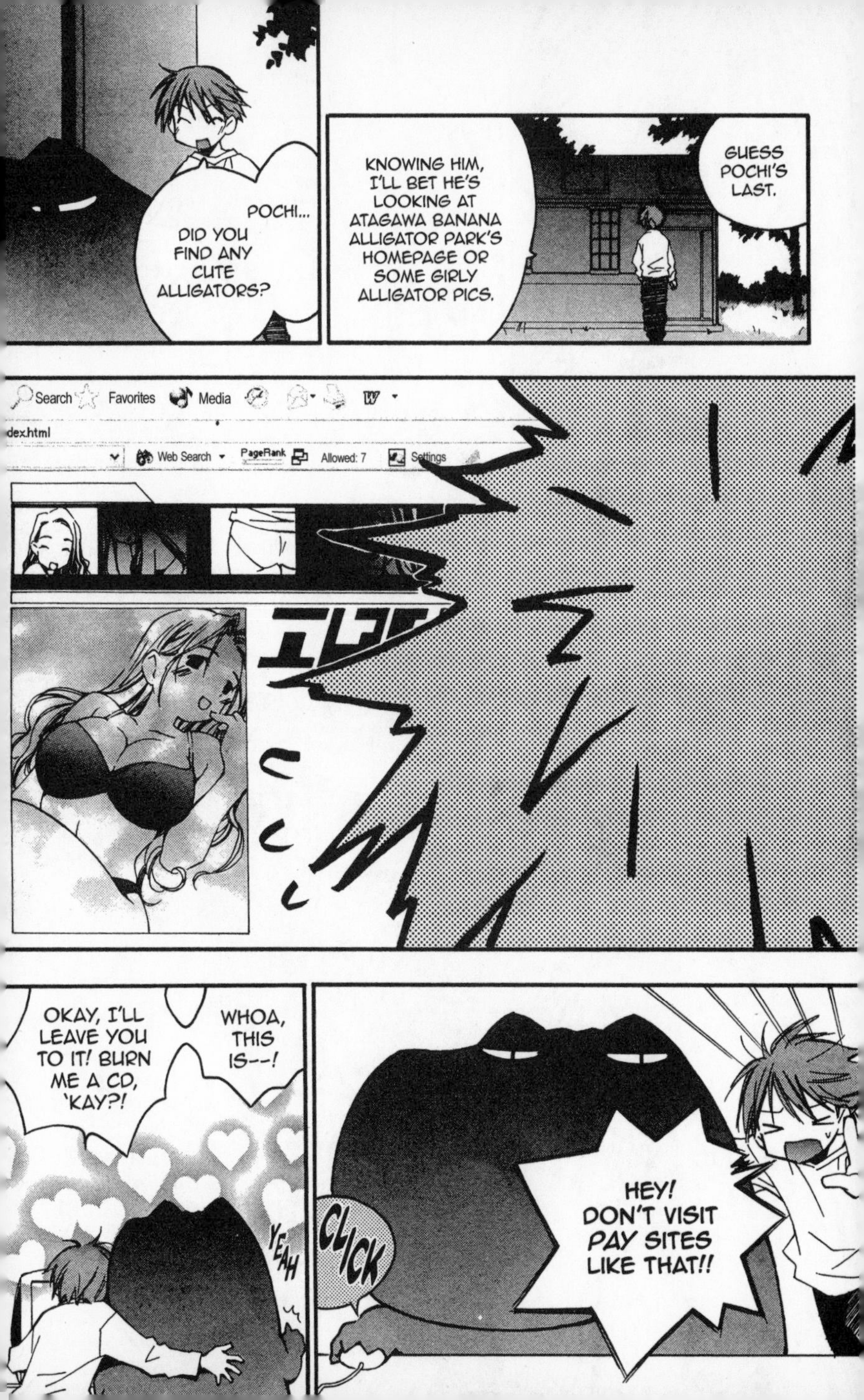
GUESS POCHI'S LAST.
KNOWING HIM, I'LL BET HE'S LOOKING AT ATAGAWA BANANA ALLIGATOR PARK'S HOMEPAGE OR SOME GIRLY ALLIGATOR PICS.
POCHI...
DID YOU FIND ANY CUTE ALLIGATORS?
Search Favorites Media
dex.html
Web Search PageRank Allowed: 7 Settings
HEY! DON'T VISIT PAY SITES LIKE THAT!!
CLICK
WHOA, THIS IS--!
OKAY, I'LL LEAVE YOU TO IT! BURN ME A CD, 'KAY?!
YEAH

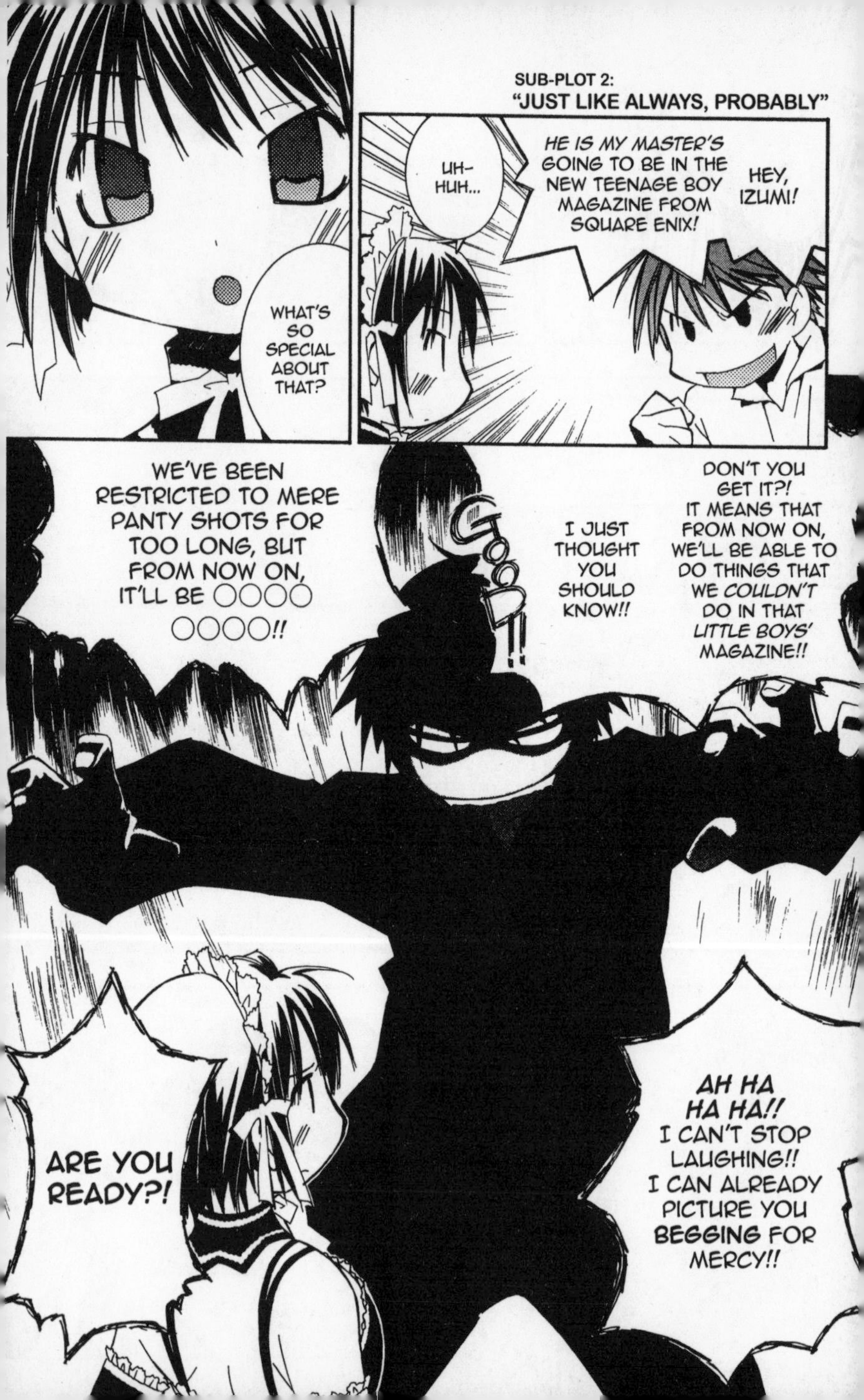
SUB-PLOT 2:
"JUST LIKE ALWAYS, PROBABLY"
HEY, IZUMI!
HE IS MY MASTER'S GOING TO BE IN THE NEW TEENAGE BOY MAGAZINE FROM SQUARE ENIX!
UH-HUH...
WHAT'S SO SPECIAL ABOUT THAT?
DON'T YOU GET IT?! IT MEANS THAT FROM NOW ON, WE'LL BE ABLE TO DO THINGS THAT WE COULDN'T DO IN THAT LITTLE BOYS' MAGAZINE!!
I JUST THOUGHT YOU SHOULD KNOW!!
WE'VE BEEN RESTRICTED TO MERE PANTY SHOTS FOR TOO LONG, BUT FROM NOW ON, IT'LL BE ○○○○ ○○○○!!
AH HA HA HA!! I CAN'T STOP LAUGHING!! I CAN ALREADY PICTURE YOU BEGGING FOR MERCY!!
ARE YOU READY?!

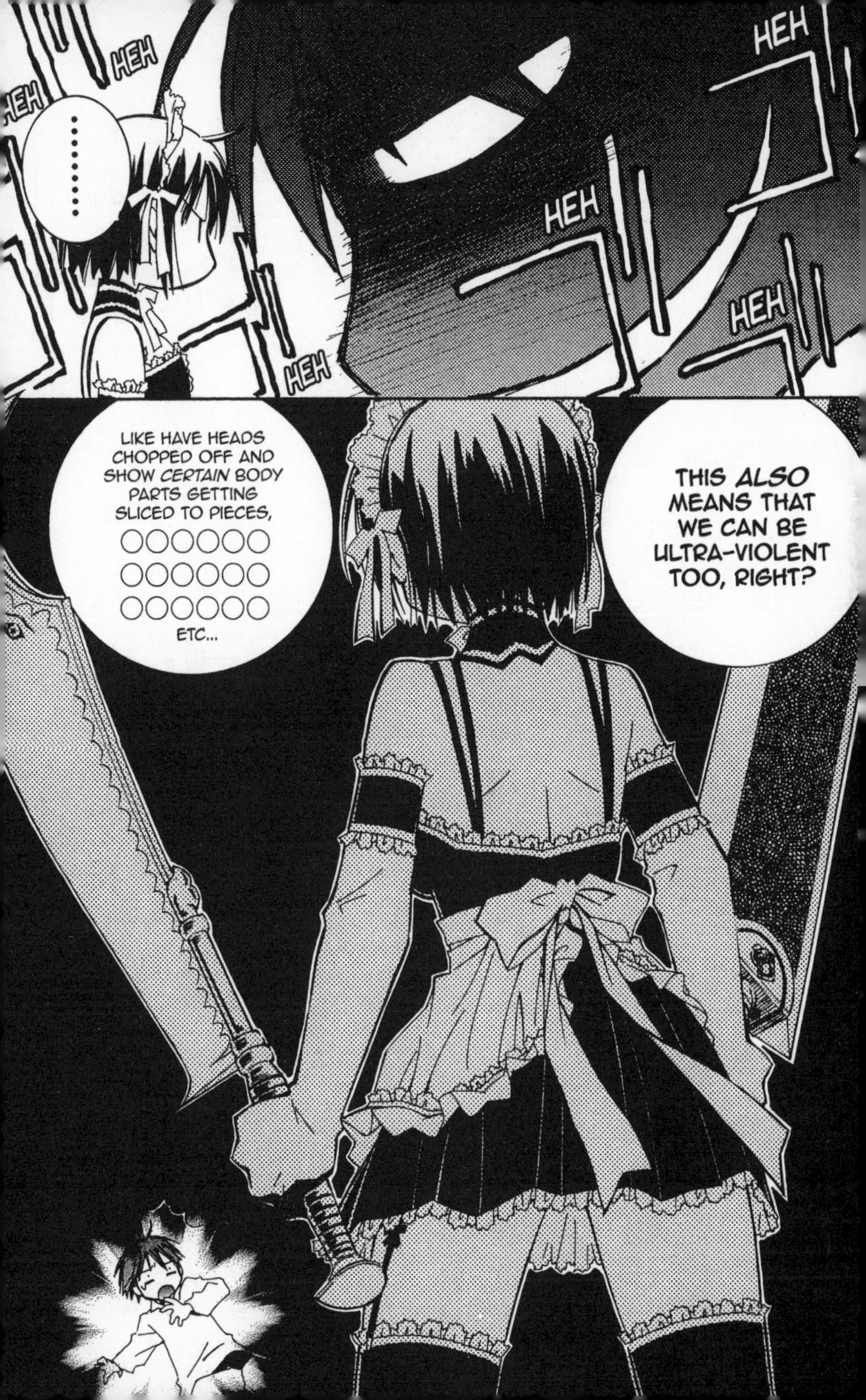
HEH
HEH
HEH
HEH
HEH
HEH
......
THIS ALSO MEANS THAT WE CAN BE ULTRA-VIOLENT TOO, RIGHT?
LIKE HAVE HEADS CHOPPED OFF AND SHOW CERTAIN BODY PARTS GETTING SLICED TO PIECES,
○○○○○○○
○○○○○○○
○○○○○○○
ETC...

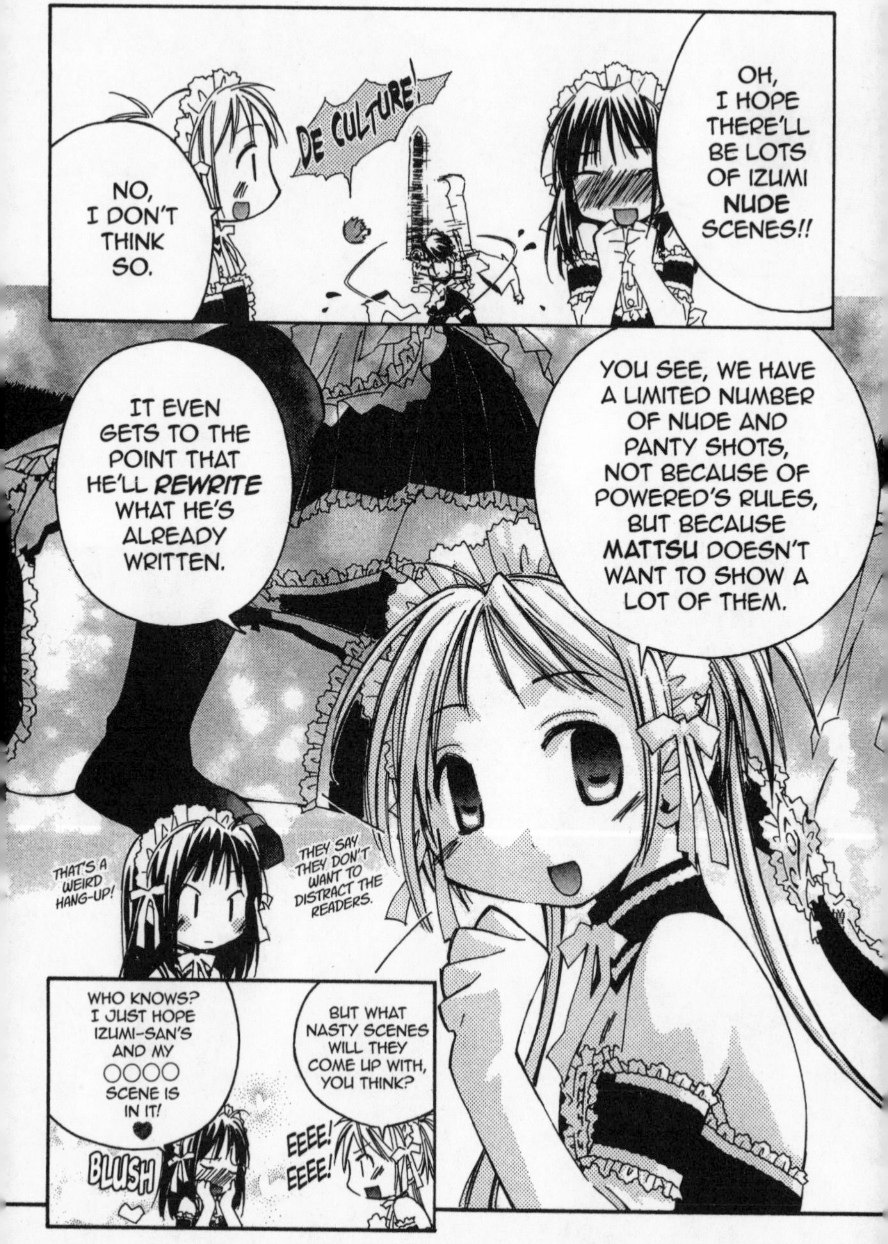
OH, I HOPE THERE'LL BE LOTS OF IZUMI **NUDE** SCENES!!
DE CULTURE!
NO, I DON'T THINK SO.
YOU SEE, WE HAVE A LIMITED NUMBER OF NUDE AND PANTY SHOTS, NOT BECAUSE OF POWERED'S RULES, BUT BECAUSE **MATTSU** DOESN'T WANT TO SHOW A LOT OF THEM.
IT EVEN GETS TO THE POINT THAT HE'LL ***REWRITE*** WHAT HE'S ALREADY WRITTEN.
THEY SAY THEY DON'T WANT TO DISTRACT THE READERS.
THAT'S A WEIRD HANG-UP!
BUT WHAT NASTY SCENES WILL THEY COME UP WITH, YOU THINK?
EEEE! EEEE!
WHO KNOWS? I JUST HOPE IZUMI-SAN'S AND MY ○○○○ SCENE IS IN IT! ♥
BLUSH

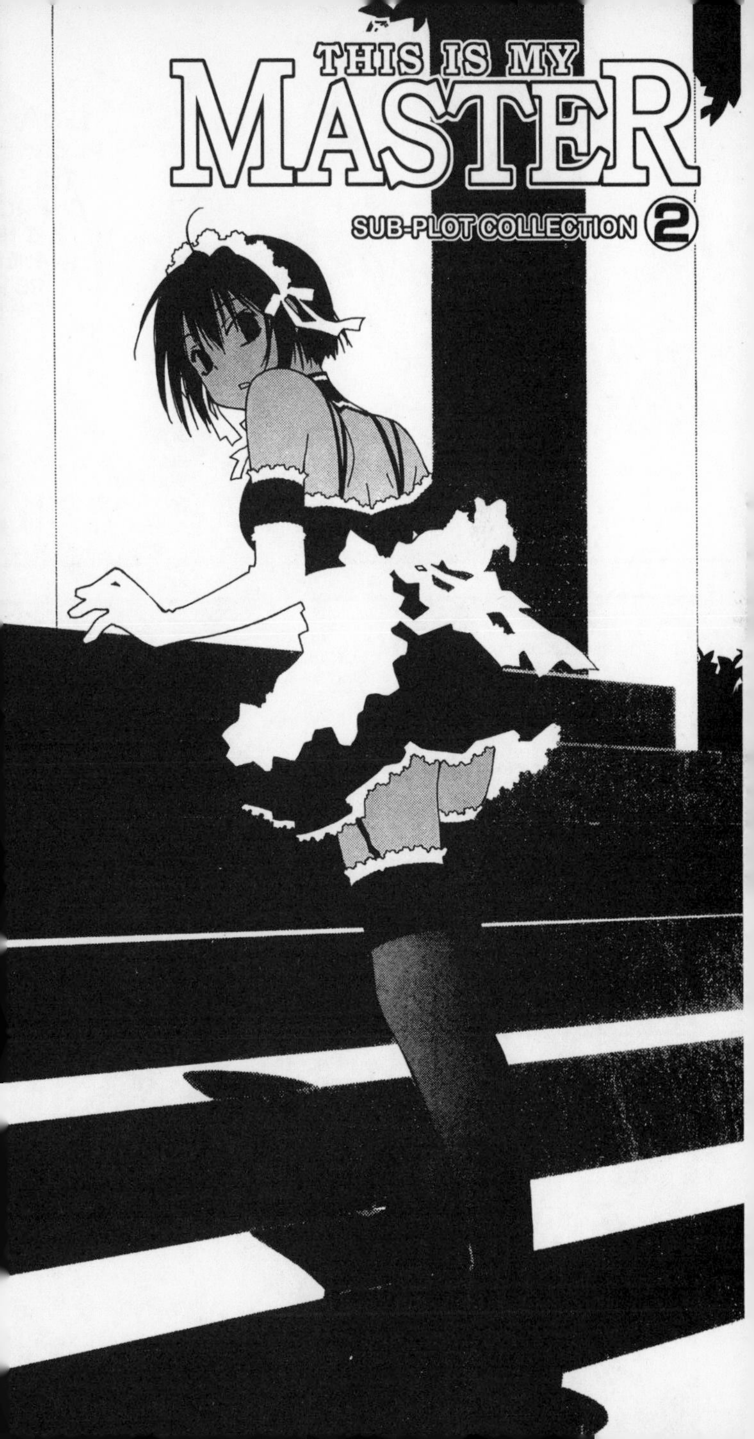
THIS IS MY
MASTER
SUB-PLOT COLLECTION 2

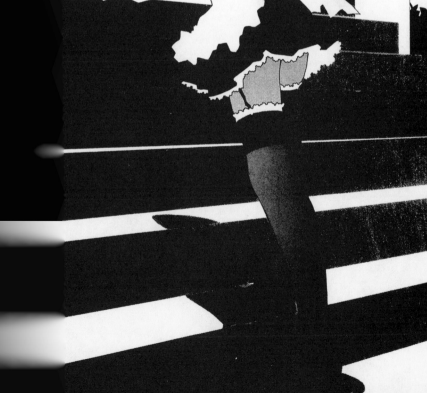

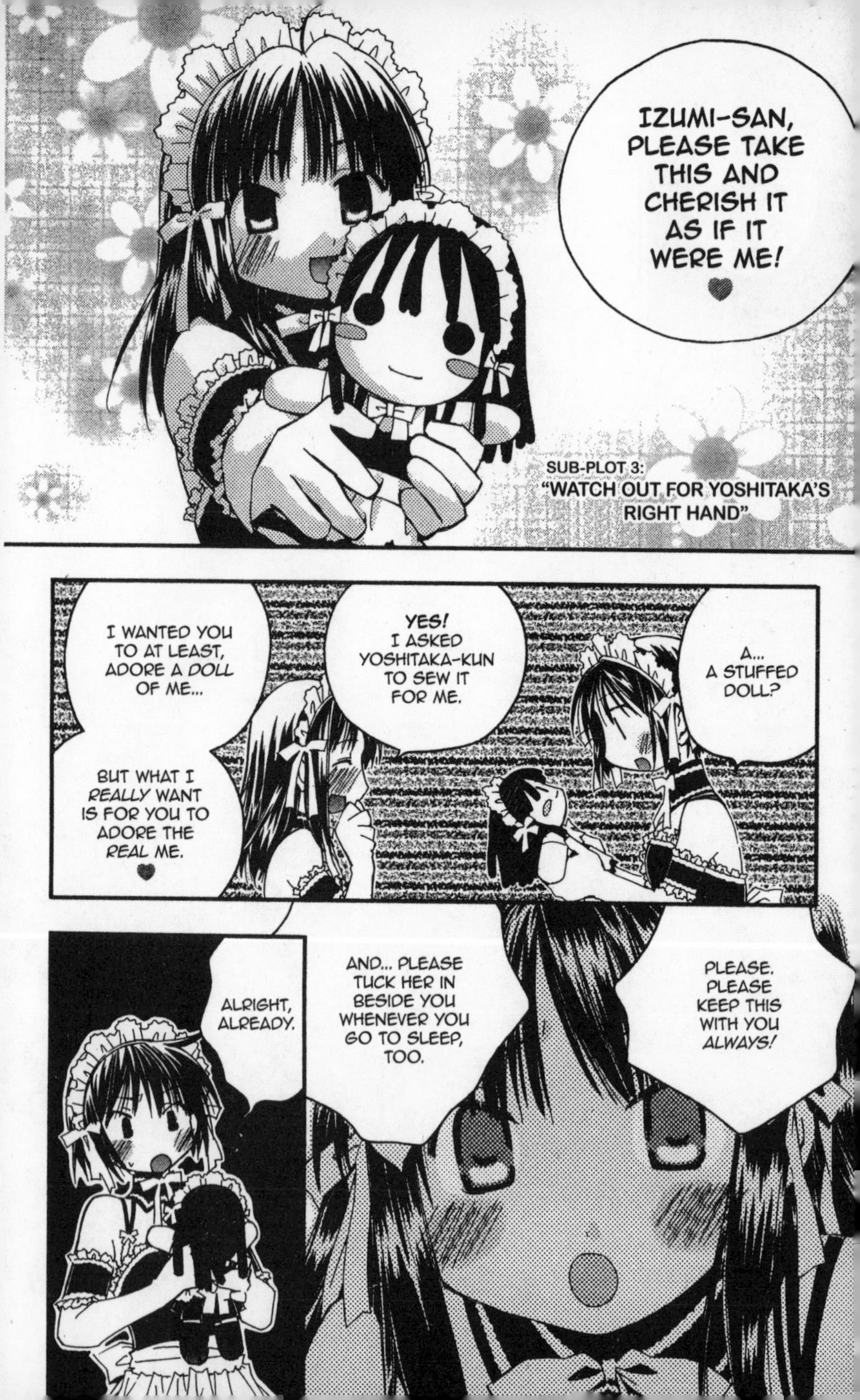
IZUMI-SAN, PLEASE TAKE THIS AND CHERISH IT AS IF IT WERE ME! ♥
SUB-PLOT 3:
"WATCH OUT FOR YOSHITAKA'S RIGHT HAND"
A... A STUFFED DOLL?
YES! I ASKED YOSHITAKA-KUN TO SEW IT FOR ME.
I WANTED YOU TO AT LEAST, ADORE A *DOLL* OF ME...
BUT WHAT I *REALLY* WANT IS FOR YOU TO ADORE THE *REAL* ME. ♥
PLEASE. PLEASE KEEP THIS WITH YOU *ALWAYS!*
AND... PLEASE TUCK HER IN BESIDE YOU WHENEVER YOU GO TO SLEEP, TOO.
ALRIGHT, ALREADY.

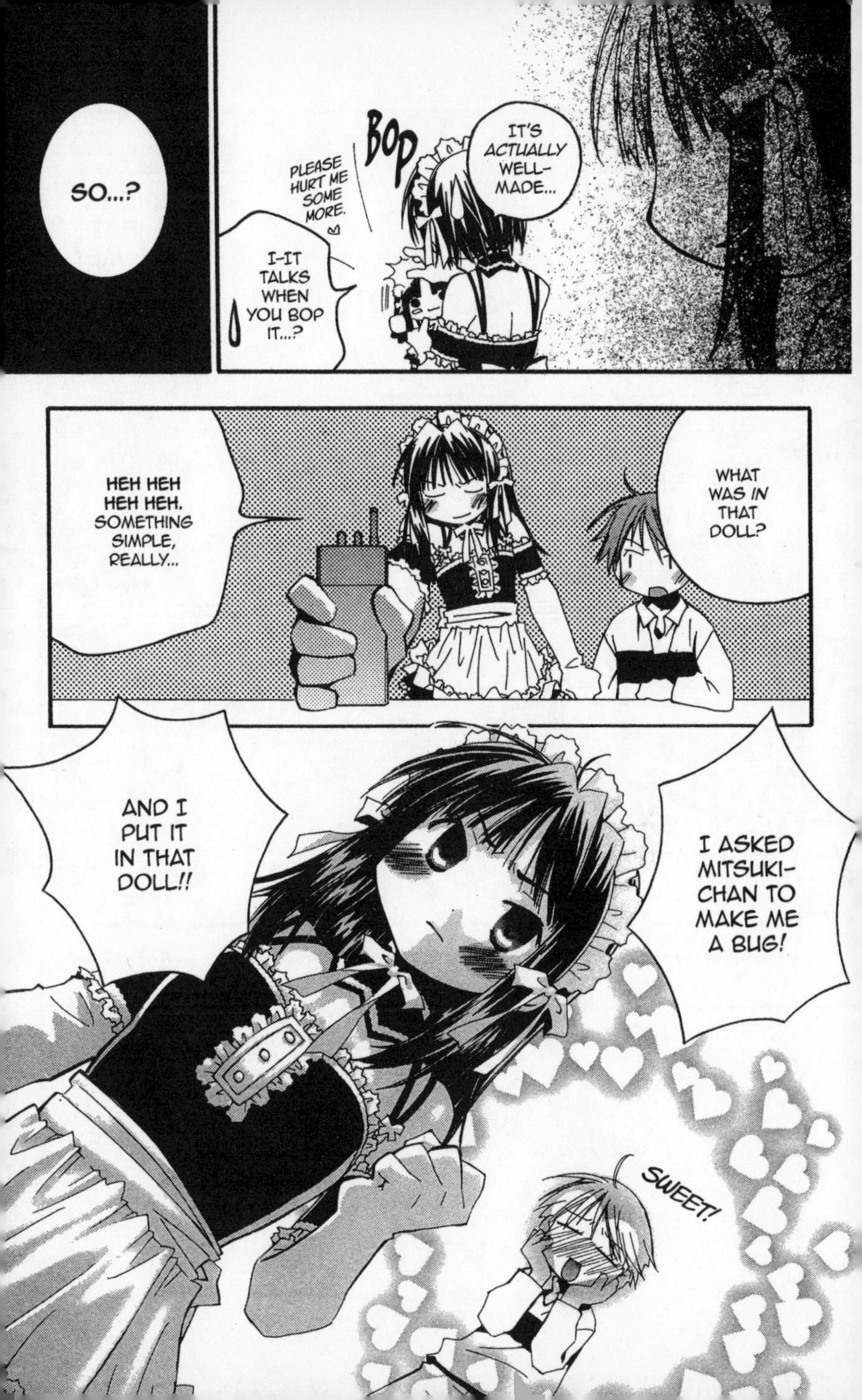
IT'S ACTUALLY WELL-MADE...
BOP
PLEASE HURT ME SOME MORE. ♡
I-IT TALKS WHEN YOU BOP IT...?
SO...?
WHAT WAS *IN* THAT DOLL?
HEH HEH HEH HEH. SOMETHING SIMPLE, REALLY...
I ASKED MITSUKI-CHAN TO MAKE ME A BUG!
AND I PUT IT IN THAT DOLL!!
SWEET!

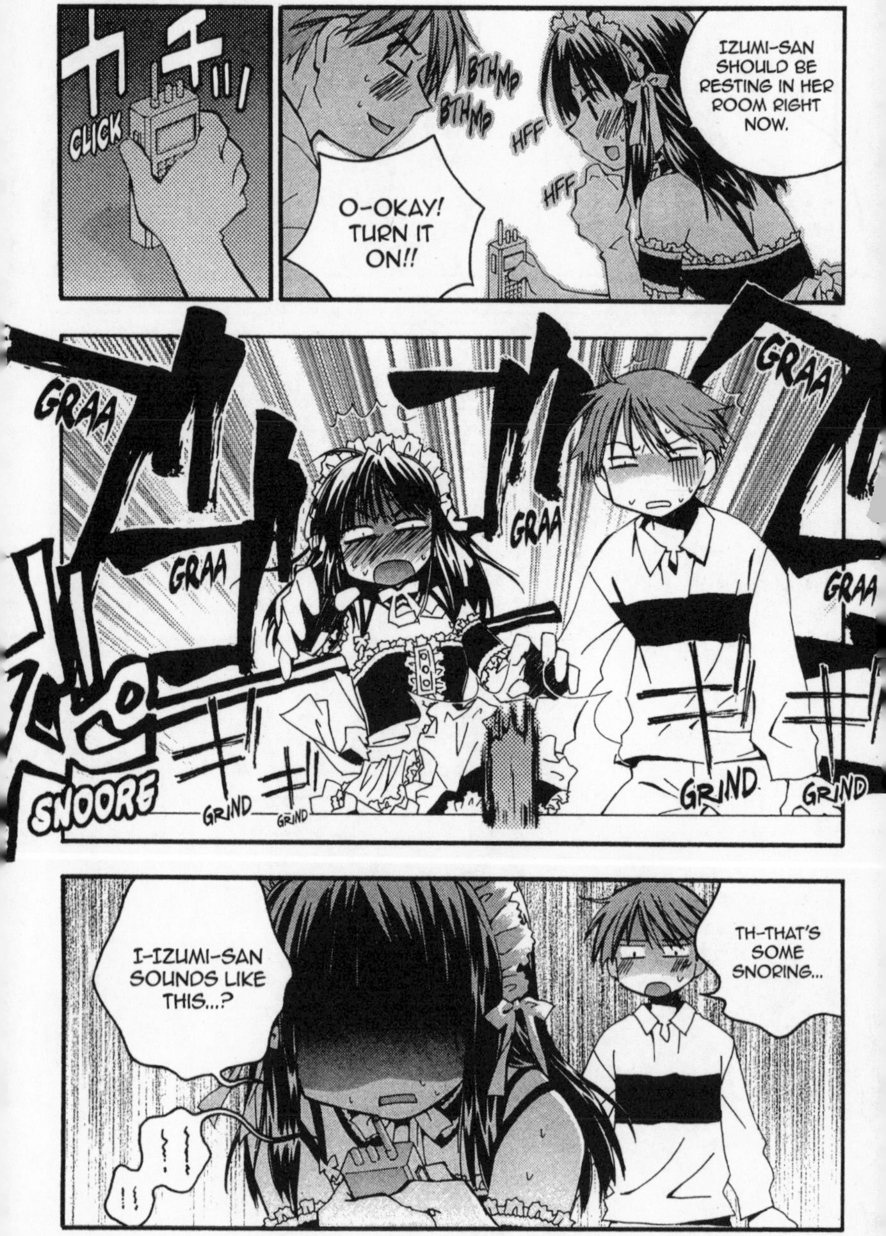
IZUMI-SAN SHOULD BE RESTING IN HER ROOM RIGHT NOW.
HFF
HFF
BTHMP
BTHMP
O-OKAY! TURN IT ON!!
CLICK
GRAA
GRAA
GRAA
GRAA
GRAA
GRIND
GRIND
GRIND
GRIND
SNOORE
TH-THAT'S SOME SNORING...
I-IZUMI-SAN SOUNDS LIKE THIS...?

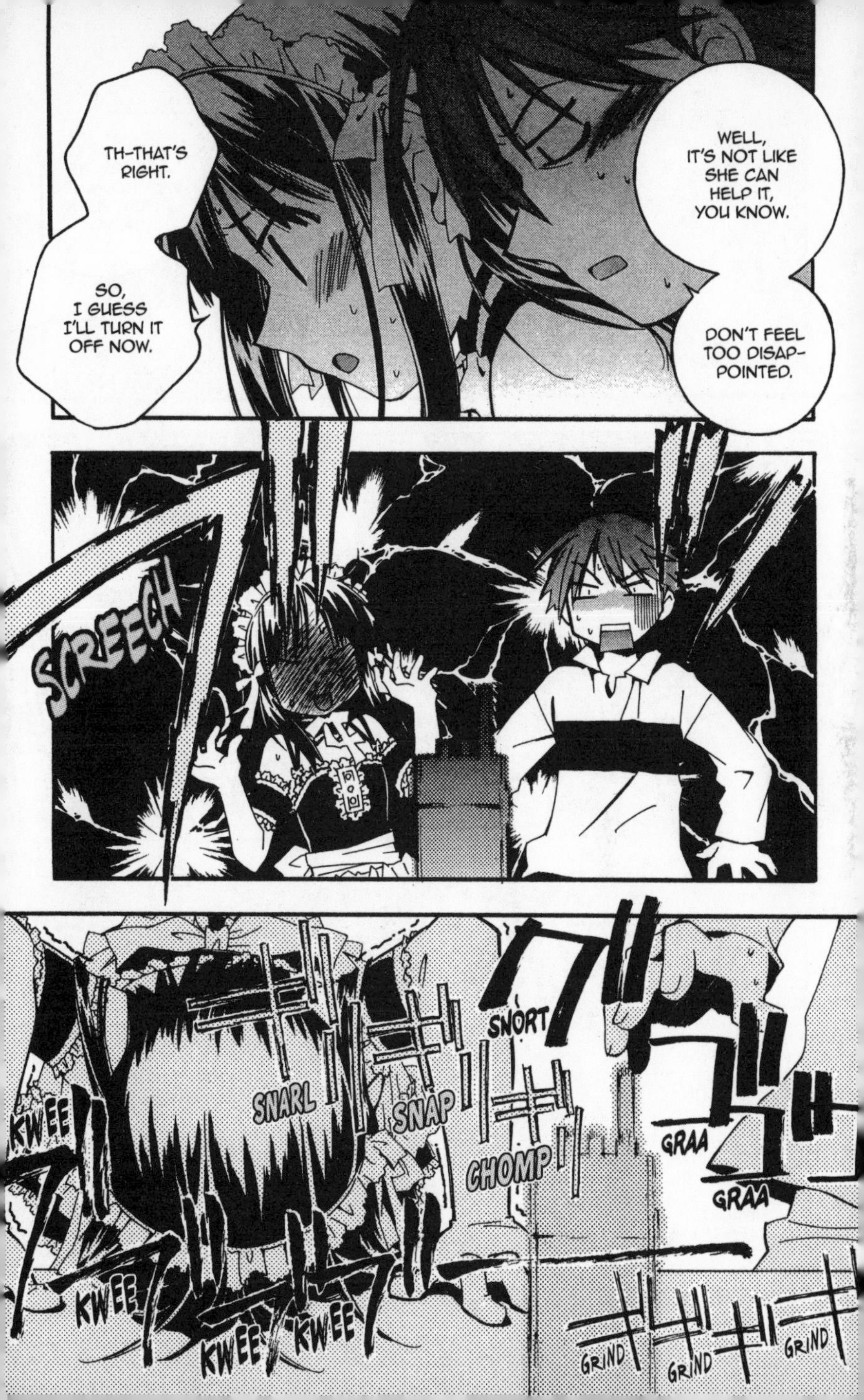
WELL, IT'S NOT LIKE SHE CAN HELP IT, YOU KNOW.
DON'T FEEL TOO DISAP-POINTED.
TH-THAT'S RIGHT.
SO, I GUESS I'LL TURN IT OFF NOW.
SCREECH
SNORT
GRAA
GRAA
SNAP
CHOMP
SNARL
KWEE
GRIND
GRIND
GRIND
KWEE
KWEE
KWEE

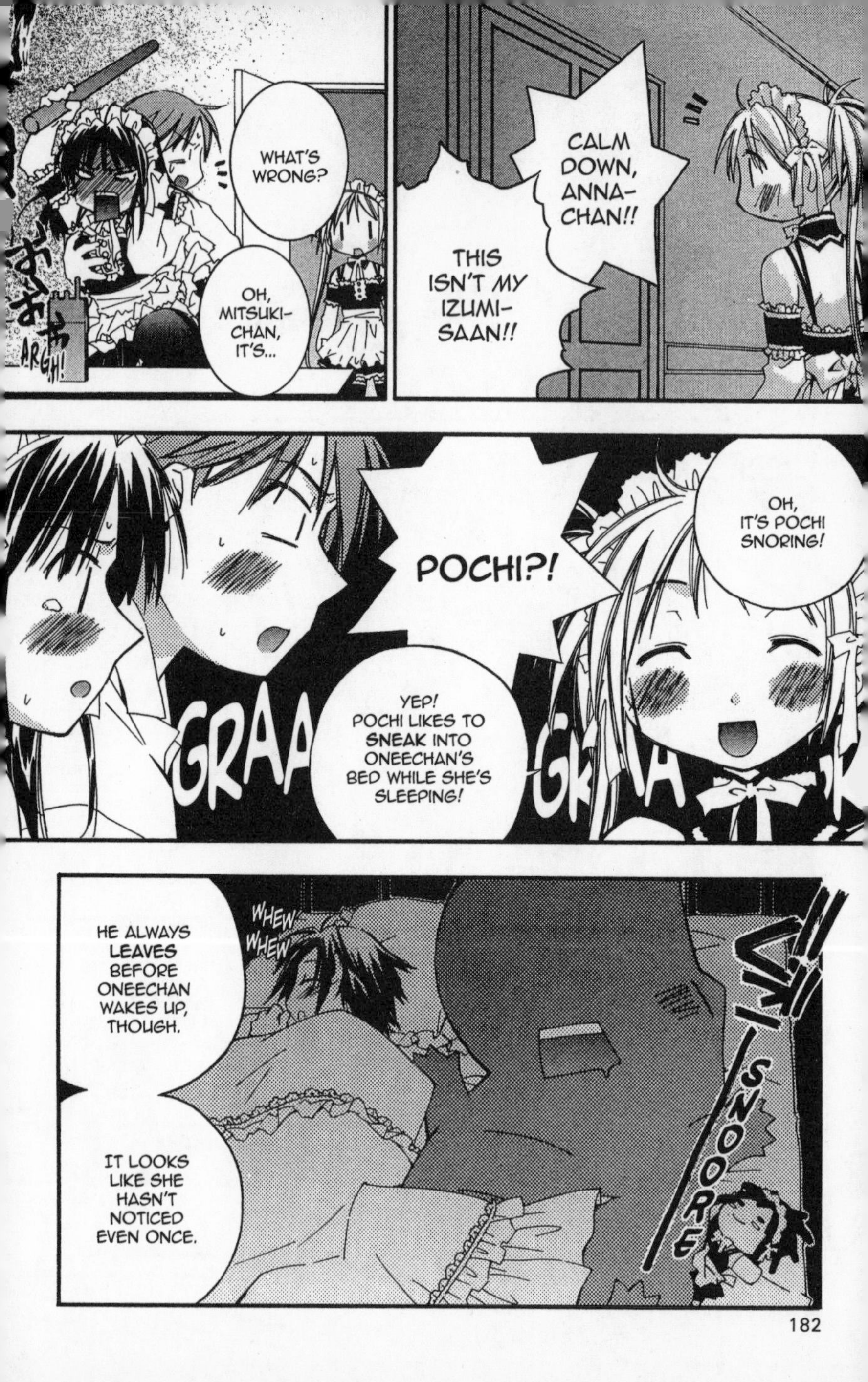
CALM DOWN, ANNA-CHAN!!
THIS ISN'T MY IZUMI-SAAN!!
WHAT'S WRONG?
OH, MITSUKI-CHAN, IT'S...
ARGH!
OH, IT'S POCHI SNORING!
POCHI?!
YEP! POCHI LIKES TO SNEAK INTO ONEECHAN'S BED WHILE SHE'S SLEEPING!
GRAA
HE ALWAYS LEAVES BEFORE ONEECHAN WAKES UP, THOUGH.
IT LOOKS LIKE SHE HASN'T NOTICED EVEN ONCE.
WHEW WHEW
SNOORE

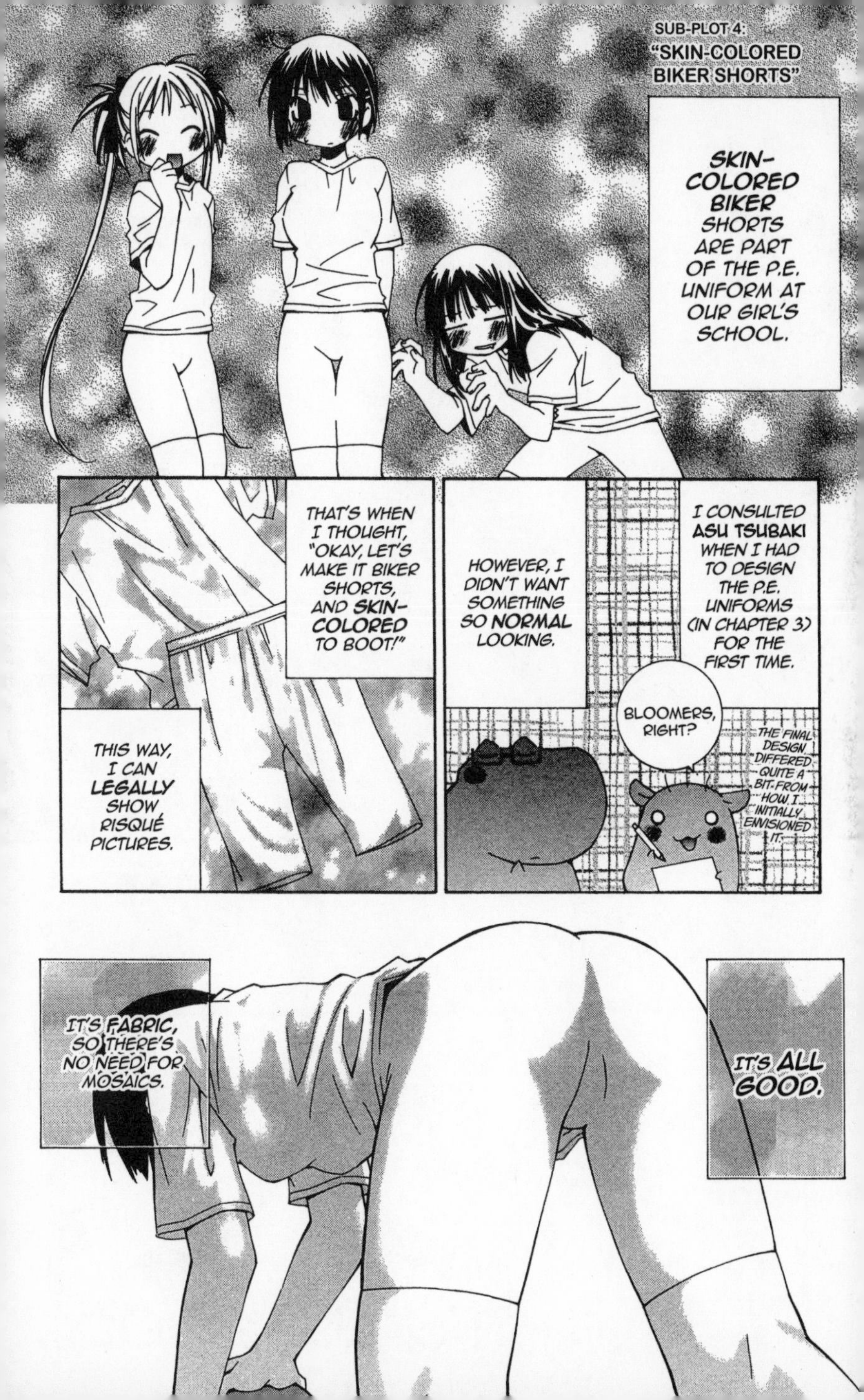
SUB-PLOT 4:
"SKIN-COLORED BIKER SHORTS"
SKIN-COLORED BIKER SHORTS ARE PART OF THE P.E. UNIFORM AT OUR GIRL'S SCHOOL.
I CONSULTED ASU TSUBAKI WHEN I HAD TO DESIGN THE P.E. UNIFORMS (IN CHAPTER 3) FOR THE FIRST TIME.
HOWEVER, I DIDN'T WANT SOMETHING SO NORMAL LOOKING.
BLOOMERS, RIGHT?
THE FINAL DESIGN DIFFERED QUITE A BIT FROM HOW I INITIALLY ENVISIONED IT.
THAT'S WHEN I THOUGHT, "OKAY, LET'S MAKE IT BIKER SHORTS, AND SKIN-COLORED TO BOOT!"
THIS WAY, I CAN LEGALLY SHOW RISQUÉ PICTURES.
IT'S ALL GOOD.
IT'S FABRIC, SO THERE'S NO NEED FOR MOSAICS.

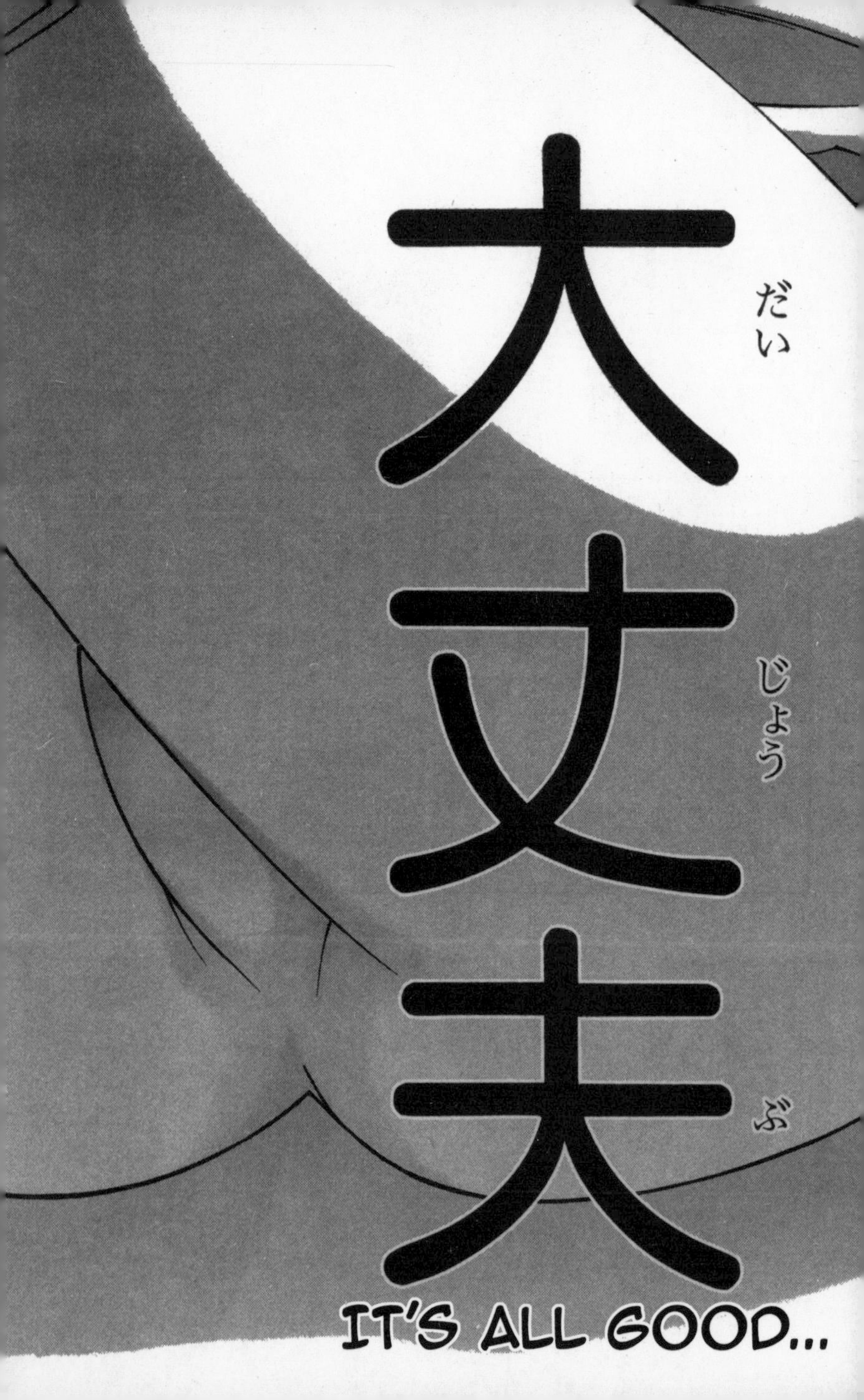

大丈夫(だいじょうぶ)
IT'S ALL GOOD...

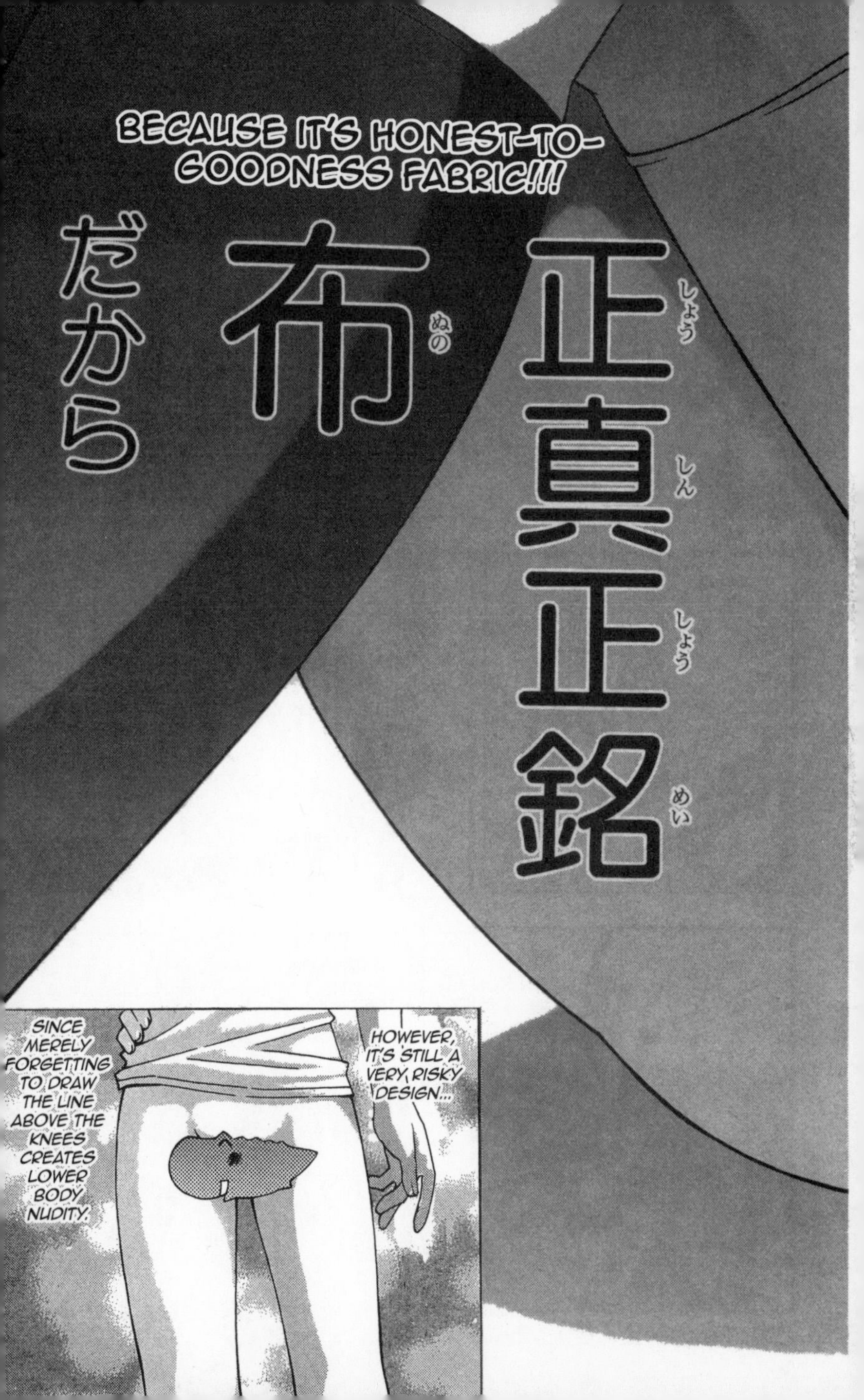
BECAUSE IT'S HONEST-TO-GOODNESS FABRIC!!!
正真正銘(しょうしんしょうめい)布(ぬの)だから
HOWEVER, IT'S STILL A VERY RISKY DESIGN...
SINCE MERELY FORGETTING TO DRAW THE LINE ABOVE THE KNEES CREATES LOWER BODY NUDITY.

SUB-PLOT 5: "MAID CATCHER"

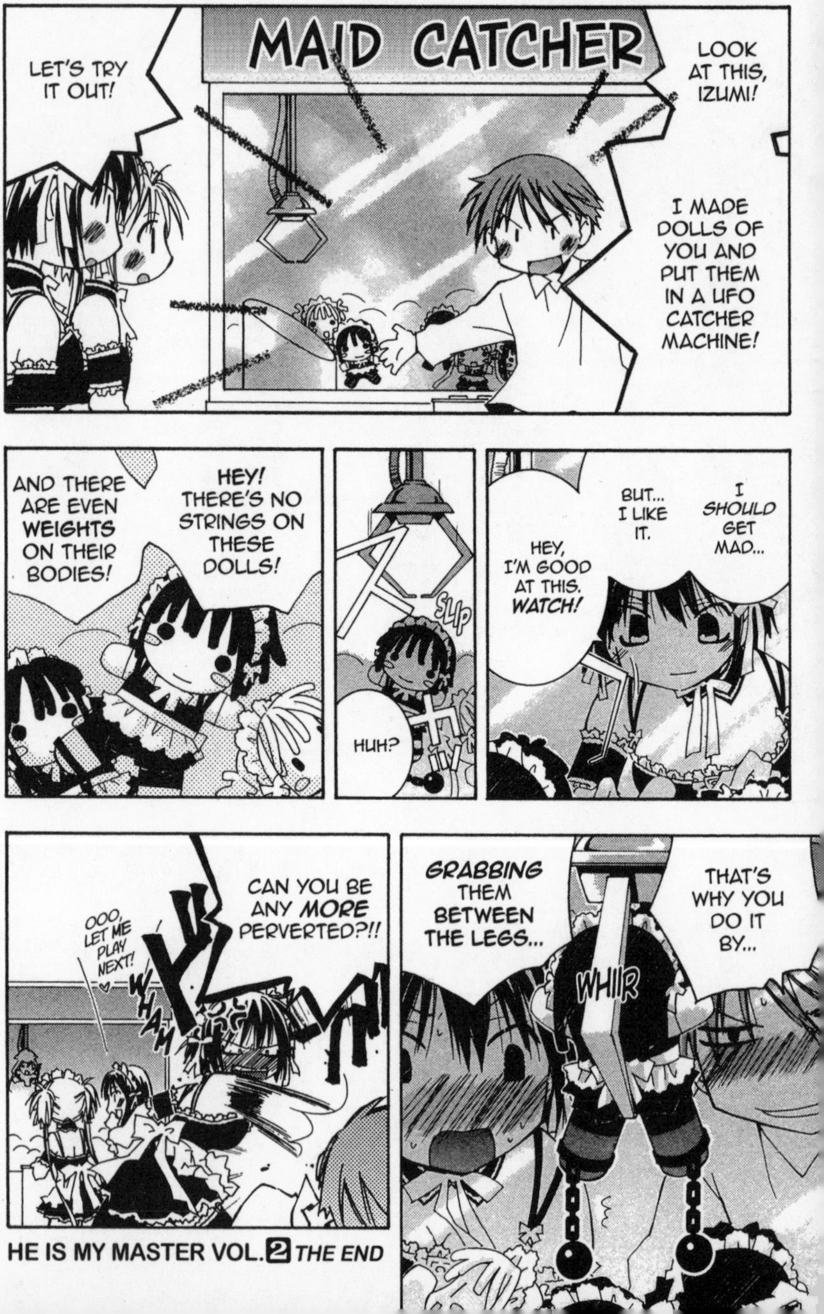
LOOK AT THIS, IZUMI!
I MADE DOLLS OF YOU AND PUT THEM IN A UFO CATCHER MACHINE!
MAID CATCHER
LET'S TRY IT OUT!
I SHOULD GET MAD...
BUT... I LIKE IT.
HEY, I'M GOOD AT THIS. WATCH!
SLIP
HUH?
HEY! THERE'S NO STRINGS ON THESE DOLLS!
AND THERE ARE EVEN WEIGHTS ON THEIR BODIES!
THAT'S WHY YOU DO IT BY...
GRABBING THEM BETWEEN THE LEGS...
WHIIR
CAN YOU BE ANY MORE PERVERTED?!!
WHAM
OOO, LET ME PLAY NEXT! ♥

HE IS MY MASTER VOL. 2 THE END

BATHS SHOULD DEFINITELY BE TAKEN AFTER THE MAIDS

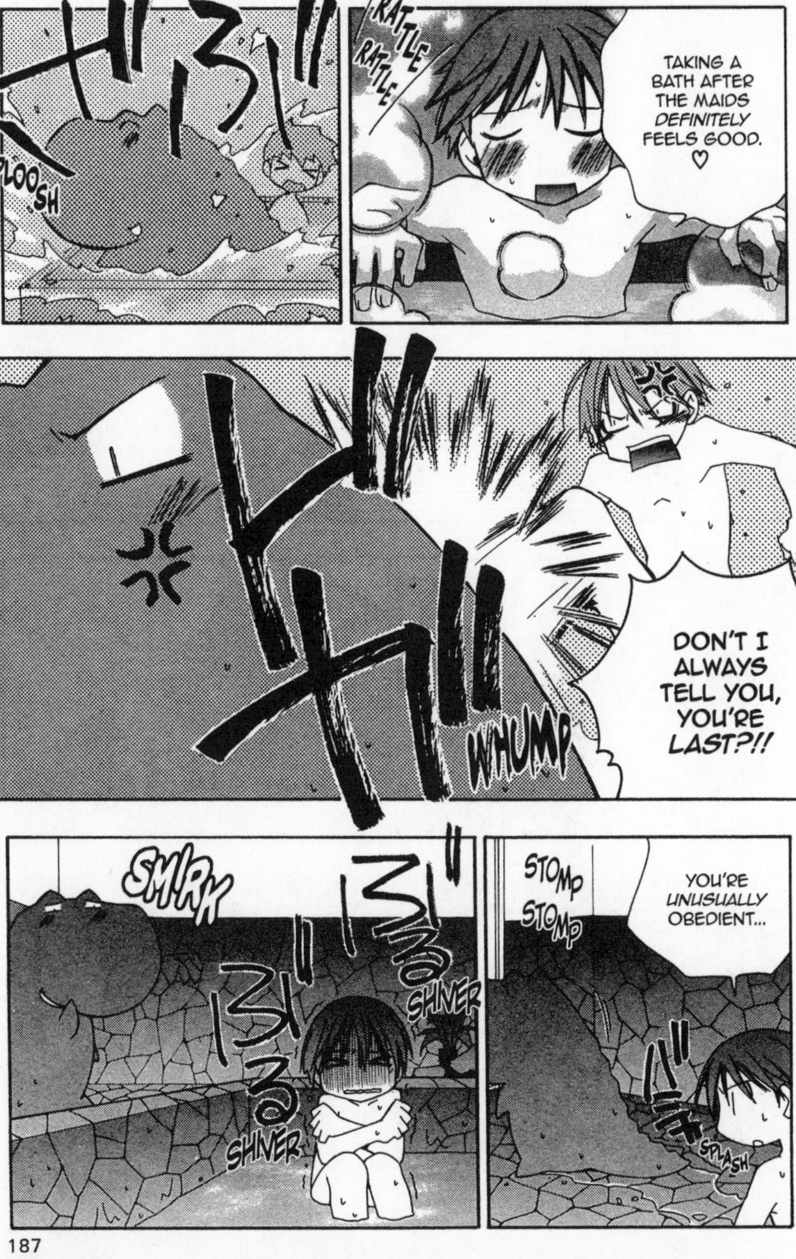

RATTLE
RATTLE
TAKING A BATH AFTER THE MAIDS *DEFINITELY* FEELS GOOD. ♡
SPLOOSH
DON'T I ALWAYS TELL YOU, YOU'RE *LAST?!!*
WHUMP
STOMP
STOMP
YOU'RE *UNUSUALLY* OBEDIENT...
SPLASH
SMIRK
SHIVER
SHIVER

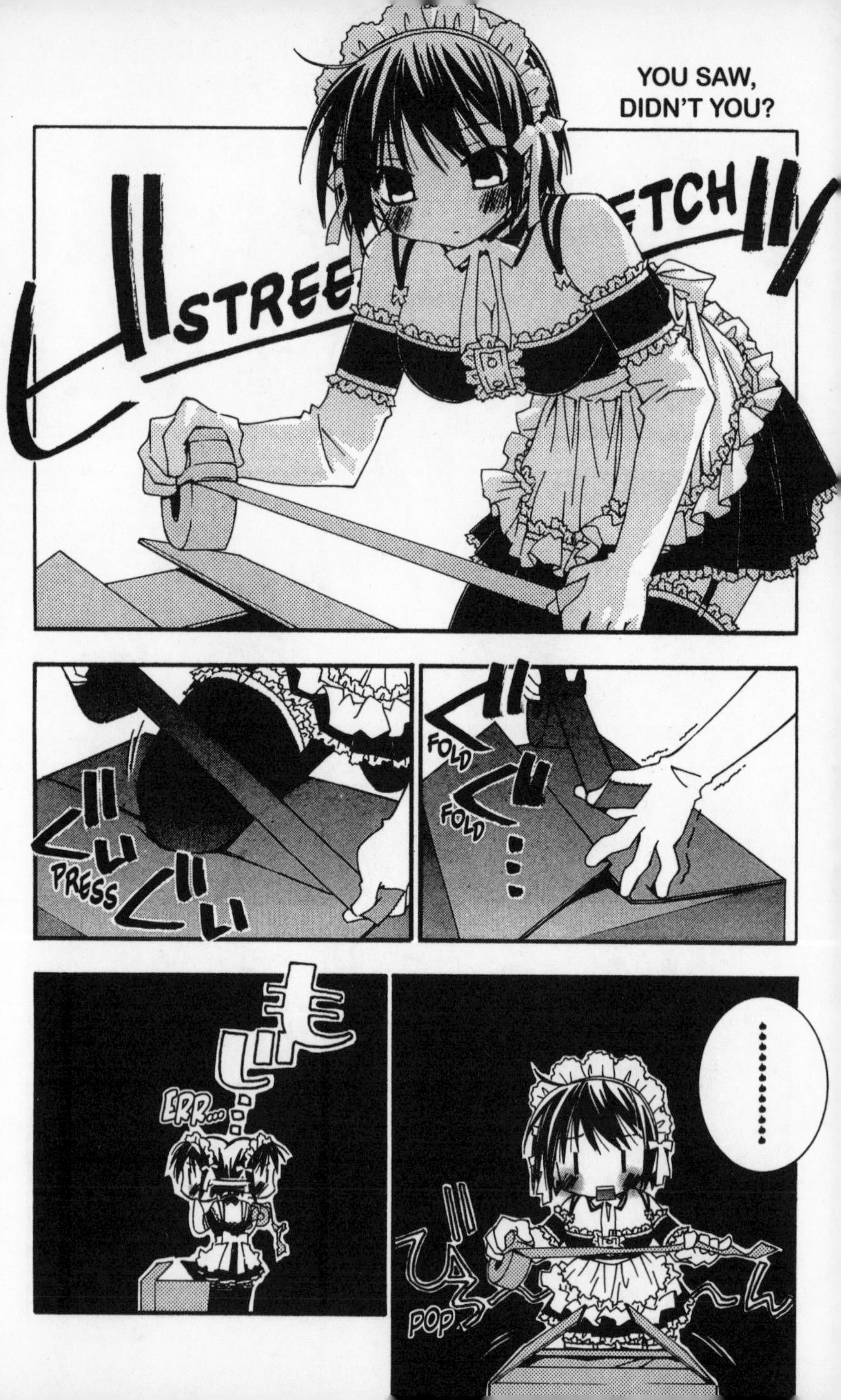
YOU SAW, DIDN'T YOU?
STREE-ETCH
FOLD
FOLD
...
PRESS
....
POP
ERR...

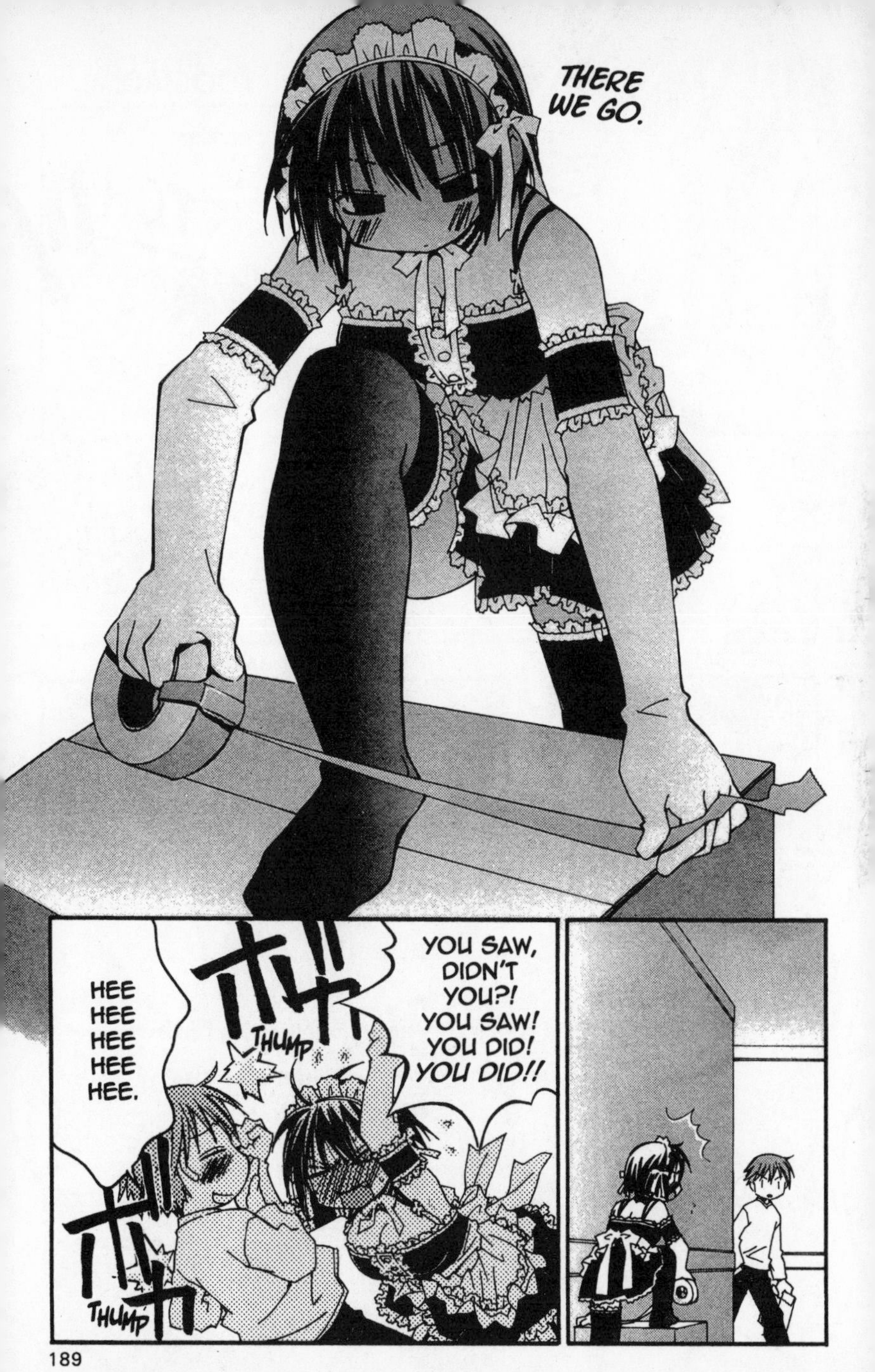
THERE WE GO.
YOU SAW, DIDN'T YOU?! YOU SAW! YOU DID! YOU DID!!
THUMP
HEE HEE HEE HEE HEE.
THUMP

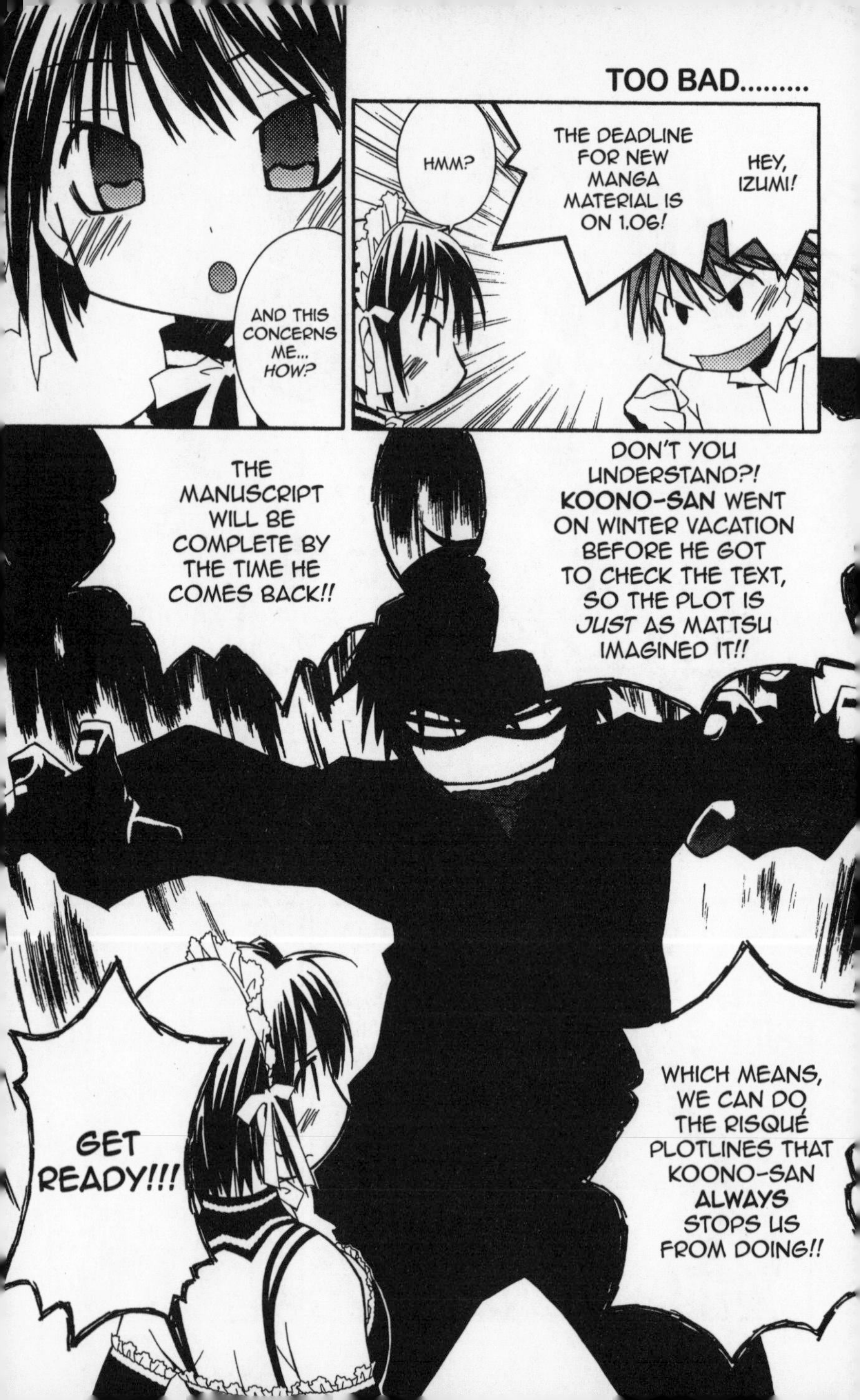
TOO BAD.........
HEY, IZUMI!
THE DEADLINE FOR NEW MANGA MATERIAL IS ON 1.06!
HMM?
AND THIS CONCERNS ME... *HOW?*
DON'T YOU UNDERSTAND?! **KOONO-SAN** WENT ON WINTER VACATION BEFORE HE GOT TO CHECK THE TEXT, SO THE PLOT IS *JUST* AS MATTSU IMAGINED IT!!
THE MANUSCRIPT WILL BE COMPLETE BY THE TIME HE COMES BACK!!
WHICH MEANS, WE CAN DO THE RISQUÉ PLOTLINES THAT KOONO-SAN **ALWAYS** STOPS US FROM DOING!!
GET READY!!!

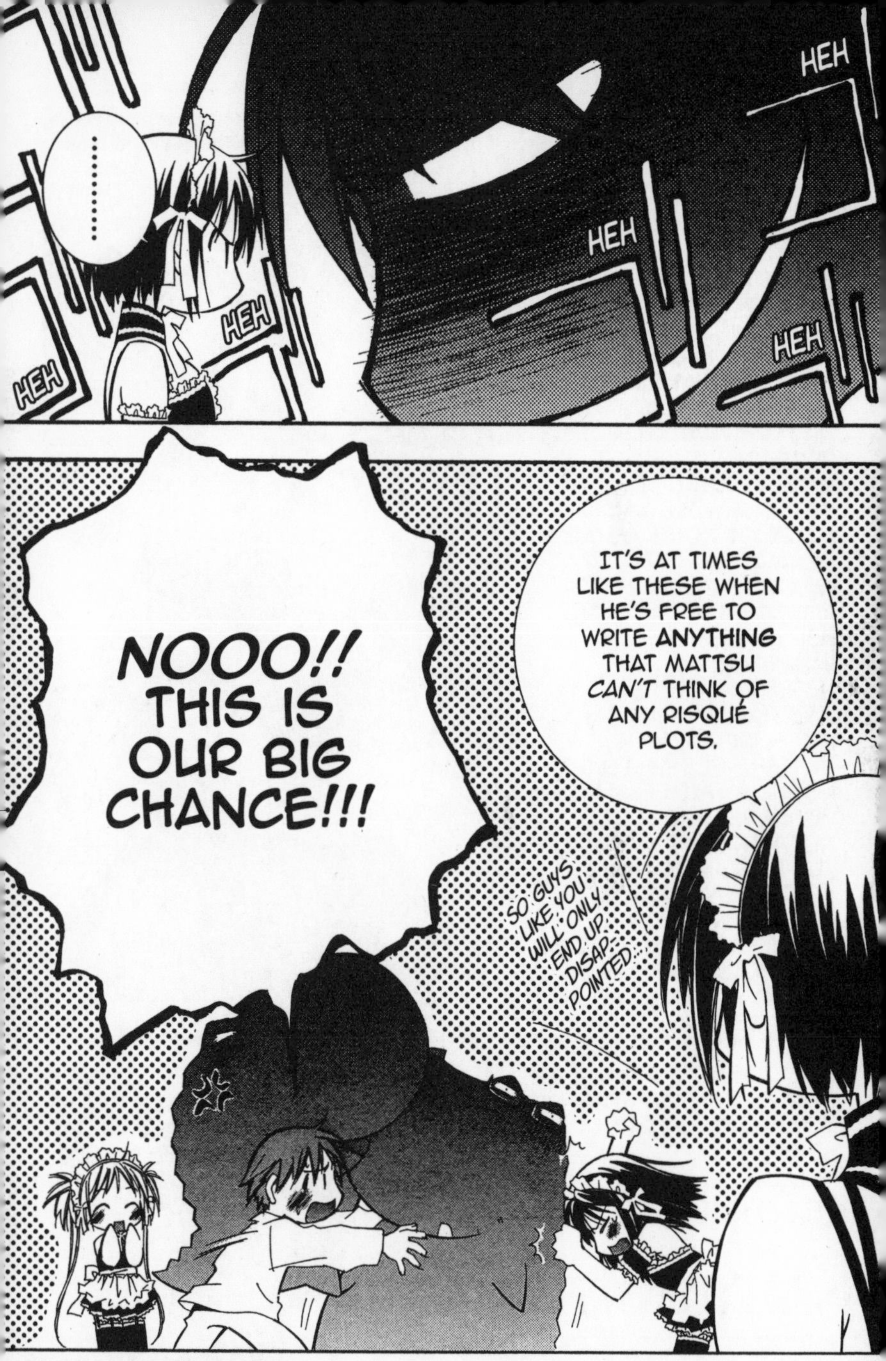
HEH
HEH
HEH
……
HEH
HEH
IT'S AT TIMES LIKE THESE WHEN HE'S FREE TO WRITE ANYTHING THAT MATTSU CAN'T THINK OF ANY RISQUÉ PLOTS.
NOOO!! THIS IS OUR BIG CHANCE!!!
SO GUYS LIKE YOU WILL ONLY END UP DISAP-POINTED...

SEE YOU NEXT VOLUME!

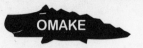

OMAKE

Comments: Mattsu

THIS IS THE GIRL WHO MISUNDERSTOOD SOMETHING AND FELL IN LOVE WITH YOSHITAKA, AND THEN MISUNDERSTOOD SOMETHING *ELSE* AND FELL IN LOVE WITH IZUMI. AT FIRST, IT WAS DIFFICULT TO DIFFERENTIATE HER PERSONALITY FROM MITSUKI'S, BUT IT'S GETTING MORE AND MORE OBVIOUS AS WE GO ALONG. HER FAVORITE BOOK IS *YURI SHIMAI*. HER DREAM IS TO IMMIGRATE TO THE NETHERLANDS AND MARRY IZUMI. IT'S SURPRISING, BUT SHE SEEMS TO BE POPULAR WITH FEMALE READERS. SHE LOVES COOKING, BUT ALWAYS MAKES FUNNY DISHES (THEY'RE *NOT* JUST FUNNY), WHICH SHE THINKS ARE ***DELICIOUS.*** SHE WORKS AS A MAID UNDER YOSHITAKA ONLY BECAUSE SHE WANTS TO BE WITH IZUMI. SHE DOESN'T THINK FOR AN INSTANT THAT YOSHITAKA IS HER MASTER.

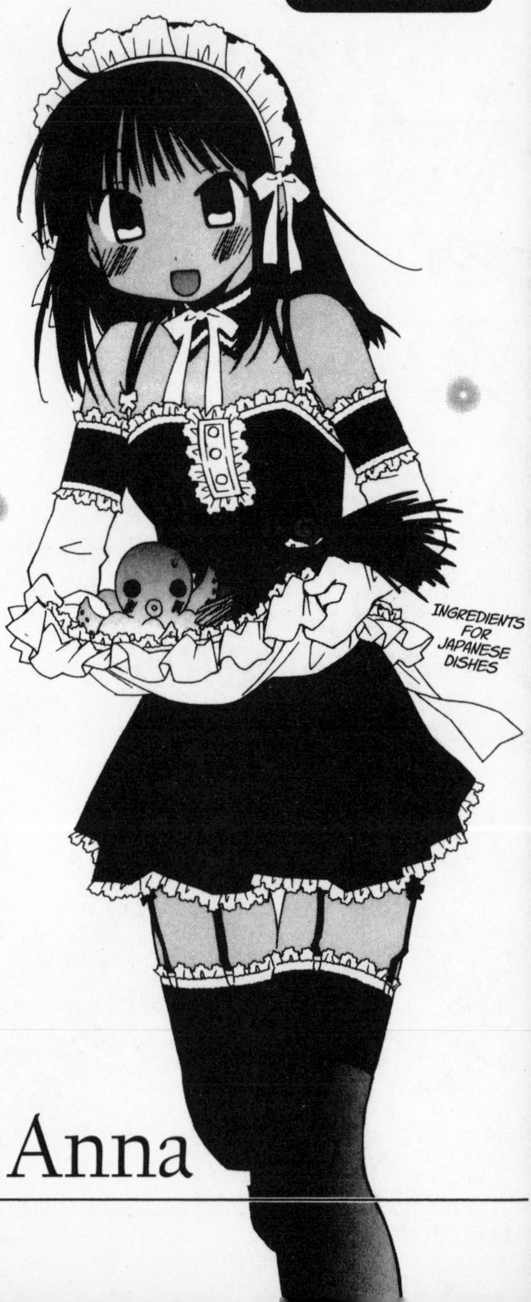
INGREDIENTS FOR JAPANESE DISHES

Kurauchi Anna

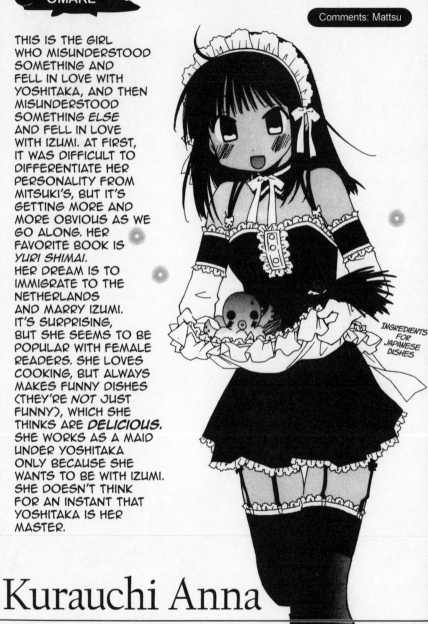

Pochi

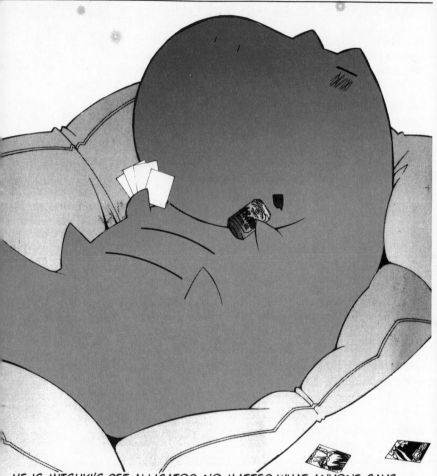

HE IS MITSUKI'S PET ALLIGATOR. NO MATTER WHAT ANYONE SAYS, HE'S *STILL AN ALLIGATOR*, NOT A GUY IN A RUBBER SUIT. HE'S A PEERLESS LOVER OF WOMEN, AND ASSAULTS THEM UPON SIGHT. HUMAN OR ALLIGATOR, HE'S OKAY WITH BOTH. HE SEEMS JUST LIKE YOSHITAKA WHEN I WRITE STUFF LIKE THIS, BUT POCHI IS MORE OF A FEMINIST. YOSHITAKA IS JUST A PERVERT. STUPID. HE'S #1 IN THE "CHARACTER YOU WANT KILLED MOST BY THE END OF THE SERIES" CATEGORY. MITSUKI IS LIKE HIS FOSTER PARENT, SO HE ONLY LISTENS TO WHAT MITSUKI SAYS. TO TELL YOU THE TRUTH, HE'S GOTTEN FATTER AND ROUNDER NOT BECAUSE HE'S LIVING THE GOOD LIFE OR BECAUSE IZUMI'S WEARING A LOT OF CLOTHES, BUT JUST BECAUSE HE WASN'T DEFORMED ENOUGH IN THE BEGINNING. BUT I USED THAT STORYLINE FOR AN EPISODE ANYWAY.

JAPANESE HONORIFICS GUIDE

To ensure that all character relationships appear as they were originally intended, all character names have been kept in their original Japanese name order with family name first and given name second. For copyright reasons, creator names appear in standard English name order.

In addition to preserving the original Japanese name order, Seven Seas is committed to ensuring that honorifics—polite speech that indicates a person's status or relationship towards another individual—are retained within this book. Politeness is an integral facet of Japanese culture and we believe that maintaining honorifics in our translations helps bring out the same character nuances as seen in the original work.

The following are some of the more common honorifics you may come across while reading this and other books:

-san – The most common of all honorifics, it is an all-purpose suffix that can be used in any situation where politeness is expected. Generally seen as the equivalent to Mr., Miss, Ms., Mrs., etc.

-sama – This suffix is one level higher than "-san" and is used to confer great respect upon an individual.

-kun – This suffix is commonly used at the end of boys' names to express either familiarity or endearment. It can also be used when addressing someone younger than oneself or of a lower status.

-chan – Another common honorific. This suffix is mainly used to express endearment towards girls, but can also be used when referring to little boys or even pets. Couples are also known to use the term amongst each other to convey a sense of cuteness and intimacy.

Sempai – This title is used towards one's senior or "superior" in a particular group or organization. "Sempai" is most often used in a school setting, where underclassmen refer to upperclassmen as "sempai," though it is also commonly said by employees when addressing fellow employees who hold seniority in the workplace.

Sensei – Literally meaning "one who has come before," this title is used for teachers, doctors, or masters of any profession or art.

Oniisan – This title literally means "big brother." First and foremost, it is used by younger siblings towards older male siblings. It can be used by itself or attached to a person's name as a suffix (niisan). It is often used by a younger person toward an older person unrelated by blood, but as a sign of respect. Other forms include the informal "oniichan" and the more respectful "oniisama."

Oneesan – This title is the opposite of "oniisan" and means "big sister." Other forms include the informal "oneechan" and the more respectful "oneesama."

TRANSLATION NOTES

32.2.2

These are names of real (and well-known) French women. *Emmanuelle Beart* is an actress and social activist; *Virginie Ledoyen* is a model and actress; *Sophie Marceau* is an actress; and *Vanessa Paradis* is an actress and singer. All are very beautiful, which is why Yoshitaka is familiar with them.

39.2

The restaurant's name *"Taberuna"* means "Do not eat" in Japanese.

57.1.2

"Yukata" are a light-weight type of kimono meant to be worn during the summer. They are usually more brightly patterned than regular kimonos.

60.4.1

The goldfish-catching game during festivals is very popular, especially among children. The goal is to catch a goldfish with a thin paper net, which becomes difficult once the paper gets wet. A good scooping technique is the trick to winning.

64.4.2

"Wasshoi" is what participants shout out when they carry festival floats.

67.5.3

Ancient Japanese burial mounds are called *"kofun."* The key-hole shaped ones are most famous, but they also come in round circles (the kind Izumi is talking about) and squares. They range from 50 to 400 meters wide.

68.4

In Japan, when people pay their respects to the dead, they light a stick of incense, clap their hands, and pray.

70.5.3

In Japan, if your parents are already dead by the time you get married, you usually bring your new spouse to the graves to introduce him/her to your parents who have passed away.

105

Jyaian is the big bully in the anime/manga *Doraemon,* and Nobita is the stupid and weak kid that Jyaian is always bullying.

110.3.2

Moomin are characters in the Swedish comic and novel series by Tove Jansson.

123.2.4

"Daccha" is what *Urusei Yatsura's* Lum from says at the end of her sentences, (i.e. I am sleepy-daccha).

129.2.3
Mitsuki is referring to Jojo from *Jojo's Bizarre Adventure.*

167.2.2
Gangan YG is a sister manga anthology magazine to *Monthly Shonen Gangan,* the magazine which runs *He Is My Master.* Its current title is simply *Young Gangan.*

168.1.5
"It's okay to die for about an hour" is a popular phrase on the Japanese internet. It means that you are "dead to the world" since you are so immersed into something.

172.4.1
"Gekiura Jyouhou" translates as "Super Behind the Scenes Information." It's intentionally spelled "GekiOra" in the panel's URL; the real URL is http://www.gekiura.com. It could also mean "Super Underground Information." The titles of the articles listed in the Guest section range from "How to Tame Poisonous Scorpions" to "How to Enjoy THC."

176.1.2
"De culture" is one of the "foreign" words that the aliens say in the Macross anime.

183.3.2
In Japan, it's against the law to show genitals in photos and drawings. They must be obscured by a mosaic pattern.

186
The crane games in arcades where you use a claw to try to pick up a stuffed toy and release it over a chute are called "UFO Catchers" in Japan, thus the "Maid Catcher" title. The stuffed toys and dolls in the machines usually have a string loop on the top, making it easier to catch with the crane.

Omake: Kurauchi Anna
"Yuri Shimai," literally "Lesbian Sisters," was a manga anthology magazine that included stories about girls falling in love, with varying degrees of explicit details.

CREATORS' CORNER

Mattsu & Asu Tsubaki

Asu Tsubaki designed the mascot character for "Kyarappa!," Gangan's gathering of characters event.

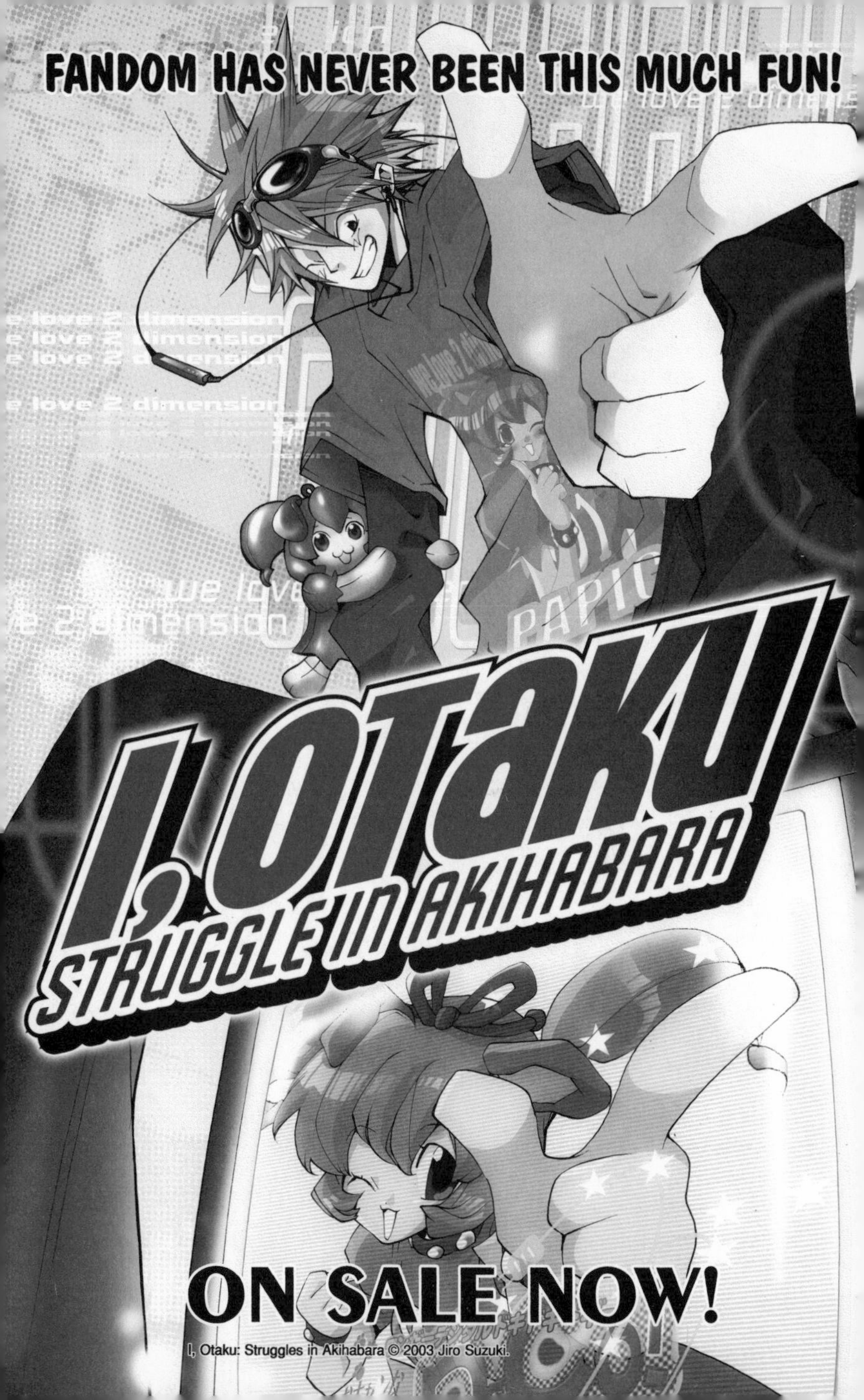
FANDOM HAS NEVER BEEN THIS MUCH FUN!
we love 2 dimension
I, OTAKU
STRUGGLE IN AKIHABARA
ON SALE NOW!
I, Otaku: Struggles in Akihabara © 2003 Jiro Suzuki.

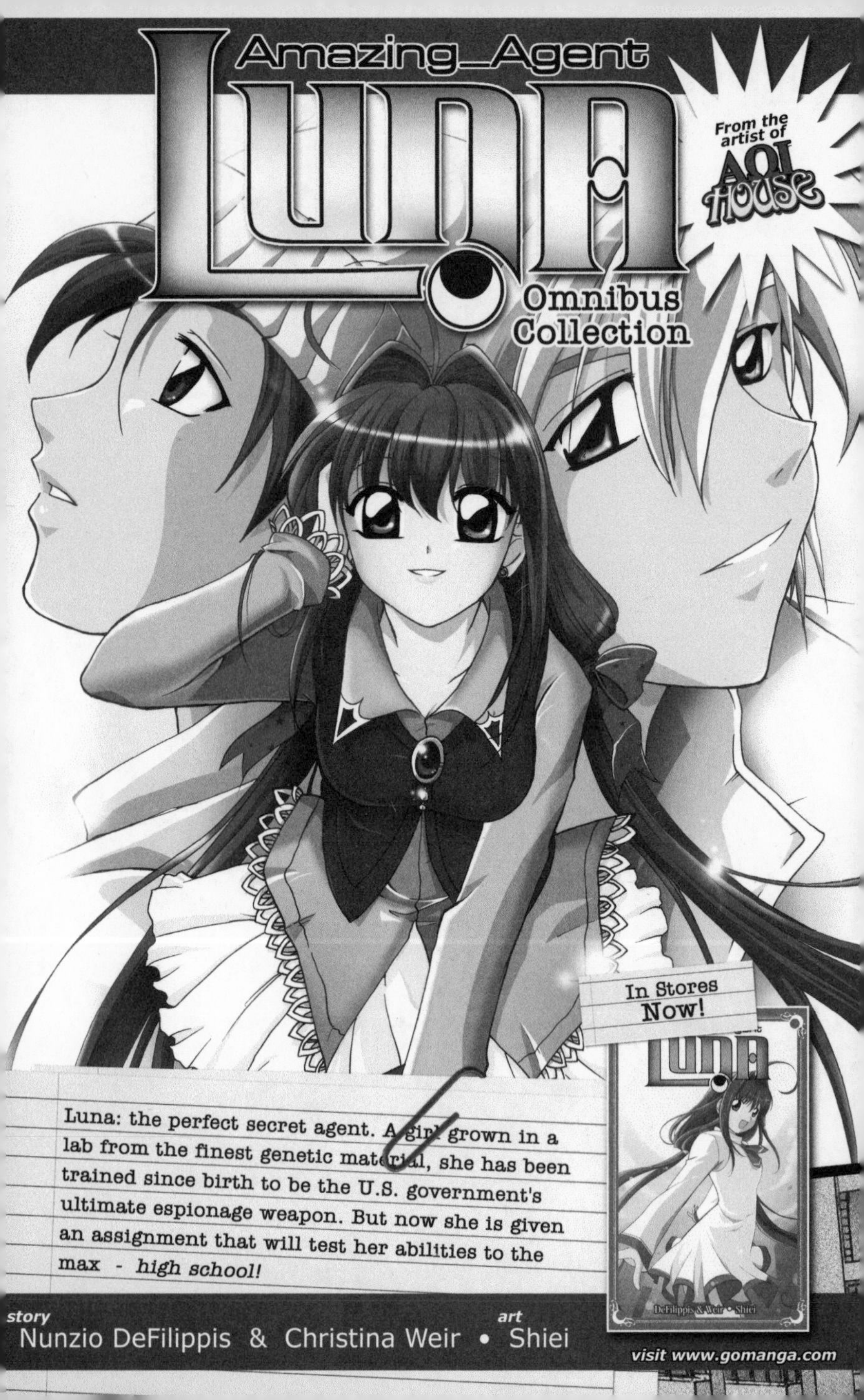
Amazing Agent
Luna
Omnibus Collection
From the artist of AOI HOUSE
In Stores Now!
Luna
DeFilippis & Weir • Shiei
Luna: the perfect secret agent. A girl grown in a lab from the finest genetic material, she has been trained since birth to be the U.S. government's ultimate espionage weapon. But now she is given an assignment that will test her abilities to the max - high school!
story
Nunzio DeFilippis & Christina Weir
art
Shiei
visit www.gomanga.com

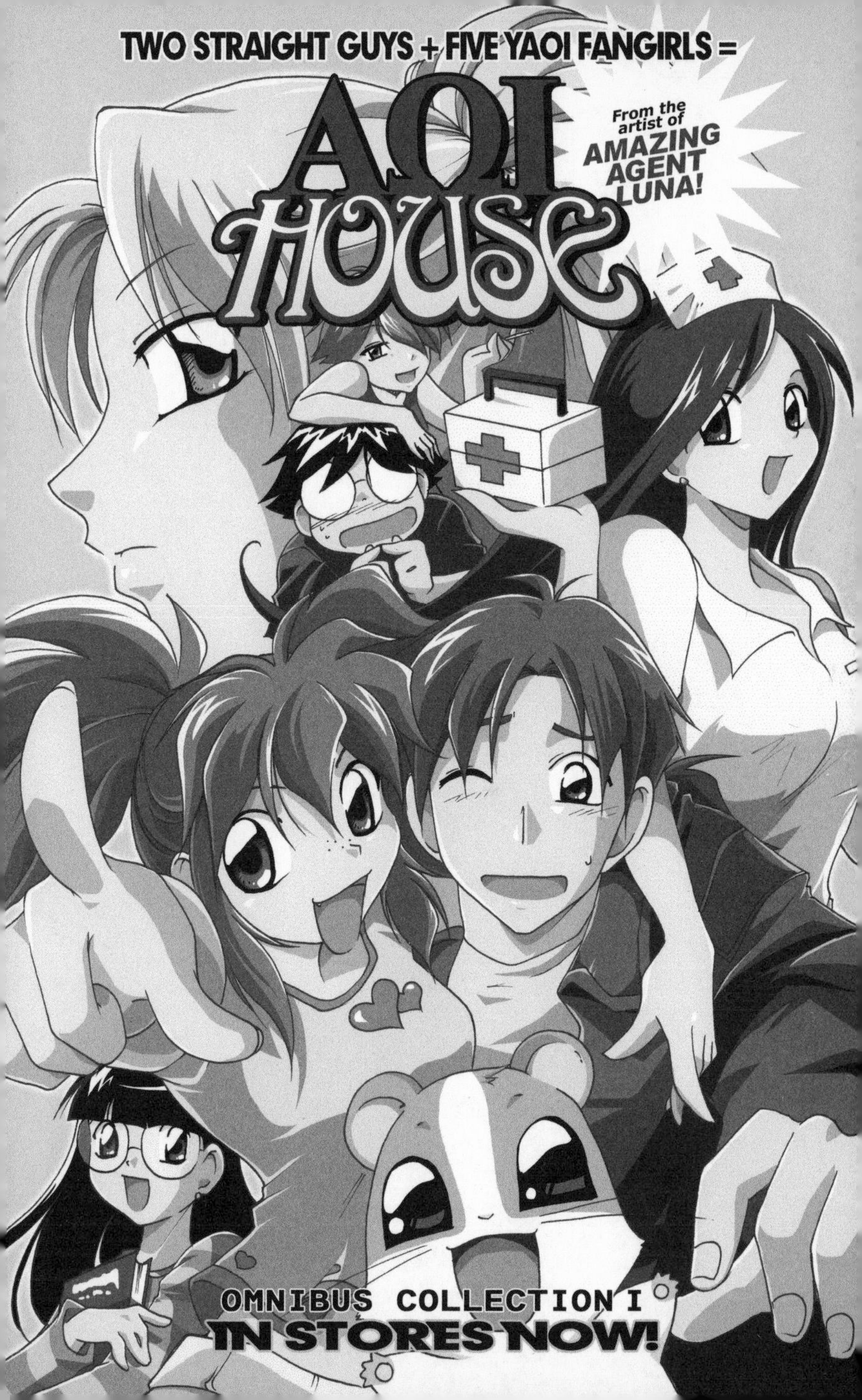
TWO STRAIGHT GUYS + FIVE YAOI FANGIRLS =
AOI HOUSE
From the artist of AMAZING AGENT LUNA!
OMNIBUS COLLECTION I
IN STORES NOW!

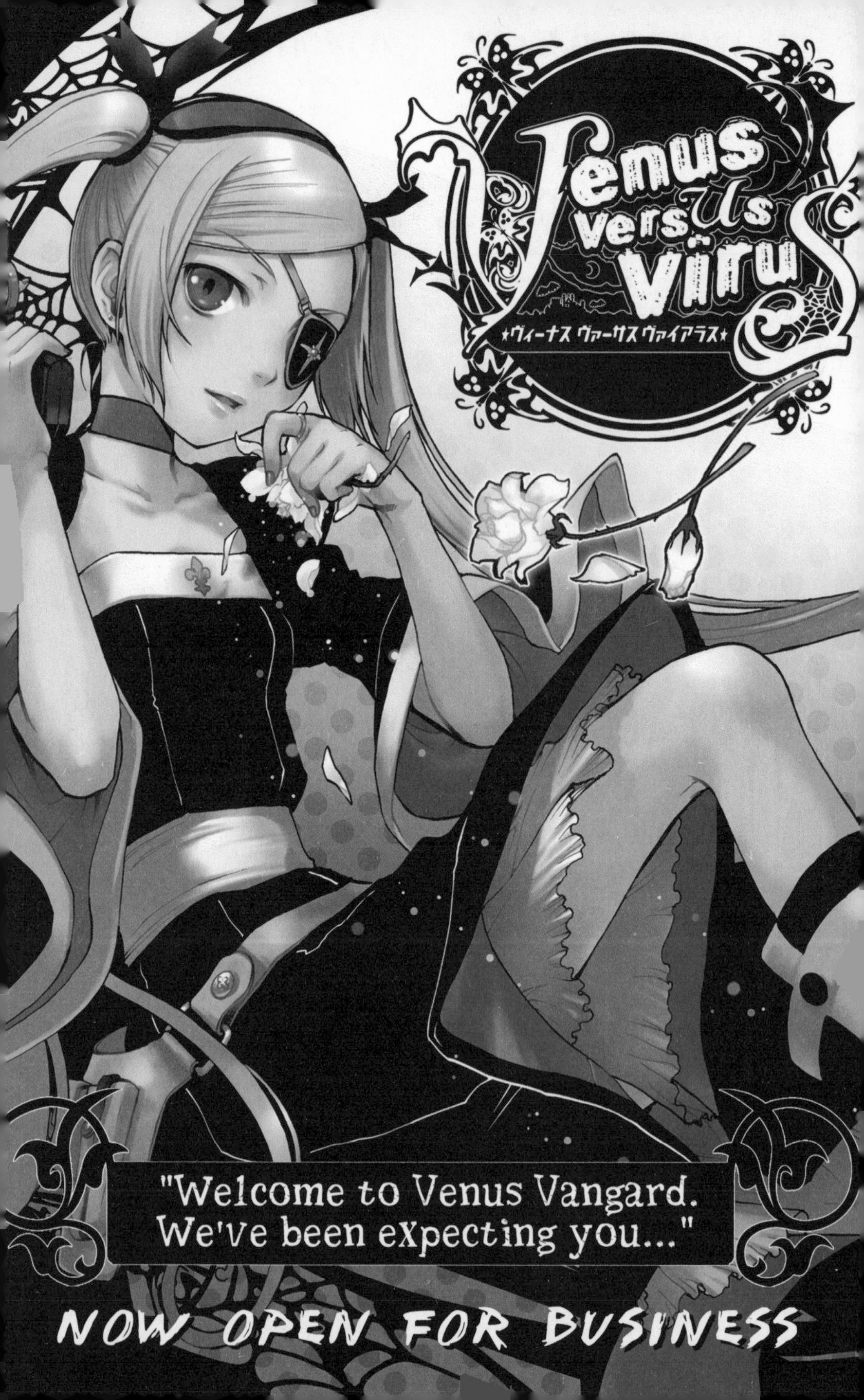
Venus versUs Virus
★ヴィーナス ヴァーサス ヴァイアラス★
"Welcome to Venus Vangard.
We've been expecting you..."
NOW OPEN FOR BUSINESS

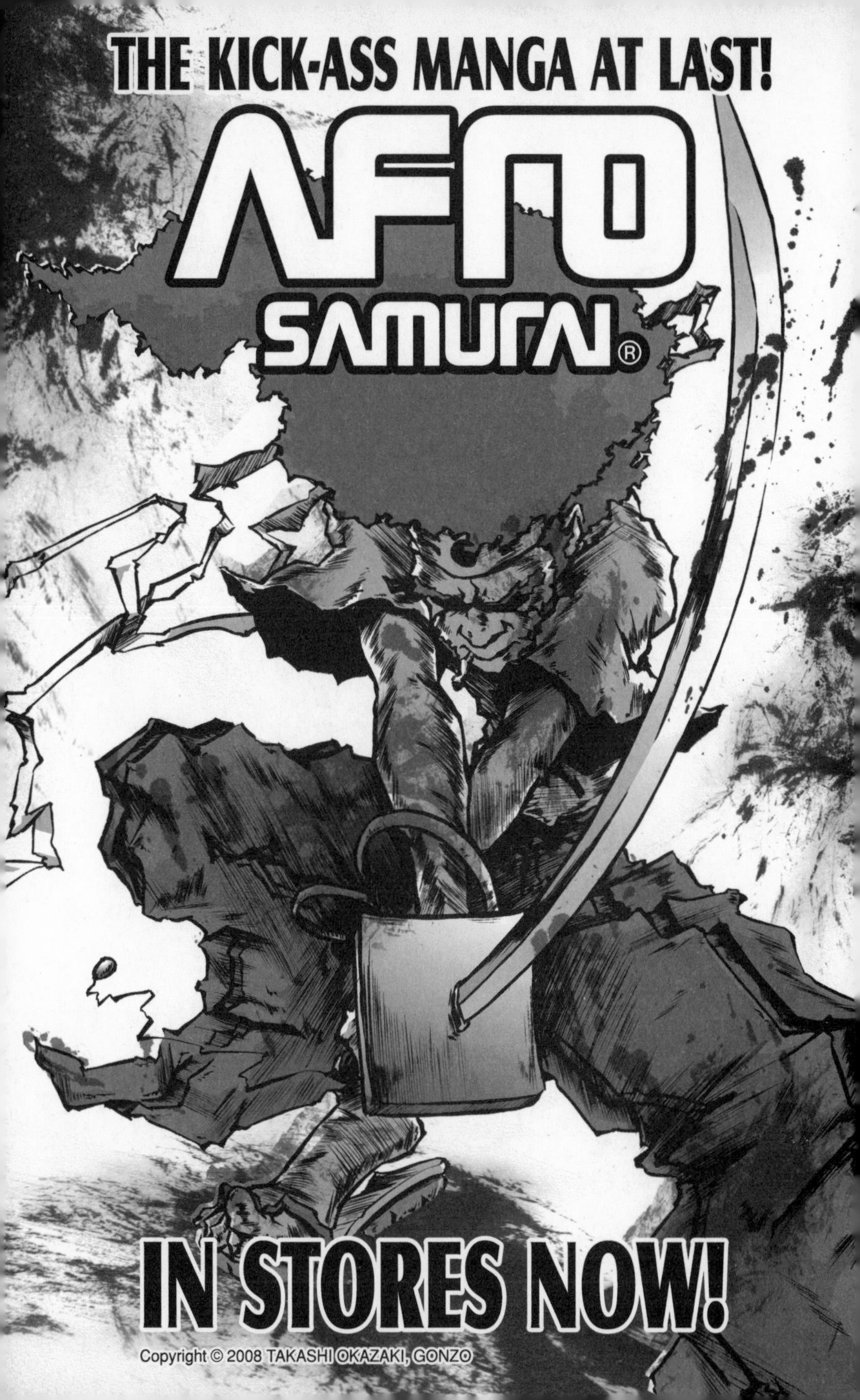
THE KICK-ASS MANGA AT LAST!
AFRO SAMURAI®
IN STORES NOW!
Copyright © 2008 TAKASHI OKAZAKI, GONZO

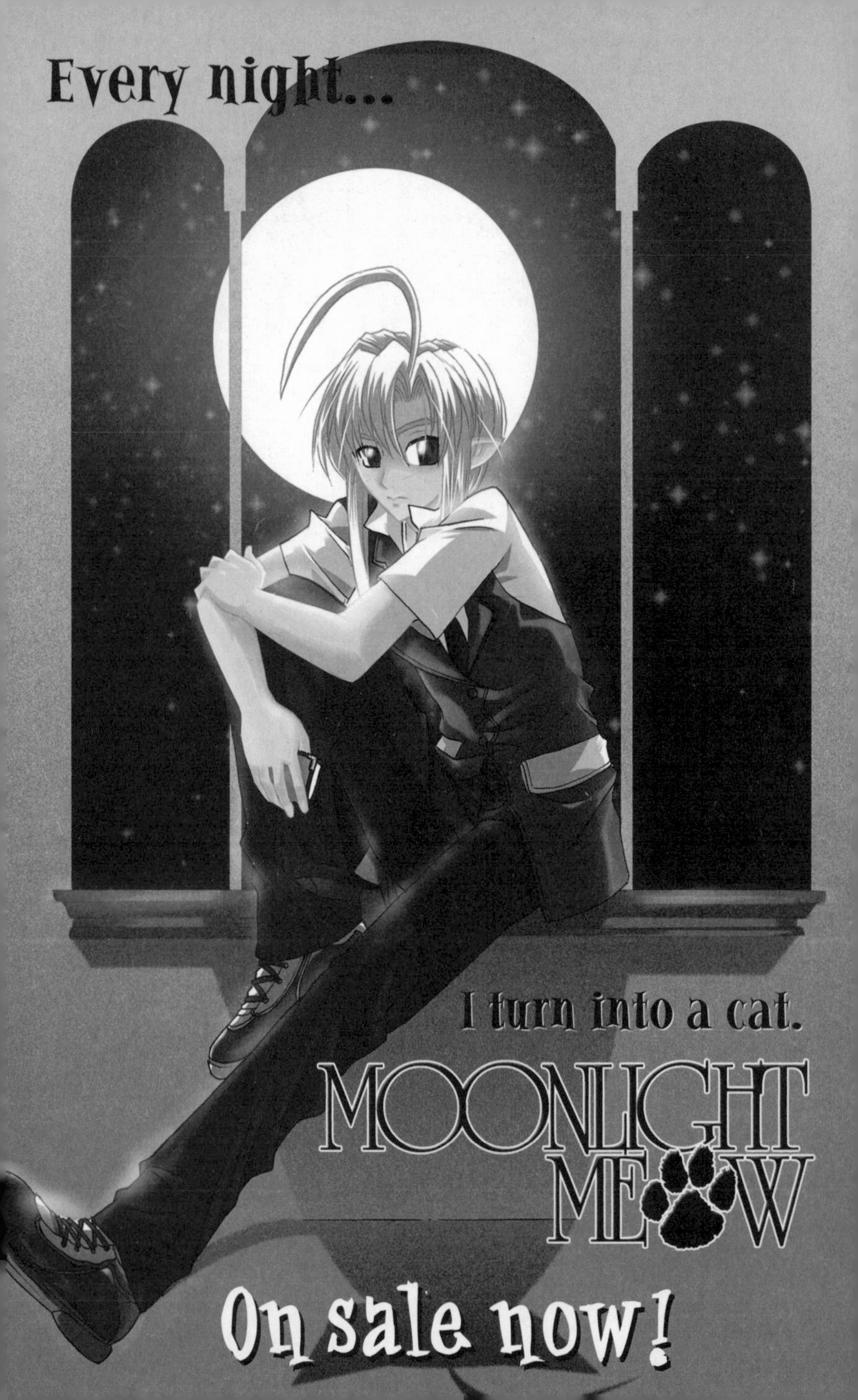

Every night...
I turn into a cat.
MOONLIGHT MEOW
On sale now!

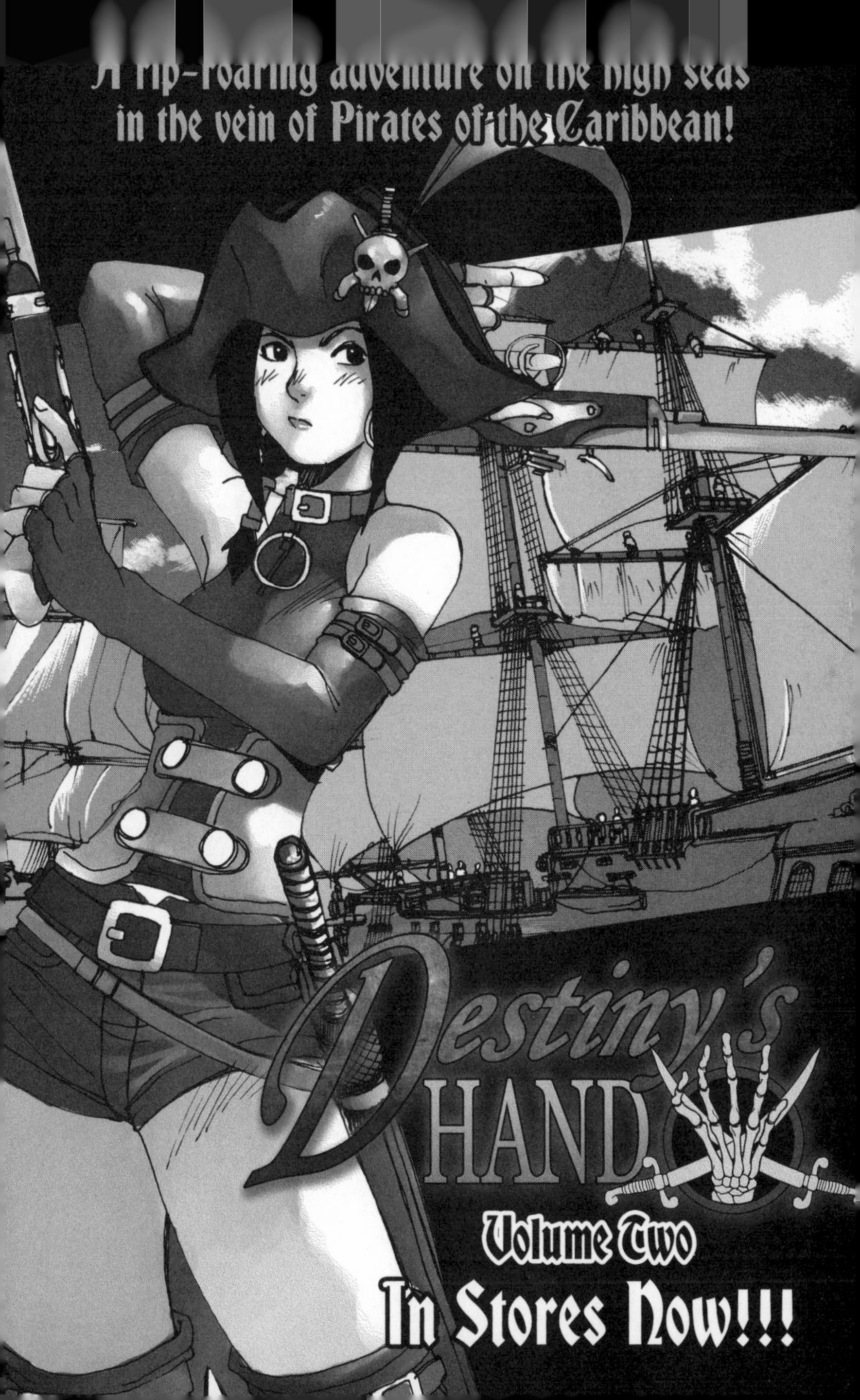
A rip-roaring adventure on the high seas
in the vein of Pirates of the Caribbean!
Destiny's
HAND
Volume Two
In Stores Now!!!

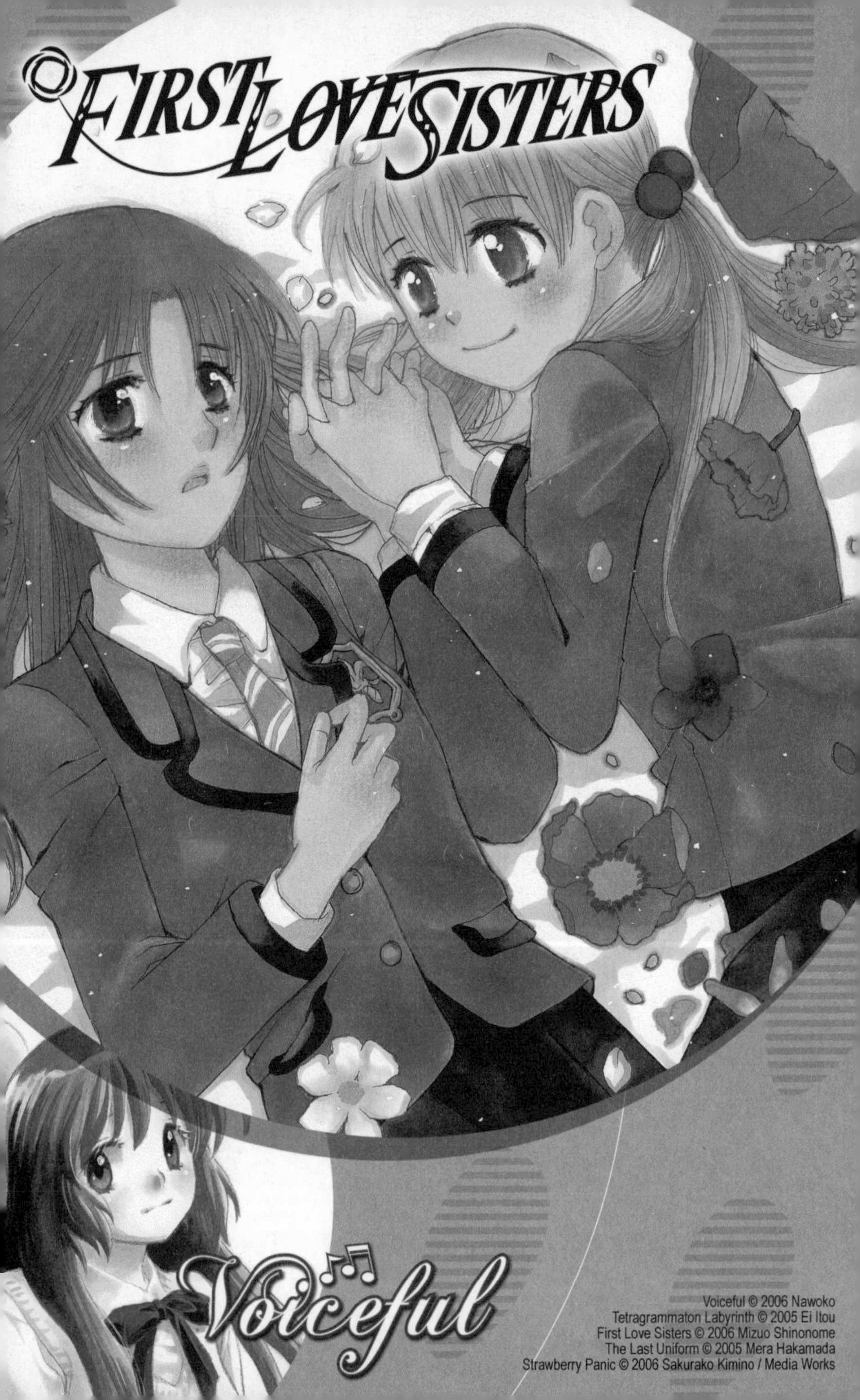
FIRST LOVE SISTERS
Voiceful
Voiceful © 2006 Nawoko
Tetragrammaton Labyrinth © 2005 Ei Itou
First Love Sisters © 2006 Mizuo Shinonome
The Last Uniform © 2005 Mera Hakamada
Strawberry Panic © 2006 Sakurako Kimino / Media Works

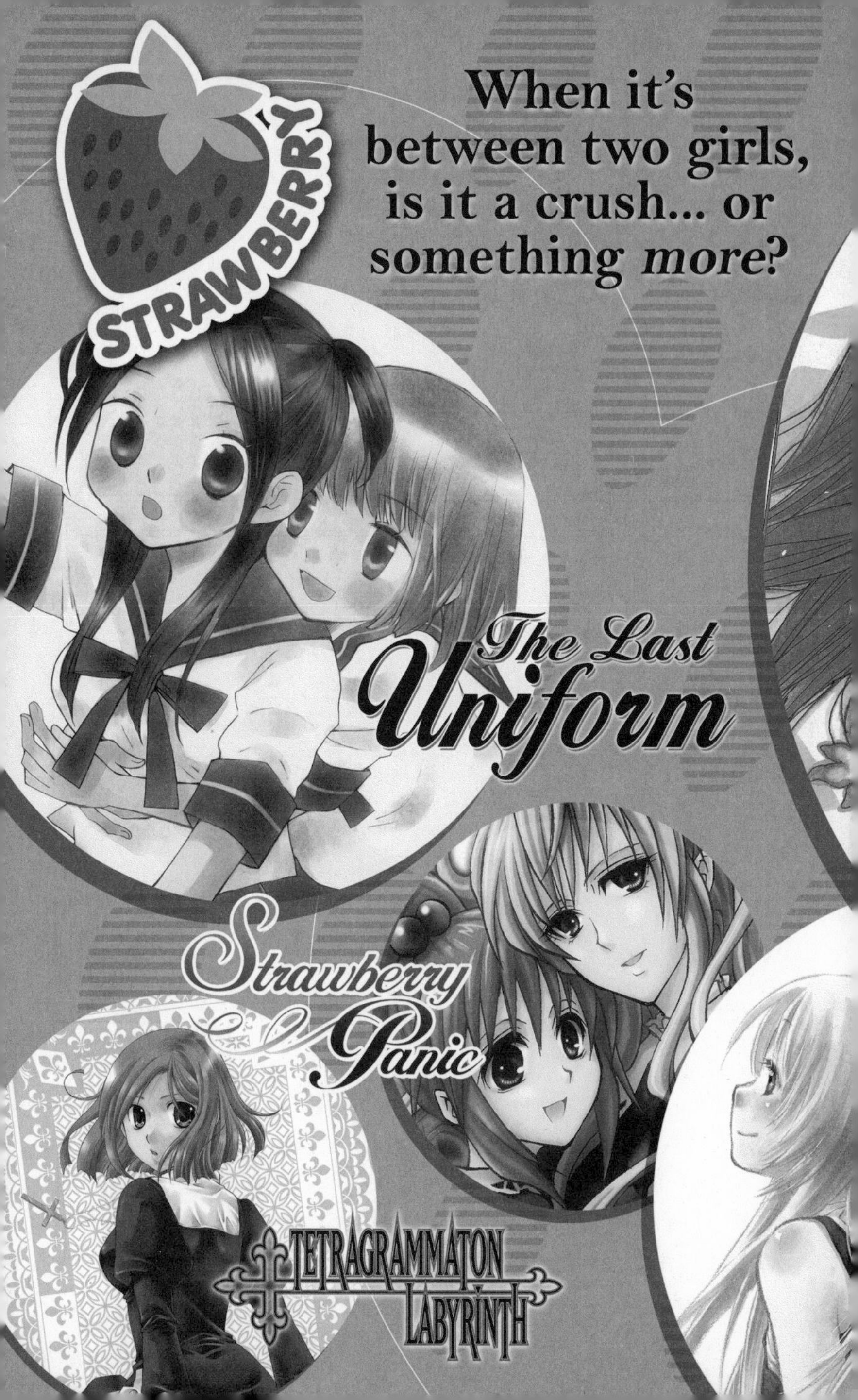
STRAWBERRY
When it's between two girls, is it a crush... or something *more*?
The Last Uniform
Strawberry Panic
TETRAGRAMMATON LABYRINTH

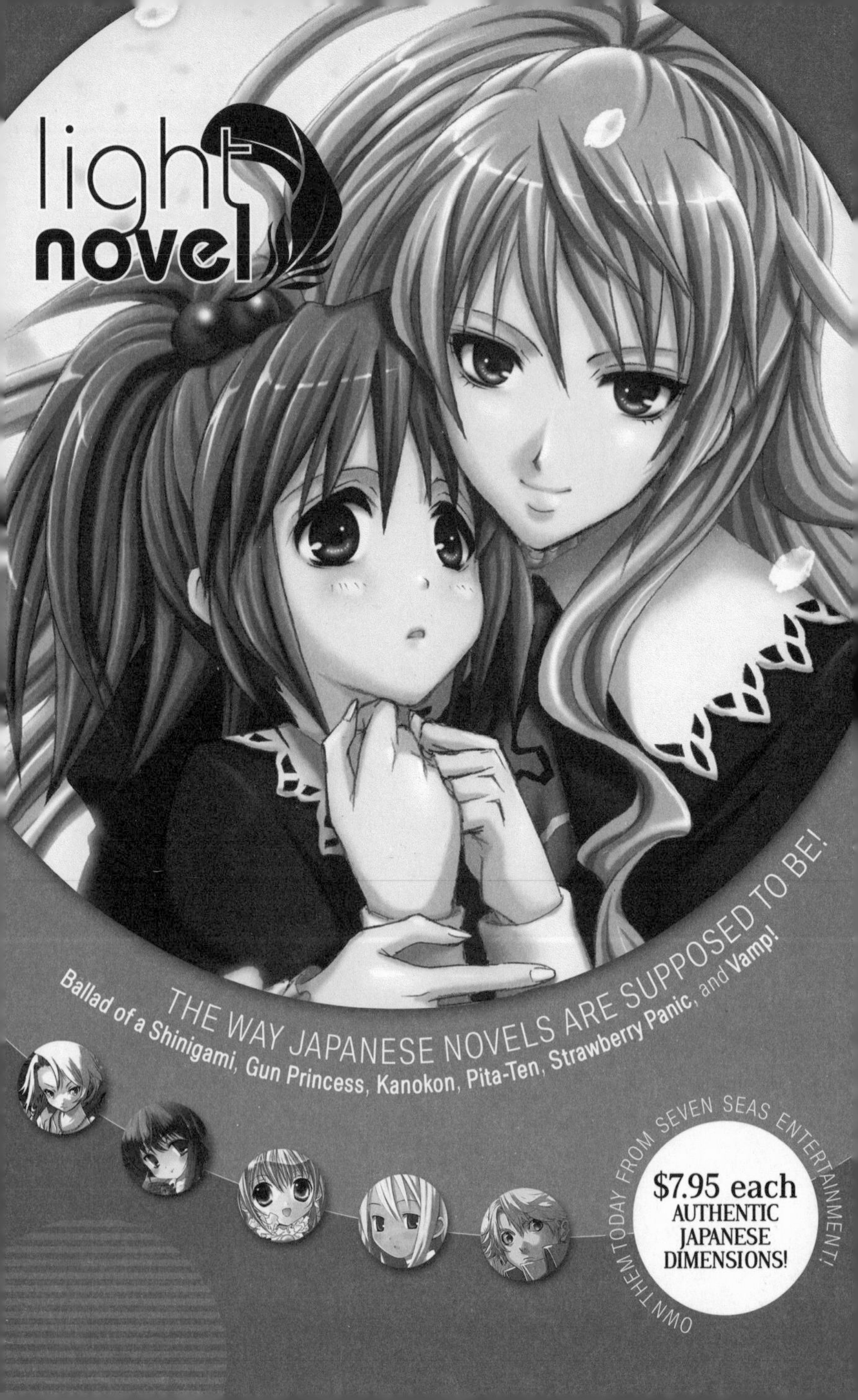
light novel
THE WAY JAPANESE NOVELS ARE SUPPOSED TO BE!
Ballad of a Shinigami, Gun Princess, Kanokon, Pita-Ten, Strawberry Panic, and Vamp!
OWN THEM TODAY FROM SEVEN SEAS ENTERTAINMENT!
$7.95 each
AUTHENTIC
JAPANESE
DIMENSIONS!

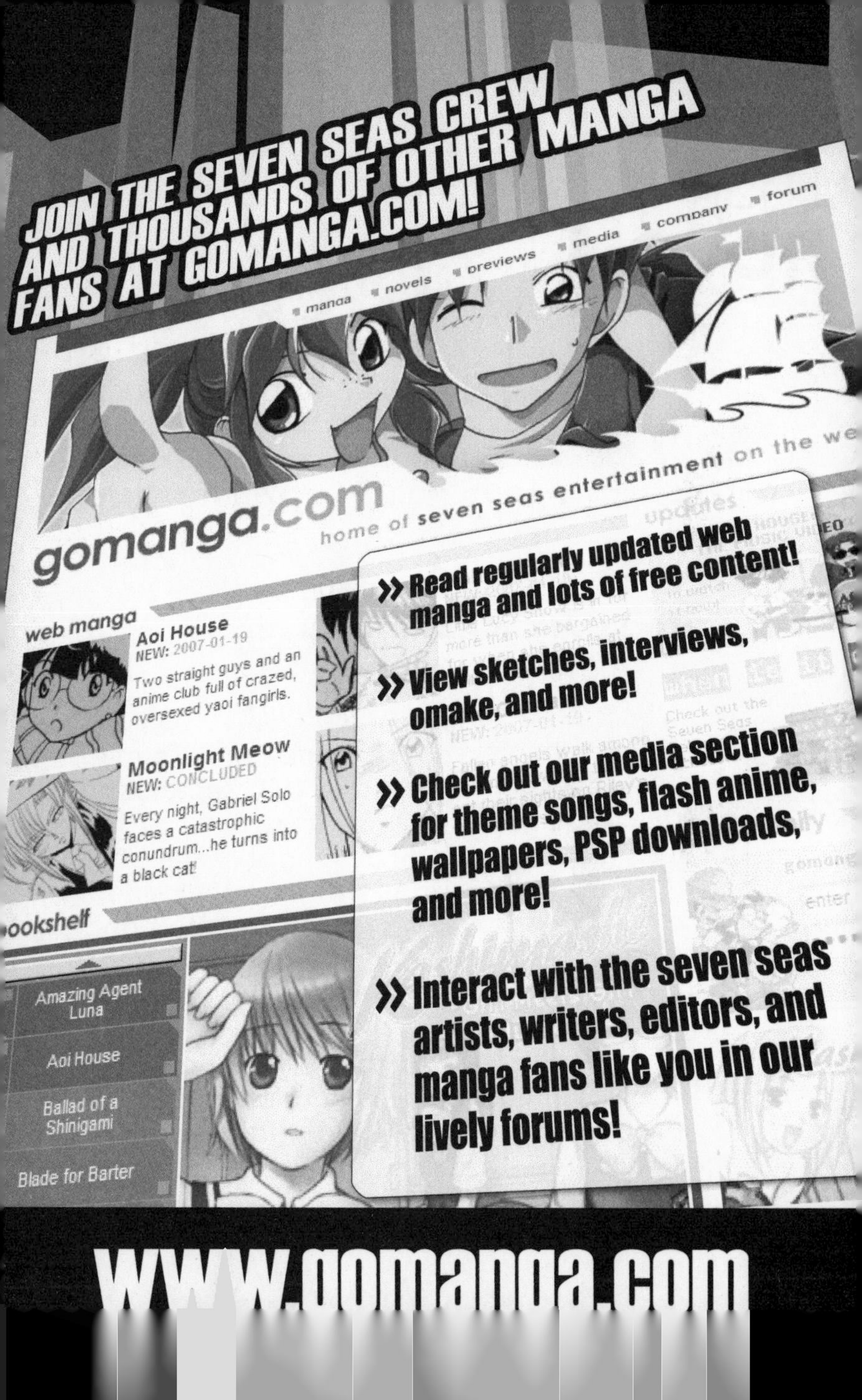
JOIN THE SEVEN SEAS CREW AND THOUSANDS OF OTHER MANGA FANS AT GOMANGA.COM!
manga
novels
previews
media
company
forum
gomanga.com
home of seven seas entertainment on the we
web manga
Aoi House
NEW: 2007-01-19
Two straight guys and an anime club full of crazed, oversexed yaoi fangirls.
Moonlight Meow
NEW: CONCLUDED
Every night, Gabriel Solo faces a catastrophic conundrum...he turns into a black cat!
ookshelf
Amazing Agent Luna
Aoi House
Ballad of a Shinigami
Blade for Barter
» Read regularly updated web manga and lots of free content!
» View sketches, interviews, omake, and more!
» Check out our media section for theme songs, flash anime, wallpapers, PSP downloads, and more!
» Interact with the seven seas artists, writers, editors, and manga fans like you in our lively forums!
www.gomanga.com

THE END

GRRKrk!!

BOSS!!

HEY, IT'S
STUPID!

YOU'RE READING THE WRONG WAY

This is the last page of
HE IS MY MASTER Volume 2

This book reads from right to left, Japanese style. To read from the beginning, flip the book over to the other side, start with the top right panel, and take it from there.

If this is your first time reading manga, just follow the diagram. It may seem backwards at first, but you'll get used to it! Have fun!